CAMPUS MARTIUS

A mosquito-infested and swampy plain lying north of the city walls, Rome's Campus Martius, or Field of Mars, was used for much of the Roman Republic as a military training ground and as a site for celebratory rituals and the occasional political assembly. Initially punctuated with temples vowed by victorious generals, during the imperial era it became filled with extraordinary baths, theaters, porticoes, aqueducts, and other structures – many of which were architectural firsts for the capital. This book explores the myriad factors that contributed to the transformation of the Campus Martius from an occasionally visited space to a crowded center of daily activity. It presents a case study of the repurposing of urban landscape in the Roman world and explores how existing topographical features that fit well with the republic's needs ultimately attracted architecture that forever transformed those features but still resonated with the area's original military and ceremonial traditions.

Paul W. Jacobs II is an independent scholar who focuses on ancient Rome and its topographical development. A graduate of Harvard College and the University of Virginia Law School, and a litigator by training, Jacobs has practiced and published in the area of voting rights, where knowledge of demographics, mapmaking, and geography is essential. He has spent extensive time in Rome and has studied the ancient city and its development for decades.

Diane Atnally Conlin is Associate Professor of Classics at the University of Colorado, Boulder. She is author of the award-winning *The Artists of the Ara Pacis* (1997) and is codirector of the University of Colorado and Comune di Roma excavations at the Villa of Maxentius in Rome. She specializes in the production and style of Roman relief sculpture. In addition to her art historical and archaeological research, Conlin has won numerous teaching awards, including a lifetime appointment as a President's Teaching Scholar.

For Fredrika, my bride of forty years, and our family, Jessica, Nick, & Peter
PWJ

For Michael
DAC

CAMPUS MARTIUS

THE FIELD OF MARS IN THE LIFE OF ANCIENT ROME

PAUL W. JACOBS II

Independent Scholar

DIANE ATNALLY CONLIN

University of Colorado

CAMBRIDGE
UNIVERSITY PRESS

32 Avenue of the Americas, New York, NY 10013-2473, USA

Cambridge University Press is part of the University of Cambridge.

It furthers the University's mission by disseminating knowledge in the pursuit of
education, learning, and research at the highest international levels of excellence.

www.cambridge.org
Information on this title: www.cambridge.org/9781107664920

First published 2014

Printed in the United States of America

A catalog record for this publication is available from the British Library.

Library of Congress Cataloging in Publication Data
Jacobs, Paul W., II, 1951–
Campus Martius : the Field of Mars in the life of ancient Rome / Paul W. Jacobs II,
independent scholar ; Diane Atnally Conlin, University of Colorado.
    pages cm
Includes bibliographical references and index.
ISBN 978-1-107-02320-8 (hardback) – ISBN 978-1-107-66492-0 (pbk.)
 1. Campo Marzio (Rome, Italy) 2. Campo Marzio (Rome, Italy) – Buildings, structures,
etc. 3. Rome (Italy) – History – To 476. I. Conlin, Diane Atnally. II. Title.
III. Title: Field of Mars in the life of ancient Rome.
DG66.J33   2015
937'.63–dc23   2014021793

ISBN 978-1-107-02320-8 Hardback
ISBN 978-1-107-66492-0 Paperback

CONTENTS

ILLUSTRATIONS

ACKNOWLEDGMENTS

This book is the result of a decade-long journey through Rome's *centro storico* searching for the evidence of its ancient past. As with any lengthy adventure, it is easy to take a wrong turn, and you are always grateful for the assistance of both passersby and fellow travelers to keep you headed in the right direction. The directions can be detailed or sketchy or just provide encouragement, but without them the trip would be much longer and, perhaps, unfulfilled. Early in the travels, I was able to tap into the formidable sense of direction and jovial support of the late William MacDonald. His scribbled postcard notes are still treasured. At various points as I wandered through the twists and turns of the project, I would reach out to Diane Favro, who was never too busy to provide advice, share source material, and encourage the effort. When the signposts in Latin or Greek were confusing and nuanced, Walt Stephenson at the University of Richmond was always there to prevent mistakes. Occasionally, doors to subterranean Rome were locked, but Angela Federico found the right persons with the keys to let me in and continue the journey. Jeffrey Becker and Ross Twele at the University of North Carolina's Ancient World Mapping Center provided extraordinary assistance with the maps of the ancient Field of Mars.

When I determined to memorialize the adventure, there was one person who was willing to stop, listen to the story, and decide that it was worth sharing – Beatrice Rehl. Without her support and that of Cambridge University Press the record of the journey would have remained unseen. As the project developed, I recognized that support under the elbow was required to get to the end, and Diane Atnally Conlin graciously agreed to join the hike. She brought in her backpack a formidable knowledge of Roman topography and history, and I am most grateful for her willingness to supply her expertise to the endeavor. With Diane came a most remarkable assistant, Joanna Schmitz, who double-checked every citation and note and searched for the perfect translation. Joanna's work was invaluable. The anonymous readers pointed us in the right direction when wrong turns were about to be taken, and we are appreciative of their help. Wendy Yohman provided her excellent word-processing skills to sew the manuscript together. I am particularly grateful to my partners at Christian & Barton for indulging my lengthy trips to Rome to allow the work to continue.

More fortunate than most, I had a fellow traveler, a partner in crime as it were, who was with me throughout the journey to climb down ladders and crawl under churches, to get me into archives and to deal with bureaucratic headaches. She queried every proposition in the book and dealt with more than a few prepositions. Having trekked along many similar trails, she knew the pitfalls and kept me from tripping. It is easy to say that without Fredrika Jacobs at my side, this book would not have happened, and it is to her and our progeny that the book is most lovingly dedicated.

Paul W. Jacobs II

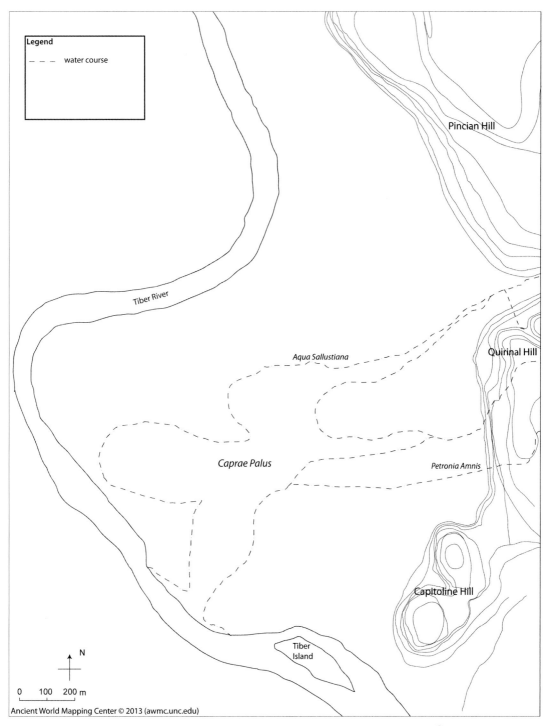

Plan 1 Campus Martius, eighth century B.C.E. Ancient World Mapping Center © 2013 (http://awmc.unc.edu). Used by permission.

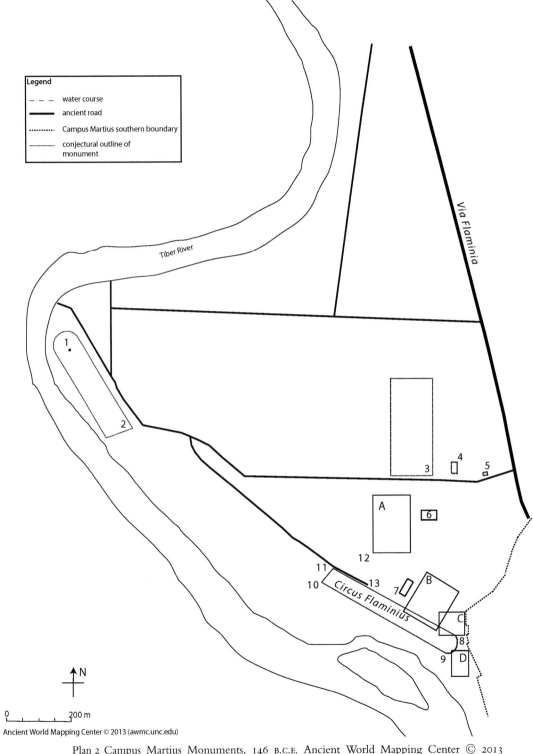

Legend

— · — water course

—— ancient road

········· Campus Martius southern boundary

——— conjectural outline of monument

Tiber River

Via Flaminia

1.

2

3

4

5

A

6

12

11

10

Circus Flaminius

13

7

B

C

8

9

D

N

0   200 m

Ancient World Mapping Center © 2013 (awmc.unc.edu)

Plan 2 Campus Martius Monuments, 146 B.C.E. Ancient World Mapping Center © 2013 (http://awmc.unc.edu). Used by permission.

Plan 2 (*continued*)

Largo Argentina Temples

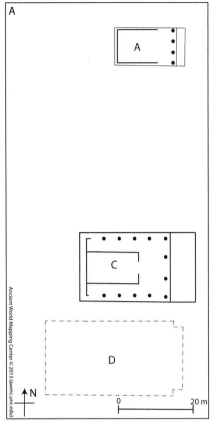

Area of the *Porticus Metelli*

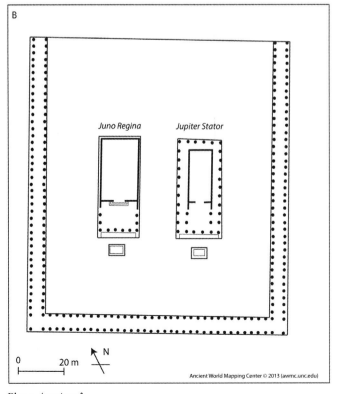

Plan 2 *(continued)*

Area of the Temple of Apollo

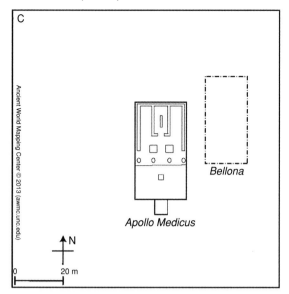

C

Ancient World Mapping Center © 2013 (awmc.unc.edu)

Bellona

Apollo Medicus

N

0   20 m

Plan 2 (*continued*)

Forum Holitorium temples

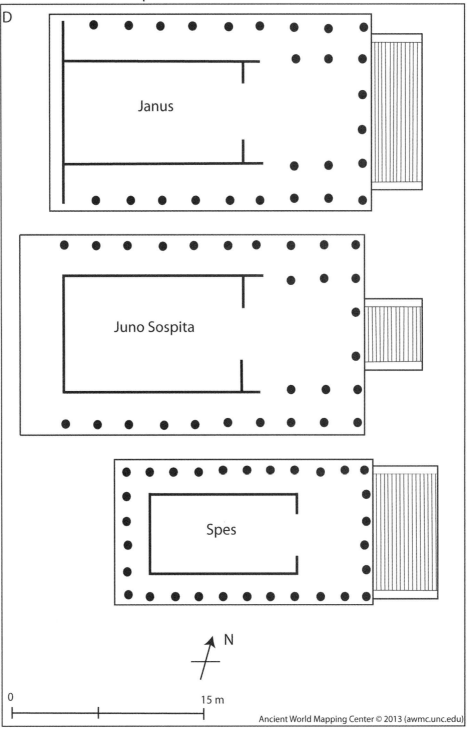

Plan 2 (*continued*)

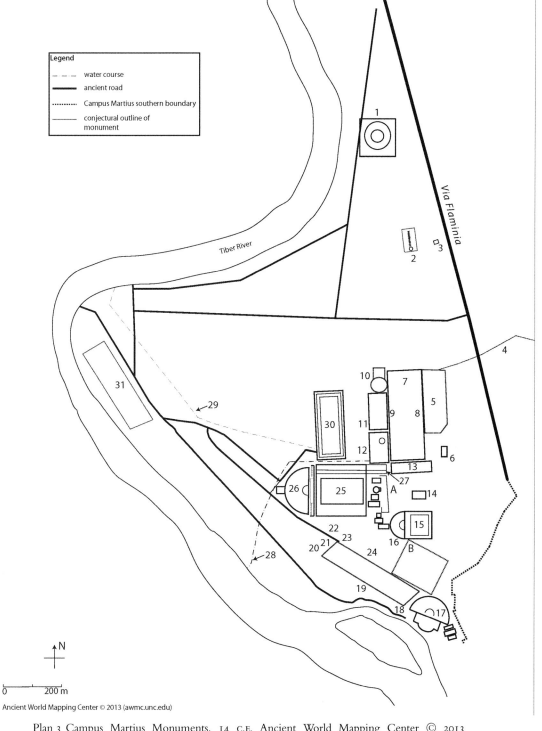

Plan 3 Campus Martius Monuments, 14 c.e. Ancient World Mapping Center © 2013 (http://awmc.unc.edu). Used by permission.

1. Mausoleum of Augustus
2. Horologium of Augustus
3. Ara Pacis
4. Aqua Virgo
5. Temples of Isis and Serapis
6. Pavilion in Villa Publica
7. Saepta Julia
8. Porticus Meleagri
9. Porticus Argonautarum
10. Pantheon (Agrippan structure)
11. Stoa of Poseidon / Basilica of Neptune
12. Baths of Agrippa
13. Diribitorium
14. Temple of the Nymphs (?)
15. Crypta Balbi
16. Theater of Balbus
17. Theater of Marcellus
18. Temple of Diana?
19. Temple of Castor and Pollux
20. Temple of Hercules Magnus Custos
21. Temple of Neptune?
22. Temple of Fortuna Equestris
23. Temple of Mars in Circus Flaminius
24. Portico of Octavius
25. Portico of Pompey
26. Theater of Pompey
27. Hecatostylon/Porticus Lentulorum?
28. Euripus Virginis
29. Euripus Thermarum Agrippae
30. Stagnum Agrippae
31. Trigarium

Inset A: Largo Argentina temples in the Augustan period
Inset B: Area of the Porticus Octaviae

Plan 3 (*continued*)

Largo Argentina Temples in the Augustan Period

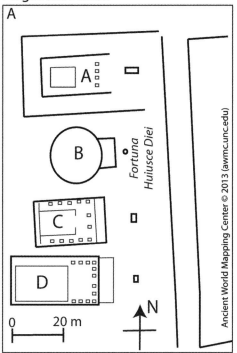

A

Fortuna Huiusce Diei

A

B

C

D

0   20 m

N

Ancient World Mapping Center © 2013 (awmc.unc.edu)

Area of the Porticus Octaviae

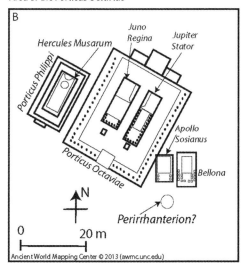

B

Hercules Musarum

Juno Regina

Jupiter Stator

Porticus Philippi

Porticus Octaviae

Apollo Sosianus

Bellona

N

Perirrhanterion?

0   20 m

Ancient World Mapping Center © 2013 (awmc.unc.edu)

Plan 3 (*continued*)

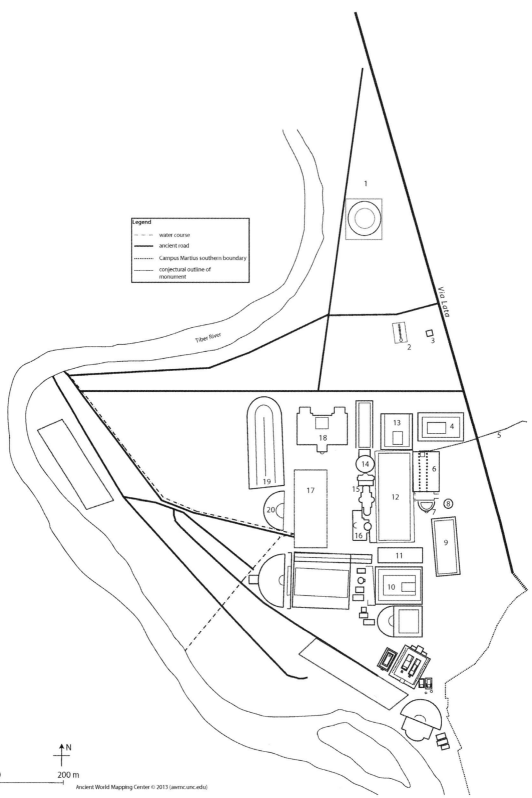

Legend
- - - water course
——— ancient road
········· Campus Martius southern boundary
——— conjectural outline of monument

Tiber River

Via Lata

1
2
3
4
5
6
7
8
9
10
11
12
13
14
15
16
17
18
19
20

N

0   200 m

Ancient World Mapping Center © 2013 (awmc.unc.edu)

Plan 4 Campus Martius Monuments, 235 C.E. Ancient World Mapping Center © 2013 (http://awmc.unc.edu). Used by permission.

1. Mausoleum of Augustus
2. Horologium of Augustus
3. Ara Pacis
4. Temple of Divine Hadrian
5. Aqua Virgo
6. Temple of Serapis
7. Temple of Isis
8. Temple of Minerva Chalcidica
9. Divorum
10. Porticus Minucia Frumentaria (?) and Temple of Nymphs (?)
11. Diribitorium
12. Saepta Julia
13. Temple of Divine Matidia
14. Pantheon (Hadrianic structure)
15. Basilica of Neptune
16. Baths of Agrippa
17. Stagnum
18. Baths of Nero and Alexander Severus
19. Stadium of Domitian
20. Odeum of Domitian

Plan 4 (*continued*)

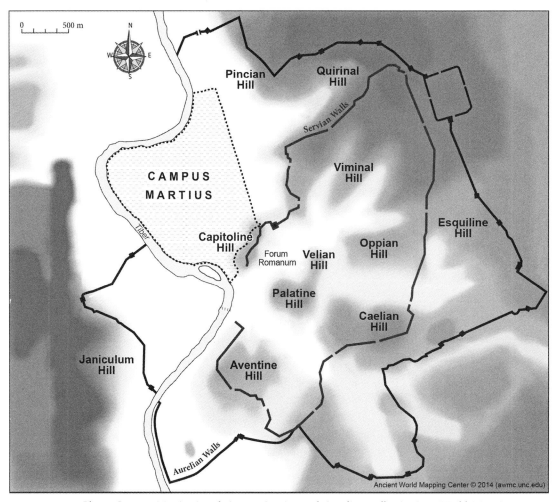

Plan 5 Campus Martius in relation to Servian and Aurelian walls. Ancient World Mapping
Center © 2013 (http://awmc.unc.edu). Used by permission.

Plate I Pantheon exterior and obelisk in the Piazza della Rotonda

Plate II Fresco from the family tomb of Titus Statilius Taurus (late first century B.C.E.) of the infants Romulus and Remus in a basket by the Tiber

Plate III Aureus of Cn. Domitius Ahenobarbus (ca. 41 B.C.E.). Reverse: Temple of Neptune?

Plate IV Head from area of the Temple of Fortuna Huiusce Diei (ca. 101 B.C.E.) attributed to Skopas Minor

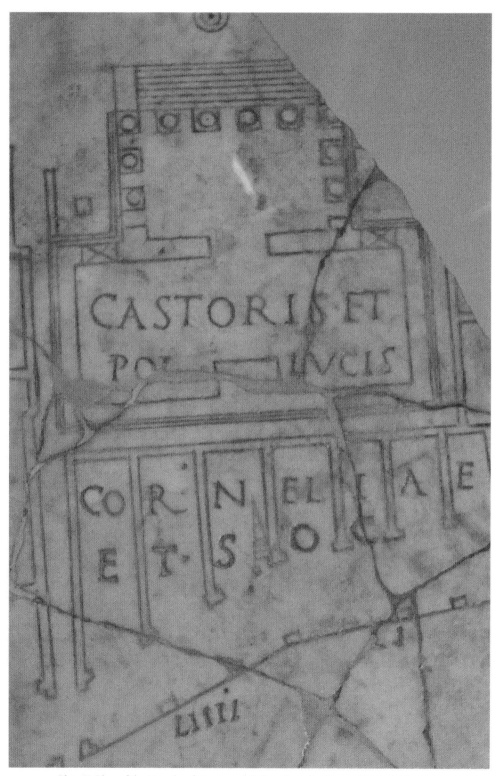

Plate V Plan of the Temple of Castor and Pollux from the Forma Urbis di Via Anica

Plate VI Temple of Apollo Sosianus (ca. 29 B.C.E.), partial restoration

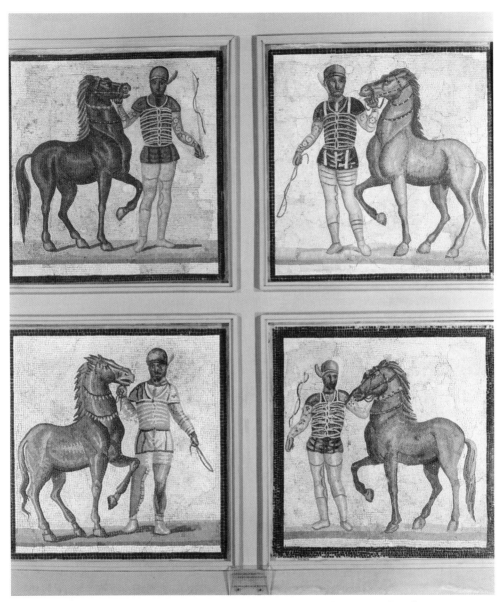

Plate VII Charioteers with horses, four mosaic sections from the Villa of Baccano, Rome (Palazzo Massimo alle Terme) (third century C.E.)

Plate VIII Vault stucco in the Theater of Marcellus

Plate IX Aureus of Septimius Severus (206 C.E.). Reverse: Stadium of Domitian

Plate X View west along the Porticus Octaviae in the direction of propylaeum

INTRODUCTION: "THIS PLACE WAS HOLIEST OF ALL"

During or just after the reign of Rome's first emperor Augustus (r. 27 B.C.E.–
14 C.E.), the Greek geographer Strabo penned his work *Geographica* and
provided a valuable description of many of the peoples and places in the
Greco-Roman world.[1] When Strabo reported the "best accredited story of
the founding of Rome," he recounted the tale, "partly fabulous but partly
closer to the truth," of Rhea Silvia, a woman forced by her uncle Amulius
to become a Vestal Virgin to assure she would remain childless, thereby preventing the birth of a potential political rival.[2] Notwithstanding her sacred
inviolability, Rhea Silvia was impregnated by the god Mars. She gave birth to
Romulus and Remus, semidivine twin boys who grew into manhood, defeated
Amulius and his sons, and established the foundations for the city of Rome.

Lacking natural defenses and usable arable land, the location for Rome's
foundation was suitable "more as a matter of necessity than of choice."[3]
For his part, Strabo forgave the early Romans for not beautifying their city,
citing their understandable preoccupation with matters of government and
war. The successors to Rome's mythical founders would eventually reduce its
vulnerability by building protective circuit walls and defensive gates as early
as the fourth century B.C.E. By the reign of Augustus, however, Strabo noted
that circumstances had indeed changed. Rome's leaders of the late republic
and the first imperial court had not neglected the city's infrastructure; rather
they filled Rome with "many beautiful structures."[4]

In fact, Pompey, the Deified Caesar, Augustus, his sons and friends, and wife and sister, have outdone all others in their zeal for buildings and in the expense incurred. The Campus Martius contains most of these, and thus, in addition to its natural beauty, it has received still further adornment as a result of foresight. Indeed, the size of the Campus is remarkable, because it affords space at the same time and without interference, not only for chariot-races and every other equestrian exercise but also for all that multitude of people who exercise themselves by ball-playing, hoop-trundling, and wrestling; and the works of art situated around the Campus Martius and the ground, which is covered with grass throughout the year, and the crowns of those hills that are above the river and extend as far as its bed, which present to the eye the appearance of a stage-painting – all this, I say, affords a spectacle that one can hardly draw away from. And near this campus is still another campus, with colonnades round about it in very great numbers, and sacred precincts, and three theatres, and an amphitheatre, and very costly temples, in close succession to one another, giving you the impression that they are trying, as it were, to declare the rest of the city a mere accessory. For this reason, in the belief that this place was holiest of all, the Romans have erected in it the tombs of their most illustrious men and women.[5]

This area known in Strabo's day as the "Campus Martius," or "the Field of Mars," was located not in the city proper but north of the Capitoline Hill, just outside of Rome's first defensive walls. Large and flat and, for much of the republican period, grassy and unencumbered by man-made structures, the Campus Martius was part of a floodplain framed by the Capitoline Hill to the south, the Tiber River to the west, the Pincian and Quirinal Hills to the east, and a narrow throat of land between the Tiber and the Pincian Hill to the north. Until the late imperial era, most of the region lay outside the *pomerium*, the mythical plow line or sacred furrow that delineated the city limits and relegated certain activities to one side (intrapomerial) or the other (extrapomerial). For example, according to long-standing republican tradition, rituals that sought divine approval for mortal actions could be performed within the *pomerium*, but Rome's own armed troops were forbidden to cross the pomerial boundary and enter the city unless expressly invited by the Senate.[6] Soldiers mustering for war and citizens gathered for census counting, centuriate assemblies, and military unit assignments were relegated to the plain of the Campus Martius, outside the sacred line. Following a successful return from campaign, Roman legions would assume military formations on the open plain in preparation for the triumphal processions that snaked their way through the narrow city streets. In addition to troop assembly, certain foreign ambassadors were temporarily housed in the Campus Martius while they waited for an invitation to cross the *pomerium*.[7] Moreover, the open field was also an ideal location for the construction of temples vowed by generals during the heat of battle with Rome's many enemies, some dedicated to foreign gods that could be worshiped only beyond the city walls. Likewise, cremation and burial rites were permitted only outside of the pomerial line; some of the most significant funerary structures were constructed in the Campus Martius, including the great mausoleum of Rome's first emperor.

The Field of Mars also was connected intrinsically to the foundation legends of the city. The Tiber that ran along its western boundary was the same flood-swollen river into which Rhea Silvia's twin sons were thrown, only to wash ashore in their cradle further downriver. Years later, according to one legend, Romulus, then Rome's sole king, ascended to heaven in a storm cloud from the center of the open field, where he had been mustering his troops for battle. Ultimately, this land "between the city and the Tiber" became, according to Livy, the property of Rome's last Etruscan king, Tarquinius Superbus.[8] After the defeat and exile of Tarquinius in 509 B.C.E., the plain was once again reclaimed by Rome's Latin citizens and dedicated to the god Mars.[9] Following the expulsion of the foreign despots, the area north of the pomerial line was known, according to Livy, simply as the Campus Martius, or "Field of Mars."[10]

As it contained few structures until the third century B.C.E., the swampy plain north of the city accommodated large crowds on a periodic and usually seasonal basis. Soldiers mustered there in the spring and received discharge orders in the fall. Citizens gathered in the field for important religious festivals tied to the war god, such as the equestrian contest known as the October Horse and the holiday Anna Perenna on the Ides of March, in addition to remembrances every July to Romulus's death. As the location for triumphal parade formations, the Campus Martius received throngs of visitors on the dates set for the celebration of military victories. Lying in a floodplain and infested with mosquitoes in late summer, the plain was deemed ideal for periodic military training and festivals but not for daily urban activities. For five centuries after Rome's mythical founding, use of the field by Rome's residents was limited.

With the advent of the Punic Wars beginning in the mid-third century B.C.E., Rome expanded its military reach throughout the Mediterranean basin and north of the Alps. This resulted in the slow demise of the annual rhythm of warfare and, with it, the requirement of seasonal musters in the Field of Mars. No longer needed entirely for unobstructed troop exercises, the Campus Martius began to attract development that complemented its military and other public uses. The plundered treasures of foreign conquest pouring into the capital during overseas military adventures funded the construction. The scale and cultural importance of the Campus Martius made it an ideal location for the conspicuous and tangible display of political ambition. It was there that leading republican citizens constructed temples to provide lasting reminders of their personal successes and public munificence. Some temples were surrounded with beautiful colonnades, creating sacred precincts in an area that could accommodate vast enclosures. The marbled spaces served as repositories for extraordinary art and provided various "firsts" for the city, including the first temple entirely of marble and the first colonnade as a victory monument.

Notwithstanding the construction of temples and occasionally temporary wooden theaters, until the mid-first century B.C.E., the use of the Campus Martius by Rome's residents remained as it had been for centuries, a place for periodic gatherings and festivals. A significant transformation of the space began, however, when one of Rome's greatest generals, Gnaeus Pompeius Magnus (Pompey the Great), dared to erect a permanent venue for theatrical shows. He chose the flat, open plain as the ideal location for his enormous stone structure. Other buildings in the Campus Martius designed for entertainment as well as for bathing followed, and by the beginning of the common era, streams of visitors came to the field on a daily basis.

With the ascension to power of Augustus, the Field of Mars began its conversion into a showcase for imperial architecture and the physical manifestation of Rome's preeminence. At the time Strabo called the location of the Campus Martius the "holiest of all," the open fields were quickly shrinking. Drained and leveled, the alluvial plain was filling from the south to the north with colonnades, theaters, an amphitheater, public baths, temples, and sacred precincts. Although the earlier martial functions of the plain were no longer critical to the success of Augustus's empire, inscriptions and carved images on triumphal arches, commemorative columns, and temple pediments proliferated throughout the Campus Martius to serve as reminders of the area's connection to the god of war and the foundation legends of Rome.

Over time, the Field of Mars was crammed with constructions of marble, concrete, and wood, until little of Mars's open field was left. Large private landholdings of famous generals such as Pompey and Marcus Agrippa were subdivided into beautiful public parks with pools and statuary and extraordinary edifices supported on carved columns and arches. Open spaces were now enclosed in colonnades, and the once flat topography developed a verticality created by buildings such as Pompey's theater and Augustus's mausoleum that reached as high as the Capitoline. Although its natural beauty was replaced by the man-made, the Campus Martius still remained highly susceptible to nature's powerful forces. Draining the marshes and raising the ground level did not prevent the terrible inundations from Tiber floods that periodically washed across the plain. Visitors to the field's numerous entertainment attractions in late summer were at risk of malaria outbreaks from the mosquitoes that frequented Rome's low-lying regions. Like many sectors of the ancient capital city, the northern plain suffered from fires that frequently razed buildings, thereby providing opportunities to build new structures with updated architectural designs and decorative programs. The interstices between temples, porticoes, baths, and theaters began to fill with commercial structures, houses, and apartment buildings. The *pomerium* shifted north, and in the third century C.E., the Aurelian Wall enclosed the Field of Mars within the city proper. The discernible features of the plain that distinguished it from the remainder of Rome were now blurred, as the Campus Martius was fully integrated into the *urbs* (city) that dominated the ancient world.

This book presents a case study of the repurposing of urban space in the Roman world and explores how uses that fit well with existing topographical features ultimately attracted architecture that forever transformed those features. It considers how the ideal topography and extrapomerial location of the Campus Martius allowed this sector to serve first as Rome's premier military assembly area and parade ground, space essential for a city-state that honored success in battle as the highest societal value.[11] Through its connections to the activities of war, the Field of Mars offered the perfect location for important foundation myths of Rome, and this, in turn, influenced the types and decorative programs of buildings constructed within it. These structures as well as the availability of open, flat terrain in an increasingly crowded urban landscape, attracted more grandiose public works, which then reshaped the topography, altering forever the once open field of the war god Mars. Chapter 1 introduces the space and major monuments through a topographical overview, defining its limits and noting the changes from a swamp to a marble wonderland. Chapter 2 considers the relationship of the campus to Mars and the myths of Rome's foundation. The variety and location of temples built most often as vow fulfillments for the battlefield successes of ambitious republican generals are considered in Chapter 3. Previously a locale for occasional theatrical performances in temporary structures built near the steps of temples, the landscape of the Campus Martius evolved into a premier entertainment zone punctuated with permanent stone theaters, a horse racing track, and a stadium for Greek-style games. These structures are the focus of Chapter 4, whereas Chapter 5 considers the development of colonnades which created large sacred spaces around temples and parks next to theaters and which were filled with sculpture and painting from conquered nations. Water, both channeled and untamed, pervasively affected the Field of Mars, and its impact on the plain and its monuments is discussed in Chapter 6. Chapter 7 considers the imperial architectural programs that unified large sections of the Campus Martius and captured the martial and mythical past of the plain for the ideological and political agendas of Rome's emperors. The concluding chapter ties the various themes together and notes that, as Rome declined, the field that once awed Strabo now sheltered some of Rome's shrinking population among crumbling buildings. The extraordinary marbled edifices became *monti* of rubble that serve as the foundation materials for a modern city that, in turn, remains a palimpsest for its ancient glory. To assist the reader in his or her understanding of the space, Appendix A lists the major monuments of the Field of Mars in chronological order and within the context of major political events, while Appendix B may be consulted for the meaning of various architectural terms employed.

CHAPTER ONE

"THE SIZE OF THE PLAIN IS REMARKABLE": DEFINING THE LIMITS OF THE CAMPUS MARTIUS IN TIME AND SPACE

TIME

For many travelers to Rome today, the center of the city is often considered the area around the nineteenth-century monument to King Victor Emmanuel II, an imposing marble structure with a high colonnade that looks north over tightly spaced buildings and a busy traffic circle. Built hard up against the Capitoline Hill, a natural landscape feature known today as the Campidoglio, this memorial to the first king of a unified Italy hides from view the hill that once dominated the ancient skyline as seen from the northern reaches of the city. But wander off to the western side of the monument, and the visitor discovers the ramped carriage steps leading to the Campidoglio, the perfectly balanced space created by Michelangelo in the sixteenth century. From this high vantage point, the modern observer's gaze extends to the northern horizon across a plain dominated by tile-roofed structures from the seventeenth through nineteenth centuries. At the viewer's right is the very straight Via del Corso running north from the Piazza Venezia, but the undulating Tiber River on the left is now hidden by trees and a floodwall (Figure 1).

Three millennia ago the Capitoline was a very different place. As a result of lava flows from volcanic eruptions over the previous 600,000 years, nearly 100,000 square meters of hilltop formed a rugged saddle of tufa resting between two higher peaks.[1] A small village of wooden huts sat on the relatively flat space between the rises, with similar villages dotting Rome's other hilltops.[2] Instead

1. View north from the Capitoline Hill with modern Corso (ancient Via Lata/Via Flaminia) on the right. (Photo: Paul Jacobs)

of an urban landscape lying to the north of the Capitoline, there was a marshy plain punctuated by woods and shallow pools of water. Caught between the Tiber River to the west and the Pincian and Quirinal Hills to the east, the flatland became a lake for many days during the seasonal inundations from the river's floodwaters. Further north, where the Tiber curves close to the hills, a small volcanic fissure hinted at the region's seismic instability. A narrow stream, later known as the Petronia Amnis, wended from the Quirinal through the marsh before emptying into the Tiber (Plan 1).[3] Few, if any, artificial features stood between the trees and wetland pools on the plain to suggest human encroachment.[4] This, however, was the area that – many centuries later – Romans would know as the Campus Martius, the Field of Mars.

According to ancient writers, the city of Rome was founded in 753 B.C.E., but there is little archaeological evidence to suggest that at that time it was much more than a cluster of humble villages.[5] While a crude stone wall enveloped the Palatine Hill to the southwest of the Capitoline, and wood and thatch huts sat along the Palatine's crest, the most famous of the city's republican gathering places, the Roman Forum, was then a mere swampy lowland populated with a smattering of small dwellings and burial plots.[6] The northern plain would have shown little evidence of human intrusion, and although a century after the city's mythical founding other areas of Rome had changed dramatically, the floodplain to the north of the Capitoline was still open and marshy with few, if any, man-made structures.[7] The villages resting on Rome's hills and tucked in its lower valleys had, by the sixth century B.C.E., expanded and converged into a city of stone, wood, and terracotta covering approximately 2.8 square kilometers. Fortified walls were under construction, and in the valley south of the Capitoline, the primitive wooden huts were cleared away to make space for the building of the Roman Forum.[8] An open sewer channel, later covered and known as the Cloaca Maxima, helped to drain the basin of the Forum.[9] On the lower of the two Capitoline peaks, the great Temple of Jupiter Optimus Maximus (Jupiter Best and Greatest) rose on a terrace approximately 3,300 square meters in area.[10] With white stucco walls, timber beams, and a wooden roof crowned by a statue of Jupiter in a chariot,[11] the enormous temple served as Rome's most significant religious structure. The open area that surrounded the temple functioned as the meeting place for Rome's first assembly, the Comitia Calata.[12]

With the *pomerium* located at the foot of the Capitoline, the open plain to the north began to be used for military musters. Roman men of fighting age assembled in the marshland every spring before heading off on a path that led north in the direction of hostile tribes in Etruria. Annual equestrian contests were also held in the field. With the possible exception of a small altar to Mars near the center of the field, it was not until two more centuries had passed that visible changes finally came to the marshy field north of the Capitoline.[13] During the fifth century B.C.E., a large clearing was prepared about 300 meters beyond the hill in which citizens would congregate every five years to be counted in a census.[14] Known as the Villa Publica, the gathering space remained free of permanent structures, although a portico and buildings were added two centuries later during a renovation (Plan 2, No. 4).[15] Soon after space was cleared for the Villa Publica, a temple was erected on the southern edge of the field. Dedicated in 431 B.C.E. to Apollo Medicus (Apollo the Healer), the temple was raised in response to a plague that had recently ravaged the city (Plan 2, Inset C).[16] The city continued to grow to the south and east with walls, temples, public buildings, aqueducts, and housing, but the northern plain was slower to see change. Roman writers do not report construction of a second significant structure in the plain before 296 B.C.E., when a temple to the war goddess Bellona was vowed and a few years later dedicated next to Apollo's temple (Plan 2, Inset C).[17]

Three decades later, the pace of construction quickened with the advent of the three Punic Wars (264 to 146 B.C.E.). The open space north of the city walls soon became a popular site for the placement of temples vowed by generals. A vegetable market, the Forum Holitorium, just to the northwest of the Capitoline and near to the temples of Apollo and Bellona, became the location for three temples (Plan 2, Inset D).[18] By the Forum Holitorium and the temples of Apollo Medicus and Bellona, a site for temporary markets and public meetings developed. Over time, the space known as the Circus Flaminius would be articulated by temple precincts and portico complexes (Plan 2). For the first time, the center of the plain became a construction site as well. In and around a sacred zone now known as the Largo Argentina (Plan 2, Inset A), temples of rather obscure water deities were erected. At least sixteen temples, or more than half of Rome's temples vowed during the period of the Punic Wars, rose on the floodplain north of the city walls.[19]

Whereas the orientation of the Circus Flaminius and the temples on its edge generally followed the path of the Tiber River to its west, the republican temples in the Largo Argentina district were built along a north-south axis, a topographical pattern that was expanded in future centuries of ancient Roman construction. The earlier dirt road used by mustering troops was monumentalized and renamed the Via Flaminia (Plan 2). It became a major Roman highway jammed with soldiers heading off to distant northern and western battlefronts, as well as farmers and merchants transporting agricultural products, imported items, building materials, and domestic animals to and from the city center. The northern marshland also became a destination point for citizens participating in Rome's numerous religious festivals. Temporary stages and bleachers were erected near temples for theatrical events connected with temple dedications and annual celebrations. A practice track for horse racing likely was cleared near the Tiber. The area around the Circus Flaminius would also attract spectators to the gathering point for triumphal parades awarded by the Senate to successful military generals.

By the beginning of the first century B.C.E., clusters of temples and some porticoes were located in the southern and central portions of the plain, reflecting the captured wealth from Rome's successful foreign conquests. The perimeter of the Circus Flaminius was now clearly defined by permanent edifices, including two temples of Hercules (Plan 2, Nos. 7 and 10) and temples of Juno Regina (Juno the Queen) and her consort Jupiter Stator (Jupiter the Stayer), both enclosed, at least in part, by the Porticus Metelli (Plan 2, Inset B). A temple of Neptune (Plan 2, No. 11), one of Mars (Plan 3, No. 23), and a temple of the twin horse tamers Castor and Pollux (Plan 3, No. 19) also rested on the edge of the circus. A portico built by Gnaeus Octavius, an ancestor of Rome's first emperor Augustus, ran along the northeast side of the Circus Flaminius, either covering over or parallel to a major street leading into the heart of the northern field (Plan 3, No. 24).[20] In the Largo Argentina region, a round temple now identified as honoring Fortuna Huiusce Diei (the goddess of the present day) was added (Plan 3, Inset A). The northern portion of the field that spread its way up to the narrow throat between the Tiber and the Pincian Hill remained open and relatively undeveloped. Because the plain was beyond the *pomerium*, burials were allowed there.

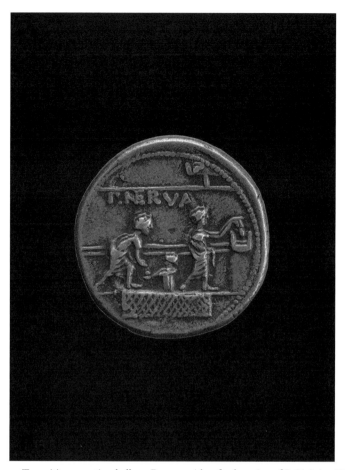

2. Two citizens casting ballots. Reverse side of a denarius of P. Licinius Nerva (113–112 B.C.E.). (Photo: Trustees of the British Museum)

The late republic in Rome was a period of great men jockeying for power with the means to use architecture as a tool to promote their political ambitions. No longer needed for military musters, the flatland north of the Capitoline had sufficient space for enormous structures to reflect the glory of outsized personalities. Moreover, because of its associations with Rome's mythic beginnings, it provided an appropriate location to realize these projects. Temporary wooden entertainment venues became larger and more elaborate, and in the mid-first century C.E. Rome's first permanent theater rose just west of the Largo Argentina. Erected by one of the republic's most successful generals, Pompey the Great (106–48 B.C.E.), the enormous stone theater was complemented by a large open space fronted on three sides by an ornate portico (Plan 3, Nos. 25 and 26). Dedicated in 55 B.C.E., Pompey's theater was then the tallest structure on the field north of the Capitoline and dominated the landscape.[21]

Nearby, Roman citizens congregated in a precinct known as the Saepta for voting (Figure 2) in the centuriate assemblies (*comitia centuriata*) and tribunal

assemblies (*comitia tribunata*). As an architectural counterpoint to the constructions of his rival Pompey, Julius Caesar (100–44 B.C.E.) conceived of a plan for
replacing the Saepta with a massive colonnaded voting precinct, which was
finally brought to fruition under the reign of Augustus (Plan 3, No. 7). While
not leaving a permanent mark on the northern plain, Julius Caesar used it for
grandiose displays, such as mock naval battles in an artificial basin called the
Naumachia Caesaris. He even conceived a plan for straightening out the Tiber
and adding land to the east bank.[22] Caesar's proposal would have allowed an
expanded plain to house Rome's growing population.[23] Although the scheme
was never implemented, the field was beginning to see private development,
much of it unauthorized.[24]

Besting Pompey for bragging rights in the field north of the Capitoline
proved elusive for Julius Caesar. Ironically, Caesar defeated his rival at the
Battle of Pharsalus in 48 B.C.E. yet was felled by assassins in an annex to
Pompey's theater. With Caesar's death came further political turmoil that
resulted in the rise of Octavian, Caesar's adopted son, who became Rome's
first emperor, Augustus. Octavian was very familiar with the open field north
of the city. In his youth, he went riding on the plain, and it was there that he
camped his troops when he marched back to Rome in 43 B.C.E. to claim his
rightful inheritance following Caesar's death.[25] After defeating the forces of
Mark Antony and Cleopatra VII at the Battle of Actium in 31 B.C.E., Augustus
began a building program that saw an extraordinary transformation of the
former marshland. Apart from addressing renovations to existing structures
such as the Saepta, now the Saepta Julia, Augustus ordered the erection of new
buildings, including his future burial site. A magnificent circular tumulus, the
Mausoleum of Augustus dominated the northern horizon and reset the limits
of the developed area to the north (Plan 3, No. 1).[26]

An undifferentiated area during the previous century, the northern part
of the plain was highly organized during Augustus's reign with structures that
related to one another, reflecting the substantial imprint of the emperor's building program. Along the Via Flaminia south of the Mausoleum, a square marble
altar complex known as the Altar of Augustan Peace (Ara Pacis Augustae) was
dedicated in 9 B.C.E. following Augustus's safe return from triumphal campaigns in Gaul and Iberia (Plan 3, No. 3). Adjacent to the altar complex was a
horologium composed of an obelisk of red-gray Egyptian granite surmounted
by a sphere, the shadow of which fell on a bronze marker inset in travertine
(Plan 3, No. 2).

Augustus's chief military commander, Marcus Agrippa (63–12 B.C.E.) was
given the task of transforming the center of the field. These projects included
completion of the Saepta Julia, construction of a building to count votes
(Diribitorium), Rome's first imperial bathhouse (Thermae Agrippae), an artificial lake (Stagnum), and the original Pantheon (Plan 3, Nos. 10, 12, 13,

and 30). In order to supply the baths and other structures in the Campus Martius with fresh water as well as supply drinking water to villas across the Tiber, Agrippa ordered the construction of a new aqueduct, the Aqua Virgo. Oriented north-south and east-west, the Augustan era additions to the Field of Mars defined the organization of construction on the plain for several centuries thereafter. Placed in a depression that has been associated with the Goat Marsh (Caprae Palus), the site of Romulus's legendary ascension to the heavens, the Agrippan projects benefited from a subterranean drainage infrastructure that made the area now suitable for large buildings.[27]

Although Pompey's theater was the first permanent entertainment venue in Rome, others were soon raised on the northern field. An amphitheater used for gladiatorial games was constructed in an unknown location and dedicated in 29 B.C.E. by Statilius Taurus, the commander of Augustus's land forces at the Battle of Actium. To the southeast of the temples in the Largo Argentina, the noble L. Cornelius Balbus, who served under Julius Caesar, built a second stone theater complex (Plan 3, No. 16). Augustus had yet a third permanent theater placed close to the temples of Apollo and Bellona, naming it for his deceased nephew Marcellus (Plan 3, No. 17). The three theaters alone created permanent seating for as many as 45,000 Romans eager to attend theatrical performances and witness wild animal hunts and gladiatorial combat. In a few short decades, the plain had been transformed from a mostly open, marshy area with temples and wooden bleachers for occasional festivals to a daily draw for citizens for bathing, shopping, and entertainment.

By the death of Augustus in 14 C.E., many of the republican temples and other public structures located around the Circus Flaminius had been refurbished and new ones added, all dedicated to the greater glory of Augustus and the imperial family. The Porticus Metelli was reconstructed, expanded, and renamed the Porticus Octaviae after the emperor's sister (Plan 3, Inset B). The Temple of Hercules Musarum (Hercules of the Muses) was surrounded now by a portico (Porticus Philippi) erected by L. Marcius Philippus, Augustus's stepfather (Plan 3, Inset B). Several restored temples, including temples honoring the gods Apollo Medicus (now referred to as Apollo Sosianus), Jupiter Stator, Juno Regina, Neptune, Mars, and Felicitas, were rededicated on Augustus's official birth date, September 23.[28]

Although the Villa Publica in the earlier centuries had extended over approximately 150,000 square meters of the northern plain, its area had been pared down considerably by this time. The Theater of Balbus, the Saepta Julia, and the Diribitorium now filled the once open space where soldiers formerly gathered and the census had been taken.[29] Colonnades enclosed gardens and, in the central portion of the plain, former marshland was being converted to tame public parks interspersed among monuments. The open fields – once vast – were rapidly shrinking.[30] Nevertheless, sufficient open parkland in the northern and western reaches must have remained because, according to Strabo, space was available to accommodate chariot racing and equestrian exercises "without interference" and there was ground "covered with grass throughout the year."

Despite the greater use of stone and concrete in the buildings in the northern plain, wooden structural timbers were employed throughout the area. This meant that fire was a constant danger in the Campus Martius, as elsewhere, in a city of about one million inhabitants. Devastating conflagrations periodically erupted there in the first century C.E., resulting in the need for reconstruction of many of the Augustan architectural monuments and providing space for new imperial projects. The Theater of Pompey was damaged by flames and repaired in 21 C.E., and the Amphitheater of Statilius Taurus was destroyed in the fire of 64 during the reign of Nero (r. 54–68 C.E.), and there is no indication that it was thereafter rebuilt. The great fire of 64 inflicted even more damage within the city walls, and the emperor temporarily used the area north of the Capitoline to house a population displaced by the flames.[31] Just a few years previously, Nero had added a second great bathhouse, complete with gymnasium, the Thermae Neronianae, just northwest of Agrippa's baths (Plan 4, No. 18).[32]

A major fire in the spring of 80 C.E. was particularly destructive to the buildings north of the Capitoline.[33] For three days and nights, flames raced through the plain. Smoke and fire poured out of the Saepta, the Baths of Agrippa, the Pantheon, the Theater of Balbus, the stage building at Pompey's theater, and many more structures.[34] The Diribitorium – headquarters for firefighters in a previous blaze – was also a victim as its giant roof of larch wood came crashing to the floor.[35] Next to the Saepta, temples less than a century old and dedicated to the Egyptian deities Isis and Serapis also burned (Plan 3, No. 5).[36] While the emperor Titus (r. 79–81 C.E.) was in Campania attending to the disaster that befell Pompeii and Herculaneum a few months earlier, fire brigades raced to douse the flames whose sparks had even reached the Temple of Jupiter on the Capitoline.[37]

Many of the structures that were charred and in a state of collapse from the fire of 80 C.E. were restored by order of the emperor Domitian (r. 81–96 C.E.). The theaters of Pompey and Balbus, the Saepta, Agrippa's baths, temples of Egyptian gods Isis and Serapis, and the Pantheon were all substantially repaired and restored. The giant horologium of Augustus was relaid to improve its accuracy.[38] Apart from reconstruction projects, Domitian left his own mark on the urban development of the plain. He reduced the Villa Publica to a small park one-tenth its previous size and erected in its center a pair of temples dedicated to the divine incarnations of his brother Titus and his father Vespasian, renaming the set of buildings the Divorum (Plan 4, No. 9). Next to that complex, the emperor commissioned the Temple of Minerva Chalcidica

(Plan 4, No. 8).[39] Just to the north of the Theater of Pompey, a smaller covered theater, the Odeum, was built (Plan 4, No. 20), as was a new venue for athletic competition known as the Stadium of Domitian (Plan 4, No. 19).

The relative wealth and political stability of the second century C.E. encouraged another spurt of construction with the addition of several buildings in the center of the once open field by Hadrian and his Antonine successors. Totally reconstructed under Hadrian, the Pantheon (Plan 4, No. 14) took the form we recognize today (Plate I). Hadrian also erected nearby a temple to his deceased mother-in-law Matidia (Plan 4, No. 13), and just east of the Temple to the Divine Matidia, Hadrian's successor Antoninus Pius (r. 138–61 C.E.) caused to be erected the Temple of the Divine Hadrian (Plan 4, No. 4). To the north a freestanding column with a base displaying a personification of the Campus Martius was erected in memory of Antoninus Pius and his wife Faustina by their adopted sons Marcus Aurelius and Lucius Verus. Near to this memorial, another tall marble column depicting battle scenes and a temple were later built to honor Marcus Aurelius (r. 161–80 C.E.).

During the reign of Alexander Severus (r. 222–35 C.E.), the Porticus Octaviae was burned and repaired, while the Baths of Nero was expanded and renamed for the emperor as the Thermae Alexandrianae (Plan 4, No. 18). The large open spaces of the Campus Martius had now vanished, and the construction of major public buildings on the once marshy plain was nearly over. The area north of the Capitoline had been filled with temples, baths, and theaters laced together with kilometers of porticoes enclosing beautiful gardens.[40] Between the imperial structures were numerous shops, warehouses, and apartments. After 800 years, the Campus Martius was finally built out. By the mid-third century C.E. there was little, if any, open space left unencumbered. The massive Aurelian Wall defined the northernmost reach of the plain by the end of that century, encompassing within its nineteen-kilometer perimeter the area that is the focus of this study as well as much of the rest of the city (Plan 5). The *pomerium* had moved north as well, reaching at least as far as the center of the plain and possibly along the Aurelian Wall.[41]

Had Strabo been alive four centuries after the Augustan era, he would have likely marveled at the increased number of marbled colonnades, sacred precincts, theaters, and very costly temples against the stage backdrop of the "crowns of those hills that are above the river and extend as far as its bed." The amphitheater he had observed was gone, but the Odeum and Stadium built after his day were active entertainment sites. What was no longer present in the fourth century C.E. to have caught a viewer's eye was the open space he had so admired, used "without interference" for "chariot-races and every other equestrian exercise," "ball-playing" and "hoop-trundling," and "the ground . . . covered with grass throughout the year." The Campus Martius was now finely woven within Rome's urban fabric.

SPACE

So where exactly in this plain was the area that the Romans called the "Campus Martius"? This question has been the subject of modern scholarly contention for generations. Roman writers do not inform the controversy because they used the term somewhat loosely in their descriptions. "Campus" generally referred to land lying outside of the *pomerium* and was sometimes, but not always, conjoined with the name of the nearest gate or associated with a particular structure or entity.[42] Occasionally, early sources employed a broadly descriptive phrase for the location of a building while describing another structure or event as located "in campo," leading some scholars to draw boundary lines around the Campus Martius on the basis of such distinctions.[43] The use of the war god's name in connection with "campus," at least in extant literary sources, was a mid-first-century B.C.E. development and even after that point not consistently employed. Firm conclusions about its use as a distinguishing spatial marker are, therefore, difficult to reach.

Gazing down at the plain from any of the surrounding hills, an ancient Roman could observe a few natural reference points – the Tiber on the west and northwest, the row of hills on the east and at least two drainage channels that flowed from the hills to the river.[44] Until the addition of man-made structures, there was nothing tangible to separate one part of the floodplain from another. Ancient writers tell us of several other discernible areas of the early Field of Mars: an oak grove somewhere north of the Tiber Island, the Caprae Palus in the center of the space, and fields of grain.[45] In the fifth century B.C.E., there were finally two structural imprints defining the space, the Villa Publica and the Temple of Apollo Medicus. It is generally thought that the path north abutting the Villa Publica and that later became the Via Flaminia served as the eastern edge of the Campus Martius (Plan 3).[46]

It has been argued that one of the two streams crossing the plain, the Petronia Amnis, formed a southern border to the Campus Martius, thereby excluding from the campus zone the large open area of the Circus Flaminus and the many temples that surrounded it.[47] Support for excluding the structures in the Circus Flaminius from the Campus Martius is found in the fact that some ancient references describe their location as "in circo Flaminio" and not "in campo Martio."[48] Counterarguments are offered that, although the Petronia Amnis may have been a northwestern boundary to the Circus Flaminius, that fact does not necessarily mean it was the border of the Campus Martius, because the Field of Mars was likely subdivided into smaller tracts whose titles identified more precise locations.[49] Moreover, some structures were noted as residing both "in circo Flaminio" and "in campo Martio."[50] Certainly, by his reference to "three theatres and an amphitheatre," Strabo clearly believed that the Theater of Marcellus at the southern edge of the Circus Flaminius was within the same campus as the theaters of Pompey and Balbus northeast of the Petronia Amnis.[51]

With respect to the western line of the Campus Martius, there is no debate that the campus did not extend further to the west than the east bank of the Tiber River. It has been suggested, however, that it stopped short of the river's edge, following the line of an ancient southeast-northwest road running from the Circus Flaminius to a bridge (the Pons Neronianus) crossing the river about 1.3 kilometers upstream.[52] The northern reach of the Campus Martius had no clear natural divider, but the bend in the river by the modern Ponte Cavour created a narrow throat of land between the Tiber and the Pincian Hill, extending just past the modern Piazza del Popolo. When it was constructed in the late first century B.C.E., Augustus's Mausoleum was the only major structure in this area. Located halfway between the river and the Via Flaminia, it likely created a strong visual signpost for the northernmost limits of the Field of Mars (Plan 3, No. 1). As with the southern border, however, this conclusion, too, is in dispute.[53] The third-century C.E. Aurelian Wall, built about a half kilometer north of the Mausoleum, would have also provided a convenient demarcation for the northern edge of the Campus Martius, but it is not clear that it served that function (Plan 5).[54]

Although it is not possible to reconcile all of the disputes over the borders of the Campus Martius, part of the debate may be due to shifting definitions of the space by ancient viewers. As natural features became obscured by man-made structures, alternate lines of demarcation likely developed, making easier the exclusion of some portions of the plain while confusing the division from others.[55] (Compare Plans 1 and 2.) Furthermore, the Campus Martius may have referred to different topographical conditions of the plain depending on context. Occasionally, the reference could be to the remaining open space as opposed to the entire built-up area.[56] Recalling Rome's panorama from his exile on the Black Sea, Ovid wrote:

> From my home, I turn my steps once more towards the beautiful city's regions and my mind surveys all those places using its own eyes. Now the fora, now the temples, now the theatres clad in marble, now the colonnades and their level grounds rise up before me, and now the grassy Campus Martius with its view of fair gardens, and the pools and canals and the water of the Virgo.[57]

There were some defining structures that separated the developed areas from the shrinking open spaces. In the late first century B.C.E., the arches of the Aqua Virgo that crossed the Via Flaminia and the north side of the Saepta Julia would have created a visual boundary line between the northern fields and the increasingly crowded southern campus.[58] About a century and a half later, that boundary had pushed north about 152 meters to the road that connected the Pons Neronianus to the Via Flaminia. The closely sited Stadium of Domitian, Baths of Nero, Pantheon forecourt, Temple of the Divine Matidia, and Temple of the Divine Hadrian dominated the southern side of that cross street whose ancient name remains uncertain.[59] (See Plan 4.) Their crowded placement must have made the fields to the north appear even more isolated.[60]

In 7 B.C.E., administrative order was imposed on the topography of the city, including the Campus Martius. In that year, Augustus reconfigured Rome's four main districts and added territory outside of the *pomerium* to create fourteen administrative regions. Composed of smaller wards known as *vici*, the regions were indicated by small stone markers, or *cippi*. Municipal services such as street maintenance and fire fighting were organized on a regional basis.[61] All of the area west of the Via Flaminia to the river's edge and from the Capitoline to at least as far north as the Mausoleum of Augustus fell within Region IX.[62] This would have included the monuments around the Circus Flaminius and the Theater of Marcellus and arguably the Forum Holitorium. Augustus's urban reorganization identified the Via Flaminia as the eastern boundary of that region. The land north of the Capitoline but east of the Via Flaminia extending to the Quirinal and Pincian Hills was relegated to Region VII.[63] The fourth-century C.E. regionary catalogs, which provide names to the various regions, do not call Region IX the Campus Martius, however; instead, the tract is called "Circus Flaminius."[64] While at one time the *pomerium* could be used as a dividing line to separate the Field of Mars from the city, that designation, too, was subject to revision with *cippi*.[65]

This study uses "Campus Martius" to identify the plain north of the city from the Via Flaminia to the Tiber's edge and from the temples of Apollo and Bellona and the Forum Holitorium to the Mausoleum of Augustus, essentially the space encompassed by Region IX. Although there were apparently some distinct areas within the large plain, the whole seems to have been viewed as more than the sum of its parts. Cicero noted, for instance, "I think, indeed, that if the Campus Martius were to be divided, and if every one of you had two feet of standing ground allotted to him in it, still you would prefer to enjoy the whole of it together, than for each individual to have a small portion for his own private property."[66] The fact that the space had certain physical attributes and was beyond the *pomerium* until at least the mid-first century C.E. more likely influenced its architectural development than any topographical labels used in Augustus's *regiones* system.

Even when viewed under the most expansive definition, the Campus Martius was no larger than many parks in the modern world's great cities, and in some cases much smaller. Measured with the Via Flaminia as the eastern edge and including the Circus Flaminius area, the Field of Mars was only about 1.7 square kilometers.[67] That is approximately half the size of New York's Central Park, or about two-thirds of the combined area of London's Hyde Park and Kensington Gardens. Paris's Bois de Boulogne is about five times larger. What the Campus Martius lacked in buildable area, it made up for in political, martial, and architectural significance.

CHAPTER TWO

GATHERING TROOPS IN THE WAR GOD'S FIELD

If you were on the Capitoline facing north on a summer's day in 717 B.C.E., you would have witnessed, according to Plutarch, a large thundercloud drifting ever lower until it touched the swampy ground in the general area where the Pantheon now stands. That ominous mist was about to envelop and carry off Rome's sacred and mythical founder, Romulus.[1] Livy described the fantastical scene occurring on the Nones of Quintilis (July 7), noting that,

> as the king was holding a muster in the Campus Martius, near the swamp of Capra [or Goat Marsh], for the purpose of reviewing the army, suddenly a storm came up, with loud claps of thunder, and enveloped him in a cloud so thick as to hide him from the sight of the assembly; and from that moment Romulus was no more on earth.[2]

On seeing Romulus's throne empty, the citizens unanimously recognized that their king had transformed into a deity; they quickly declared Romulus to be a god and the son of a god.[3] This story is revealing in several respects: it suggests a popular recollection of the Campus Martius as a place to muster troops; it notes the early topography of the area as marshy; and, by describing Romulus's ascension, it creates the conditions for a sacred space. As discussed later in this chapter, many centuries after this mythical event, Romans were still making an annual pilgrimage to the Caprae Palus on a holiday called the Nonae Capratinae (Nones of the Goat), possibly to celebrate Romulus's apotheosis.[4]

MUSTERING FOR BATTLE

To contemporaries of Livy or Plutarch, there were few, if any, visual cues afforded by the field, then covered by temples, baths, and colonnades, to indicate to them that large numbers of soldiers would have once massed there and witnessed an apotheosis or, indeed, gathered together for any other purpose. Yet the memory of the Campus Martius as a mustering ground persisted, as evidenced by two stories Livy recounted. In 458 B.C.E., the Roman people urged Cincinnatus to come to the aid of the city and lift the siege laid by the Aequians against the camp of the hapless consul L. Minucius Esquilinus. Cincinnatus, then out plowing his fields, was convinced to drop his tools, don his toga, and assume emergency dictatorial powers. Before dawn the following day, he met the assembled citizens in the Forum and issued instructions that before sunset each man of military age was to assemble in the Campus Martius with his equipment and supplies. Cincinnatus's command was heeded. By sunset the battle-ready troops were assembled on the Field of Mars. The army promptly marched from there to the battlefield and, in short order, defeated the Aequians.[5] Similarly, Livy recorded how, in preparation for battle against the Volscians in 446 B.C.E., "the standards were fetched from the treasury by the quaestors that very day, and being carried to the Campus Martius, headed the line of march from the mustering ground."[6]

From the city's earliest days, the flat plain north of the city walls provided an ideal location for the gathering of troops. First and foremost, it was outside the *pomerium* and, therefore, the plain was a permissible collection point for Rome's army.[7] Second, at 1.7 square kilometers in size, the area between the river and the later-built Via Flaminia provided more than enough space for assembling many citizens, whether for military or enumeration purposes. Third, the military provided protection to those gathering to vote, and because the Campus Martius was used for that purpose, the army's presence amid the election activities was appropriate.[8] Fourth, after the completion of the Via Flaminia in the late third century B.C.E., soldiers who gathered in the Campus Martius could mobilize quickly to engage Rome's enemies located north of the capital.

While the field was well established by the fifth century B.C.E. as a mustering ground for the city's army, it was not the only location for assembling troops outside the *pomerium*. Livy's account of preparation for battle against the Gauls in Latium in 350 B.C.E. notes that, rather than assemble in the Campus Martius, all young men were ordered to appear by the Temple of Mars located along the Via Appia, south of the city.[9] Because the Gauls were camped along the Alban Mount by which the Appian Way passed, it is reasonable that armies heading southeast from Rome would gather outside the *pomerium* on the southern side of the city rather than circumnavigate the perimeter of the walls from

3. Detail, *suovetaurilia* from the Paris/Munich reliefs (formerly known as the Altar of Ahenobarbus) (first century B.C.E.). Louvre, Paris. (Photo: © RMN-Grand Palais / Art Resource, New York)

the Campus Martius. However, because the army was assembled in the Field of Mars for reasons other than just receiving its marching orders, there may have been a combination of various martial activities that made the space the primary military gathering location.

For instance, the campus was the site of the census that took place every five years for the purpose of dividing the male citizenry into appropriate military units.[10] Rome's legendary sixth-century B.C.E. king, Servius Tullius, was credited with holding the first census to organize the army into wealth-based military units known as centuries. Livy recounts that once the initial census was completed, Servius issued a proclamation commanding all Roman citizens, "to assemble at daybreak, each in his own century, in the Campus Martius."[11] Once assembled, enrolled citizens witnessed a *lustrum*, a blood offering to the god Mars, signaling the completion of the census and intended for purification. Magistrates sacrificed a pig, a sheep, and a bull in an exceptionally sacred ceremony known as the *suovetaurilia*.[12] A famous marble relief in the Louvre, reportedly found in the area of the Circus Flaminius, depicts a lustration with the three sacrificial animals (Figure 3).[13] In 443 B.C.E., officials called censors were first used to conduct the census. Eight years later, the Villa Publica was established to provide a fixed location on the Campus Martius at which citizens could gather and be counted.[14] Centuriate assemblies, or *comitia centuriata*, also met on the plain to choose their commanders and vote for war or peace.[15] Cassius Dio recorded that all soldiers were required to attend the assemblies.[16] As John Rich has written, it was "no accident that, when the people met to elect their chief magistrates, who commanded the army, they assembled outside the city on the Campus Martius – the field of Mars, the war god."[17]

Although Livy claims that Servius Tullius enrolled 80,000 citizens in the first military census, the army in the field was much smaller.[18] It originally consisted of at least one legion (from *legio*, meaning "to levy") of sixty centuries, each composed of approximately 100 infantry soldiers for a total of 6,000 heavily armed infantry plus 2,400 *velites*, soldiers with light weaponry.[19] For much of the republic, the size of a century fluctuated, but in Polybius's day a legion was composed generally of 4,200 soldiers and 5,000 in times of special danger.[20]

By the end of the fourth century B.C.E., the army contained four legions or approximately 16,000 men,[21] a size that could be easily organized in the open field north of the *pomerium*.

The requirement that the military gather outside of the *pomerium* was a centuries-old tradition; however, there were no obvious physical boundary markers for the *pomerium* other than stone *cippi* until the so-called Servian Wall was built in the fourth century B.C.E. (See Plan 5.)[22] Although Livy credits the sixth-century B.C.E. king with constructing the wall and thereby extending the *pomerium* to the approximate limits of the enclosure,[23] it is widely accepted that the eponymous reference to Servius Tullius is incorrect and that the wall postdated the sack of the city by the Gauls in 390 B.C.E.[24] Approximately eleven kilometers in length, the fortification enclosed just under five square kilometers of the city, or two and one-third times the area of the Campus Martius, encircling all or part of the original seven hills of Rome.[25] The pomerial line delineated the ritually defined boundary, but it was the stone ramparts themselves that provided the physical barrier preventing uniformed soldiers from entering the city without senatorial permission. When viewed in conjunction with the Villa Publica established a half century earlier, the Servian Wall must have clearly delimited the Campus Martius as a space important to Rome's strong and developing military traditions.

Even though it was considered most prudent to keep armed soldiers outside of the city walls, it was risky, because it made other areas of Rome vulnerable to attack when its forces were mostly concentrated on the northern plain. Although the Tiber River and the nearby foothills of the Apennines might have provided some sense of security from northern invaders, this was not actually the case. As the Gallic sack of Rome in 390 B.C.E. demonstrated, the northern plain was easily bypassed by attackers who simply laid siege to the city from other, more vulnerable points.[26] To prevent sneak attacks, sentries flew a red flag from the Janiculum Hill to signal that no enemy was in sight.[27]

Beginning in the mid-fifth century B.C.E., a pattern of annual warfare began to develop. Rome was at war for fifteen of the twenty-five years from 440 to 416 B.C.E., and thereafter, during the century and a half from 415 B.C.E. to the beginning of the First Punic War in 264 B.C.E., there were only thirteen years when Rome was not fighting its enemies.[28] During the fifth century, the battles were conducted in alliance with other tribes and with a limited geographic reach as Rome fought the Volsci, the Aequi, and the southern Etruscans.[29] As one author has noted, Rome was a "frontier-town," with the Tiber that ran the length of the Campus Martius and beyond serving as the border with territory controlled by Etruria.[30] By the fourth century B.C.E., however, the Romans were battling in the Samnite Wars for supremacy of the Italian Peninsula and, thus, fighting further and further from their home base.

Nevertheless, with exceptions such as the lengthy siege of Veii resulting in its capture in 396 B.C.E., until the start of the First Punic War in 264 B.C.E., Roman warfare generally had what has been called an "annual rhythm," with most campaigns restricted to the summer months.[31] The Campus Martius would have been part of this seasonal cycle, witnessing the collection of troops in the spring and their discharge every fall.

The three Punic Wars and several military confrontations with the Greek kings in the eastern Mediterranean far from Rome brought significant changes to the yearly military musters and to the use, therefore, of the Campus Martius. As many as ten legions were deployed to fight Rome's distant enemies and, as a result, permanent, manned garrisons were created.[32] By the beginning of the Second Punic War in 218 B.C.E., service in the military had generally changed from part-time, seasonal campaigns to year-round duty,[33] although at that time the soldiers made up what has been termed a "peoples' army," with as much as 26 percent of the male population participating in the war.[34] An elected magistrate returning to Rome in the fall brought with him only those soldiers who had finished their years of service. In the spring, his successor would head out to meet his troops with new recruits in tow.[35]

Some historians believe that since campaigns were often conducted far from Rome in the third century B.C.E., the procedure for declaring war was altered, too, and it seems likely that the martial functions of the Campus Martius may have changed. Livy wrote that during the time of the kings, Roman priests, known as *fetiales*, would ceremonially cast a spear into enemy territory prior to the formal declaration of war in Rome.[36] The priest would travel to the disputed territory and demand redress for a perceived wrong. Then, according to Livy, if after thirty-three days his requests failed to accomplish the desired result, the *fetialis* returned to Rome for consultation. After approval from the Senate, the priest would once again depart for the enemy lines, tossing a spear across the border to signal the official commencement of war. Although Livy claimed that the practice was continued by later generations, the several examples of *fetiales* going to the enemy to declare war in the fourth and early third centuries B.C.E. make no mention of the spear-hurling ceremony.[37] Late Roman commentators explained that the practice became impractical when enemies were pushed further and further from the city limits and that as a result the ritual was revised around 280 B.C.E. with senatorial legates throwing a spear into specially designated "enemy territory" located in the area later known as the Circus Flaminius.[38] In an act of war declaration against Mark Antony and Cleopatra, Augustus hurled a spear from a location near a war column, or *columna bellica*, in the area of the Temple of Bellona, the war goddess.[39] Whether the use of the southern end of the Campus Martius as mock enemy territory was simply a bit of drama started by Augustus or was begun more than two centuries earlier, the fact that the space was outside of the *pomerium* would have made it appropriate for that purpose.[40]

As the theaters of war spread beyond the Italian Peninsula in the third century B.C.E., Rome needed to move its troops farther and faster. Likely in anticipation of renewed fighting with the Carthaginians, the Via Flaminia was constructed in 220 B.C.E. to cut roughly north-south through the plain along a previous path. Once completed, the road would come to demarcate clearly the eastern edge of the Campus Martius.[41] When the censor Gaius Flaminius Nepos finished the highway, it stretched approximately 362 kilometers from the Porta Fontinalis in the Servian Wall by the Capitoline to the Milvian Bridge and then north to Ariminum, ancient Rimini.[42] The new road facilitated the quick march of troops north through the Italian Peninsula and ultimately to Spain, a strategically important territory during the Second Punic War.[43]

When the Third Punic War ended in 146 B.C.E., the whole of the Mediterranean basin was under Roman control.[44] Rome's soldiers, now scattered far and wide, no longer marched home at the end of a season of battles. By the early first century B.C.E., the annual levies of citizens for war appear to have stopped, and with the military reforms under the consulship of Gaius Marius in 104 B.C.E., landless citizens, the so-called *capite censi*, were accepted into an army now better organized into units called cohorts.[45] During the reign of Augustus the citizen army finally disappeared, replaced by professional soldiers serving for as long as twenty-five years.[46] In the first century B.C.E., the function of the Field of Mars as a gathering point for the deployment of soldiers abroad must have greatly diminished, although its use for musters had not stopped altogether. In 82 B.C.E., Sulla rushed his army back to Rome to oppose the forces of Marius inside the city. He had his army camp before the northern gates in the campus to await his orders.[47] Years later when Octavian advanced on the forces of Crassus that were held up in the capital city, he ordered his troops to establish a stronghold in the Campus Martius.[48] In these instances of civil war, the field was useful as a staging area for troops to engage in military intimidation of those within the walls rather than as a gathering point from which to march out to challenge foreign enemies.

Although construction projects in the plain began to encroach on the areas available for military exercises during the first century B.C.E., nonetheless sufficient space remained for that purpose if required, both within enclosed spaces and in open fields. The Villa Publica was large enough to house approximately 4,000 prisoners of war during the early part of the century.[49] The Saepta voting precinct could accommodate perhaps as many as 70,000 people at one time.[50] It is important to note that most of the northern part of the plain remained completely undeveloped until the building program of Augustus. Although musters for battle preparation were now rare, the open space in the Campus Martius continued to be used during the first century B.C.E. as a military exercise area and parade ground.[51] Writing a paean to peace during the first half of the first century B.C.E., the poet Lucretius despaired of "legions swarming round the Field of Mars [*campi*], rousing a mimic warfare – either side strengthened with large auxiliaries and horse, alike equipped with arms, alike inspired."[52] Varro described walking among the shade trees of the Villa Publica where "the cohorts encamp for a consular review, and here they display their arms."[53] In his youth, the future emperor Augustus would practice riding and other military exercises in the Campus Martius.[54] The imperative for a wide-open space had diminished, but at least until the late republic it was available for large military gatherings.

Rome's navy also utilized the Field of Mars. Archaeological evidence for the Roman naval arsenal and shipyards (*navalia*) along the Tiber's edge has been excavated upstream of the modern Ponte Sant'Angelo and tentatively dated to the fourth century B.C.E.[55] The *navalia* consisted of covered docks with peaked roofs over each ship.[56] After a naval battle in 338 B.C.E., ships of the Latin tribes that were not destroyed were brought back to the *navalia*,[57] and the naval forces of the consul Lutatius Catulus likely launched from the *navalia* in 242 B.C.E. during the First Punic War, ultimately returning home in triumph.[58] As with the army, the navy's use of the campus as a gathering point decreased with the onset of the imperial era. In the case of sailors, however, the reason had more to do with navigational limitations than changes in conscription. Silt began to obstruct the Tiber's mouth, prompting larger boats to be maintained at Puteoli in the south and at the nearby port at Ostia. The ship sheds, though, were not abandoned. Pliny notes that they were employed to house animals destined for games in the Circus Maximus, a use that also fit well with the changes in the function of the Field of Mars during the imperial period to a center of entertainment and recreation.[59]

The topographical characteristics of the Campus Martius that made it appropriate for collecting soldiers, whether for battle or political purposes, also presented certain limitations. As discussed in more detail in Chapter 6, the low, flat plain was prone to flooding in the late fall to early spring and generally marshy, particularly in the central area where the Pantheon now stands. Summer months saw swarms of mosquitoes and the risk in early fall of malaria. The seasonal nature of warfare during the early and mid-republic correlated with the topographical challenges presented by the low ground of the plain. Following the selection of new consuls each year, soldiers were collected every spring after the end of the winter rains to go off to do battle and returned in the fall after the dangers from mosquitoes abated but before the rains of late fall.[60]

Whatever difficulties a swampy plain presented to gathering an army at certain times of the year, the nearby hills overlooking the Campus Martius provided excellent vantage points from which officers and magistrates might observe military formations down below. Rome's army remained outside the *pomerium*, in large part because armed soldiers were not to be fully trusted, and just as the magistrates might watch the red flag of warning on the Janiculum, so too, the soldiers' actions could have been viewed from a hilltop.

Rome's armies also participated in the city's public pageantry and, in that sense, the Field of Mars was a stage for citizens to observe martial preparedness and entertainment. For instance, Livy noted that having defeated the Volscians and killed more than 13,000 of their men in 461 B.C.E., the Roman army under the leadership of the consul Lucretius laid out all of the captured booty in the plain for three days for public inspection and for reclamation by anyone recognizing his property.[61] When the last of the Macedonian line of Alexander the Great, Perseus of Macedon, was defeated in the Third Macedonian War, his flagship was brought to Rome. The city's population lined the Tiber's banks as the massive ship with sixteen banks of oars came up river to its berth at the *navalia*, laden with "splendid armor [and] royal fabrics."[62] In a separate event, Plutarch reported how the aged and somewhat corpulent general and consul Marius would draw a crowd by donning his armor and going to the campus to engage in equestrian games with much younger men.[63] Moreover, Octavian's spear toss into the symbolic "foreign" territory by the Temple of Bellona most certainly attracted an interested audience.

Whether viewed from the hilltops or up close, the military activity on the Campus Martius that likely transfixed most observers was the triumph. When significant battlefield success had been achieved, a conquering general and his victorious men could be awarded a military parade that would assemble with arms in the field and, in this rare instance, cross the pomerial line into the city. The triumphal procession helped accentuate the significance of the plain north of the *pomerium* as a center of activities associated with warfare in contradistinction to the city as a refuge of peace. A general who crossed the *pomerium* without having been awarded a triumph by the Senate lost his right to obtain that honor.[64] Fragmentary inscriptions carved at the time of Augustus, the *Fasti Triumphales*, record more than 200 military triumphs reaching back to Rome's mythical founding in the eighth century B.C.E.[65]

Because the Field of Mars was used for centuries as an important location to collect and send troops off to battle and to celebrate their return, it is not surprising that the space reflected myth and legend. However, by the time Livy recounted the story of how Romulus, a son of Mars, rose to heaven while surrounded by his mustered troops, soldiers had stopped using the campus for war preparations. Similarly, triumphs of conquering generals had ceased and were only an imperial prerogative. The field itself had been transformed from a marshland to a thriving center of entertainment and recreational activities. At that point in Rome's history, the story of Romulus's apotheosis could only confirm the Campus Martius as part of the city's foundation myth. Conclusions regarding the field's mythical significance during the early and mid-republican periods require consideration of the development of the stories surrounding Mars and Romulus.

MARS AND HIS FIELD

As a deity worshiped by the Romans, Mars appears to date to the beginning of the republic in the late sixth century B.C.E. and, perhaps, even earlier to the monarchy. A stone inscription dedicated to Mars likely dates to circa 500 B.C.E.,[66] and an ancient college of priests, the Arval Brotherhood, invoked Mars in the earliest surviving extended Latin text.[67] By the early third century B.C.E., his image began to appear on coins.[68] "Mars" may have been derived from various iterations of the name such as "Mavors," "Mamers," and "Marmor" found throughout the Italian Peninsula.[69] The god was extraordinarily significant to the Romans, second only to Jupiter as their patron.[70] Livy noted that Rome's second king, Numa, appointed *flamines* or priests for Jupiter, Mars, and Quirinus, and Ovid wrote that Mars was worshiped "above all gods."[71]

The antiquity and significance of Mars to the Romans is found in his connection to the calendar, a connection that reflects on his ties to the Campus Martius. Mars was the only god in the old Roman calendar for whom a month was clearly named, and it was his month March that began the year.[72] Until 153 B.C.E. consuls entered their official duties on March 1, the *feriae Marti*, commemorating the date when Mars's sacred shield, or *ancile*, fell from heaven.[73] To celebrate this event, the members of the *Salii Palatini* retrieved shields from the Regia in the Roman Forum and struck the *ancilia* with short spears or sticks as they marched through the streets of Rome singing hymns. This festival continued until the 24th of the month. On March 14, a horse race, the Equirria, was held in the Field of Mars. Although this was the first horse race of the calendar year, the Equirria was connected to a day of racing conducted two and a half weeks earlier (February 27), also on the Campus Martius. Both races were held in honor of Mars and, according to legend, had been initiated by Romulus.[74] As described by Ovid, "The day has kept the appropriate name of Equirria, derived from the races which the god himself beholds in his own plain [*in campo*]."[75] On the Ides of March another festival, Anna Perenna, was celebrated in the Campus Martius. Plebs would go out to the Field of Mars in pairs for a day of feasting and drinking, either in the open or in pitched tents.[76] Likely derived for the term to complete the circle of the year, *annare perennare*, Anna Perenna was depicted as an old hag representing the old year while Mars represented the new. Mars was generally associated with the patrician class, and the holiday celebrated by the plebs mocked the war god who was tricked into making love to the ugly Anna.[77] The last festival of the month of March was the Tubilustrium (March 23) during which military brass instruments were purified for use in summoning the *comitia curiata*, the curiate assemblies claimed to have been started by Romulus to validate the kings' *imperium* and later the consuls' *imperium*.[78]

Perhaps the most famous festival dedicated to Mars that took place in the Campus Martius was not celebrated in the month of March and was not even marked on the calendar. This was the ritual of the October Horse that took place on the Ides of October. Since the sixth century B.C.E.,[79] two chariots, each pulled by two fast horses, would race at some still undetermined location in the Campus Martius.[80] A horse of the winning racer would be sacrificed to Mars, killed, according to one ancient source, with a spear.[81] The tail and head were then cut off, with the former carried to the Regia so that its blood could drip on the sacred hearth and the latter fought over by two neighborhoods for the honor of displaying it.[82] As early as 300 B.C.E., a Greek writer named Timaeus sought to explain the significance of the then centuries-old ceremony by relating it to the wooden-horse legend of the Trojan War.[83]

Attempts to connect these various festivals together and to draw conclusions about the nature of the Roman god Mars have generated contentious scholarly discourse. Some have cast Mars as an agricultural god, others as a god of war, and some historians have argued for both.[84] Because the October Horse was characterized by at least two ancient writers as a "war horse" and the race occurred at the end of the campaign season, the sacrifice has been interpreted as a *lustrum* for the army as it lay down its weapons for the winter. It was tied, according to this theory, to the Equirria that opened the military campaign season.[85] It has also been suggested that the October Horse was associated with the harvest season and that Mars was from earliest times an agricultural deity whose name was invoked in lustrations for farmers.[86] The two theories are not mutually exclusive. The October Horse may have started as an agricultural harvest custom that changed over time to celebrate the end of the military season, "just as Mars originally perhaps the protector of man, herds, and crops alike becomes ... a deity of warriors and war horses of the yearly renewed strength of a struggling community."[87] For the purposes of this study, what is most significant is that for as long as Romans were gathering in the Campus Martius to go to war and to return from battle, festivals were celebrated there in honor of Mars, creating and continuously reinforcing a special, sacred link between the deity and the space.[88]

Despite the long association of the campus with military activities as well as with festivals connected to the war god, structures dedicated to Mars appear to have been few. There is thought to have been an altar to the war god (Ara Martis) in the Campus Martius, but no temple is known to have been associated with it.[89] The date of the establishment of the Ara Martis is unknown, although the writer Festus claimed it went back to the time of King Numa in the late eighth century B.C.E., 250 years before the first verifiable monument to Mars.[90] No remains have yet been found, nor has its location been definitively determined, but a reference in Livy to the construction of a portico in 193 B.C.E. from the Porta Fontinalis to the Ara Martis suggests by context that the altar was in the area of the Villa Publica (Plan 2, No. 5).[91] Livy noted that newly elected censors "as the custom was from olden times, took their seats on curule chairs by the altar of Mars."[92] As elusive as its location and age of construction is the date of the altar's disappearance. One historian believes that the Ara Martis was rebuilt after the fire of 80 C.E. and was located in the Divorum, the then remaining space of the earlier Villa Publica (Plan 4, No. 9).[93]

The first known temple dedicated to Mars and associated with the Campus Martius was erected circa 133 B.C.E. by Junius Brutus Callaicus.[94] According to Pliny, it contained giant statues of Mars and of Venus, both by the famed fourth-century B.C.E. sculptor Scopas, and was located in the Circus Flaminius.[95] If the Circus Flaminius is understood to be part of the Campus Martius, then Cassius Dio's report that "the temple of Mars in the field of the same name was struck by lightning" in 9 C.E., may refer to Callaicus's temple (Plan 3, No. 23).[96] Nearby and just south of the Circus Flaminius was a temple of Bellona, a goddess of war, vowed in 296 B.C.E. by Appius Claudius Caecus, the builder of the Appian Way (Plan 2, Inset C).[97] Although her name derives from the Latin word for war (*bellum*), Bellona is not precisely a female counterpart to the war god Mars. Mars was the personification of physical combat as was Bellona, but she was involved as well in war preparation, diplomacy, and war victory.[98]

Writing in the first century B.C.E., the Roman architect Marcus Vitruvius Pollio advised that "the temple of Mars should be . . . out of the city, that no armed frays may disturb the peace of the citizens, and that this divinity may, moreover, be ready to preserve them from their enemies and the perils of war."[99] Certainly, the Campus Martius met this Vitruvian principle for the placement of a temple of the god of war, but it was not the only place that worked. Two hundred fifty years before the Temple of Mars in the Circus Flaminius was built, one to the war deity was founded on the southern side of the city along the Via Appia. It was by this temple, vowed by T. Quinctius when Rome was under attack from the Gauls and dedicated in 388 B.C.E., that, thirty-eight years later, the Roman army was levied before a campaign just south of the city outside the Porta Capena. This same location served as the beginning point for a parade of the *equites* every July.[100]

Why was the northern plain not selected instead by Quinctius for his temple, or chosen by later generals to honor the war god until Callaicus built his temple in the Circus Flaminius in the late second century B.C.E.? As we will explore in the next chapter, the location chosen for temples depended in large part on the idiosyncratic agendas of the patrons, and in part on the evolving identities of the deities honored with such structures. Mars may have been avoided, in part, for the reason noted by one author that the god produced a blind fury, and hence bore the epithet *Mars caecus*. Such ferocity needed to be directed to victory, and "with the outcome still in doubt, the general appeals to a divinity less involved in the intoxicating detail of action."[101] At least in the fourth century B.C.E., the dearth of temples of Mars in the northern field, or those to any other deity for that matter, may also have had something to do with contemporary perceptions of the campus as an area that was best left open for military use. Until the beginning of the third century, the only known structures *in campo* were the Temple of Apollo Medicus at the far southern edge and the open space associated with the Villa Publica and the nonstructural saepta voting precinct (Plan 2, No. 3 and Inset C). By the mid-third century B.C.E., however, temples were being constructed in the central Campus Martius (the modern Largo Argentina), thereby diminishing any possible restrictions to building a temple of Mars simply on the grounds that the open space was needed for military assemblies (Plan 2, Inset A).

One author suggests that it was the early Ara Martis itself that provided the Field of Mars its name and since, as Ovid indicates, the entire field was the domain of Mars, arguably additional temples were unnecessary.[102] Ovid, however, was writing at the turn of the first century C.E., and there is little to support the conjecture that an altar from centuries earlier provided the eponymous reference to the entire field or that ancient sacredness obviated any further need for a temple of the war god. The perceived lack of a temple of Mars may have been why Suetonius indicated that Julius Caesar intended to build one on the spot of his naumachia.[103] Although the basin was filled after Caesar's death, the temple was never built.[104] In short, despite the space's significance to the military, the available evidence suggests that no republican general commissioned a temple of the war god in his own field until the second century B.C.E., after numerous other deities had a claim to real estate in the Field of Mars.

ROMULUS ON THE CAMPUS: APPEARANCE AND DISAPPEARANCE

It has been conjectured that Rome's founding by twins is a tale of the mid- to late fourth century B.C.E. created in conjunction with laws that successively allowed power sharing between patricians and plebeians (367 B.C.E.) and then required a consul be elected from each group (342 B.C.E.).[105] In 300 B.C.E., the brothers Gnaeus and Quintus Ogulnius, serving as tribunes, pushed through a law that permitted plebeians to have representation equal to patricians in the pontifical and augural colleges.[106] It was under the direction of the Ogulnii brothers that the road out to the Temple of Mars on the Via Appia

4. Silver didrachm (third century B.C.E.). Reverse: She-wolf and suckling twins Romulus and Remus. British Museum. (Photo: © Trustees of the British Museum)

discussed earlier was paved. That temple is known to have had a statue of Mars accompanied by wolves in 217 B.C.E., although it is not known if they were she-wolves.[107] Livy notes that in 295 B.C.E. the brothers also set up a statue of the she-wolf with the "infant founders of the city" by the fig tree where they were exposed.[108] This monument of the suckling twins who founded the city may be viewed as a celebration of the new equality.[109] A quarter century later in 269 B.C.E., coins depicting a she-wolf were being minted (Figure 4). During approximately the same period, a Greek writer in Syracuse made the first known literary reference to Rome's founding by Romulus and Remus.[110]

Early in the development of the legend of Rome's founding, Romulus and Remus were connected to Mars. The war god was viewed as a force of nature and had ties to both wolves and woodpeckers, animals that figure in the legend of the twins being saved at birth.[111] In the same passage in which Livy describes the monument of the she-wolf and twins erected by the Ogulnii, he notes the brothers' construction of the paved walkway to the Temple of Mars on the Via Appia.[112] Romulus and Remus became identified as sons of Mars through the rape of their mother Rhea Silvia, a story that was told circa 200 B.C.E. by the historian Fabius Pictor.[113] The twins were also subjects of two plays by the historical dramatist Naevius, who wrote sometime after 220 B.C.E., one on the birth and raising of Romulus and Remus and the second on the overthrow of Amulius.[114] By the end of the first century B.C.E., the tradition was firmly established.[115] Later Plutarch would claim that in order to honor Mars, Romulus, in turn, had named the month of March after the deity.[116] Images of the twins with the she-wolf were common throughout the imperial era (Plate II and Figure 5).

The temple of Quirinus, the divine name for the deified Romulus, located on the Quirinal Hill, was vowed in 325 B.C.E. and dedicated in 293 B.C.E., and it has been conjectured that the story of the death and apotheosis of Rome's first king was created in conjunction with the dedication.[117] The epic poet Ennius (ca. 239–169 B.C.E.) noted that Romulus lived in heaven with the gods who gave him birth.[118] It is unclear as to when the details of the location of the death in the Campus Martius were added, but they probably were established by the time Fabius Pictor wrote at the beginning of the second century B.C.E., roughly the same period that the story of Rome's founding had become canonical.[119]

Writers in the Augustan age supply two details for the location for Romulus's apotheosis on the Field of Mars. The first account suggests that Romulus's death occurred while he was reviewing his troops outside of the city.[120] As noted previously, the likeliest place for this activity would be the Campus Martius, possibly in the area of the Villa Publica.[121] The second clue is that the apotheosis occurred *in campo ad Caprae paludem*, or "in the Campus Martius, near the swamp of Capra,"[122] an area identified as the low area in the central Campus Martius that would later become the site of Agrippa's Pantheon and the earlier Villa Publica.[123] Romulus's legendary death on July 7, the Nones of Quintilis, may have been selected to coincide with a preexisting holiday, the Nonae Capratinae. On the other hand, the Nonae Capratinae may have been established to celebrate the site of the king's apotheosis. Plutarch's text allows for both possibilities. In one account in Plutarch, on the Nones of Quintilis, handmaidens, dressed in the clothes of their mistresses, ran out to the Campus Martius, conducted a mock battle, and then dined in huts constructed of fig tree branches while waited on by matrons.[124] According to Plutarch, the holiday may have obtained its name from the wild fig or *caprificus* and was an ancient festival, still celebrated in his day.[125] The alternative theory for the holiday's history in Plutarch is that the Nonae Capratinae was derived from the word for she-goats or *caprae*, which was also the name of the marsh where

5. Altar relief from Ostia depicting she-wolf nursing Romulus and Remus with personification of Tiber and shepherds (late first century–early second century C.E.). Museo Nazionale Romano, Rome. (Photo: Album / Art Resource, New York)

Romulus disappeared into a cloud, and therefore the festival celebrated his apotheosis.[126] If that were the case, the Nonae Capratinae could not go back further than the middle of the fourth century B.C.E. when the Romulus legend probably developed. More likely, the date for Romulus's death was picked to correspond to a preexisting holiday, which, as two scholars have noted, was a day of "dissolution and reversal."[127] Certainly by the death of Augustus in

14 C.E., the holiday celebrated on the Field of Mars carried associations with both the death of the son of Mars and military victory.[128]

If the legend of Romulus's apotheosis was established alongside the dedication of the temple of Quirinus at the beginning of the third century B.C.E., it appears that the story was further embellished during the first century B.C.E. with the added detail of the resurrection of Rome's founder. According to Plutarch, after his apotheosis, Romulus was seen walking along a road by a patrician Julius Proculus. Romulus told Proculus that he was returning to heaven as the deity Quirinus, a name that Plutarch confirms was associated with the god Mars.[129] An early first-century C.E. inscription makes clear the accepted deification.[130] In Ovid's account of the tale, Romulus appeared dressed in a robe and announced to Proculus, "Bid the pious throng bring incense and propitiate the new Quirinus, and bid them cultivate the arts their fathers cultivated, the art of war."[131] When the *Salii Palatini* danced through the city streets in the month of March beating the *ancilia*, they were divided into two groups, one representing Mars, the other Quirinus.

Although Roman historians during the early empire recognized these myths as "fabulous," they were not willing to dismiss entirely their historical authenticity. As Plutarch notes, "Although most of these particulars are related by Fabius and Diocles of Peparethus, who seems to have been the first to publish a 'Founding of Rome,' some are suspicious of their fictitious and fabulous quality; but we should not be incredulous when we see what a poet fortune sometimes is, and when we reflect that the Roman state would not have attained to its present power, had it not been of a divine origin, and one which was attended by great marvels."[132]

Clearly, however, the tales were employed and sometimes embellished for political expediency. The tale of Romulus's resurrection dates back only to the mid-first century B.C.E., and the use of the name of the patrician Julius Proculus suggests it may have been fabricated to promote the ties between Rome's founder and Julius Caesar and his family.[133] Julius Caesar appears to have attempted to capitalize on another part of the Romulus legend, namely, the connection between Rome's founder and the Trojan wanderer, Aeneas. During the late fifth century B.C.E., a Greek historian, Hellanicus of Lesbos, wrote that Rome was founded by Aeneas and named after "Rhome," a refugee from Troy, who, along with other Trojan women, burned their ships on the Italian Peninsula to end the voyage.[134] By the fourth century B.C.E. Roman patrician families were claiming Trojan descent.[135] Roman incorporation of the story of Aeneas into the city's foundation legend is thought to date to the third century B.C.E.[136] Fabius Pictor linked Aeneas with Rome's founders by establishing a chronology of several generations between the Trojan and the founder of Alba Longa and his descendants, the twins Romulus and Remus.[137] The relationship varied over time, with a contemporary of Fabius Pictor believing Romulus to be the grandson of Aeneas, while an ambassador to Rome in 193 B.C.E. wrote that Aeneas had four sons, two of whom (Romulus and Remus) founded the city.[138] By the first century B.C.E., the story was firmly established, with Livy documenting the death of Aeneas, the founding of Alba Longa by his son Ascanius, and the reign of his grandson Silvius and his descendants down to Rhea Silvia and her twin sons.[139] The tradition was carried further by Strabo, Ovid, Plutarch, and, of course, Vergil.[140] With the connection of Rome to Aeneas in full force by the time of his political ascendancy, Caesar drew the genealogical line down to *gens Iulia*. Before battle Caesar sacrificed to the mother of Aeneas (Venus) and to the father of Romulus (Mars), and after his defeat of Pompey the Great, he traveled to Troy.[141] The associations of the Iulii with Rome's founders were amplified, as discussed later, by his adopted son and successor Octavian/Augustus.[142] As a paean to Augustus, Vergil's *Aeneid* tied it together by predicting the future grandeur of Rome under the Iulii: "Wars shall cease and savage ages soften... *Quirinus with his brother Remus, shall give laws.*"[143] Romulus became Quirinus reunited with his brother in peace, both the sons of Mars.[144] The story of Romulus and the founding of Rome remained an important theme throughout the imperial era.

THE NAME OF THE FIELD

Although it has been suggested by some modern scholars that an altar to Mars provided the name for the campus, Romans of the early imperial era associated the topographical name with an episode in the early history of the city. According to Livy, the Field of Mars received its name when the land "lying between the city and the Tiber" was seized in 509 B.C.E. from Rome's last king, Tarquinius Superbus, after his followers attempted to regain for him the throne and his royal property. When the revolt failed, his lands outside the city walls were seized and "consecrated to Mars and became the Campus Martius."[145] Plutarch states that it was the better part of the campus that had belonged to Tarquinius Superbus and was dedicated to Mars, which suggests, perhaps, that the former king's lands did not include the entire field.[146]

The property was seized at harvesttime and because, according to Livy, religious reasons forbade the consumption of the crop that grew on it, the grain was then cut to the ground and tossed in the Tiber.[147] Plutarch suggests that the consecration to Mars came first, and, therefore, it was that act that made the grain holy and unfit for consumption.[148] He further notes that not only the sacred grain but also entire trees on the former monarch's grounds were cut down, an act that left the place "wholly untilled and barren for the god of war."[149] The grain cast in the river became stuck in the mud of the low summer flow and blocked the passage of other flotsam that then accumulated over time and formed the Tiber Island.¹⁵⁰ The story reverberates in the July celebration on the Campus Martius of the Nonae Capratinae that occurred just before the grain harvest when "an abundant crop could guarantee once again the maintenance of the social order."¹⁵¹

Although Livy claims that the property's eponymous reference to the war god gained currency at the time of the expulsion of the last king of Rome, he also uses the phrase *in campo Martio* to describe the space when used by an earlier king Servius to hold the first census.¹⁵² The anachronistic reference by Livy may not be surprising when it is considered that extant texts indicate that ancient historians writing about Rome, both Greek and Roman, used only the words *campus* and its Greek equivalent *pedion* (πεδιον) without the additional reference to Mars until the mid-first century B.C.E.¹⁵³ Even then *campus* with the addition of *Martius* is not consistently used.¹⁵⁴

Why were ancient references to the plain as the Field of *Mars* only recorded relatively late? It may have been that the space was already intimately connected to the war god through musters, triumphs, holiday celebrations, and an altar; the full name could go unstated in the same way that telling a neighbor that one is going to the "mall" conveys sufficient information as to its location without using the formal title. This was, after all, the largest open "field" outside the city walls, and its use for gatherings of soldiers and ceremonies tied to Mars went back hundreds of years. There is, however, another possibility. As we saw in the overview of the area's development in the preceding chapter, and as will be discussed in more detail later, by the mid- to late first century B.C.E., the once empty space was beginning to fill with structures. It did not look so much like a "field" as it had in the past centuries, except perhaps in its northern reaches, and activities connected with war and Mars were waning. Troop assemblies on the plain were diminished, if not completely eliminated, and triumphal parades, such as Pompey's great triumph of 61 B.C.E., while still spectacular, were fewer and further between. The structures connected with Mars and the martial activities of the troops and triumphant generals were therefore reduced to the point that perhaps the term "field," as a shortened version of the more descriptive "Field of Mars" was seen as insufficient.

At the same time, however, new associative links were being forged. Various foundation myths connecting Mars, Romulus, and even Aeneas to one another gradually obtained canonical status. Such connections were ripe for exploitation by those Roman leaders vying for enhanced political power at a time when the traditional republican institutions of government were waning. Pompey crowned his new theater with a temple dedicated to Aeneas's mother, Venus Victrix, while Caesar, who tied his family to the Trojan hero, answered Pompey's grand structure with plans for the massive Saepta Julia. It is argued that Caesar even wanted to straighten the Tiber to increase the size of the Campus Martius, and as noted earlier, he possibly planned to fill in his

6. Relief fragment depicting the pediment of the Temple of Quirinus (late first century C.E.). (Photo: with permission of the Ministero dei beni e delle attività culturali e del turismo – Soprintendenza Speciale per i Beni Archeologici di Roma)

naumachia in the western Campus Martius and to construct a temple of Mars.[155] To further emphasize his ties to Rome's founders, Caesar was reported to have dressed in the manner of Romulus and set up a statue of himself in the temple of Quirinus, the deified Romulus.[156] The dictator also took the title *pater patriae*, likely in reference to Rome's founder who had the title *pater*.[157] These associations were not lost on the writers of the day. Cicero, who, as we have seen, was now adding the word "martius" to "campus," took umbrage at Caesar for equating himself with Quirinus.[158]

Caesar's successor, Augustus, visualized his connections to Rome's foundation legends by embroidering them on the urban fabric. In 16 B.C.E. the emperor restored and rededicated a temple of Quirinus that displayed sculptures on its pediment of Romulus and Remus taking auspices (Figure 6).[159] Twenty-seven years earlier, still with the name Octavian, Augustus had marched up the Via Flaminia to the city walls, and on August 19, 43 B.C.E., Caesar's heir was first elected consul in the Campus Martius. It was in the Campus Martius, according to Cassius Dio, that Augustus saw six vultures present during a meeting with citizens, and then another twelve appeared to him while he was addressing the army. "Comparing [the sight] with Romulus and the omen that had befallen him, [Augustus] expected to gain that king's sovereignty also."[160] Augustus eventually brought the war god within the city limits with the construction of the Temple of Mars Ultor (Mars the Avenger) in the Forum of Augustus, finally dedicated in 2 B.C.E.[161] With its eight Corinthian columns lining the facade, the temple portico contained freestanding sculptures of both Romulus ("carrying on his shoulders the arms of conquered leaders") and Aeneas ("and many an ancestor of the noble Julian line").[162] The pediment displayed Mars in the center and a seated figure of Romulus.[163] In addition to his new grand temple of Mars, Augustus rebuilt the temple of Jupiter Feretrius on the Capitoline, a temple thought to have been erected by Romulus that contained the first king's spoils of war (*spolia optima*).[164] Down in the area of the Circus Flaminius, Augustus also rebuilt the temple of the goddess of war, Bellona. On the Palatine, he constructed a house near the so-called hut of Romulus, an eighth-century B.C.E. timber and thatch structure that the Romans believed was the first king's archaic home. By the Palatine's southwestern slope, he repaired and monumentalized the cave where legend recorded that the she-wolf had once suckled and protected Romulus and Remus.[165] Augustus's important generals also apparently desired to be associated with the legends of Rome's founding. Frescoes discovered in the tomb of the commander of Augustus's land forces at Actium, T. Statilius Taurus, narrate the foundation cycle from Aeneus to the twins (Plate II).[166]

Augustus's extensive public building program was executed in large part by Marcus Agrippa, a man both Vergil and Propertius appear to have associated with the mortal Remus in his close partnership with Augustus, the immortal Romulus.[167] Agrippa's original Pantheon was located in the area of Romulus's ascension from the Caprae Palus and may have contained a statue of Rome's founder.[168] Writing more than two centuries after Agrippa's construction, Cassius Dio, who was clearly confused about some elements of Agrippa's Pantheon, nevertheless recorded that the Augustan structure also contained cult statues of Mars and Venus,[169] which indicates that the original building may have been dedicated to those deities.[170]

Another Augustan monument in the Campus Martius closely associated to the foundation legends was the altar to Augustan peace, the Ara Pacis Augustae. After Augustus's return from Gaul and Spain in 13 B.C.E., the Senate decreed the monumental altar's construction. It was erected along the Via Flaminia in the northern Campus Martius and dedicated on January 30, 9 B.C.E. Although the identification of the friezes on the reconstructed altar is not beyond doubt, the northwest panel on the exterior of the precinct wall has generally been interpreted as depicting the discovery of the infants Romulus and Remus by their adoptive father Faustulus, with the god Mars in attendance.[171] The southwest panel has generated more controversy with a long-standing scholarly tradition identifying the main figure as Aeneas in the act of sacrificing a sow.[172] Thus, Augustus, through both panels, is tied to the canonical foundation stories. Recent scholarship has argued, not without disagreement, that the veiled and bearded figure traditionally identified as Aeneas is instead an image of Rome's legendary second king, Numa Pompilius.[173] If Numa rather than Aeneas, the figure would have nevertheless reinforced important associations of Augustus with the Campus Martius and Rome's early legends. As noted earlier, Roman writers attributed the construction of the Ara Martis in the Campus Martius to Numa; it was at the Ara Martis that Numa sacrificed to Mars to honor the treaty between the Sabines and the Romans. In addition, Numa enacted a law that established the rules for going to war and the use of the *fetiales* described previously.[174] Whereas Romulus was the warrior king, Numa was viewed as a peacemaker. The Campus Martius was the space from which Romans for centuries thereafter marched to war and usually returned in victory and the concomitant cessation of hostilities. Augustus returned to the Field of Mars having vanquished his enemies and ushered in an era of peace. A reinterpretation of the Ara Pacis's southwestern mythological panel as a scene depicting Numa does in fact create a more balanced iconographic presentation of the attributes of Rome's first emperor.[175]

Even the imperial title of Augustus taken by Octavian was associated with Rome's founder. Although according to Suetonius it was suggested that Augustus receive the title of Romulus as a "second founder of the city," the appellation was rejected, likely because it carried monarchical connotations.[176] Nevertheless, the nomenclature of "Augustus," selected as "not merely a new title but a more honorable one," was believed by Suetonius to have had an etymological connection to the auguries by which Romulus was chosen as Rome's first leader.[177] According to Ovid, Augustus's achievements had now surpassed those of the founder of Rome, and so Ovid noted that Romulus "must yield pride of place" and the title "Father of the World" (*pater orbis*) to the first emperor.[178] The concept of Augustus as successor to Romulus and worthier of praise than Rome's founder did not end with the death of the first emperor. Augustus died on August 19, 14 c.e., the anniversary of the date he was first elected consul and that of his own reported experience of the vulture augury tied to the selection of Romulus. Images of Augustus's prominent ancestors "beginning with Romulus himself" were carried in his funerary procession.[179] In his funeral oration, Augustus's adopted son and successor, Tiberius, praised the accomplishments of the first emperor of Rome: "Yet what deed like this can be cited of Alexander of Macedon or of our own Romulus, who perhaps above all others are thought to have performed some notable exploit in youth?

But these men I shall pass over, lest from merely comparing them with him and using them as examples – and that among you who know them as well as I – I may be thought to be detracting from the virtues of Augustus."[180]

In a clear allusion to the apotheosis of Romulus, Cassius Dio describes how the deceased emperor was transported on a bier through the Campus Martius where his body was consumed in the flames of a funeral pyre and "an eagle released from it flew aloft, appearing to bear his spirit to heaven."[181] Even the story of the sighting of the deceased Romulus is retold with Augustus in the place of Rome's founder. Dio notes that his widow Livia "bestowed a million sesterces upon a certain Numerius Atticus, a senator and ex-praetor, because he swore that he had seen Augustus ascending to heaven after the manner of which tradition tells concerning Proculus and Romulus."[182] At about the same time, the self-penned list of deeds by the emperor, the *Res Gestae*, was affixed to his Mausoleum in the northernmost reaches of the plain. In the *Res Gestae*, Augustus referred to the location of the Ara Pacis Augustae as the Campus Martius.[183]

CONCLUSION

Although Livy recorded that the apotheosis of Romulus in the presence of his troops occurred in the eighth century B.C.E., evidence suggests the legend did not start circulating until four centuries later. Before the fourth century B.C.E., the northern plain likely had associations with Mars, but not with the foundation legends. The links to Mars were probably made especially strong through the field's use for musters, triumphs, and military festivals and, possibly, its altar. It was not, however, unique in that regard. The area just south of the city walls along the Via Appia contained a temple of Mars and served as a gathering place for troops as early as the fourth century B.C.E. By the third century B.C.E., the connections of the mythical founders of Rome with Mars and to the space north of the *pomerium* were slowly strengthening. Concurrently, the requirement of a large open plain for war preparation was diminishing. Armor that had been donned for protection before battle was relegated to costume for mock military engagements, and the *navalia* gave way to the entertainment venue known as the *naumachia*. What open space remained in the early imperial era, mostly in the northern portion, was used in a simulacrum of warfare, not in preparation for the real thing. Suetonius provided the following description of a mock battle by the emperor Claudius: "He gave representations in the Campus Martius of the storming and sacking of a town in the manner of real warfare, as well as of the surrender of the kings of the Britons, and presided clad in a general's cloak."[184]

Indeed, there appears to have been an inverse relationship between the use of the area for war footing and its mythological ties to the war god and the glorification of military engagement. The manifestations of those connections of Mars to the northern field, however, were gradual and relatively late in date. Apart from the possible Ara Martis, the first religious structure reliably dedicated to Mars to be built in these northern reaches was not constructed until late in the second century B.C.E. Even then the first temple to Mars was raised only on the area's edge in the Circus Flaminius, notwithstanding the fact that throughout the middle and late republic the Campus Martius was the preferred site of numerous manubial temples. The failure to honor the war god properly in his own field may have been recognized by Julius Caesar around the same time that writers began identifying the space formally as the Field of Mars. In the late republic, Rome's foundation legends were made more immediate through various fictitious genealogical connections to the city's leading families. As the republic transitioned into an empire, little could be seen of the empty plain where Cincinnatus had once ordered Rome's youth to gather with spears at sunset. The marshland had been filled with temples, theaters, and amphitheaters but was recognized clearly as the Campus Martius, the Field of Mars.

CHAPTER THREE

"VERY COSTLY TEMPLES": THE CAMPUS MARTIUS AND REPUBLICAN TEMPLE CONSTRUCTION

A SECOND-CENTURY RIVALRY

Despite having been elected consul a few days earlier on February 18, 188 B.C.E., Marcus Aemilius Lepidus was very displeased.[1] The day after his selection along with co-consul Gaius Flaminius, six praetors were chosen, and now the Senate would decide to which region of the expanding empire each would be sent. War was brewing with the Ligurians in the northern part of the Italian Peninsula, and the Senate decreed that the two consuls should proceed in that direction to keep the peace. Lepidus objected, arguing to the Senate that "it was improper that both consuls should be shut up in the valleys of the Ligurians while Marcus Fulvius [Nobilior] and Gnaeus Manlius for two years now [as consuls], the one in Europe, the other in Asia, were lording it as if they were the successors to Philip [of Macedon] and Antiochus [the Great]."[2] Lepidus had a particular grudge against Fulvius, who had managed to thwart his efforts to become consul two years earlier.[3] The sole activities of the former consuls, Lepidus claimed, were threatening tribes against whom no war had been declared and enriching themselves by "selling peace for a price."[4] Either send the newly elected consuls to Europe and Asia to replace Fulvius and Manlius, he pleaded to the Senate, or bring those soldiers home. Unfortunately for Lepidus, the Senate chose the latter course. With their term starting on the New Year on March 1, 187 B.C.E., Aemilius Lepidus and his co-consul Flaminius were ordered north to battle the Ligurians.[5]

Rather than going to the pleasant cities of Asia for an easy tour of duty assured by the "feebleness of the enemy and the wealth of its kings,"[6] Lepidus found himself situated in a hilly and rough landscape of northern Italy with narrow, winding roads where the lightly armored Ligurians hid, ready to ambush his men.[7] As Livy noted, "This enemy was born, as it were, to keep alive the military discipline of the Romans during the intervals between their great wars."[8] Lepidus's Ligurian campaign was anything but a great war. The posting was grim, set in a poor area with few pickings for plunder. Even the traditional civilian camp followers stayed home.[9] Lepidus passed the time by burning farms and villages and goading small groups of Ligurians to leave their mountainous redoubt and meet his men in the open. Ultimately, the enemy obliged. During the engagement, Lepidus reportedly made a vow to the goddess Diana that, if she led him to victory, he would build a temple in her honor.[10] Having been favored with a win, albeit against a relatively small force, Lepidus crossed the Apennines to take on the Ligurian tribes on the other side.[11] Finding another pocket of resistance, he vowed another temple, this time to the queen of the heavens, Juno Regina. Again, he received divine favor and routed the enemy.[12]

The two goddesses to whom Lepidus prayed for victory and promised temples in return shared mythological characteristics. Derived from Greek deities, Juno and Diana had been worshiped on the Italian Peninsula for centuries by the time of M. Aemilius Lepidus's prayers, and they were seen as protectors of soldiers as well as promoters of fertility.[13] Each had been honored with her first Roman temple on the Aventine Hill.[14] Additionally, Juno's first temple also had been built after a battlefield vow, and, as we shall see, Lepidus's act of battlefield piety followed two centuries of Roman tradition.[15]

With two victories under his belt and two temples to erect, Lepidus headed back to Rome. He had reason to move quickly. Word had been received that his old nemesis, Fulvius Nobilior, had just returned to the capital from Aetolia and was pressing for the award of a triumphal parade, an extraordinary honor granted only by the Senate and only for significant victories.[16] Lepidus anticipated such a move and had his agents in the Senate assert that it was improper for a triumph to be awarded before the current consul could return and weigh in on the issue.[17] The Senate rebuffed the effort, and the celebration was scheduled for January. Rightfully fearful that Lepidus would press the attack once in Rome, Fulvius Nobilior pushed forward the date to December 23, 187 B.C.E., and thus was able to parade through Rome's streets with a remarkable triumph before Lepidus could get back to the city. Later the next year, Fulvius continued the festivities with ten days of entertainment with actors and athletic competition. Like the triumphal procession, these events were another tribute awarded for major wartime success.[18]

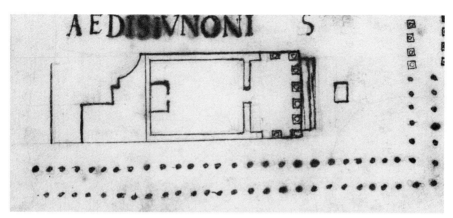

7. Detail, Vat. Lat. 3439 f.23r. Temple of Juno Regina after the Severan Marble Plan (sixteenth century). (Photo: with permission of Biblioteca Apostolica Vaticana, with all rights reserved)

Temporarily outwitted by his rival's ephemeral honors, Lepidus nevertheless was able to memorialize his victories over the Ligurians with permanent shrines. This was accomplished by the construction of the vowed temples of Diana and Juno Regina. The two temples were dedicated on December 23, 179 B.C.E., a year in which, ironically, he served as co-censor with Fulvius Nobilior and on the eighth anniversary of Fulvius's earlier triumph.[19] The two temples were placed along the edge of the Circus Flaminius, a location that, as we shall see, was likely along the triumphal parade route. The Severan Marble Plan, a third-century C.E. stone map of the city, reveals that the temple to Juno Regina was situated along the southeast side, but the precise location of the one to Diana has not been determined (Figure 7, and Plan 2, Inset B).[20] In what may have been an attempt at self-promotion at the expense of his rival, Lepidus not only dedicated both temples on the same day in December but, on the previous day, dedicated a temple vowed in battle by a deceased relative.[21]

Fulvius, though, was not going to be outdone. Less than fifty meters to the northwest of Lepidus's temple of Juno Regina on the long north side of the Circus Flaminius, a temple containing nine bronze statues of Muses taken during Fulvius's Ambracian campaign as well as a statue of Hercules with a lyre was dedicated.[22] The temple, shown later on the Severan Marble Plan as Hercules Musarum, was additionally embellished by Fulvius with a small bronze shrine, said to date to the time of King Numa, as well as a calendar (Figure 8, and Plan 2, No. 7). Because Numa was celebrated as the reformer of the calendar, the dedication may be seen as an honorary reference to Rome's second king.[23] The ancient sources do not tell us if, like Lepidus, Fulvius vowed the temple during battle. It nonetheless has been convincingly argued that this was the case since the construction of the Temple of Hercules Musarum was underway, if not completed, at the time he was co-censor in 179 B.C.E.[24]

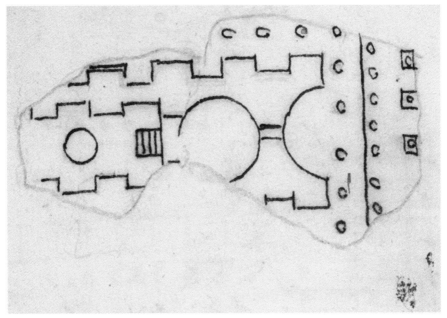

8. Detail, Vat. Lat. 3439 f.22r. Temple of Hercules Musarum after the Severan Marble Plan (sixteenth century). (Photo: with permission of Biblioteca Apostolica Vaticana, with all rights reserved)

Why were these temples of Hercules, Diana, and Juno Regina placed on the southern fringe of the Campus Martius in the Circus Flaminius and not somewhere else? No literary evidence offers an answer to this question or, indeed, illuminates the reasons for siting any republican temple within Rome.[25] Nevertheless, the patterns of temple location, placed in their historical contexts, provide clues that allow reasonable conjecture on this issue and also inform the discussion of topographical development in general in the Campus Martius.

CONSTRUCTING TEMPLES IN REPUBLICAN ROME

There were three essential ways that proposals for the construction of temples were initiated during the republic. They could be vowed by generals in battle, suggested by the officials (aediles) charged with maintaining public buildings, or decreed by the Senate after consultation with the set of Greek oracles known as the Sibylline Books.[26] Of the forty-eight temples built in Rome between the end of the sixth century and the middle of the first century B.C.E. whose method of foundation has been identified, more than half were the result of battlefield vows.[27] The middle republic was the most prolific period for temples vowed by generals, with eleven vowed in a twenty-one-year span, between 201 and 180 B.C.E.[28] With respect to those temples promised on the battlefield, there were three steps that tradition required to be completed. First came the *vota nuncupata*, or vow made by a magistrate.[29] Second was the *locatio*, a term that had two possible aspects: site selection and award of the construction contract.[30] The third element in temple building was the *dedicatio*, or dedication of the completed structure. Each step played an important role in the process and likely influenced temple placement in order to magnify the honor brought to the general, the state, and the god.

A variety of battlefield circumstances inspired such vows. Some were offered in hope of victory during the heat of battle, and divine benevolence required reciprocation.[31] This was the case with the first vowed temple in the Campus Martius, the temple of the goddess Bellona, constructed just to the southeast of the area where the Circus Flaminius was later built (Plan 2, Inset C). In 296 B.C.E., while in the midst of a chaotic skirmish with the Etruscans and Samnites, the consul Appius Claudius Caecus reportedly raised his arms with his palms to the sky and cried, "Bellona, if today thou grant us the victory, then do I vow thee a temple."[32] This action appears to have inspired his men and promoted discipline up and down the lines: the enemy was routed. Another example of inspiring soldiers with a battlefield vow occurred in 197 B.C.E., when the consul Cornelius Cethegus vowed a temple to Juno "the Savior" (Juno Sospita), a protector of soldiers in battle, which was later built on the southwest edge of the Campus Martius in the Forum Holitorium (Plan 2, Inset D).[33] As Livy notes, when Cethegus vowed to construct the temple "if the enemy should be routed and put to flight that day, the soldiers shouted out that they would bring about the fulfillment of the consul's vow and the attack on the enemy began."[34] Sometimes vows were made when the victory of the engagements were never really in doubt, such as those made to Diana and Juno Regina by Lepidus during his battles with the Ligurians. In other cases generals promised to raise a temple after the bloodshed had stopped, in thanks to a god for victory.[35] In all events, the vow was a sacred act, and a general who was cavalier in his obedience to religious ritual risked dire consequences on the battlefield, including his own demise.[36]

Why a particular god was called on in the midst of battle is uncertain, but the choice could have consequences for temple location. For instance, some scholars have accepted the proposition that if a temple was built to honor a foreign cult, it had to be placed outside the pomerial line.[37] If indeed this was the case, it is doubtful that a vowing general would be ignorant of the tradition and of its implications for site selection when considering the deity from whom to seek assistance.[38] Applying an extrapomerial rule for temples vowed to foreign deities would not necessarily place them in the Campus Martius, only outside the city, but some gods identified as "foreign" had temples in the Campus Martius, including Apollo and Feronia.[39] Apart from the possible limitations on the placement of temples of foreign deities, the first-century B.C.E. architect Vitruvius spelled out a few rules concerning temples of particular gods. As noted in Chapter 2, temples of Mars should be located outside the city where the god could "preserve the [citizens] from their enemies."[40] Temples of Vulcan, the god of fire and smitheries, should "be away from the city, which would consequently be freed from the danger of fire; the divinity presiding over that element being drawn away by the rites and sacrifices performing in his temple."[41] Temples of Hercules, "if there be neither amphitheatre nor gymnasium . . . should be near the circus." Temples of Apollo should be placed near the theater, and those of Isis and Serapis should be honored in the marketplace.[42] These rules conflating the religious and the practical were articulated in the late republic, and it is not known whether Vitruvius was summarizing traditional principles that would have been considered at the time the temples in the Campus Martius were vowed and constructed. The extent to which a vowing general consciously selected a deity in order to provide a reason for placing a temple in a particular location or made the choice for other reasons, and subsequently was confined by his decision, is unknown. It is possible that suggestions – subtle or otherwise – with respect to a temple vow, were made to the consul at the time of his election to office. As the Senate retained supreme authority in religious matters, the consul may have had guidance as to the god whose help he should beseech, providing collective advance influence over temple location.[43]

After a general returned to Rome, the *locatio* would commence. There is significant debate as to whether the Senate had to ratify the vow made by the magistrate before the temple could be built, with one scholar arguing that a temple could not become part of the state religion, effectively blocking assistance for its construction, if the Senate did not approve of the vow.[44] This issue is problematic, as we have but one known example where a temple vow was submitted for ratification to the Senate (which did, in fact, approve it) and one example where the Senate rejected a magistrate's vow (but it was for games, not a temple).[45] If the Senate did play a role in approval of vowed temples, consensus between general and the Senate must have been very high.[46]

Implicated in the question of the Senate's role in approving the construction of the temple is the source of the funds to build these costly structures. Most scholars believe that temples vowed in battle were financed with the general's retained war booty or *manubiae*.[47] While it was expected that most captured wealth would be turned over to the state treasury, a part, the *manubiae*, could be kept by a general for his own use, whether that be for personal aggrandizement or expenditure on his soldiers, officers, and even friends.[48] Beginning in the fourth century B.C.E., *manubiae* were used for the public good as well, being expended on such diversions as games and spectacles, but primarily financing the construction of buildings, which were almost always temples.[49] By one count, from the fourth century B.C.E. to the beginning of the Second Punic War in 218 B.C.E., 80 percent of Rome's temple construction was financed with the magistrates' *manubiae*.[50] Numerous battles during this period provided both the opportunities for generals to vow temples and the captured booty with which to finance them,[51] creating what has been described as the golden age of temple construction by generals.[52] Although it has been argued that war booty empowered a general to build a temple where he saw fit, the Senate is known to have played a role in at least some such projects, and it likely could not be ignored with impunity.[53]

The final stage in the construction process was the *dedicatio*, a ceremony that often took place some years after the vowing of the temple. The *dedicatio* had to be performed by someone with proper legal authority. Often the consul who vowed the structure would dedicate it while serving as censor.[54] Although the Senate could play a role through the appointment of special officials known as *duumviri aedi dedicandae* to perform dedications, most often vowed temples were dedicated by the magistrate who had promised the structure on the battlefield or by close kin. Of seventeen temples where both the person vowing and the one dedicating are known, twelve were dedicated by the vowers or by their kinsmen.[55] That was the case with respect to M. Aemilius Lepidus, who dedicated three temples in 179 B.C.E., two vowed personally and a third that had been vowed by his deceased relative. The Temple of Hercules Musarum built by Fulvius Nobilior likely adds another to the list. While vowing a temple helped secure a general's place in history, the dedication, often accompanied by games and great ceremony, brought immediate glory. Lepidus, for instance, obtained funds from the Senate to help finance games in connection with the dedications, holding them over five days – three for Juno and two for Diana.[56]

Of the approximately eighty temples constructed in republican Rome, about twenty were built in the Campus Martius, but most in the Field of Mars were not erected until the period of the Punic Wars. The first, the Temple of Apollo Medicus, dedicated in 431 B.C.E. following an outbreak of plague, sat alone on the edge of the later-built Circus Flaminius for 137 years until a second, the Temple of Bellona, was placed next to it.[57] The only other known "structure" in the Campus Martius during this period was the Villa Publica and, perhaps, the Altar to Mars, but as the Villa Publica was likely nothing more than a cleared area at that date, the Apollo Medicus temple is the first major architectural structure known to have occupied the Field of Mars.

When the Temple of Bellona was vowed and erected, the central Campus Martius was used primarily for the census and for collecting and training troops for battle. Between the time of its construction at the beginning of the third century B.C.E. and the advent of the wars with the Carthaginians three decades later, twelve temples were promised in battle and subsequently built in Rome, but none in the Campus Martius.[58] With the First Punic War, however, came a perceptible shift favoring greater construction of temples on the edge of and, indeed, in the heart of the Field of Mars. Of approximately thirty-one temples identified with vow dates during the period of the three Punic Wars, about

9. South wall of the Church of S. Nicola in Carcere with the imbedded columns of the Temple of Juno Sospita. (Photo: Paul Jacobs)

half are believed to have been located in the campus.[59] Three nodes (areas of concentration) of temple construction developed there during this period: the Forum Holitorium and the Circus Flaminius on the southern end, and the area we now call the Largo Argentina in the central Campus Martius.

The Forum Holitorium is of uncertain date and the structures that were erected prior to the Punic Wars are unknown, although one ancient writer claimed it was Rome's earliest vegetable market.[60] In 260 B.C.E., however, the first of three temples promised to the gods during the period of the Punic Wars was vowed and later built there.[61] Dedicated to Janus and vowed by the consul C. Duilius, this first temple honored the victory over the Carthaginian fleet off the coast of Sicily.[62] Fast on the heels of the construction of that temple came another. Vowed to Spes, the goddess of hope, it was placed in the Forum Holitorium in line with that of Janus, but at a sufficient distance to allow for a later temple to be erected between them.[63] Although its date of completion is unknown, the Temple of Spes was in existence by 218 B.C.E., when Livy records that it was struck by lightning.[64] In 194 B.C.E., construction of the Temple of Juno Sospita filled the gap between the temples of Janus and Spes.[65] Its foundations are thought to be within the Church of S. Nicola in Carcere with the remains of the Temple of Janus to the north and that of Spes to the south (Figure 9, and Plan 2, Inset D).[66]

Within a decade of the construction of the Temple of Janus in the Forum Holitorium, foundation blocks were laid in the heart of the Campus Martius, in the area of the modern Largo Argentina, for temples of other gods. Although

10. East side of temples in the Largo Argentina. (Photo: Paul Jacobs)

the podiums and columns of several temples came to light there in the early twentieth century, debate still rages over the identity of each; hence, they are usually described as temples A through D (Figure 10; Plan 2, Inset A; and Plan 3, Inset A). A temple raised to honor Juturna, goddess of fountains and springs, is thought to have been built in approximately 242 B.C.E. in the Largo Argentina. Both temples A and C have been proposed for its location.[67] After the destruction in 241 B.C.E. of the Etrurian city of Falerii, about fifty kilometers north of Rome, the cult of Juno Curitis was brought to Rome, and a temple in her honor was built in the area of the Largo Argentina. Temples A and C, too, have been offered as the remains of her shrine.[68] Additionally, they have been suggested as the location for a temple to the fertility goddess, Feronia.[69] Another candidate for the temples found in the Largo Argentina is that dedicated to the Lares Permarini (Lares of the Sea), the result of a vow in 190 B.C.E. made by L. Aemilius Regillus while engaged in a decisive naval battle against the ships of Antiochus the Great.[70] As noted previously, it was dedicated eleven years later in 179 B.C.E. by his relative, M. Aemilius Lepidus, who had a lengthy inscription carved over the door detailing the enemy's defeat.[71] Two sites have been proposed for its construction: Temple D in the Largo Argentina and a small temple about 150 meters to the east across from the later-built Theater of Balbus.[72]

The third location, the Circus Flaminius, became the most concentrated area for republican temples in the Campus Martius. A public square created by C. Flaminius Nepos when he was censor in 221 B.C.E., the circus was located within an area previously known as the "Flaminian Field" (*prata flaminia*) that Livy tells us was used as early as the fifth century B.C.E. for public gatherings such as plebian councils.[73] Despite the use of the term "circus," the Circus Flaminius had neither architectural elements nor permanent seating, and the appellation confused even ancient writers.[74] Its long axis went from southeast to northwest, following the line of the river and that of two earlier temples (of Apollo Medicus and Bellona) beyond the southeast side. Lacking a clear architectural structure, the space was defined by the buildings that enclosed it, with the first known structure being, perhaps, a temple erected by Flaminius himself (Plan 2, No. 10), dedicated to Hercules Magnus Custos (Hercules the Great Guardian).[75] The circumstances of the founding of the temple of Hercules, as well as its name, remain a mystery, in large part because the books of Livy's history dealing with this time period are missing.[76] The precise location and details of the temple are also unknown, although it may have been sited on the western end of the Circus Flaminius.[77] Soon after the circus's establishment and the completion by Flaminius of his temple of Hercules Magnus Custos, a temple of the sea god Neptune was possibly constructed in the area. It was raised as early as 206 B.C.E. as Cassius Dio notes that one of the portents for that year was the profuse sweating of the doors and altar of such a temple.[78] A gold coin issued a century and a half later depicts a temple that may represent a reconstructed version of the earlier shrine to the sea god (Plate III).[79]

Details about the next three temples built in the Circus Flaminius – of Diana, Juno Regina, and Hercules Musarum – are more certain, putting three and possibly five temples on the perimeter of the open space by the end of the first third of the second century B.C.E. There was, however, room for more. By 146 B.C.E., a temple of Juno's consort, Jupiter Stator, was located next to hers, the result, perhaps, of a vow by the praetor Q. Caecilius Metellus, who erected a portico that year following his successes during the Fourth Macedonian War (150–148 B.C.E.) and at least partially enclosing the two temples.[80] Somewhere between the three temples in the Forum Holitorium and those in the Circus Flaminius, a temple of Pietas was dedicated in 181 B.C.E. (Plan 2, No. 8). The identification of its precise location remains in debate. Pliny claimed it stood where the Theater of Marcellus was later built, at the southeast corner of the circus, and this corresponds with Cassius Dio, who wrote that Julius Caesar tore down the temple in 44 B.C.E. to make way for the theater, an act claimed to be very unpopular with the Roman people.[81] The Temple of Pietas had been vowed by the consul M. Acilius Glabrio as he fought and then defeated the forces of Antiochus III the Great at the Battle of Thermopylae in 191 B.C.E., bringing back a sizable amount of plunder.[82] His son, who was serving as *duumvir*, dedicated the temple in 181 B.C.E. and honored his father by placing beside it a large, gilded statue of the elder Glabrio, the first of its kind in Rome.[83]

With the close of the Third Punic War in 146 B.C.E., the golden age of temple construction during the republican era came to a close. Three specific areas for temples had been established in the Campus Martius. Two of them – the Forum Holitorium and the Circus Flaminius – were loosely linked by three temples:

11. West side of the Temple of Fortuna Huiusce Diei (Temple B, Largo Argentina). (Photo: Paul Jacobs)

those of Apollo Medicus, Bellona, and Pietas. In the period from the final defeat of the Carthaginians to the advent of the empire, three more temples embellished the vicinity of the Circus Flaminius, and one was constructed in the area of the Largo Argentina, further concentrating republican religious structures in those two nodes of the Field of Mars. In 133 B.C.E., D. Junius Brutus Callaicus, who conquered western Iberia, used his war spoils to build in the area of the Circus Flaminius the Temple of Mars discussed in Chapter 2.[84] Later, perhaps around the turn of the first century B.C.E., a temple of the twin horsemen Castor and Pollux was erected on the edge of the Circus Flaminius, again on the southwest side (Plate V).[85]

In the early first century B.C.E., a round temple was squeezed between temples A and C in the Largo Argentina. Known by the letter *B*, it is the one temple in the area whose true identity garners the greatest consensus (Figure 11, and Plan 3, Inset A). It is recognized to be dedicated to Fortuna Huiusce Diei.

Vowed by Q. Lutatius Catulus on July 30, 101 B.C.E., at the Battle of Vercellae in northern Italy, the *aedes* contained extraordinary art, including two draped figures and a colossal nude by the fifth-century B.C.E. Athenian master Phidias, and seven nudes by a contemporary, Pythagoras of Samos.[86] The monumental head of Fortuna found on site has been attributed to Skopas Minor (Plate IV).

Several factors converged to create the blossoming of temples in the Campus Martius from the beginning of the Punic Wars into the first century B.C.E. First, an extraordinary influx of money and art treasures from foreign conquest provided the means to construct and embellish costly stone monuments. Second, it became fashionable for such resources to be deployed in the erection of temples in a way that had not been previously seen. It has been suggested that in the fourth century B.C.E. there were more fortifications built in Italy than temples, but by the second century B.C.E., almost three times more temples than fortifications were raised. Temples composed almost half of all public structures erected during the second century B.C.E.[87] Third, as Rome was growing quickly, space within the city for construction projects would have become more precious, making extrapomerial development more attractive.[88] Specifically, the Campus Martius was recognized as available for temple placement, likely because its use for military mustering was decreasing with longer service abroad. In just two decades between 194 and 173 B.C.E., seven temples were dedicated in the Campus Martius.[89] The extraordinary associations of the Field of Mars with military preparation together with its ties to the foundation legends must have made it singularly attractive for the placement of temples resulting directly from military vows, much more than other available sites also outside the *pomerium*.

While these factors might justify the appeal of the Campus Martius, they do not fully explain the clustering of the temples in the southern Campus Martius from the Circus Flaminius to the Forum Holitorium and the distinct node further north, in the area of the Largo Argentina. Different elements may have influenced each location. With respect to the Circus Flaminius, it has been suggested that certain temples make appropriate companions, and it is possible that the placement of one temple would influence the location of others. Jupiter Stator was long associated with Juno Regina, and it was natural for its placement to be adjacent to that of his consort.[90] It has also been argued that, as co-censors in 179 B.C.E., the once-rivals M. Aemilius Lepidus and M. Fulvius Nobilior were reconciled and that it was appropriate for the latter's temple to Hercules Musarum to be erected only meters from Lepidus's Juno Regina.[91] This theory is wholly dependent, however, on the notion that M. Fulvius Nobilior did not begin construction of his temple until the year he was censor and after Senate approval, points that are controverted.[92]

Perhaps the one factor that made the Circus Flaminius and the Forum Holitorium so attractive to generals vowing temples in battle was the area's ties to the triumphal route. Extraordinarily important events of religious, military, and political significance, the *triumphales* were not granted lightly. According to Plutarch, their origins date to the time of Romulus.[93] As noted previously, 200 triumphs were recorded from the mid-eighth century B.C.E. to the end of the republic. The general parading through Rome's streets was, at least for a day, viewed as omnipotent, and for life he carried the title of *vir triumphalis*, a man of triumph.[94] According to the early first-century C.E. writer Valerius Maximus, 5,000 enemy combatants had to be slain in order to qualify for a triumph, but this rule was not strictly enforced.[95] There were relatively few triumphs awarded until the late third and early second centuries B.C.E.[96] Only twenty-two triumphal parades occurred in the fifth century B.C.E., while during the middle republic one in every three consuls celebrated a triumph.[97] Between the years 200 and 167 B.C.E., they averaged more than one a year.[98] Generals who were granted triumphs sponsored eleven of sixteen temples built in the Campus Martius from the commencement of the Punic Wars to the final defeat of the Carthaginians.

The wealth of foreign lands that supplied the source financing the construction of vowed temples and their ornamentation was first on conspicuous display during the victorious general's triumph. M. Fulvius Nobilior's triumphal parade in December 187 B.C.E. celebrating his defeat of the Ambracians displayed golden crowns weighing 112 pounds as well as other gold objects weighing 243 pounds, 1,083 pounds of silver, 785 bronze statues, and 230 marble statues.[99] The triumph twenty years later by Lucius Aemilius Paullus for his victory over Perseus of Macedon at Pydna required a full day to parade the looted statues and paintings displayed in 250 chariots.[100] Perhaps the most extraordinary description of a triumph is that of the remarkable pageantry associated with the triumphal return to Rome of Pompey the Great after his defeat of Mithridates VI, the King of Pontus in northern Anatolia. This was Pompey's third awarded triumph, and he was now the conqueror of enemies on all of the known continents.[101] Describing the spectacle that occurred at the end of September 61 B.C.E., the writer Appian noted that for two days Romans watched "two-horse carriages and litters laden with gold or with other ornaments of various kinds, also the couch of Darius... the throne and scepter of Mithridates Eupator himself, and his image, eight cubits high, made of solid gold, and 75,100,000 drachmas of silver coin; the number of wagons carrying arms was infinite, and the number of the beaks of ships. After these came the multitude of captives and pirates, none of them bound, but all arrayed in their native costumes."[102] Marching in the procession were 324 satraps, sons, and generals of the kings who had fought against Pompey followed by large tableaux of the battles. Aristobulus, the King of Judea, was brought in captivity from Jerusalem and walked in the procession followed by a team of African elephants pulling a chariot in which stood Pompey himself wearing the cloak of Alexander the Great.[103] Although not all or even most

12. Pavilion in the Villa Publica (?). Reverse side of denarius of P. Fonteius Capito (ca. 59–55 B.C.E.). (Photo: Trustees of the British Museum)

triumphs had such conspicuous displays of war booty, those that did must have left a lasting impression on the spectators.[104]

Despite the colorful descriptions of the triumphal parades, the route taken by the general and his wagons of gold and silver is woefully incomplete. We know that they started outside of the city and to the north in the Campus Martius, but the precise location eludes modern determination. The best description of the gathering place for a triumph comes not from the republican period but from Josephus recounting the triumph in 71 C.E. of Emperor Vespasian and his son Titus celebrating the conquest of Jerusalem.[105] According to Josephus's account, the *triumphatores* spent the night in the central Campus Martius in or by the Temple of Isis, possibly in a building on the grounds of the Villa Publica (Figure 12), just east of the Saepta Julia and Pantheon, before moving on to the Portico of Octavia on the eastern side of the Circus Flaminius where official ceremonies commenced:[106]

All the soldiery marched out, while it was still night, in proper order and
rank under their commanders, and they were stationed on guard not at
the upper palace but near the Temple of Isis. For it was there that the
emperor and prince were resting that night. At break of day Vespasian and
Titus emerged, garlanded with laurel and dressed in the traditional purple
costume, and went over to the Portico of Octavia. For it was here that the
senate, the leading magistrates, and those of equestrian rank were awaiting
their arrival. A platform had been erected in front of the colonnade, with
thrones of ivory set on it. They went up to these and took their seats.
Straightaway the troops broke into applause, bearing ample testimony one
and all to their leaders' valor. They were unarmed, in silken costume,
garlanded with laurels. Acknowledging their applause, although the men
wanted to continue, Vespasian gave the signal for silence.

When it was completely quiet everywhere, he rose, covered most of
his head with his robe, and uttered the customary prayers. Titus prayed
likewise. After the prayers, Vespasian briefly addressed the assembled
company all together and then sent the soldiers off to the traditional
breakfast provided by the emperors. He himself meanwhile went back to
the gate that took its name from the fact triumphs always pass through
it. Here he and Titus first had a bite to eat and then, putting on their
triumphal dress and sacrificing to the gods whose statues are set up by
the gate, they sent off the triumphal procession, riding out through the
theaters so that the crowds had a better view.[107]

Whether Vespasian and Titus followed a route different from that used by
the many *triumphatores* before the advent of the empire is simply unknown,
although it is generally thought today that the Circus Flaminius served as
the initial collecting point for the beginning of the parade, at least after its
development in 221 B.C.E.[108] If initiated in the Circus Flaminius, the triumphal
parade would have then moved past the temples of Apollo Medicus and Bellona
and the temples in the Forum Holitorium, perhaps entering the city through
the Porta Carmentalis.[109] The procession may have then passed through the
Circus Maximus, entering the Roman Forum from the south end and wending
its way up the Capitoline to the Temple of Jupiter Optimus Maximus.[110]

Livy's descriptions of the Senate's debates over awarding triumphs occurring
in the nearby Temple of Bellona also lend weight to the theory that this area
marked the seminal point for these processions.[111] The Temple of Apollo next
to that of Bellona was also used by the Senate to consider requests by generals
for triumphal parades, including that of M. Fulvius Nobilior, an effort that, as
we saw earlier, was opposed by the agents for his rival M. Aemilius Lepidus.[112]
The cumulative evidence indicates that those temples placed in the Circus
Flaminius and along the line running from the temples of Bellona and Apollo
to the Forum Holitorium stood within direct view of triumphal parades.
It is not clear when the Circus Flaminius was first used for the formation

of triumphal parades, but certainly the formalization of the public space by Flaminius must have encouraged that activity.[113]

In short, generals who vowed sacred structures during battle, deployed large amounts of war booty in their construction financing or ornamentation, and sought and achieved triumphs could further burnish their glory by placement of these temples along the triumphal route. Indeed, one general, Aulus Atilius Calatinus, placed temples in two spots along the triumphal route – one honoring Spes in the Forum Holitorium and another dedicated to Fides (goddess of trust) on the south side of the Capitoline, at the end of the triumphal route[114] – allowing him to memorialize his name with two structures in prime locations. Atilius Calatinus's good works would have been clearly visible to future *triumphatores* as they marched past. Even to the extent that state funds and not *manubiae* financed temple construction, the high degree of consensus that prevailed in these matters suggests that a general would not be denied the desirable opportunity to place his temple along the triumphal route. Although display of captured wealth in temples may have been of greater significance to a general than the temple itself,[115] the fact that a temple was chosen to be vowed by generals who thereafter sought personal glory in triumph and, more often than not, participated in elaborate dedication ceremonies indicates an interest in a location that future *triumphatores* would have to pass. A small but telling piece of evidence for this proposition is that while Fulvius placed a bronze shield in his temple of Hercules, Lepidus had a Ligurian shield placed in the Temple of Juno Regina, a clear reminder to future passersby of their military victories.[116]

Although the triumphal route provided an appealing stretch of real estate for temples in the southern Campus Martius, there is little to support the proposition that it reached further north into the central area of the field.[117] Nevertheless, there were other reasons a general looking for a temple site would find the central Campus Martius appealing. Since the fifth century B.C.E., the Villa Publica – near, if not adjacent to, the temples in the Largo Argentina – provided a gathering place for the census and military levies. The centuriate assemblies met to vote in the nearby Saepta. Military leaders seeking a space wherein to remind future crowds of citizens and soldiers of their victories and good deeds could hardly find a more fitting space.[118] Vowed temples could also be useful campaign tools for generals or their kinsmen running in elections.[119] Indeed, as the Circus Flaminius was not developed until 221 B.C.E., the area by the Villa Publica likely had early appeal to conquering generals laden with treasure from battles with the Carthaginians. Despite arguments that, for generals seeking temple placement in the public eye, the area around the Villa Publica with its infrequent centuriate assemblies would be less attractive than the crowded fora and circus, as many as four temples were placed in the area of the Largo Argentina before the construction of the first ones in the Circus Flaminius.[120]

13. Temple on the Via delle Botteghe Oscure (Temple of the Nymphs?). (Photo: Paul Jacobs)

Apart from the proximity to the Villa Publica, the temples in and near the Largo Argentina honored gods with relationships to one another, providing clues to site selection. For instance, as discussed in Chapter 6, a few temples of water deities – Juturna, Feronia, the Lares Permarini, and a temple of the Nymphs – were clustered together (Figure 13).[121] The proximity of the Tiber and the alluvial nature of the topography of the central Campus Martius, in particular the low-lying waters of the Goat Marsh, made this area appealing for honoring that element. Alternatively, Catulus's selection of the Largo Argentina to honor Juturna after a naval victory may have been due to a desire to be within view of the Villa Publica, and the fulfillment of his vow then started a trend of clustering water-related temples in this area.[122] Associations with Rome's foundation legends provide a plausible explanation for the presence of certain other temples in the area. Plutarch notes that the name for the deified Romulus, Quirinus, may come from the word for spear (*quiris*) and is tied etymologically to Juno Curitis who carries a spear and whose temple was located in the area of the Theater of Pompey.[123] Vulcan's temple located in the Campus Martius was, according to Plutarch, used by Romulus to hold meetings with senators, although its construction actually occurred four centuries after the city's mythical founding.[124] Juturna, in turn, was connected to the Vulcanalia, a festival that acknowledged the protective employment of water to combat the constant dangers of Vulcan's fire.[125] In short, the legends of the gods and their celebration interweave to suggest tantalizing possibilities for the siting of vowed temples in the area of the Largo Argentina. The fact remains, however, that the Largo Argentina, Circus Flaminius, and Forum Holitorium were all in view of significant public gathering places associated with the military and so were all appropriate places to honor gods whose aid was invoked in battle. The sacred structures resonated the field's long history as a mustering ground.

THE TEMPLES AND THEIR DESIGNS

Before the Punic Wars, temples constructed in the Campus Martius reflected traditional architectural elements used by the Etruscans and other tribes of the Italian Peninsula. Characterized by tall bases or podiums with two or four wide-spaced columns supporting a deep porch (*pronaos*) and accented with molded terracotta ornamentation, these so-called "Etrusco-Roman" temples included the earliest versions of temples A and C in the Largo Argentina.[126] Both structures sat on high podiums of volcanic tufa, and both were *tetrastyle* (four columns fronting the *pronaos*). Temple A, with columns only in the front (*prostyle*), was much smaller than C, which also had five columns down each side (*peripteral*).[127] At the southern edge of the Campus Martius, the fifth-century B.C.E. Temple of Apollo Medicus and the early third-century B.C.E. Temple of Bellona would have exhibited similar characteristics.[128]

The complicated alliances of the later Punic Wars led Rome's military to the east where victories allowed the generals to send back more than captured wealth and enemy soldiers; they also carried to Rome the architectural elements of the Greek mainland that began to be incorporated into temple design.[129] There was no rapid conversion but rather a synthesis of the two styles. For instance, in the Forum Holitorium, the temples of Janus, Juno Sospita, and Spes combined the tall platforms and deep porches of older Roman architecture with the more numerous and closely placed columns characteristic of Greek temples.[130] Each had six columns (*hexastyle*) across the *pronaos* with Juno Sospita and Spes displaying eleven columns down each side.[131] With a combined total of eighteen columns across their fronts, the three temples suggested, according to one scholar, a "portico-like front to a common sacred area."[132] If so, it was hardly a uniform portico as the porches were of different heights and Janus and Juno Sospita had Ionic columns as might be found in Greece while Spes's columns were still in the Tuscan style.[133]

In the Circus Flaminius, the Temple of Juno Regina erected by M. Aemilius Lepidus and the Temple of Jupiter Stator, built several decades later by Metellus, incorporated even more Hellenistic elements. Juno Regina had six tall, fluted columns with Ionic capitals across the front. Filled with beautiful Greek statuary, including a statue of Diana by Cephisodotus, son of the famed Praxiteles, as well as a marble statue of the god of medicine, Aesculapius, the temple reflected Roman appreciation of Greek design and decoration.[134] Designed by a Greek architect, Hermodorus of Salamis, the Temple of Jupiter Stator was also hexastyle and peripteral with a narrow *cella*.[135] More importantly, it was the first temple in Rome to have been built entirely of marble, a material later used in copious amounts during the imperial age.[136] Hellenistic influence continued when Hermodorus designed another temple located on or near the Circus Flaminius, the Temple of Mars.[137]

New ideas were not exempt from alteration, however, as Vitruvius remarks on the recombination of elements in the design of the nearby Temple of Castor and Pollux, which bore a transverse *cella* and six-columned porch (Plate V).[138] Another example of the synthesis of Roman aesthetic with Hellenistic architectural ideals is found in the rendering on the Marble Plan of the temple to Hercules Musarum, also along the Circus Flaminius. The Marble Plan shows the temple to Hercules Musarum to have been a Greek-style round temple (*tholos*) resting on a rectangular platform requiring an axial approach and bearing a staircase of five steps (see Figure 8).[139] The last temple built in the Largo Argentina, Temple B (Fortuna Huiusce Diei), was also a *tholos*, surrounded by eighteen Corinthian columns and approached by stairs set on an axis that conformed to an earlier, traditional plan (see Figure 11).[140]

By the end of the third century B.C.E. and with the conclusion of the Second Punic War, Rome was filling with structures to meet a growing population. Edifices from this time still reflected the traditional Etrusco-Roman architectural styles criticized by Macedonian generals.[141] Over time, however, many of the republican temples in the Campus Martius were altered in accordance with the increasingly popular Greek style. Temples A and C in the Largo Argentina began with Tuscan Doric columns but ended with those in the Corinthian style. In the case of Temple A, the base was increased in size, columns were increased in number along the front of the *pronaos* from four to six, and they were added along the sides and back where none had previously been.[142] Although the original temples in the Largo Argentina were built at different ground levels, during the late second century B.C.E. and again in the first century C.E., the ground level was raised to a uniform height, reducing the height of the temple platforms and providing a more Hellenistic portico-like appearance to the complex.[143]

In the area of the Circus Flaminius, the Temple of Apollo underwent a radical transformation during the late first century B.C.E. The Temple of Apollo

14. Aedicula from the cella of the Temple of Apollo Sosianus (ca. 32 B.C.E.). (Photo: Paul Jacobs, published with permission of Roma, Musei Capitolini, Centrale Montemartini)

Medicus as rebuilt by Fulvius Nobilior in 179 B.C.E. had four columns across the front and two on the side, but the triumviral general C. Sosius placed six Corinthian columns along the front, six engaged columns along the back of the *cella*, and a combination of ten full and engaged columns along each side.[144] Three of its beautiful marble columns may be seen today, reerected on site (Plate VI), and remnants of its decorative elements from the *cella* are on view in Rome's Museo Centrale Montemartini (Figure 14). The name of the temple changed as well and became known as Apollo Sosianus. The temple of the goddess of war, Bellona, next to the Apollo *aedes* was rebuilt in marble and travertine with six Corinthian columns along the front and nine along the sides.[145] The temples of Juno Regina and Jupiter Stator were refurbished with libraries in the late first century B.C.E. by Augustus's sister Octavia.[146] (Compare Plan 2, Inset B, and Plan 3, Inset B.) When the porticoes surrounding the temples in the Circus Flaminius are considered in combination with the temples themselves, the sum reflects not only an assimilation of Hellenistic architectural aesthetic but also the development of a new, distinctly Roman style of the imperial age.[147]

CONCLUSION

Although for centuries the Campus Martius remained relatively free of structures as the space within the *pomerium* began to fill, in the late third century to the mid-second century B.C.E. it witnessed a significant change. This period of the Punic Wars saw consuls and praetors leading Rome's legions in distant places and seeking divine intervention to assure victory. With temples vowed and the riches of conquered foreign kings at their disposal, and with no clear military imperative to leave the Campus Martius free of brick and stone, returning generals found the field north of Rome to be an attractive location for honoring the gods who brought them victory. Although the role of the Senate in the decision of temple site selection is debatable, certainly a consensus must have developed that the Field of Mars was now an appropriate place in which to erect these structures. Perhaps in some cases the gods honored in the Campus Martius were not to be worshiped within the walls, clarifying perhaps the decision for their temples' extrapomerial location. More significant, however, must have been the fact that for a people almost continuously at war, temples vowed in battle were a natural fit for a space tied to both military activities and foundation myths. Clustered along the triumphal route or within clear view of the location for civic events, the temples were not randomly placed but were situated with care to maximize the connection between the vowing general and the military significance of the Field of Mars. Filled with the spoils of war and over time incorporating the Hellenistic architectural traditions, which were appropriated as deliberately as foreign captives paraded in chains, these monuments helped to organize the Campus Martius for future uses while maintaining traditions supporting the military impulses behind foundation legends such as Romulus's apotheosis among his gathered troops.

CHAPTER FOUR

"CHARIOT RACES," "THREE THEATRES," "AN AMPHITHEATRE," AND MORE: ENTERTAINMENT IN THE CAMPUS MARTIUS

Having climbed the slope of the steps of a wooden amphitheater, Corydon, a creation of the poet Titus Calpurnius Siculus, vividly describes taking his seat in the upper level among the poor in their unbleached cloaks and near the benches where women were allowed to view the spectacle below.[1] If the events set out in his eclogue took place in 57 C.E., as many scholars believe, then the poet Calpurnius had likely observed the Campus Martius from the recently completed structure built in less than a year under the orders of Emperor Nero.[2] Employing a veritable forest of wood, including the largest larch tree ever brought to the capital, Calpurnius/Corydon tells us that the amphitheater rose on interwoven beams above the flat plain of the Campus Martius in two curved sections, creating an oval arena on the center floor.[3]

From Corydon's words, we might imagine Calpurnius at the amphitheater surveying the crowd and incidents to include in his work. Before the show grabbed his attention, perhaps he looked out across the Field of Mars and saw in the distance the Capitoline Hill, appearing not much taller than the amphitheater itself.[4] From his high perch atop the theater, the poet would also have seen a remarkable sight. Once a marshy military exercise ground, the plain was now the premier entertainment district within a bustling, urban landscape. Captured in Calpurnius's view from this impressive, albeit temporary entertainment site, would have been the even more extraordinary and permanent stone theaters and amphitheater constructed by great men during the waning days of the republic. These massive edifices significantly influenced the trans-formation of the topography of the Campus Martius. The Amphitheater of Statilius Taurus was then approaching its ninth decade of hosting gladiatorial and animal exhibitions. Constructed a century before Nero's temporary struc-ture was raised, the curved walls of Rome's first and largest stone theater, the Theater of Pompey, would also have been visible. Indeed, it rose higher than the amphitheater where Calpurnius sat. About half a kilometer southeast of Pompey's theater, another theater sat close to the riverbank, this one built by Augustus to honor his deceased nephew Marcellus. Yet a third theater and its attached portico, built by a general from Hispania, Lucius Cornelius Balbus, stood approximately equidistant between the other two. The view from the top seats of the amphitheater might have included other nearby venues for occasional sporting events, such as a *trigarium*, or practice track for horse races, and the Saepta Julia, which was used sometimes for gladiatorial combat and gymnastic competition.

Turning his attention from the skyline to his immediate surroundings, Calpurnius might have marveled at both the amphitheater's ornamentation and the performance staged below. Just above him, an awning, described by Pliny as blue with stars, fluttered in the breeze.[5] It covered only part of the audience, with the equestrians and tribunes sitting near the arena floor exposed to the sun and sky.[6] In order to awe the audience with a display of imperial wealth, Nero added gilded arcades to this building of wood, as well as a marble wall separating the seats from the arena floor. The low wall, or *balteus*, ringing the cross aisle of the amphitheater was encrusted with gems. On the day of Calpurnius's visit, ticket holders watched a display of wild beasts, and Corydon lists animals such as bison, bears, "sea calves," and hippopotamuses among the entertainment. As with similar shows, nets were placed along the edge of the arena floor to protect the viewers from danger. But these were not just ordi-nary woven ropes. Nero had them made of gold wire suspended from huge white tusks, each reportedly longer than a plow. For added spectator protec-tion, ivory cylinders on wooden axles were placed around the arena ready to spin and throw off sharp claws if an animal attempted to lunge at the closest viewers. Trapdoors were built into the floor to deliver the animals leaping to the surface in a cloud of yellow sand and dust, surprising and delighting the spectators.[7]

This show, described by Calpurnius in his *Eclogues*, was the type of spectacle that Romans expected in the Field of Mars in the mid-first century C.E., but the venues in which they were held had developed slowly and with designs and materials varying according to the type of entertainment. The earliest events, such as horse racing, continued over time with – at best – temporary seating. Other diversions, such as theater performances, were ultimately staged in massive stone structures that were to last for centuries, leaving a permanent mark on the landscape of the Campus Martius.

VENUES FOR "CHARIOT RACING AND OTHER EQUESTRIAN ACTIVITIES"

Apart from the pomp and pageantry associated with the triumphal parade, the earliest form of organized spectator events in the Campus Martius appears to have been three days of horse racing.[8] The Equirria, held in the Campus Martius on February 27 and on March 14, have been associated with the annual military campaign season and must be of very early origin.[9] Occasionally, horse races occurred in Rome without chariots, and it is not clear whether the Equirria contests were run with or without chariots.[10] We do know that the October Horse was a competition among *bigae*, two-horse chariot teams. Held on October 15 somewhere in the Field of Mars, the October Horse may date to the sixth century B.C.E.[11]

The open, flat terrain of the Campus Martius during the republic lent itself well to equestrian events, and its use for that purpose would not have interfered with military training exercises. In fact, such activities reinforced the space's connection to the horses of war. The Field of Mars, however, was by no means the only suitable area of the city for the sport.[12] Southwest of the Campus Martius, a long, narrow valley between the Palatine and Aventine Hills proved ideal for a track, and it was here that Rome's oldest and largest racetrack, the Circus Maximus, was established.[13] Achieving its greatest size and magnificence during the reign of Emperor Trajan (r. 98–117 C.E.), the Circus Maximus at that time was a stone stadium three stories high with arcades and engaged columns along the exterior perimeter of the lowest level. Its seating accommodated an estimated 150,000 to 250,000 spectators to cheer the chariot drivers racing along an oval track approximately 550 meters long and 80 meters wide.[14] Along the center of the track ran the *spina* that became in the second century C.E. a *euripus*, a marbled basin filled with water over which bridges were placed at regular intervals leading to islands containing sculpture, obelisks, and pavilions.[15]

Horse racing was first associated with votive offerings by triumphant generals and was presented periodically as part of the *ludi Romani* or Roman games.[16] In 366 B.C.E., these occasional games became an annual September event with chariot races known as *ludi circenses*, or circus games.[17] Although the races took place in the Circus Maximus, the festival had strong ties with the early uses of the Campus Martius. Dedicated to Jupiter Capitolinus, the *ludi Romani* celebrated peace at the end of the military season, when soldiers returned from war to the Field of Mars. A lengthy procession led by the sons of citizens nearing the age for military service, followed by charioteers and other athletes, wended from the Campus Martius to the Capitoline, through the Forum to the Circus before the start of the games themselves.[18]

After the mid-fifth century B.C.E., state money was used to supply racehorses for the games.[19] It was perhaps at that point in time that organized groups of drivers formed, with colored tunics to distinguish each team: Red (*russata*), White (*albata*), Blue (*veneta*), and Green (*prasina*) (see Plate VII).[20] In addition to the *bigae*, there were chariots pulled by three horses (*trigae*) and, most popularly, by four horses (*quadrigae*).[21] The Circus Maximus was large enough for each team to field three *quadrigae* at a time, allowing twelve charioteers driving forty-eight horses to race at once.[22] At the time of Augustus, there were seventeen days of public chariot races on the calendar. By the mid-third century C.E., there were sixty-six days annually.[23] At that time, there were as many as twenty-four races in a day, each lasting about fifteen minutes. Although drivers likely competed several times, a large number of fresh horses would have been needed on race day.[24]

While the Circus Maximus had many days of equestrian events, we know of very few in the Campus Martius. In addition to the two Equirria and the October Horse, one other festival with horse racing, the *ludi Taurii*, has been clearly associated with the Field of Mars, but it was held only once every five years in the Circus Flaminius, and without chariots.[25] Another annual festival, first mentioned in 216 B.C.E., the *ludi Plebeii*, was held every November with theatrical performances as well as three days of circus games, and while one ancient writer indicated that it was run in the Circus Flaminius, doubt has been cast on that site as the games' location for very long.[26] Notwithstanding these few known equestrian events, in the early imperial era, when the southern and central Campus Martius were filling with structures, Strabo wrote that the plain still afforded "space . . . without interference . . . for the chariot-races and every other equestrian exercise."[27] Was Strabo simply referring to the few races known or acknowledging that there were more? If the latter, where were they raced?

Although called a "circus," the Circus Flaminius space was used generally as a public square for markets, assemblies, and triumphal gatherings.[28] Lacking permanent spectator seating, it did host one chariot-less race every five years and perhaps, for a while, the *ludi Plebeii*. Doubt has been cast on its use for other races, and the confined space of the Circus Flaminius would have limited chariot races to a scale much smaller scale than those held in the Circus Maximus. No more than about 500 meters on its long axis before temples confined the space, the open area within the Circus Flaminius shrank considerably by the late second century B.C.E.[29] Indeed, once surrounded by buildings, the available space would have confined a track to less than half of the length of the Circus Maximus, allowing four-horse chariot teams to race down the long side in about half a minute.[30] Temporary wooden viewing stands would have constricted the tight space even further. This suggests that any races were more likely observed from the surrounding temple steps and porticoes. Unlike the Circus Maximus, the Circus Flaminius was too narrow to accommodate twelve *quadrigae* at a time. Nonetheless, it was certainly wide enough to allow at least one four-horse chariot for each of the four teams.[31]

Because the October Horse was run with *bigae*, the space within the Circus Flaminius was likely sufficient to hold the annual contest, but references to the race in a fourth-century C.E. calendar suggest a wholly separate location for the October Horse, perhaps a kilometer north of the Circus Flaminius where the Tiber begins to narrow the Campus Martius (see Plan 2).[32] Whether the Equirria contests were held in this same location is simply unknown.

Some scholars have also argued for the existence of a practice track in the Campus Martius near the Tiber called a *trigarium*, a name possibly derived from the three-horse chariot team.[33] Given the large number of charioteers and horses that participated in Circus Maximus races and the competitive spirit among the four teams, a workout facility appears logical. A dedicated practice area for racing could have been in use year-round, perhaps occasionally with Strabo watching from the sidelines. Strabo states that the charioteers raced "without hindrance," and as he gives no precise location, it is possible that there was no permanent seating.[34] At best, there would have been a wooden viewing stand, possibly erected only on festival days. As for its position, it is unlikely that the central area of the Campus Martius was suitable for the *trigarium* because by the early imperial era it was fast filling with structures whose exact locations have been identified. One proposed area for the track is the western side of the Campus Martius, near the present-day Via Giulia, following the northwest-southeast line of the Tiber (Plan 3, No. 31).[35]

Although no direct physical evidence has been found that situates a racetrack in the western Campus Martius, an inscription found in the area refers to horse stables for the Green team. Known collectively as the *Stabula IIII Factionum*, the stables for all four teams were likely separated but in close proximity to each other. They provided shelter and fodder for the large number of horses required for racing days in the Circus Maximus and likely facilitated daily practice in the *trigarium*.[36] The importance of horse racing and the excesses of the imperial age came together in this location. According to ancient writers, Caligula (r. 37–41 C.E.), an enthusiastic fan of the Green faction, caused an ivory paddock and marble stall to be built at the Green stables for his favorite horse, Incitatus.[37] According to Suetonius, the emperor often spent the night there, and just before race day, Caligula would deploy his soldiers to enforce silence in the surrounding area to prevent Incitatus from being disturbed.[38]

In addition to races on tracks, the Campus Martius provided space for more informal equestrian activities. We know, for example, that the young

Octavian used to engage in riding and military exercises in the field and Marius donned armor and participated in mock battles on horseback.[39] Until the Augustan building program in the late first century B.C.E., the central and northern portions of the Campus Martius remained open space that could accommodate these activities. Even during Strabo's day, the northern reaches were just beginning to see development, and apart from chariot races, the "other equestrian exercise" could occur there "without interference."[40]

While the Campus Martius was likely viewed as little competition for the extraordinary racetrack that was the Circus Maximus, it appears to have provided an important venue for a few races tied to the sanctity of the space such as the October Horse, to have supported the Circus Maximus with practice facilities and paddocks, and, at least through the Augustan principate, to have offered the casual horseman a splendid recreational area among its still-open spaces and manicured parks.

FROM TEMPLE STEPS TO STONE SEATS: SPACES FOR THEATER

Though it would seem that the earliest form of public entertainment in the Campus Martius left no permanent imprint on the space, the next type of performances staged there ultimately shaped the landscape in ways still visible. The scenic games (*ludi scaenici*) evolved into theatrical events held in massive stone theaters that remained mostly intact until the end of the empire. According to Livy, the first of the *ludi scaenici* came to Rome in the mid-fourth century B.C.E. "This was a new departure for a warlike people, whose only [earlier] exhibitions had been those of the circus."[41] The scenic games were a simple combination of music and movement and appear to have been introduced through contact with the Etruscans to the north. At the first Roman Games, according to Livy, "Without any singing, without imitating the action of singers, players who had been brought in from Etruria danced to the strains of the flautist and performed not ungraceful evolutions in the Tuscan fashion."[42] The Romans also likely were exposed at this time to the slapstick comedy performed with masks by their southern neighbors, the Oscans, as well as to the farcical dramas known as *phlyakes* performed in the Greek colonies on the Italian Peninsula.[43] The first scripted dramas did not arrive in Rome for another century, until just after the close of the First Punic War.[44] Two decades later, the first historical dramas, or *fabulae praetextae*, were performed, and in the period between the First and Second Punic Wars, some festivals became associated with scenic entertainment.[45] The *ludi scaenici* were not wholly separate from the *ludi circenses* discussed earlier, because both could be employed as part of the same festival, as with the *ludi Romani* and the *ludi Plebeii*.[46] By the mid-second century B.C.E. there were approximately twenty days of *ludi scaenici* on the calendar, and by the time of Augustus in the late first century B.C.E. there were fifty-six days set aside for theater, showing the grow-ing popularity of the performing arts at the end of the republic.[47] Beacham has summarized the situation well: "Public demand for entertainment encouraged prudent politicians and rulers as well as ambitious patrons to provide generous sponsorship and support."[48]

It is believed that the first theaters in Rome were little more than wooden stages set up in the Forum, the Circus Maximus, or before a temple. Generally tied to religious festivals, *ludi scaenici* would be performed in the vicinity of a temple, the god of which was honored by the celebrations.[49] When a stage was erected in front of a temple, the steps leading to the podium often doubled as seating.[50] Although ancient literary sources do not provide explicit evidence for annual festival plays held at the temples in the Campus Martius, given the explosion of temple construction occurring in the plain just as *ludi scaenici* were coming to Rome, it is reasonable to presume that they were. We do know that a contract was awarded by Aemilius Lepidus for the construction of a theater near the Temple of Apollo in 179 B.C.E., likely to be used in connection with the *ludi Apollinares* held every July. In this case, however, rather than employing the improvised seating of temple steps, audience seats were to be constructed along with a stage. The theater seating possibly remained in place for several years and was reused for other performances, although it has been questioned whether the structure was actually built at all.[51] The dedication six years later of the Temple of Fortuna Equestris (in the general vicinity of the later-built Theater of Pompey) also included four days of theatrical entertainment, although the location of the performances is not identified.[52]

Scenic games were limited neither to temple dedications nor to annual religious celebrations, but were sometimes performed in conjunction with triumphs, as in 167 B.C.E. when *ludi scaenici* were held on a large stage, complete with an orchestra for dancers, in the Campus Martius.[53] Indeed, triumphal parades that formed up in the Campus Martius sometimes brought to the viewers lining the route a theater in motion with "a chorus of musicians and pipers, in imitation of an Etruscan procession, wearing belts and golden crowns, and they march evenly with song and dance."[54] Julius Caesar sponsored stage plays, which were performed "by actors of all languages" in every ward of the city as part of the quadruple triumphs celebrated in 46 B.C.E. Suetonius tells us that in one such play a Roman knight "acted a farce of his own composition, and having been presented with 500,000 sesterces and a gold ring, passed from the stage through the orchestra and took his place in the . . . rows" reserved for knights.[55] Particular favorites of the Roman audiences were mimes, plays with lascivious and mocking themes, and pantomimes, solo dancing by masked actors accompanied by music and often based on Greek themes.[56]

At the same time that the Romans viewed performances in simple, impro-vised venues or watched them pass along the parade route, theatergoers elsewhere on the Italian Peninsula and in Sicily enjoyed such spectacles from stone seats built into the curve of a slope, both natural and man-made. The audiences faced a raised stone stage (-*pulpitum*) with tall scene buildings (*scaenae frons*) as a background and set.[57] The large theater in Pompeii, for instance, dating to the second century B.C.E. was built against a lava and earth slope and had a seating area (*cavea*) approximately forty-nine meters wide with a stage placed almost two meters higher than the orchestra.[58] Some of the theaters were large enough to seat as many as 14,000 theatergoers, although most held far less.[59] Not all shows outside of Rome were performed in large permanent venues, however. The *phlyakes* were held on temporary wooden stages with decorated cloth or wooden backdrops, and it is thought that the first Roman theaters were possibly modeled on these Greek structures.[60]

Not until Pompey the Great erected his enormous concrete and stone theater, dedicated in 55 B.C.E., did Romans see in their capital a permanent structure for theatrical entertainment similar to those found elsewhere in Italy. Numerous causes have been offered for this state of affairs, but generally scholars have settled on attempts by the aristocracy to maintain control over theatrical performances for various reasons. These include a desire to restrict shows to specific holidays, fear that a conspicuous display through construction of massive buildings would engender resentment by the lower classes, and the inappropriateness of the permanent glorification of a wealthy benefactor.[61] The impracticality of building a permanent theater for each honored god and the poor quality of concrete available in Rome for use in large structures have also been offered as explanations for the existence of only temporary theaters in the Campus Martius before the mid-first century B.C.E.[62]

In 154–150 B.C.E., an attempt by the censors to build a permanent theater was thwarted after materials had been gathered and construction almost completed. Using the stated reason that permanent theaters were "useless and injurious to public morals," the Senate on the urging of the statesman Scipio Nasica brought the project to a halt.[63] To make the point, a law was passed at that time prohibiting sitting at public games within a mile of the city. Moreover, any theater seating that had been erected as of this date in Rome was now off-limits.[64] According to Appian, writing more than 200 years after the fact, the demolition was carried out either to eradicate a likely source of intrigue or to keep Romans from becoming accustomed to Greek recreation.[65] Because Greek theatrical performances were not prohibited, the latter reason rings hollow. As Gruen suggests, it may have had more to do with the desire of the magistrates to use temporary theaters to keep drama dependent on their annual approval.[66]

Even within the temporary theaters, rules were developed to impose social order and reinforce conservative norms of morality. Until the beginning of the second century B.C.E., members of the various classes and both sexes intermingled at performances, but in 194 B.C.E. special seats near the stage were reserved for Senate members.[67] At some point men and women were segregated during performances, and when dividing the viewers did not resolve upper-class concerns about the theater promoting unacceptable moral behavior, other measures were taken. In 115 B.C.E., for instance, actors and all theater personnel were temporarily banned from the city.[68] Stricter rules for audience class divisions were adopted under Augustus through a law known as the *Lex Iulia Theatralis*.[69] Theatrical performances appear to have become caught in the culture wars, with plays considered by some in the upper class as subversive and interjecting dangerous foreign ideas.[70]

Despite efforts to control theatrical displays, the simple wooden affairs for performances at religious holidays had evolved into elaborate edifices by the first century B.C.E. Awnings were added and stages were embellished with silver, gold, and ivory ornamentation.[71] Perhaps the most extraordinary "temporary" theater in Rome during the republic was the one constructed in 58 B.C.E. by Aemilius Scaurus. Standing for several years in the Campus Martius, the wooden theater held approximately 20,000 spectators.[72] It had a *scaenae frons* with 360 columns divided evenly among three levels.[73] The columns on the lowest level were of marble, those on the second of glass mosaic surmounted by gilt wood columns on the third. It was further decorated with 3,000 bronze statues. Five years later, a tribune erected two large wooden theaters, likely in the Campus Martius, whose semicircular seating were back-to-back, allowing two separate performances to occur simultaneously. In an amazing feat of engineering, the *caveae*, resting on pivoting platforms, were turned in the afternoon, even with the audience in place, transforming the double *caveae* into an amphitheater suitable for gladiatorial combat.[74] Writing more than a century after the fact, Pliny the Elder was contemptuous of the way in which the audience was placed in such danger:

> Here [C. Scribonius] Curio staged fights between gladiators – although the Roman people found themselves in even greater danger than the gladiators, as Curio spun them around. It is difficult to know what should amaze us more, the inventor or the invention, or the sheer audacity of the conception. Most amazing of all is the madness of a people rash enough to sit in such treacherous and unstable seats! What contempt for human life this shows! . . . Here the whole Roman people, as if put on board two ships, were supported by a pair of pivots and watched themselves fighting for their lives and likely to perish at any moment should the mechanism be put out of gear![75]

With temporary structures becoming more and more elaborate and plays gaining in popularity, the time was ripe in the mid-first century B.C.E. for another attempt to count Rome among the numerous other cities in Italy that allowed stone and masonry venues for theatrical performances. The grip of the conservative Senate over the physical development of the city was weakening as power increasingly concentrated in the hands of a few wealthy men who used conspicuous display as a political tool.[76] Nevertheless, it took the stature of Rome's then greatest general to bring about the completion of Rome's first permanent theater. With its flat expanse, the Campus Martius provided the ideal location. According to Plutarch, Pompey the Great developed the idea of constructing a permanent stage and seating in 63 B.C.E. while viewing a stone theater at Mytilene on the island of Lesbos.[77] With extraordinary spoils from his eastern campaign at his disposal, Pompey returned to Rome two years later with conceptual drawings for Rome's first permanent theater and the means to realize them.[78] Construction for the massive structure began following his third triumph in 61 B.C.E. It was completed six years later and was unlike anything Rome had seen previously built. Although supposedly inspired by the Greek theater Pompey had admired on his campaign, the structure was far grander, becoming and remaining the largest theater built by the Romans.[79] The *cavea* was approximately 150 meters across, or eight times as large as the one on Lesbos, and rose from the flat earth of the central Campus Martius instead of being built up against a hillside in the Greek style.[80] At an estimated height of approximately 44 meters, it stood 18 meters higher than the modern Capitoline piazza, and including the appended quadriportico, the area of the theater was more than half that of the Capitoline hill.[81] As Sear observed, Pompey's theater "established a new type of civic building, a totally integrated and unified structure, independent of its surroundings because of its exploitation of concrete vaulting," the end product of previous efforts elsewhere in Italy to free stone *cavea* from earthen support.[82] The seating capacity at the time it was built is unknown, but by the fourth century C.E., and after several renovations, the theater is thought to have held between 11,000 and slightly more than 17,000 spectators.[83]

To assure its permanence, the structure was built of concrete walls 1.5 meters thick and faced in stone.[84] Theatergoers entered through forty-four arched passageways along the outer wall.[85] The third-century Severan Marble Plan shows an elaborate *scaenae frons* with two deep, semicircular niches flanking a central rectangular one, all fronted by a colonnade (Figure 15).[86] The decorative elements around the exterior of the *cavea* are unknown, but with respect to the interior, beautiful statuary has been excavated in the vicinity, allowing for the possibility that Pompey's theater held sculptures in the tradition of Scaurus (Figures 16 and 17).[87] The solidity of Pompey's grandiose theater achieved the goals of its patron. Almost 500 years later, in the fourth century C.E., the theater was still noted to be one of the tallest structures in the city.[88] Even today, its footprint is reflected in the curve of the buildings resting on its arcades (Figure 18).

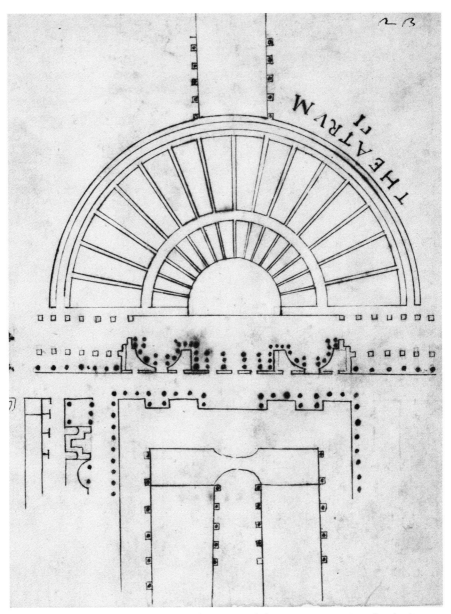

15. Detail, Vat. Lat. 3439 f.23r. Theater of Pompey and the connecting portico after the Severan Marble Plan (sixteenth century). (Photo: with permission of Biblioteca Apostolica Vaticana, with all rights reserved)

Along the top curve of the *cavea*, Pompey built a temple of Venus Victrix, and at least by the reign of Claudius, there were four additional shrines above the seating area.[89] Tertullian, a second-century C.E. writer, claimed that when it came time to dedicate the structure, Pompey issued invitations not to the dedication of the theater but instead to the Temple of Venus, asserting that the theater was merely a stairway to the temple. This was, according to

16. Satyr (ca. second century C.E.) found in the vicinity of the Theater of Pompey. Palazzo Nuovo, Capitoline Museums. (Photo: Vanni / Art Resource, New York)

17. Seated muse (late republican) found in the vicinity of the Theater of Pompey. (Photo: Paul Jacobs with permission of Roma, Musei Capitolini, Centrale Montemartini)

18. Location of the cavea of the Theater of Pompey, Via di Grotta Pinta, Rome. (Photo: Paul Jacobs)

Tertullian, an excuse for Pompey to avoid the opprobrium associated with permanent theater structures, putting it in the same category as manubial temple construction.[90] The invitation may have been made in jest, as recognition of a proscription that had little application to someone of his stature and power. Though he was harshly criticized for building the theater, had there been a serious attempt to thwart its construction, it would have been made before the concrete had set.[91]

On the eastern side of the colonnaded park behind his theater and flanking the back of the temples in the Largo Argentina, Pompey constructed a meeting room (*curia*) used by the Senate, in which stood a large statue of Pompey himself. Because he was proconsul, Pompey could meet with the senators outside the *pomerium* in a space that he built.[92] Ancient sources tell us that on the eve of his battle with Julius Caesar at Pharsalus, Pompey dreamed of walking into his theater complex to the sound of applause and of decorating the Venus Victrix with the spoils of war, but Pompey never returned to receive the adulation.[93] Instead, a golden throne for Caesar would grace the theater.[94] Four years later, however, on the Ides of March, 44 B.C.E., Caesar met his demise in the *curia* behind the theater, at the foot of Pompey's statue.[95] Later, Augustus removed the statue, placing it on a marble arch behind the *scaenae frons*. He then walled up the *curia*.[96] The meeting room was converted to a latrine that is visible today behind Temple B in the Largo Argentina (Figure 19).[97] Stretching more

19. Latrine on the west side of the Largo Argentina. (Photo: Paul Jacobs)

than 300 meters from the modern Largo Argentina to the Campo dei Fiori, the theater and portico complex occupied an extraordinary amount of prime real estate in the heart of the central Campus Martius, rising above the plain to the approximate height of the Capitoline Hill. It dominated all of the structures nearby. The Theater of Pompey was, according to Dyson, a "manubial shrine, a place of entertainment, and a porticus, where programmatic sculptures and spoils of victory would be combined for the glorification of the *imperator*."[98] Even when viewed at a distance, it reminded residents and visitors to the city of the tangible munificence of Rome's great generals, as well as the vagaries of political and military fortune, and that the Campus Martius itself was a large stage for the presentation of these themes.

For centuries, Pompey's theater presented spectacles, not only on the stage but also in the *cavea*. To display his status as sole ruler in the manner of a

Hellenistic monarch, Julius Caesar wore a crown with rays to a performance there, and at a rededication of the theater, Emperor Claudius first made sacrifices to the gods at the temples above the *cavea* and then with great solemnity walked down the steps to his seat as the audience sat in silence.[99] Pompey's structure was often on the itinerary of foreign visitors to Rome such as Germanic tribal kings in 58 C.E.[100] To impress the visiting King of Armenia in 66 C.E., Nero had the interior of the theater gilded and raised over it a purple awning or *vela* that displayed golden stars and a portrait of the emperor riding a chariot.[101] During one extravagant third-century performance, the stage accidentally caught fire.[102] Whatever concerns republican aristocrats had with the potential of permanent theaters to lessen their control over social order, the emperors of Rome were able to take full advantage of Pompey's imposing theater as a stage from which to project the power of the principate. This, in turn, assured that the center of the Campus Martius remained for centuries an important venue for imperial political display.

It remains a matter of speculation why Pompey chose the Campus Martius as the location for Rome's first stone theater. A number of factors – geographic, religious, political, and perhaps technological – plausibly informed the choice. First, the theater may have been erected on property that Pompey owned, since Plutarch tells us that he built a small house for himself directly behind the theater, "like a small boat towed by a ship."[103] Second, because the complex, including the portico, was enormous, a large, open space such as the Campus Martius was necessary if it were to be built on flat ground instead of against a hill in the manner used by the Greeks.[104] Third, by the time Pompey built his theater, the structural materials and engineering techniques were available to raise a concrete and stone structure on flat, marshy soil without fear of collapse.[105] Fourth, to the extent that he did wish to emphasize the religious elements of the architecture, namely the Temple of Venus Victrix ("Giver of Victory") crowning the *cavea*, one effective way was to place it directly west and in the sight line of the existing temples in the Largo Argentina. Fifth, the Campus Martius was now a well-accepted venue for the display of success on the battlefield, and Pompey celebrated his conquests by decorating his structure with marble personifications of the fourteen nations he conquered as well as honoring the "Giver of Victory."[106] Sixth, by overlooking those temples built by earlier triumphators and being near the Villa Publica where assemblies occurred, Pompey's Venus Victrix and perhaps companion *aedes* created a visual assertion of the general's lofty status above the benefactors of the earlier republican temples. Finally, as the back of the *cavea* was on a tangent to a major thoroughfare that connected to the Circus Flaminius, easy access for spectators was available. For a powerful general desiring to construct a building of religious, political, and theatrical significance, the Campus Martius was prime real estate on all fronts.

Whatever the motivation for Pompey's site selection, the physical impact of his complex on the central Campus Martius has proved extraordinary. When viewed in context with the preexisting temples and porticoes stretching east from the Largo Argentina to the Villa Publica, Pompey's theater complex established a strong east-west axis that imperial builders would cross at a right angle, helping to imprint an orthogonal pattern on the central Campus Martius. Whereas prior construction in the area of the Circus Flaminius worked with the landscape by following the bend in the river, Pompey's theater defied the natural surroundings and conquered them.

The construction of Pompey's theater also generated a political reaction by the general's rival, Julius Caesar, who considered building his own structures in the Campus Martius. At an unknown location in the Field of Mars, Julius Caesar planned to build a temple of the war god "greater than any in existence," but it was never realized.[107] He also conceived an idea to replace the republican voting precinct located near Pompey's theater – the Saepta – with a new one to be framed in a mile of porticoes. It was not completed during his lifetime.[108] As a more direct physical challenge to Pompey's complex, Caesar proposed the construction of his own stone theater. Although early plans called for building against the Tarpeian Hill, Caesar ultimately selected the southern Campus Martius, clearing land to the southeast of the Circus Flaminius, "to build a theater as Pompey had done."[109] He did not live to see the theater rise from the ground, however, and the work was completed by his successor, Augustus, and named for the latter's late nephew and son-in-law, Marcus Claudius Marcellus (Figure 20).[110]

The Theater of Marcellus stood in approximately the same location as the temporary stage contracted by M. Aemilius Lepidus more than a century earlier for use with the *ludi Apollinares* by the Temple of Apollo.[111] There were clear challenges to erecting a theater in a location described by Sear as "the most hallowed theatrical setting in Rome."[112] The building site was tightly confined within an area framed by the Circus Flaminius, the temples of Apollo and Bellona, the Forum Holitorium, and the Tiber. Some space was gained when the Temple of Apollo Medicus was rebuilt with a shorter porch and its steps were placed on the side. Nonetheless, the temple still came within 6 meters of the theater's facade.[113] As if the space between the Temple of Apollo and the theater was not tight enough, a small, round temple approximately 4.5 meters in diameter stood midway between the two larger structures, centered with the front of the temple and the theater's central barrel vault (Plan 3, Inset B, and Figure 21).[114] The space between the theater and the Portico of Octavia was only 2.2 meters, and the edge of the stage building was but 12 meters from the river's edge.[115] Augustus may have contributed to the tight fit by buying up additional land from private owners in order to achieve an even larger footprint for the structure.[116]

20. Northeast side of the Theater of Marcellus with the Temple of Apollo Sosianus on the right. (Photo: Paul Jacobs)

Despite the physical constraints, the theater site afforded the soon-to-be emperor certain benefits. Although Augustus did not pretend his theater was simply an appendage to a temple, by being within a few meters of two pre-existing temples, those of Apollo and Bellona, the theater was provided with appropriate religious connections without concern that additional *aedes* should be built as part of the project.[117] It has been advanced, however, that two other

21. Fragment of a round temple found in the vicinity of the Temple of Apollo Sosianus (Perirrhanterion?). (Photo: Paul Jacobs with permission of Roma, Musei Capitolini, Centrale Montemartini)

temples believed destroyed by the theater's construction may have been incorporated into the exedra behind the theater.[118] Just as Pompey's quadriportico provided convenient shelter to an audience in the event of inclement weather and offered attendees a place to stroll before and after performances, the Portico of Octavia only a few feet behind the *cavea* of the Theater of Marcellus may have served a similar function.

Construction of the theater placed a monument of Augustus not just on the triumphal route, but also in it. There was no longer a practical way for a triumphal parade with chariots and wagons forming in the Circus Flaminius to move to the city gates without going right through the theater and past a large statue of Augustus erected after his death.[119] The theater overwhelmed the republican triumphal structures in the area. Such dominance of the visual field, combined with the calculated imperial reconstruction of existing buildings around the Circus Flaminius, sent out a clear signal that the good works of republican triumphators no longer held sway.[120]

Because the Theater of Marcellus was wedged between other buildings and the river, its diameter was by necessity smaller than that of Pompey's structure. Yet it held between 2,000 and 3,500 more people than the gargantuan edifice down the way.[121] To accommodate a higher capacity in a smaller diameter, the builders used a tall, steep *cavea* that faced southwest, a direction that likely was not very comfortable on a hot summer afternoon.[122] The exterior of the *cavea* was built of travertine and composed of three levels. On the first two levels, forty-one arched openings were flanked by engaged columns: Doric on the lowest level, Ionic above that (Figure 22). Although the third level decoration disappeared in the Middle Ages, it is believed to have displayed Corinthian columns separated by square windows.[123] Just inside the lowest level of the facade, a curved arcade 3.5 meters in width ran the length of the outer *cavea* and was punctuated with radial vaults through which the audience members could access their seats.[124] Delicate stuccowork in the barrel vaulting is still visible (Plate VIII). While the Marble Plan shows the Theater of Pompey had an elaborate stage with semicircular and rectangular niches, it indicates that the Theater of Marcellus had a very plain, rectangular *scaenae frons* with no similar indentations.[125] An ancient writer notes, however, that it was decorated with four large, marble columns that had once stood in the temporary theater of Aemilius Scaurus.[126] Behind the stage building on the riverside, a colonnade connected two large halls, each with a basilica design. Beyond the colonnade, the Marble Plan discloses a courtyard or terrace surrounding two small, square structures with what appear to be altars in front of them.[127]

The first known use of the Theater of Marcellus was for celebration of the Secular Games (*ludi saeculares*) in 17 B.C.E., at least four years before the theater's official dedication.[128] These were games that were to be held every 110 years, and by the late first century B.C.E., they had developed strong mythical

22. Detail, Theater of Marcellus. (Photo: Paul Jacobs)

connections to the Field of Mars. According to Roman mythology, the games trace their origins to a sacrifice performed in the Campus Martius to a god of the underworld, Dis Pater, and his consort, Proserpina.[129] One hundred sixty years had passed since the last Secular Games when Augustus reinstituted the *ludi*, employing as venues three theaters in the Field of Mars: the Theater of Marcellus for Greek stage plays, the Theater of Pompey for Greek-style games such as boxing and foot races, and a temporary wooden venue erected along the Tiber for what were described as "Latin" games, possibly Roman theater.[130]

Between the first events in the Theater of Marcellus and its official dedication in 13 or 11 B.C.E., a third stone theater was completed in the Campus Martius. In 13 B.C.E., the proconsul L. Cornelius Balbus, who celebrated a triumph in 19 B.C.E. after defeating a North African tribe, dedicated with great fanfare his theater situated just sixty meters southeast of the Largo Argentina.[131] The alignment of his theater was roughly parallel to the Saepta and the Augustan structures to the north, reinforcing the north-south axis of the orthogonal grid developing in the central Campus Martius. Just to the north of the temples on the north side of the Circus Flaminius (Hercules Musarum, Juno Regina, and Jupiter Stator), the theater was located between the Theater of Pompey and the Theater of Marcellus (Plan 3, No. 16). Balbus's structure was the smallest of the three, seating between 7,700 and 8,400 spectators (less than half the capacity of Augustus's building) and measuring only two-thirds the diameter of the Theater of Pompey.[132] It was, nevertheless, finely decorated and may have been inspired in its design and decorative elements by theaters nearby. In contrast to the four notable marble columns in the Theater of Marcellus, for instance, Balbus had, according to Pliny, four alabaster columns placed in his.[133] Similar to Pompey, Balbus built a rectangular annex behind the *scaenae frons*. Identified in the regionary catalogs as the Crypta Balbi, the portico, portions of which are still visible in a museum built on the site, may have included a covered passageway (Plan 3, No. 15).[134] While, unlike the Theater of Pompey, there is no temple clearly associated with Balbus's theater, the Marble Plan indicates a small building within the annex. It has been suggested that this may designate a temple, a notion reinforced by the later construction of a church on the site, consistent with the practice of placing early churches over Rome's pagan temples.[135]

Although Balbus managed to dedicate his theater while Augustus was in Gaul and prior to the official celebrations in the Theater of Marcellus, the opening ceremonies were less than auspicious, as the Tiber overflowed its banks and flooded the central Campus Martius, making Balbus's theater accessible only by boat.[136] The floodwaters receding from the theater's entrance might be seen as a metaphor for the end of an era for conspicuous display by republican generals in the Campus Martius. No longer would battlefield vows for victory by patrician men-in-arms routinely result in elaborate parades and dedications of significant monuments. In fact, Balbus's triumph was the last granted to a nonmember of the imperial household and his theater, the last large structure erected without imperial sanction. While this would impact construction and celebrations throughout Rome, it had particular meaning for the Campus Martius, which had seen its open field selected time and again by successful generals as an ideal space for the fulfillment of personal vows and promotion of personal glory. Now the ultimate approval of the types and locations of major structures to be placed in the Campus Martius rested with the emperor and was used to project imperial power and prerogatives, as we will see in Chapter 7.

After his return to Rome in 13 B.C.E., Augustus, showing that he could not be upstaged, hosted his own, extraordinarily elaborate dedication of the theater in honor of his nephew. The show included a performance by Roman patrician boys of a mock military exercise known as the Troy Games, both a clear evocation of Rome's foundation legends and a reminder of the former use of the Field of Mars for martial training.[137] Hearkening back to the elaborate dedicatory celebration of the nearby Theater of Pompey four decades earlier, Augustus employed the Circus Maximus, as Pompey had done, for a *venatio* with 600 animals from Africa. Two other decisions emphasized his authority: Augustus had Pompey's statue placed in the *scaenae frons* of the deceased general's theater, and he ordered that a golden image of his nephew should be placed in a curule chair in the *cavea* of the Theater of Marcellus for display next to the officials managing the annual *ludi Romani*.[138]

With three stone theaters in the Campus Martius, the Field of Mars was now clearly the center of the performing arts, and the public's enthusiasm for theatrical entertainment only increased. Temporary wooden structures continued to be erected for special events there, and other buildings in the northern plain originally erected for other purposes were occasionally employed for entertainment. The approximately 56 days devoted annually to theatrical performances in the late first century B.C.E. grew by the fourth century C.E. to 101.[139] There should be no thought, however, that on performance days the majority of Romans spent their time at the Campus Martius theaters. Collectively, the three stone theaters could accommodate between 30,000 and 45,000 spectators, or less than 5 percent of Rome's population of approximately one million during the empire. Even then it is not likely that shows were held concurrently.[140] Moreover, racing still attracted the biggest crowds, and the Circus Maximus could accommodate more than five times the capacity of the three theaters combined. Yet the impact of these theatrical venues on the Campus Martius was extraordinary. A space that had once been open for military exercises and then dotted with temples now had more than 100,000 square meters of concrete and stone for performances and related activities.[141] Topographically, the theaters added a clearly vertical dimension to the once-flat plain. Unlike Greek theaters built into hillsides, Rome's three stone theaters rose high above the surrounding structures and parks, creating a skyline for the city in the Field of Mars.

Had Strabo lived into the late first century C.E., he could have added a fourth theater to his list of places for performances in the Campus Martius. At approximately the same time that Domitian built his stadium (ca. 86 C.E.), to be considered shortly, he caused to be erected a music hall known as the Odeum (Plan 4, No. 20).[142] It possibly stood less than 100 meters north of the Theater of Pompey, identified like the latter structure by the curve of the buildings now standing on the foundations of its *cavea*.[143] Musical performances separate and apart from dramatic performances had not generally been part of Rome's games, but Domitian used his Odeum as a venue for singing and lyre playing and for Greek and Latin prose competitions as part of the Capitoline Games (Agon Capitolinus).[144] Holding about 7,000 spectators and partially roofed, the Odeum was smaller than most entertainment sites in the city.[145]

Still later, the emperor Hadrian would add a large hall for rhetoric and poetry readings. Known as the Athenaeum, its remains may have been uncovered in recent excavations in the southeast edge of the Campus Martius in the Piazza Venezia.[146]

The theaters of the Campus Martius and their appended porticoes remained important to the cultural life of Rome for centuries and were repaired as needed, sometimes after significant damage, and at great expense. The Theater of Marcellus was restored by Vespasian who, at its rededication, revived musical entertainment and awarded large sums of money to tragic actors and musicians.[147] Alexander Severus repaired the theater in the third century C.E. with the proceeds from taxes.[148] Despite occasional dismantling (some of the theater's blocks were taken to repair the nearby Pons Cestius as early as 370 C.E.), use of Augustus's structure continued until at least the fifth century C.E. Similarly, the Theater of Pompey was repaired several times: by Domitian after the fire of 80 C.E., at least three times in the third century C.E., and once in the fourth century C.E. The last known effort at repair occurred in the early sixth century C.E.[149] Balbus's theater was also repaired after the fire of 80 C.E. It remained in use in the fourth century C.E. and, perhaps, into the early fifth.[150] Domitian's small Odeum hosted musical events into the fifth century C.E., when Polemius Silvius described it as one of the wonders of Rome.[151]

"... AND AN AMPHITHEATRE"

Coinciding with Rome's military expansion, gladiatorial combat came to Rome, according to ancient sources, in 264 B.C.E. as part of private funeral games.[152] Though Valerius Maximus states that such games were first held in the Forum Boarium, about a 100 meters south of the edge of the Campus Martius, funeral games were more often held in the Roman Forum.[153] These games also could include *ludi scaenici*, new to Rome a century earlier. Unlike plays offered as part of public games, contests by gladiators remained private affairs until 42 B.C.E.[154] These staged fights were known as *munera*, gifts to honor an ancestor. Often paired with a *venatio*, they could be highly extravagant events.[155] To honor his deceased father, Julius Caesar held games with 320 pairs of gladiators wearing armor made of silver.[156] For his daughter's funeral, he had a wooden amphitheater built, possibly in the Campus Martius, and staged gladiatorial fights and wild beast hunts.[157] In 22 B.C.E., Augustus forbade the praetors newly charged with providing games from sponsoring gladiatorial fights without express senatorial approval, and even then such games could be held no more than twice a year, with no more than sixty pairs of combatants.[158] Private *munera* also required special permission.[159] Augustus sponsored few gladiator shows himself, with only eight being held during his four-decade reign. They must have been extraordinary, however, as he employed a total of 10,000 combatants.[160] By the fourth century C.E., gladiator fighting was only on 10 of the 177 days set aside for public games. The practice was finally stopped in the early fifth century C.E., at least a century before the Theater of Pompey staged its final theatrical productions.[161]

Unlike plays that employed a stage-building backdrop, gladiatorial shows could be viewed from all sides, and the displays in the Roman Forum were held in an arena created by wooden stands encircling the combatants and holding up to 15,000 spectators. Timbers were placed on columns to create balconies to enhance the view.[162] Known at first as *spectacula*, or places for spectators to congregate and watch a performance, these structures later were called *amphitheatra*, meaning "theater on both sides."[163] The forum was not the only site where temporary arenas were erected for gladiators. As noted earlier, two temporary wooden theaters that pivoted into one oval grandstand for a gladiatorial contest were constructed in 53 B.C.E. for funeral games, likely in the Campus Martius.[164] As with theaters, Rome lagged behind other cities on the Italian Peninsula with respect to erecting permanent amphitheaters. The first known stone amphitheater in Italy was in Pompeii and dates to around 70 B.C.E. Space for the structure was carved out of the Campanian soil with the excavated earth used to support the concrete and brick *cavea*.[165] Rome did not see its first permanent amphitheater until four decades later.

The arguments discussed previously for the slowness of stone theaters to make their appearance in the capital city likely applied to other permanent entertainment venues, including amphitheaters.[166] When a stone venue for gladiatorial events was finally built in 29 B.C.E., a location in the Field of Mars was chosen. The site selection was appropriate for several reasons. First, amphitheaters were often built as part of Roman military garrisons, and the Campus Martius provided strong ties to military musters.[167] Second, it was constructed from the *manubiae* of a successful general who could follow in a long tradition of using the Field of Mars to display aristocratic munificence. The general, Statilius Taurus, had commanded Octavian's land forces at the Battle of Actium, and as the first significant structure in Rome to be dedicated after Actium, the amphitheater fit within Augustus's program to encourage loyal aristocrats to erect great structures.[168] Third, erected a little more than two decades after Pompey's theater, Taurus's building, like the earlier theater, could take advantage of the open, flat ground of the Field of Mars to sink its foundations and support bleachers of stone and concrete.

The second of the permanent entertainment venues in the Campus Martius, the Amphitheater of Statilius Taurus, preceded the theaters of Marcellus and Balbus by more than a decade. Although Statilius Taurus was encouraged by Augustus to construct the facility and the emperor used the amphitheater for some of the twenty-six wild beast hunts he sponsored during his reign, it was not particularly favored by later emperors.[169] Caligula used Statilius Taurus's structure to stage gladiatorial fights, but he did not care much for it, preferring instead to employ the Saepta Julia for such shows.[170] In fact, Caligula planned to build an amphitheater next to the Saepta but never realized the project.[171] The emperor Nero, too, may have been less than enamored with the structure for hosting entertainment, as he went to the trouble of constructing nearby the extraordinary wooden amphitheater described by Calpurnius Siculus at the beginning of the chapter.

The Amphitheater of Statilius Taurus did not survive Nero's reign. Severely damaged in the fire of 64 C.E., along with many structures in the Campus Martius, it was not rebuilt, perhaps because the damage was simply too extensive. It has been proposed that despite its stone and concrete superstructure, the amphitheater had wooden seating that contributed to its destruction in the conflagration.[172] Its ruins have never been located, and much debate surrounds its location. One suggestion is that it stood just east of the Via Flaminia outside of the Campus Martius proper. Another places it near the river between the theaters of Pompey and Marcellus.[173] Ruins seen in the eighteenth century beneath a church in the area of Monte dei Cenci and thought at one time to have been the site of the Theater of Balbus are now offered as evidence of the amphitheater's presence.[174] As Strabo saw the amphitheater in the same general area as the "three theatres," this hypothesis has much merit. Whatever the reason, Statilius Taurus's amphitheater was not rebuilt, and wherever its precise location, the Romans were not going to go long without a permanent venue for gladiatorial games. The Campus Martius, however, was not to be the site for a new amphitheater. Fifteen years after the destruction of Statilius Taurus's building, another stone amphitheater was nearly completed where Nero had earlier constructed a large lake as part of his pleasure house, the Domus Aurea.[175] Dedicated under Titus in 80 C.E. and known for centuries as the Flavian Amphitheater, the structure was used for gladiatorial combat and other games until the sixth century C.E. Ultimately, it became known by its modern name, "the Colosseum."[176]

A STADIUM FOR GREEK GAMES

Greek-style athletic competitions were periodically held in Rome during the republic. Marcus Fulvius Nobilior, for instance, included a boxing match in his triumphal games celebrated in 186 B.C.E.[177] Both boxing and wrestling were popular during the republic, but other Greek games such as running, jumping, and discus throwing, less so.[178] Gymnastic competition was featured in the dedicatory games for Pompey's Theater, and a half-century later, Augustus proudly noted in his testament that three times he brought together athletes from all over the Roman world.[179] As with other forms of entertainment displayed in the Campus Martius, games with athletes were first held in structures built of wood. Julius Caesar built a temporary facility for three days of athletic competition in 46 B.C.E., and Augustus erected wooden seats in the

Campus Martius for similar events in 28 B.C.E.[180] Nero created games to be held every four years called the Neronia that included gymnastics along with musical competitions and equestrian contests. The gymnastic events were held in the Saepta Julia.[181] It was not until the reign of Domitian, however, that a permanent structure dedicated to athletic competition was built. Known as a "stadium," this new architectural type hailed from Greece and was seldom seen on the Italian Peninsula or further west.[182]

First used to celebrate the Agon Capitolinus in 86 C.E., the Stadium of Domitian held up to 30,000 spectators, making it one of the largest structures for Greek games built in the ancient world (Plan 4, No. 19). The seats were raised on two tiers of travertine and brick in a style similar to the Colosseum completed a few years earlier by Domitian's brother, Titus. Unlike the oval shape of the Roman amphitheater, Domitian's stadium, following the Greek style, had parallel bleachers running the length of the track connected by a curved seating area on one end and a smaller seating area perpendicular to the long sides on the other.[183] The stadium is depicted on the reverse of a gold coin minted in 206 C.E. to celebrate the sixtieth birthday of the emperor Septimius Severus (Plate IX). Shown from a bird's-eye view, the stadium on the coin is represented with two levels of arches with figures, likely statues, on the upper tier.[184] The palmettes depicted along the outer rim of the structure may indicate an awning that provided welcome shade to the sports fans in attendance.[185] Within the pictured stadium, athletic competition is in progress and has been interpreted as displaying Greek-style games with a runner, boxers, a victory ceremony, and a wrestler and, to the far right, the seated emperor.[186] Despite its general use for gymnastic contests and foot races, Domitian's stadium apparently became a primary location for gladiatorial shows after the Colosseum was severely damaged by a lightning strike and ensuing fire in 217 C.E.[187] Rebuilt in 228 C.E. by Emperor Alexander Severus, the stadium still astonished visitors to Rome more than a century later as one of the "adornments of the city."[188] Domitian had the stadium constructed just north of the Odeum and in line with the Theater of Pompey, further strengthening the north-south axis of the central Campus Martius. The outline of the structure is preserved in the shape of one of modern Rome's largest and most famous gathering spots, the Piazza Navona. Remnants of its arcade on the curved north end remain visible (Figure 23).

THE SAEPTA AND DIRIBITORIUM: FROM VOTING TO GAMES

Just as an entertainment venue such as the Stadium of Domitian might host events for which it was not originally built, permanent structures in the Field of Mars that were constructed for uses other than games were found to be appropriate sites for competition when no longer needed for their original

23. Archway on the north side of the Stadium of Domitian. (Photo: Paul Jacobs)

purposes. Such was the fate of the Saepta, the republican voting precinct the reconstruction of which was originally conceived by Julius Caesar but ultimately completed and dedicated by Agrippa in 26 B.C.E. as the Saepta Julia (Plan 3, No. 7). Possibly part of the Villa Publica, the earlier space accommodated up to 70,000 voters divided into thirty-five tribes. The tribes were separated by fences – in Latin, *saepta* – hence the name for the building.[189] It was also popularly known as the *ovile*, a sheep enclosure.[190] With the emperor appointing government officials who had previously been chosen by election, the need for a voting precinct declined, but the nine-acre space, with internal fences removed, proved ideal for entertainment. Rome's first emperor hosted funeral games in honor of Agrippa there in 12 B.C.E., with gladiators fighting in single combat as well as in teams.[191] Augustus used the Saepta again for displays of gladiatorial combat in connection with the dedication of his temple of Mars Ultor a decade later.[192] Emperor Caligula also used the space for gladiatorial shows during which he exhibited pairs of boxers from among the best in Africa and Campania to fight.[193] Claudius held gladiator fights there with wild beasts as part of the annual celebrations of his ascension as emperor.[194]

As with other entertainment venues in the Campus Martius, the Saepta Julia combined political theater with games. Describing the Greek-style athletic contests that Nero held in the Saepta Julia, Suetonius noted, "At the gymnastic contest, which [Nero] gave in the Saepta, he shaved his first beard to the accompaniment of a splendid sacrifice of bullocks, put it in a golden box adorned with pearls of great price, and dedicated it in the Capitol. He invited the Vestal Virgins also to witness the contests of the athletes, because at Olympia the priestesses of Ceres were allowed the same privilege."[195] The Saepta burned in the fire of 80 C.E. and was rebuilt, but we do not know the extent to which it was later used for athletic competition.[196]

Next to the Saepta stood the Diribitorium, a structure commenced by Agrippa and used to count the votes cast in the adjacent Saepta (Plan 3, No. 13). Rectangular in shape and approximately 5,000 square meters in area, it was, at the time, the largest space in Rome completely under the cover of a roof.[197] As with the Saepta Julia, the need of the Diribitorium for voting functions diminished with the end of the republic. Though too small for large spectacles, the Diribitorium offered a more intimate setting for small theatrical events. When Rome's weather was too hot to stage *ludi scaenici* in the theaters open to the sky, Caligula had benches built in the Diribitorium so that shows could be staged under the building's protective roof.[198] Unfortunately, the roof came crashing down in the fire of 80 C.E. and was never rebuilt.[199] The extent to which the structure, now exposed to the elements, was used for entertainment after that point is not recorded. Like the Stadium of Domitian standing about 300 meters to the west, the axes of the Saepta and Diribitorium ran north-south, parallel to the Stadium, once again enforcing the orthogonal grid imposed on the central Campus Martius (Plan 4).

WHERE THE RABBLE GATHERED

Within the beautiful structures of the Campus Martius that were created for entertainment as well as within those that were ultimately employed for that purpose teemed boisterous fans who energized the various venues, particularly during sports events. These passionate spectators were not only entertained with events on the stage and arena floor but often treated to free food and wine and significant door prizes that heightened the excitement.[200] Writing in the fifth century C.E., Cassiodorus queried, "Who expects seriousness of character at the spectacles? It is not exactly a congregation of Catos that comes together at the circus. The place excuses some excesses. And besides, it is the beaten party which vents its rage in insulting cries."[201] The fourth-century C.E. Roman historian Ammianus Marcellinus penned the following description of the crowds that shuttled from horse races to theatrical events:

> Let us now turn to the idle and slothful commons.... These spend all their life with wine and dice, in low haunts, pleasures, and the games.... You may see many groups of them gathered in the fora, the cross-roads, the streets, and their other meeting-places, engaged in quarrelsome arguments with one another, some (as usual) defending this, others that.... If from [the chariot races in the Circus Maximus] they

come to worthless theatrical pieces, any actor is hissed off the boards who has not won the favor of the low rabble with money. And if this noisy form of demonstration is lacking, they cry in imitation of the Tauric race that all strangers – on whose aid they have always depended and stood upright – ought to be driven from the city. All this in foul and absurd terms, very different from the expressions of their interests and desires made by your commons of old, of whose many witty and happy sayings tradition tells us. And it has now come to this, that in place of the lively sound of approval from men appointed to applaud, at every public show an actor of afterpieces, a beast-baiter, a charioteer, every kind of player, and the magistrates of higher and lower rank, nay even matrons, are constantly greeted with the shout "You should be these fellows' teachers!"; but what they ought to learn no one is able to explain.[202]

While imposed decorum relegated female spectators to the upper reaches of the bleachers, and occasionally they were banned from the stands altogether, until the beginning of the third century C.E. women could participate in athletic competition, including gladiatorial combat.[203] Cassius Dio records that these events created an extra level of rowdiness that resulted in such contests being banned in 200 C.E. in order to enhance crowd control.

There took place also during those days a gymnastic contest, at which so great a multitude of athletes assembled, under compulsion, that we wondered how the course could contain them all. And in this contest women took part, vying with one another most fiercely, with the result that jokes were made about other very distinguished women as well. Therefore it was henceforth forbidden for any woman, no matter what her origin, to fight in single combat.[204]

These descriptions indicate that with the development of theaters and sports venues, an area that began as a military training ground and sacred space to honor the gods was, by the imperial era, a distinctly secular area, teeming with the quotidian. Once a bucolic field suitable for contemplation of the good deeds of republican generals, the northern plain was now filled with structures attracting rowdy crowds with baser interests.

The Campus Martius also saw a not-unexpected seamier side, as the high-traffic areas around the places for entertainment supported prostitution. Brothels were located in the arcades of the Stadium of Domitian, and prostitutes frequented the areas around the theaters. One writer communicated a licentious (and likely contrived) story about the third-century C.E. emperor, Elagabalus. He "rounded up into a public hall all the prostitutes from the Circus, Theatre [of Pompey], the Stadium [of Domitian], the baths and everywhere else they frequented."[205] Though the accuracy of this report as regards the emperor's actions is up for debate, the writer, in wishing the scandal to be believed,

would have used realistic details so that the prevalence and location of prostitution found herein can be taken as a reliable sketch of the business in the
Campus Martius. In fact, the presence of brothels in the arcade of the Stadium
is corroborated by the tradition of St. Agnes's martyrdom. In 304 c.e., during
the reign of Diocletian, Saint Agnes, attempting to remain pure in her love
of Christ, died a martyr by burning in the Stadium of Domitian after being
raped in one of the brothels located among its arcades.[206]

CONCLUSION

Having served as Rome's military mustering ground, the Campus Martius
naturally attracted the temples and triumphs that reflected the glory won in
battle by republican generals. These buildings, in turn, made it appropriate that
dedicatory games and annual celebrations to the gods be held in this space.
The marshland's openness easily accommodated horse races tied to specific
events such as the October Horse with room to spare for a large practice track
and paddocks to support the more common races in the Circus Maximus.
When the city required large structures for entertainment, whether temporary
or permanent, the still-open field north of the city provided a perfect fit,
topographically and symbolically. The musters were mostly gone and the
clutter found elsewhere in Rome had not yet intruded. By incorporating
or being built in close proximity to republican temples, venues for theatrical
performances, still touted as gifts to the populace from triumphant generals,
in one sense continued a tradition of public munificence. Yet they also raised
the bar for display and generosity to such a degree that only those with full
command of the levers of state could create such structures. Towering above
the other structures in the former marshland, the three stone theaters and
amphitheater and the later Odeum and Stadium vied with the Capitoline
for attention. Use of porticoes as ancillary appendages to theaters not only
provided practical protection from the elements but also contributed to a
growing network of colonnades tying the amusement centers together as
discussed further in the next chapter. By offering performances throughout
the year, the edifices for entertainment, along with the bathhouses to be
discussed in Chapter 6, guaranteed a constant flow of people to and from the
Field of Mars and resultant commercial activity. With structures that attracted
large crowds, the Field of Mars was now more tightly integrated into the
growing Roman urban landscape.

The Campus Martius was not the only area of Rome where its citizens could
turn for amusement, of course. The Circus Maximus west of the Palatine was
built long before Pompey dedicated his theater, and the Colosseum rose south
of the Roman Forum more than a century after Statilius Taurus constructed
his amphitheater. But nowhere else in Rome was there such a concentration

of crowd-pleasing sites that used storytelling and spectacle as a substitute for citizen participation in the affairs of war. Where Roman men once lined up with their military units to march to battle or by tribe to cast their ballots, now, during the imperial era, people of all ages and classes and both men and women gathered to be entertained. Mars's field was transformed into a place to witness the simulacrum of battle rather than to prepare for the battle itself. Foundation legends rooted deeply in the field's marshy soil now reverberated over the same ground from stages anchored on foundations of concrete.

CHAPTER FIVE

"COLONNADES ABOUT IT IN VERY GREAT NUMBERS": THE PORTICOES OF THE CAMPUS MARTIUS

With the onset of winter in 169 B.C.E., Perseus, the King of Macedonia, was wary that the forces of Rome would attack his poorly defended kingdom. Earlier that year, envoys from Rome had traveled through the Peloponnese and Aetolia south of Macedonia, shoring up the support of allied cities. Now, Perseus expected the worst.[1] Knowing that the Illyrians along the modern Dalmatian coast to his west had been wavering in their support for Macedonia and could provide Rome with a pathway to his kingdom, Perseus decided to take the offensive. Waiting until the winter solstice when the snows protected him from invasion across the western passes from Thessaly, Perseus invaded Illyricum, capturing a Roman garrison.[2] With one success under his belt, Perseus continued to attack and overran eleven other Roman forts.[3] A powerful Roman response was now assured.

With war against the Macedonians clearly on their minds, the Romans chose their two consuls and six praetors for the upcoming year. Lucius Aemilius Paullus was elected consul and directed to lead the forces against Macedonia. Gnaeus Octavius was chosen as a praetor and tasked with conducting Rome's naval operations.[4] In April 168 B.C.E., shortly after the Latin Festival concluded, the fleet departed east.[5] Octavius's warships traveled up the east coast of Greece to Heracleum, Meliboea, and the island of Samothrace.[6] At these locations, Octavius would have seen extraordinary Hellenistic architecture, particularly at Samothrace with its remarkable sanctuary complex composed of altars, a circular theatrical area, banquet rooms, a monumental gate, and a colonnade.[7]

Approximately 104 meters long, the Samothrace colonnade was one of the largest in Greece. Two aisles were created by two rows of columns, one down the center of the enclosed space and the other along its eastern edge.[8] The western length and the ends were enclosed. The colonnade sat next to a fountain crowned by the famous Nike of Samothrace, now in the Louvre. Situated on a hill, the marbled colonnade would have afforded Octavius with a panoramic view across the entire complex.[9] It was at Samothrace that Octavius captured the King of Macedonia, placing Perseus in his flagship and sending him on to the consul Aemilius Paullus camped on the Macedonian mainland.[10] With the last of the Antigonid kings captured and the Third Macedonian War over, Octavius loaded his ships with plundered bronze shields, statues, paintings, and vessels made of gold, silver, bronze, and ivory and headed back to Rome.[11]

In a procession of ships, first the conquered and then the conquerors traveled up the Tiber to Rome. Prisoners now, Perseus and his family were followed by the triumphant consul Aemilius Paullus, sailing in a captured royal galley with sixteen banks of oars. A few days later Gnaeus Octavius landed with his fleet and the Macedonian treasure.[12] The victorious consul and praetors were each awarded a triumph. In contrast to the triumph of Aemilius Paullus with its procession of the defeated Macedonians and their millions of sesterces in treasure, Octavius's triumph was a relatively simple affair without prisoners or captured loot.[13] Although his celebration was modest, Octavius used his *manubiae* to create a stone memorial to his role in the defeat of the Macedonian king. As many generals before him had done, Octavius chose to erect his structure in the Campus Martius, and like Fulvius Nobilior and M. Aemilius Lepidus a decade earlier, he selected more specifically the Circus Flaminius, where the edifice would be passed by future triumphant processions. Indeed, during the intense debate in the Senate over whether or not to award a triumph to Aemilius Paullus, the senators recognized that if the parade were not granted, the royal prisoners and their treasure would sit in the Circus Flaminius and go no farther.[14] As a starting point for triumphal display, this was a prime location for a general's commemorative building. Departing from the precedents of the earlier consuls who regularly commissioned temples as part of their triumphal celebrations, Octavius erected a colonnade (Porticus Octavia) in the Circus Flaminius.[15] Although no ruins of Octavius's colonnade remain, it likely stood on the northeastern side next to the Temple of Neptune, an appropriate location to honor an admiral's victory (Plan 2, No. 13).[16]

Octavius's colonnade marked the first use of a colonnade in Rome as a war memorial, and it was designed to impress. It certainly caught the attention of Pliny the Elder, who noted that the structure's columns had capitals of Corinthian bronze and it was appropriately called the Corinthian portico. Velleius Paterculus records the portico as "the most splendid of all."[17]

Why Octavius chose to construct a colonnade is unrecorded, but it is tantalizing to conjecture that the enormous and well-sited one at Samothrace influenced his choice.[18] Pliny's description of Octavius's colonnade as a double portico (*porticum duplicem*), a phrase that might refer to the number of aisles, wings, or stories, supports the supposition.[19] The single-wing colonnade on Samothrace contained a double row of columns, although any number of Hellenistic colonnades the praetor observed during the campaign could have served as models. The Romans in the Third Macedonian War were allied with Eumenes II, King of Pergamon, who constructed in his capital a decade earlier an L-shaped colonnade with two stories and a double aisle.[20] Whatever the Roman structure's ultimate architectural inspiration, Octavius would have seen numerous examples throughout the Greek world that were built as monuments to the greater glory of their patrons.[21] The significance of Octavius's commemorative colonnade was not lost on his descendant Octavian, Rome's soon-to-be emperor Augustus. In 33 B.C.E., Octavian rebuilt the colonnade and placed within it the Roman standards recaptured from the Illyrians, the tribe that Perseus had attacked a century and a half earlier.[22] It was apparently Octavian's first gift to the Roman people not begun by Julius Caesar and was worthy of highlighting in the *Res Gestae*.[23] By the time of Augustus, however, extraordinary colonnades existed throughout Rome. Monumental colonnades had become, as John Senseney noted, "a building block of Republican and Imperial urbanism."[24] This new trend was most evident on the Field of Mars.

Although Gnaeus Octavius's colonnade was the first such structure erected as a victory monument, it was not actually the first building of this type in Rome, nor even the first in the Campus Martius. That distinction was held by one built by the consul under whom Octavius served. In 193 B.C.E., Aemilius Paullus along with M. Aemilius Lepidus in their roles as curule aediles oversaw the construction of a covered walkway that ran from a gate in the Servian Wall, the Porta Fontinalis, to the area of the Altar of Mars in the Campus Martius (*a Porta Fontinali ad Martis aram*).[25] Although no definitive traces of this colonnade have been identified in the Campus Martius, it appears to have been constructed as a ceremonial walkway for the ritual journey to the Altar of Mars by the censors whose headquarters, the Atrium Libertatis, were located in the vicinity of the Porta Fontinalis.[26] As the altar likely stood in the Villa Publica, the walkway probably crossed the brook that ran through the southern Campus Martius, the Petronia Amnis, and, thus at that point was a covered bridge.[27] Arriving at the altar through the colonnade, the censors would have conducted the *lustrum* at the conclusion of the census.[28] A costly undertaking financed from fines collected for illegal grazing, the walkway may have provided the name of the southern portion of the Campus Martius known as the Aemiliana.[29]

In the same year that they authorized the construction of the porticus from the Porta Fontinalis to the Altar of Mars, the two curule aediles caused a utilitarian structure to be built down on the eastern bank of the Tiber River southwest of the Aventine by the Porta Trigemina. Called the *porticus extra Portam Trigeminam*, it likely served the purpose of sheltering pedestrians and traders with no significance as a monument.[30] Several other utilitarian structures called porticoes were built in the same time period and were similar in purpose, including one built by M. Fulvius Nobilior in the vicinity of the Navalia on the bank of the Tiber in 179 B.C.E., the same year that he constructed the Temple of Hercules in the Circus Flaminius.[31] Octavius's colonnade constructed a decade later moved the architectural form in a new direction in terms of both funding and purpose. Later victorious republican generals and then emperors followed Octavius's example.

A colonnade of the type visible to a Roman during the Third Macedonian War was known in the Greek-speaking world as a *stoa*, a term that the Greeks used at first to describe a freestanding, single-wing, covered structure similar to the one at Samothrace, generally closed on one length by a solid wall, while open on the opposite side with one or more screens of columns.[32] By the second century B.C.E., however, the term was applied to a variety of colonnaded structures throughout the Hellenistic world such as the L-shaped *stoa* at Corinth and the multileveled colonnades at Pergamon.[33] Often located by religious sites, the *stoa* provided shelter from the elements and contained dedicatory inscriptions and sometimes statues in niches.[34] Use of a lengthy colonnade as a connector road similar to Rome's first one, built *a Porta Fontinali ad Martis aram*, has few obvious Greek antecedents, and the covered walkways that proliferated throughout the Roman Near East are later in date.[35]

By the time of Augustus, the freestanding, single-wing *stoa* had given way, even in Greek cities, to colonnades more fully integrated with other structures and spaces.[36] Employing the term *stoai* to describe the crowded collection of colonnades that littered the Campus Martius in the early decades of the first century C.E., the Greek-born geographer Strabo would have seen them employed as covered streets, attached to theaters, surrounding temples and parks on four sides (*quadriporticus*), and serving as art galleries and shopping spaces.[37] Roman writers such as Pliny and Livy used the term *porticus* to describe these beautiful colonnades as well as the plainer brick arcades that lined the Tiber. Some inscriptions, such as Augustus's testament that were written in both Greek and Latin, employed the terms *stoa* and *porticus*, respectively, to describe the same structure.[38] Here, the English term portico will be used interchangeably with colonnade to refer generally to the variety of gallery-like structures supported by columns along at least one side that proliferated throughout the Campus Martius from the second century B.C.E. onward.

The use of porticoes to memorialize the glorious deeds of their builders caught on in Rome. Two decades after Gnaeus Octavius constructed his colonnade, a second manubial portico was built at the southeast end of the Circus Flaminius. This one also honored a victory over the Macedonians. Constructed by Q. Caecilius Metellus Macedonicus following his annexation of Macedonia in 146 B.C.E., the Porticus Metelli served as a sacred precinct boundary, enclosing at least partially, and perhaps completely, the temples of Jupiter Stator and Juno Regina (Plan 2, Inset B).[39] Not simply the structure but also the contents served to celebrate Metellus's achievements in the Fourth Macedonian War. The portico provided an appropriately grand setting for what J. J. Pollitt described as "one of the most famous and [he suspects] influential monuments of Hellenistic art" – a captured collection of twenty-five equestrian statues commemorating Alexander the Great's fallen comrades at the Battle of Granicus (334 B.C.E.), designed by Alexander's court artist, Lysippos.[40] The statues were arranged facing the temples in the area between the Porticus Metelli and the two shrines. At some point after the portico's construction, perhaps in the early first century B.C.E., a seated bronze statue of Cornelia, mother of the Gracchi, was added to the space.[41] It was one of the earliest publicly displayed statues of a woman in Rome.[42]

A few decades after the dedication of the Porticus Metelli, the siting of commemorative porticoes began to move north in the Campus Martius. In 110 B.C.E., the consul M. Minucius Rufus constructed a portico in the vicinity of the Largo Argentina sanctuary to honor his victory over a Balkan tribe.[43] Later called the Porticus Minucia Vetus, this structure possibly was a *quadriporticus* completely enclosing about 5,000 square meters of the sacred area (Plan 3, Inset A).[44]

Until this point, porticoes had been used as military monuments and as defining elements of sacred spaces. One-half century later, a significant change occurred when the most famous portico in the Campus Martius, the Porticus Pompeii, was constructed west of the Porticus Minucia Vetus and just east of the Theater of Pompey (Plan 3, No. 25). Behind and attached to the theater's stage building, a rectangular walkway enclosing parkland more than 24,000 square meters in area was walled on its outer perimeter and supported by a colonnade on the inner sides.[45] As Pompey found inspiration for his theater during his travels in Greece, so, too, he likely saw porticoes used in conjunction with theatrical spaces.[46] The Augustan architect Vitruvius, who devoted an entire chapter to porticoes in book 5 of *De architectura libri decem*, associated Pompey's portico with colonnades in Athens, Smyrna, and Tralles that were related to theaters.[47] Although Vitruvius praises the utilitarian benefits of a portico built near or behind a theater "so that when sudden rains interrupt the performances, the audience has a place to gather outside the theater, and the performers have a place to rehearse," that purpose likely was of greater need for Greek theaters built into hillsides than for Pompey's freestanding theater with its protective stone superstructure.[48] Built in conjunction with his theater, Pompey's *quadriporticus* provided strollers a delightful respite from the Roman sun and, we are told, a quiet spot for amorous assignations.[49] Cut off from the noise of the urban bustle, visitors walking through the colonnade could view extraordinary examples of Greek paintings and sculpture lining the outer walls that were punctuated by rectangular and semicircular exedras.[50] Although Metellus's portico was known for a statue of the noble Roman woman Cornelia, Pompey's colonnade housed a rare grouping of statues of females who have been described as courtesans but may have been women poets.[51] Pliny listed numerous paintings by famous Greek artists Nikias, Pausias, and Antiphilus as having been displayed throughout the portico.[52] Looking out through the spaces between the columns, visitors would have gazed upon a park that mimicked a sacred grove with uniformly trimmed plane trees growing in rows down the center of the open area, the expanse punctuated with fountains and sculpture; gold and purple textiles from Pergamon fluttered in the breezes.[53]

Vitruvius reports that apart from being visually pleasing, a *quadriporticus* such as Pompey's had distinct health benefits:

> The central spaces between the porticoes and open to the sky should be adorned with gardens because open-air walkways are of great benefit to health: for the eyes, first of all, because the subtle and light air from green plants flows in as the body exercises and clears the vision, carrying off the dense moisture from the eyes and leaving the sight fine and the image sharp. Furthermore, as the body heats up by moving around the walkways, the air, sucking away moisture from the limbs, reduces fullness and diminishes them by dissipating whatever the body has absorbed beyond what it can bear.[54]

According to the Severan Marble Plan, another single-wing colonnade was connected to the northern side of Pompey's portico and possibly projected beyond the eastern edge.[55] Opening north to the street instead of enclosing a courtyard, it would have provided a very different experience from the quiet stroll through the *quadriporticus* behind the attaching wall. As shown on the Marble Plan, the north-facing portico had two aisles with the inner aisle's columns set closer together and semicircular niches along the inner wall. The line of the roof extended past the outer row of columns. The remaining letters of its name [OSTYLVM] identified on the Marble Plan suggest that this was the Hecatostylon, the common name for the 100-columned structure that was destroyed in a fire in 247 C.E. (Plan 3, No. 27, and Figure 24).[56] Attached to but separated from Pompey's portico by its south wall, the Hecatostylon may have communicated with Agrippa's baths just to the north as well as with a park

24. Hecatostylon, Severan Marble Plan fragment (Stanford #39ac). (Photo: with permission of Forma Urbis Romae Project, Stanford University and Roma, Antiquarium Comunale)

just west of the baths.[57] The original formal name may have been the Porticus Lentulorum, a structure built either at about the time of the construction of Pompey's *quadriporticus* or in the early imperial era when Augustus was still encouraging Rome's great families to contribute beautiful architecture to the city.[58] A portico built during Augustus's reign and containing statues of all nations (Porticus ad Nationes) stood in the area of the Theater of Pompey and possibly was the same structure as the Porticus Lentulorum and Hecatostylon.[59] Pliny indicates that a statue of Hercules stood at the entrance to the Porticus ad Nationes, suggesting it was, in fact, a *quadriporticus*.[60]

Four decades after Pompey dedicated his Theatrum Pompei, Cornelius Balbus built his theater complex just to the southeast. Emulating the great general, he added a *quadriporticus* behind the *scaenae frons*. Identified in the fourth-century C.E. regionary catalogs as the Crypta Balbi, the three-sided structure enclosed a courtyard of approximately 6,800 square meters (Plan 3, No. 15). The meaning of the term *crypta* is uncertain, although it is thought that originally the complex was similar to a structure in Pompeii identified as a *cryptoporticus* that had a covered gallery with a series of windows surrounding a colonnaded walkway.[61] There were niches in the external walls of the Crypta Balbi that were later filled with brick. Excavations have revealed an exedra on the east side of the complex, shown on the Severan Marble Plan with columns across the front (Figure 25). In a manner similar to the Porticus of Pompey, the

25. Theater of Balbus, Severan Marble Plan fragment (Stanford #30abc). (Photo: with permission of Forma Urbis Romae Project, Stanford University and Roma, Antiquarium Comunale)

exterior solid wall of the Crypta Balbi provided a more contemplative space than the colonnades that were open to the street. During the reign of Hadrian, the Crypta Balbi was rebuilt with a second story. The exedra on the east side of the portico was converted to a latrine.[62]

At the same time that the Theater of Balbus and the Crypta Balbi were under construction, the sister of Augustus, Octavia, completed the rebuilding of the Porticus Metelli, a project initiated by her son Marcellus before his death in 23 B.C.E.[63] The porticus was located just a few meters from the site of the theater later to be dedicated to Marcellus. While it is uncertain if the original Porticus Metelli was a *quadriporticus*, the Porticus Octaviae clearly had four sides serving as a sacred precinct boundary for the temples of Jupiter Stator and Juno Regina, as well as a shelter from the sun and rain. Following the same footprint as its republican predecessor, at least on the southern side, the Porticus Octaviae appears to have been much grander; its marble facade on the Circus Flaminius was marked by a monumental entrance staircase and gate (*propylaeum*) in the Corinthian order and arched openings in the walls that led to the interior, colonnaded walkways (Plan 3, Inset B).[64] Today, the *propylaeum* is seen as projecting both within and without the line of the portico with four columns on each side (Plate X), but the design on the third-century Marble Plan shows six columns and no interior projection (Figure 26).[65] Although the original Porticus Octaviae was constructed with a solid inner wall that hid the temples below the roofline from sight of those facing the structures from

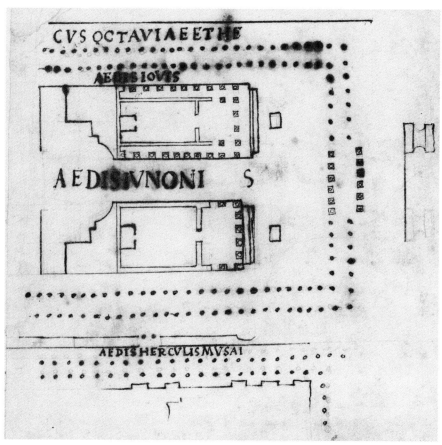

26. Detail, Vat. Lat. 3439 f.23r. Porticus Octaviae enclosing the temples of Jupiter Stator and Juno Regina after the Severan Marble Plan (sixteenth century). (Photo: with permission of Biblioteca Apostolica Vaticana, with all rights reserved)

the Circus Flaminius, by the time of the Marble Plan the wall had been replaced with a row of columns allowing a clear view of the two temples behind the porticus.[66] This would have created a significant alteration to the space, reincorporating the temples into the open and bustling Circus Flaminius. The entire *quadriporticus* appears to have been raised up on a podium, a design feature that often characterized sacred colonnaded precincts in both Greek and Roman architectural traditions.

The *quadriporticus* framed 16,000 square meters comprising a complex that Pliny called the *Octaviae opera*. It included, in addition to the two temples, a library of both Greek and Latin works (*bibliotheca Porticus Octaviae*), an assembly space (*curia*) where, on at least one occasion, the Senate met, and lecture halls (*scholae*).[67] Moreover, the complex was decorated with a wide array of celebrated paintings and sculptures, although it is uncertain if paintings were displayed in the portico itself, an issue that would have been resolved at the time the wall facing the Circus Flaminius was opened with columns.

A famous painting of the Trojan princess Hesione by the Greek painter Antiphilus was displayed, and in keeping with the Alexander theme initiated with the installation of the *Granicus Group* in the portico's earlier iteration, one of the lecture halls within the complex reportedly displayed a painting of Alexander the Great and his father Philip with the goddess Athena, also by Antiphilus.[68] Hercules, who was honored nearby in the Circus Flaminius with two temples, Hercules Musarum and Hercules Custos, was worshiped within the borders of Octavia's portico as well. Pliny notes that the *Octaviae opera* contained paintings by Androbius illustrating Hercules' apotheosis and the story of King Laomedon, whose daughter Hesione was rescued by Hercules from Poseidon's wrath.[69] A marble statue of Venus said to have been carved by Phidias and a Cupid by Praxiteles were located in the *Octaviae opera*, as well as statues of Aesclepius and Diana by Cephisodotus and Juno by Dionysius, all three of which appear to have stood inside the Temple of Juno Regina.[70] In 80 C.E., the year after Pliny perished in the pyroclastic catastrophe at Pompeii, the Porticus Octaviae burned in the fire that swept through the Campus Martius. While it is known that the structure was rebuilt, most likely by Domitian and then, after another fire, by Septimius Severus and Caracalla, the fate of its famous art and library collections is unknown. The visible remains of the *propylaeum* and columns are from the later reconstructions (Figure 27).[71] The Porticus Octaviae illustrates well the intertwined functions of porticoes in the Campus Martius at the end of the first century B.C.E. As well as serving as a resplendent memorial to deceased members of the imperial family, a *porticus* could be equipped with galleries and spaces for political meetings, intellectual discussion, and the display of famous art collections.

Likely following the same line as the Porticus Metelli on the northern side of the Circus Flaminius and constructed about six years before the Porticus Octaviae replaced Metellus's structure, another *quadriporticus* surrounded the Temple of Hercules Musarum, defining the northern length of the circus in the late first century B.C.E. Built at approximately the same time that the second-century B.C.E. temple was restored in 29 B.C.E., the portico as well as the temple reconstruction work was financed by Augustus's stepfather, L. Marcius Philippus (Plan 3, Inset B).[72] Described primarily as a picture gallery, and similar to the Porticus Octaviae next door, the *porticus* contained works by the painter Antiphilus, including a Father Liber, a young Alexander, and a Hippolytus terrified by a bull.[73] As shown on the Marble Plan, the Porticus Philippi had, at least by the second century C.E., a wide double portico, with the columns along the inner edge standing closer together than those of the outer row.[74] An outer wall enclosed the complex, obscuring the Hercules temple from the Circus Flaminius. If the Porticus Octavia (of Gnaeus Octavius) was in line with the Porticus Philippi and the Porticus Octaviae, then the three colonnades would have stretched for about 290 meters along one side of

27. Propylaeum of the Porticus Octaviae, south side. (Photo: Paul Jacobs)

the Circus Flaminius and presented a certain uniformity to grouped sacred precincts.[75] With a theater at its southern edge, two major porticoes filled with extraordinary Greek art along its eastern line, and backing on another theater and portico complex, the Circus Flaminius was, in the early imperial era, an important cultural node in the Campus Martius. These structures helped to define a space that had previously been unconfined and presented a kind of viewing platform along the edges of the space for witnessing the assembly of triumphal chariots and wagons.

Around the Theater of Marcellus to the southeast, colonnades continued along the base of the Capitoline Hill on the east side of the Forum Holitorium. On the west side of the vegetable market, the columned *pronaos* of each of the three temples of Janus, Spes, and Juno Sospita lined up such that they provided the suggestion of a continuous portico, giving a visitor the sense of a colonnade on both sides (Plan 2, Inset D).[76] Unifying space through continuous colonnades, and particularly with uniform proportions, was a technique that Vitruvius encouraged. His ideal portico consisted of a colonnade with the width of the two interior aisles equal to the height of the outside columns.

As the portico roof sloped, the interior columns were to be higher by one-fifth than the exterior columns.[77] The variety of colonnades found in Rome indicates that the ideal principles of Vitruvius were not always followed and, as with the temples in the Forum Holitorium, the sense of a colonnade could be conveyed by simply lining up columned porches.

The boom in portico construction in the late first century B.C.E. extended north of the Circus Flaminius to the central Campus Martius. Soon after Pompey dedicated his theater, Julius Caesar proposed turning the nearby and centuries-old voting precinct, the Saepta, into a marbled space for casting ballots surrounded by a mile of porticoes.[78] A perimeter of that length would have enclosed a space six times the space within Pompey's portico and one-tenth of the entire Campus Martius. Ultimately, however, the Saepta Julia was completed by Agrippa with a perimeter half the length of that proposed by Caesar and enclosing just half again as much space as Pompey's portico.[79] The precinct had porticoes running down the east and west sides, but not on the north or south ends. Although Cassius Dio records that the Saepta was surrounded by porticoes, other evidence indicates that the southern end was adjoined to the Diribitorium by a broad corridor without columns and the northern end had a lobby separated from the voting hall by a connecting wall with eight doorways through which voters could enter.[80] The Porticus Argonautarum followed the western line, and the Porticus Meleagri stood along the eastern line. Separated by the 120-meter width of the Saepta, the two porticoes would have been at their longest 310 meters, the length of the voting precinct (Plan 3, Nos. 8 and 9).[81]

Completed by Marcus Agrippa in approximately 25 B.C.E., the Porticus Argonautarum was named after a painting depicting the story of Jason and the Argonauts displayed somewhere inside or in the vicinity of the walkway.[82] Later references in Martial's *Epigrams* suggest the portico was immediately rebuilt after the devastating conflagration in 80 C.E. and remained very popular for strolls and informal meetings, as well as a shopping area for luxury goods.[83] It is possible that the Porticus Argonautarum served similar functions in Agrippa's day; despite being an independent structure, there is no doubt it was also used on occasion as a place for shelter and gathering during the political and entertainment activities that are recorded to have taken place in the Saepta Julia. Although its dimensions and overall design remain uncertain, a surviving portion of its western wall next to the later built Hadrianic Pantheon indicates that it was constructed of brick-faced concrete and covered in marble with regularly placed rectangular niches that possibly held statues (Figure 28).[84] Its close proximity to the east side of the Pantheon's drum suggests that pedestrian traffic between the Saepta and Hadrian's structure funneled through the colonnade.

Though the Porticus Meleagri is identified through three fragments of the Marble Plan and mentioned in the late antique regionary catalogs, the date of

28. Portion of the western wall, Porticus Argonautarum. (Photo: Paul Jacobs)

its construction is not secure. However, given the numerous illustrious building projects nearby – the Saepta Julia (dedicated in 26 B.C.E.), Porticus Argonautarum (ca. 25 B.C.E.), the Diribitorium (dedicated in 7 B.C.E.), the Pantheon (ca. 27 B.C.E.), and Baths of Agrippa (ca. 25 B.C.E.) – the Porticus Meleagri was likely constructed during the final decades of the first century B.C.E. as part of imperial efforts to monumentalize the area and specifically to serve a the eastern border for the Saepta Julia. Like the Porticus Argonautarum, the Porticus Meleagri probably derived its name from publicly displayed artwork, in this case paintings or sculptures illustrating the myth of another of the Argonauts, Meleager.[85]

During the late republican and early imperial era, the Field of Mars was not singular as a site for the construction of spectacular porticoes. Perhaps the most important use of *quadriporticus* architecture in the city was to define the perimeters of the imperial fora located within the *pomerium* to the southeast of the Campus Martius. Enclosing temples, lawcourts, and public administrative space, the porticoes of the Forum Iulium and Forum Augustum, and still later the Forum Traiani and Forum Transitorium, helped to create a unified urban complex in marble.[86] Together, the Forum Iulium and Forum Augustum enclosed more than 22,000 square meters within their colonnades, which, while impressive, is still but three-fifths of the area enclosed by the Saepta Julia alone.[87] Indeed, when all of the major *quadriporticus* constructions with known dimensions and extant at the time of Augustus are considered, those in the Campus Martius enclosed as much as three-fourths of the colonnaded space or more than 100,000 square meters.[88] These figures do not include the single-wing porticoes such as the Hecatostylon that, when added, helps explain why Strabo singled out the Field of Mars for its numerous colonnades.

The emperors after Augustus continued to populate the Campus Martius with porticoes. Sometime in the mid- to late first century C.E., a second Porticus Minucia was constructed. Known from the regionary catalogs as the Porticus Minucia Frumentaria, this portico is likely the *quadriporticus* indicated on the Marble Plan just east of the Largo Argentina and possibly was an extension of the earlier Porticus Minucia Vetus (Plan 4, No. 10).[89] Surrounding an earlier built temple, perhaps the Temple of the Nymphs, the portico possibly served a mostly utilitarian function as a grain distribution point. Those entitled to collect a monthly wheat dole came to one of forty-five stations either within the *porticus* or perhaps in the arcade on the west side to wait their turn.[90] In a manner similar to the entertainment sites described in Chapter 4 and the baths to be discussed in Chapter 6, the portico helped assure that the imperial Campus Martius would attract a constant flow of visitors to the once open field. While not likely ever used as a place of refuge, a large, centrally located *porticus* where provisions could be stored would have met the practical safety aspects of an enclosed colonnade as articulated by Vitruvius, who noted that they provided protection in time of war and that during emergencies they could be used for the allocation of rations.

> During such emergencies, the walkways are opened up and rations are allocated to individuals according to their tribes. Thus open-air walkways offer two excellent advantages: a place of health in peacetime, and, secondly, a place of safety in time of war. For these reasons the layout of walkways, put in not only behind the scene building of the theater, but also in the precincts of all the gods, can offer great benefits to cities.[91]

Possibly at the same time as the construction of the Porticus Minucia Frumentaria, the emperor Domitian constructed a less utilitarian colonnade just east of the Saepta Julia in what was left of the now shrunken Villa Publica (Plan 4, No. 9). Known as the Divorum, the portico as shown on the Marble Plan measured 15,000 square meters and was entered through a triple arch on the north and a less definable columned entrance on the south. The colonnade enclosed two small facing temples on the northern edge as well and, similar to the portico of Pompey, may have had rows of large trees along the eastern and western sides.[92] Adjacent to the Saepta Julia on the north, the emperor Hadrian enclosed a temple to the memory of his mother-in-law, Matidia, within a portico (Plan 4, No. 13). As represented on a second-century C.E. medallion, the portico had a high colonnade on the first story and a second story that may have been vaulted. It was likely a *quadriporticus* with walls along the outer perimeter, enclosing the sacred precinct within a space approximately 6,500 square meters.[93] Close by, Hadrian's successor, Antoninus Pius erected a temple to his deified (adoptive) father and likely enclosed it within a large colonnade more than twice as large as the space dedicated to Matidia (Plan 4, No. 4).[94] Excavations have uncovered fluted columns of *giallo antico* marble with Corinthian capitals.[95]

As late as the fourth century C.E., porticoes were still being built in the Campus Martius. A large portico just west of the Baths of Agrippa, and possibly in the vicinity of a temple of Bonus Eventus, may have been constructed in this period. Large Corinthian capitals possibly from the portico were found in the nineteenth century.[96] From a fourth-century C.E. inscription, we also learn of a Porticus Maximae that may have followed a street from the Circus Flaminius to the Pons Aelius, now the Ponte Sant'Angelo, a distance of more than 1,000 meters. Columns of granite with marble capitals have been located along its route and may belong to this colonnade of the late empire.[97] According to Lanciani, it was possible at this point in time to walk from the imperial fora through the Campus Martius to the Vatican, a distance of more than 3,000 meters, under the cover of colonnades.[98]

The reasons that the Campus Martius received so many porticoes and Romans enclosed so much area within thousands of meters of column-lined walkways cannot be known with certitude. Nevertheless, we may look to both the topography and the prior and contemporaneous development of the space for answers. The flat and largely undeveloped space within the Field of Mars provided a base on which colonnades could rise without the cost and political issues associated with tearing down existing structures. A *quadriporticus* required a large expanse of level ground such as found in the Campus Martius. The colonnades could serve as the defining perimeters of sacred spaces and, with the proliferation of manubial temples in the Campus Martius during and in the wake of the Punic Wars, would add those important lines to religious precincts already constructed or under construction in the field north of the city. Perhaps as importantly, they allowed successful generals laden with the bounty of foreign conquest to apply their *manubiae* to another form of architecture that not only faced the triumphal parade route but also served as the repository for the exhibition of captured treasures. The emperors continued this tradition and added to and embellished existing republican colonnades, while also constructing new ones even more resplendent.

As theaters, baths, and pleasure parks attracted an increasing number of visitors to the former marshland, the colonnades served as a marketplace for hawkers of both quotidian and luxury goods that ranged from wigs to inlaid furniture, goblets, and jewelry.[99] When theatergoers were caught in rainstorms during the open-air performances, porticoes provided fast shelter. To those wandering among the marbled edifices of the imperial Field of Mars, the colonnades could serve as geographic markers and meeting points. Writing in the late first century C.E., the poet Martial humorously described the desperation of one Selius wandering through the Campus Martius in search of someone to take him to dinner so he does not have to eat at home. He begins at the Porticus Europae, which may be the Porticus Vipsania located on the eastern edge of the Field of Mars.[100] The hungry Selius next runs to the Saepta Julia and then to the Porticus Argonautarum, but has no success. He doubles back to the nearby Temple of Isis and then heads a few blocks south to the Hecatostylon. Still unable to find anyone willing to take him to a meal, Selius searches among the double row of trees in Pompey's portico. Failing in that effort, he meanders back to the Porticus Vipsania to again try his luck there.[101] Martial's readers would have understood his reference to the "roof supported by a hundred columns" as the Hecatostylon and recognized "the gift of Pompey and the double wood" as the tree-lined portico behind his great theater.[102] These were well-known meeting places and part of the imperial urban fabric.

To get from one colonnade to the next, however, Selius would have been forced to travel by foot. Moreover, he could not have easily found a direct route. By the end of the first century C.E., what had been mostly open space in the central Campus Martius was subdivided into numerous rectangles and semicircles pushed hard up against each other with little maneuverable room for street traffic. The subdivisions were created in large part by the porticoes themselves that enclosed or were attached to the temples, theaters, and parks. Relatively wide streets such as the Via Flaminia bordered the space and forced pedestrians to enter the porticoes and travel their length or cut across the rectangular enclosures to speed their journey. The alternative was an even more circuitous route through narrow streets that wound around the massive marbled structures.

In this configuration, the porticoes, and in particular the quadriporticoes, in the Field of Mars about which we have literary and archaeological evidence performed more often as "way stations" than connective armature (to use MacDonald's terminology), serving as "social structures, made for pausing or resting, an architecture of invitation, of the opportunity to quit, for the moment, the activity of the pavement."[103] There were likely porticoes in the

Campus Martius that did function as part of the city's armature, although the architectural evidence is sketchy.[104] Perhaps the best example would be the fourth-century C.E. Porticus Maximae that may have connected the Circus Flaminius with the Pons Aelius to the north. While the Theater of Marcellus acted as a significant bottleneck for traffic at the southern end of the campus, the route of the Porticus Maximae linked a major market and parade assembly ground with a bridge across the Tiber. The *porticus a Porta Fontinali ad Martis aram* that led from the city gate to the Altar of Mars might be considered another channel for foot traffic although, at least originally, it served as only a ceremonial connector to an isolated religious site. For the most part, however, the porticoes and specifically the quadriporticoes in the central Campus Martius between the Via Flaminia and roads on the western side near the Tiber did serve as resting points for those attempting to negotiate the now crowded and built-up space. Diverted perhaps from their intended destination, visitors to Pompey's portico and similar spaces in the Campus Martius discovered "an ordered world against which the chaotic untidiness of life might be measured."[105]

CHAPTER SIX

BETWEEN THE AQUA VIRGO AND THE TIBER: WATER AND THE FIELD OF MARS

To Vergil, it was the majestic "Father Tiber"; to Statius, the "prince of rivers"; to Dionysius Periegetes, the "most kingly of rivers"; and to Martial, the "sacred Tiber."[1] Encapsulating these ancient assessments, a recent study describes the Tiber as the "center of traditional stories of the foundation of Rome in which it appeared as a benevolent collaborator."[2] The great river carried the basket bearing the twins Romulus and Remus as well as the sacred grain of Tarquinius Superbus that formed the Tiber Island.[3] For Romans it was both source and receptacle of divine power. In Vergil's *Aeneid*, the river's associated god Tiberinus appeared to Aeneas and prophesized the future site of Rome along the river's banks.[4] Sacred springs such as the Cati fons drained into the Tiber (by way of the Petronia Amnis and other rivulets), and Ovid wrote that nymphs and naiads haunted the river's shoreline.[5]

Occasionally, the Tiber overflowed its banks, and while Plutarch wrote that citizens regarded one of its highest floods, which occurred during the brief reign of Otho, as a "baleful sign," this was not always so.[6] Interpreting the Tiber's floodwaters in 27 B.C.E. as a positive omen, soothsayers prophesized that Augustus would "hold the whole city under his sway."[7] For much of the year, however, the river remained safely contained within its banks. Pliny the Elder described the Tiber as the "tranquillest purveyor of the produce of the whole globe."[8] Livy wrote that it carried on its placid surface the "fruit of inland places" and the "seaborne produce from abroad," and as Juvenal recorded, the river brought the languages and customs of distant countries to the capital.[9]

In places the current flowed calmly enough to allow swimming. Cato the Elder taught his son to swim in the Tiber, and soldiers would take a dip following military exercises.[10] Generally praised in the ancient sources, the Tiber nevertheless had its more dangerous side. The Tiber's heavy winter flows not only led to the often destructive flooding of low-lying areas of the city but also likely contributed to the presence in the late summer and fall of "tertian fever," a malady known today as malaria. The river further served as the depository for the refuse of sewers, baths, and distant streams connected to the city by aqueducts.[11] As Nicholas Purcell has aptly summarized, the Tiber was to Romans "their blessing and their curse, ambiguous from mouth to source."[12] Nowhere in the city was this truer than in the Campus Martius, whose long, winding western border was etched by the Tiber's flow.

WATER FROM THE WEST

From the embankment by the Mausoleum of Augustus to the Pons Fabricius behind the remains of the Theater of Marcellus, the river wends its way south then west and then south again for 2.9 kilometers, 1.5 kilometers longer than the path between parallel points along the very straight Corso, the modern Via Flaminia. The Tiber, therefore, constituted a lengthier border to the Field of Mars than the eastern boundary. This extended border was occasionally a dangerous one. Runoff from more than 15,000 square kilometers of Italian hills drains into the Tiber, and during the winter and spring rains, its waters swell. Before the construction of the late nineteenth-century floodwall, the Tiber would occasionally overflow its banks when it reached the city. Ancient Rome was located precisely where the river's floods reached their maximum level.[13] When the torrent coursed through the channel toward the plain north of Rome, the Campus Martius was among the first areas to suffer the effects of relentlessly rising water.[14] As a low-lying marsh, the Field of Mars was only about three to five meters above the Tiber's normal level.[15] Accordingly, a "minor" flood surrounded all of the central Campus Martius monuments, including the Theater of Pompey, the Theater of Balbus, the Saepta Julia, the Pantheon, and the Largo Argentina temples, while a "major" inundation reached all the way to the Via Flaminia, covering all of the Campus Martius.[16]

How often the Tiber overflowed its banks is a matter of debate, because ancient records are, at best, anecdotal and spotty. Only fifteen floods are recorded in Rome in the four centuries preceding the reign of Augustus, although six more are noted just in the four-decade rule of Rome's first emperor.[17] On the basis of modern data and the best-documented ancient sources, however, Gregory Aldrete argues that flooding in Rome occurred to a height of thirteen meters above sea level about every four years and to a height of at least fifteen meters above sea level approximately every nineteen years.[18] Put another way, Romans could count on much of the Campus Martius submerged under three meters of water twice a decade. According to Livy, there were two great floods in the year 215 B.C.E.; in 189 B.C.E. alone, the Tiber flooded the Campus Martius twelve times.[19] The duration of the inundations obviously varied. Cassius Dio reports that the floods of 27 and 23 B.C.E. each made the city navigable by boat for three days, while the flood of 5 C.E. allowed boat passage for an entire week.[20]

The ancient descriptions of Tiber overflows paint a scene of devastation in the low-lying areas of the city. In the flood of 241 B.C.E., several unidentified buildings were knocked down by the torrential force of the floodwaters or collapsed because of waterlogged, destabilized foundations.[21] A flood in 69 B.C.E. caused disruption of the grain supply and subsequent starvation, and the force of the floodwater itself could be lethal: "Many were swept away in the public streets, a larger number cut off in shops and in their beds."[22] Pliny the Younger described vividly the loss of property from floods: "Those who live in highlands out of the reach of these terrible storms have witnessed, here, the household paraphernalia and weighty furniture of the wealthy, there, the simple tools of the farm, over there, oxen, plows, and the plowmen themselves, here, herds set free and straying, jumbled among the trunks of trees, or the beams and roofs from villas, and all of it floating about randomly and widely."[23]

The problem of flooding in Rome was not unique to the northern plain. Streams ran through the valleys that separated the hills of the city, eventually draining into the Tiber. The Petronia Amnis discussed in Chapter 1 flowed from a spring on the western side of the Quirinal Hill and then cut a course through the widening northern plain before reaching the river north of Tiber Island (Plan 1).[24] Springs and streams also burbled through the lower ground of the Roman Forum as well as through the valley between the Palatine and the Aventine where the Circus Maximus was constructed. The lowlands were composed of impermeable clays that held water near the surface, leading to swamplike conditions.[25] Livy notes that Rome's early settlers found only "forests and marshes."[26] The Circus Maximus area would flood when the Tiber was about five to seven meters above normal, and the fora would suffer inundation when the river was ten to twelve meters above normal.[27] Floodwaters in 12 C.E. were high enough to disrupt games in the Circus Maximus, which were temporarily transferred to the still-dry area of the Forum of Augustus immediately north of the Roman Forum.[28] Indeed, all of the city's flatland between the hills was continually in peril of flooding from a major rise of water cresting the Tiber's banks. In 241 B.C.E., nearly all the low-lying areas of the city were submerged, and again in 189 B.C.E., including the plain of the Campus Martius.[29] In 27 B.C.E., the Tiber "overflowed and covered all of Rome that was on low ground, so that it was navigable for boats," and in 15 C.E. floodwater "flooded the lower levels of the city."[30]

The few anecdotal reports of floods from ancient writers that can be tied to precise dates do not provide a clear pattern of flood stage seasonality. Ovid notes that the infants Romulus and Remus came to rest downstream during the winter floods, and the Equirria held in March occasionally relocated to the Caelian Hill because of flooding in the Campus Martius.[31] A flood in 13 B.C.E. occurred on July 4 at the time when Augustus returned to Rome from his western campaigns.[32] The flood of 12 C.E. that forced the move of games from the Circus Maximus to the Forum of Augustus occurred around May 12.[33] More accurate records of water levels and flooding during the past several centuries support the view that most floods of the Tiber in ancient times occurred from the late winter to the early spring.[34]

To add to the misery of a swampy, occasionally flooded environment were the pests that lived in such places, especially mosquitoes, and the disease they carried – malaria. Romans were all too familiar with the problems of mosquitoes in marshy environments. Columella, a first-century C.E. writer on agriculture, advised that buildings should not be too close to a marsh "because it throws up an evil odor during the summer heat and produces insects armed with dangerous stings, which swoop upon us in dense swarms."[35] Romans did not completely understand the connection between mosquitoes and malaria, but they did know that swamps contributed to deadly spikes in body temperatures.[36] Writing in the first century B.C.E., Varro noted that "care must also be taken in marshy areas ... because certain small animals breed there. These animals cannot be seen with the naked eye and enter the body through the mouth and nostrils in the air and cause severe disease."[37] Nineteenth-century epidemiological studies in Rome provide some indication that floods contributed to populations of malarial mosquitoes that peak in mid- to late summer, making August the month of greatest risk for contracting the disease.[38] The poet Juvenal suggested that malaria took its greatest toll in the fall.[39]

Despite the inundations that washed over the Campus Martius in the late fall to early spring months and the disease-bearing mosquitoes that infested the plain in the late summer, the Romans persevered, turning the Field of Mars into a monumental complex of temples, colonnades, theaters, baths, and stadiums. Why did they remain so steadfast? One answer is the Roman attitude toward natural events combined with the practical needs of an expanding city and improving engineering and construction skills.[40] Romans viewed the Campus Martius as both sacred and economically valuable real estate; disease and flooding could be mitigated or, in the very least, accommodated by all manner of construction projects. The historical, religious, and practical importance of the northern plain ensured that the Field of Mars would not be left undeveloped. Moreover, the slow, incremental development of the Campus Martius over several centuries allowed for necessary modifications to infrastructure by greater use of stone and water-resistant mortar that could withstand the challenges of an alluvial environment. Certainly, in the worst situations, the plain could be temporarily abandoned because the low-lying region was within a fast walk of hilltop retreats from which the devastation below could be witnessed.[41] People whose lives were lost in floods were, according to Cassius Dio, those "who did not take refuge in time on the highest points."[42] The hills of Rome also provided some protection from mosquitoes in the summer.[43] According to Cicero, "The site that Romulus chose . . . was a healthful spot in a plague-ridden region: the hills not only receive a breeze, but they bring shade to the valleys."[44]

When the Campus Martius was simply a military mustering ground and voting precinct, the conditions presented by the wetland soil and seasonal flooding were relatively easy to avoid. Armies vacated the area in the spring following the worst months for floods and ahead of the arrival of mosquitoes. They returned in the fall in advance of the winter rains that swelled the Tiber and after the summer swarms of insects diminished. Moreover, in addition to the attractiveness of the open space of the Field of Mars for military maneuvers, the Tiber provided the area particular benefits. Vegetius, a fourth-century C.E. writer on military science, while discussing the importance of soldiers learning to swim, noted, "The ancient Romans . . . chose the Field of Mars as the most commodious for their exercises on account of its vicinity to the Tiber, that the youth might therein wash off the sweat and dust, and refresh themselves after their fatigues by swimming. The cavalry also as well as the infantry, and even the horses and the servants of the army should be accustomed to this exercise, as they are all equally liable to the same accidents."[45]

Horse racing and religious celebrations that were hosted in the Campus Martius in the spring and fall also fell outside the most dangerous months, although, as noted previously, the Equirria was accommodated elsewhere when the racetrack was flooded. The situation changed, however, when permanent structures began to rise in the Field of Mars. Drainage now needed to be considered. The Romans had extensive experience with removing water. Since the time of Rome's last king, Tarquinius Superbus, Rome's largest drainage conduit, the Cloaca Maxima, channeled water to the Tiber from the valley between the Quirinal and the Esquiline, an area that included the Roman Forum.[46] As its qualifier *maxima* implies, the sewer line was huge: large enough to fit a hay wagon. When later improved by Agrippa, the cloaca was navigable by boat.[47]

Similar networks of pipes and ditches would have been necessary to remove standing water from the Campus Martius. Evidence indicates that there were, in fact, significant sluice lines through the Field of Mars, although nothing as massive as the Cloaca Maxima. Certainly some surface water and runoff was captured by the Petronia Amnis, which later joined with another channel as part of the reworking of Rome's sewer system by Agrippa.[48] Ancient lines have been discovered in the area of the Pantheon and the Baths of Agrippa, as well as in the southern Campus Martius, indicating that the Romans made significant efforts to remove the surface water that accumulated in the Field of Mars.[49] Given the fact that Agrippa's Pantheon was built in the lowest part of the Campus Martius, some drainage must have been installed in its vicinity by the time of its construction in 27 B.C.E.[50] Vitruvius recognized that quadriporticoes were often built in low-lying regions and provided directions for draining the space inside of the colonnades.[51]

Beginning in the early imperial era, surface water may have also collected in the Stagnum Agrippae, a large artificial lake fed primarily from the Aqua Virgo's waters that passed through the Baths of Agrippa built just to the east.[52] The Stagnum itself drained to an artificial canal that ran for about 800 meters before emptying into the Tiber somewhere between the modern Ponte Vittorio Emanuele and Ponte Sant'Angelo (Plan 3, No. 29).[53] Called today the Euripus Thermarum Agrippae, the concrete channel was less than 2 meters deep and possibly followed the route of a stream that drained the marshy Caprae Palus. A section of the channel is still visible beneath the Palazzo della Cancelleria.[54]

Although the drainage system did not prevent flooding, it did at least allow construction on marshy soil. Cattails and other marsh grasses gave way to large stone buildings, colonnades, and paving blocks. Ironically, covering the marshes with an impervious stone surface aggravated the effects of floodwater rising in narrow streets.[55] During flooding, the drainage to the Tiber would back up, speeding the rise of water in the Campus Martius.[56] Pliny the Younger noted with respect to a flood during the reign of Trajan, "Although drained by a spillway made by the foresight of the emperor, the river covers the valleys, swims into the fields and entirely covers over the flat ground."[57]

Although the Romans had the technology to contain the Tiber's floodwaters through use of a floodwall, there is no evidence that they attempted to do so.[58] That effort would not begin in earnest for 1,900 years. One early plan to redirect the Tiber was likely intended to increase land for Rome's growing population rather than for flood control and might not have provided protection from flooding in any event. Cicero wrote that Julius Caesar had a grandiose plan to divert the Tiber north of the Milvian Bridge and channel it over 1.6 kilometers through an artificial drainage line west of the Vatican Hill.[59] The plan was never implemented, of course, and it might have been opposed on both religious and practical grounds had a serious effort been put forth.[60] The ancient citizens of Rome did, however, undertake solutions to the flooding problem. Suetonius reported that Augustus attempted to solve the problem by dredging the river's rubble-filled bed. Obviously, the effort failed over the long term. The city's low-lying areas, including the Campus Martius, continued to flood.[61] Tiberius set up a commission of five members to regulate the Tiber in an effort to eliminate both winter floods and summer droughts. Despite this measure and later attempts to control the river, there is no record that imperial engineers successfully deployed any means of reversing the river's natural proclivities.[62]

Though failing to stop the floods, the Romans undertook various construction techniques that mitigated the impact of inundations in the Campus Martius. First and foremost, they erected massive brick and mortar as well as stone buildings that could withstand the effects of rising water. For instance, Hadrian's Pantheon, located in the lowest area of the Campus Martius (the former Caprae Palus), was constructed with a drum of brick-faced concrete 6.2 meters thick.[63] The concrete foundation walls of Pompey's theater, also on the edge of this same depression, were 1.5 meters thick, faced in quasi reticulate on top of large blocks of tufa.[64] While the ancient writers describe the devastation of structures in the Campus Martius resulting from a series of fires, there is no similar evidence that the major monuments in the Field of Mars suffered significantly from the Tiber's overflow.

Although soaking floodwaters could degrade the walls and foundations of wooden buildings or those built with poor-quality brick and concrete, the public baths, temples, and permanent theaters of the Campus Martius were sufficiently impermeable to water, and thus maintained their structural integrity.[65] In addition, some buildings remained dry on the interior because they were raised on bases above the flood level. For instance, the temples in the Forum Holitorium close to the Tiber's edge and the nearby Temple of Apollo Sosianus perched on podia approximately fifteen meters above sea level, or above all but the worst inundations in the Campus Martius.[66] A building type that did suffer heavily during Rome's floods was the apartment complex (insula). Often of shoddy construction, the foundations of these structures could be jeopardized after several days of soaking in floodwater.[67] Tacitus wrote that in the flood of 69 C.E., "Apartment houses had their foundations undermined by the standing water and then collapsed when the flood withdrew."[68] During the fourth century C.E., there were numerous insulae in the Campus Martius, and while there are no extant descriptions of flood damage to apartments in the Field of Mars per se, they must have been as prone to destruction as those located in other parts of the floodplain.[69]

Rising ground levels due to constructions in the Campus Martius would have mitigated the impact of floodwaters, but as we know from the numerous floods in the area until the construction of the floodwall that follows both banks of the river, it certainly did not thwart the Tiber's seasonal inundations. The Pantheon of Hadrian, for instance, was built on a foundation approximately

29. Detail, Temple of Divine Hadrian, Piazza di Pietra, Rome. (Photo: Paul Jacobs)

2.5 meters higher than the original temple constructed by Agrippa.[70] Much of the northern plain was raised approximately 1.2 and 2.4 meters between the reigns of Vespasian and Hadrian.[71] In addition to the natural accretion, this artificial fill has caused the ground level of the Field of Mars to rise to the point that most of the extant ancient monuments have their foundations several meters below modern street level. The base of the Temple of the Divine Hadrian is 5 meters beneath the pavement (Figure 29) and the street elevation behind the Pantheon has risen 10 meters.[72] The Flavian pavement in which the horologium meridian is set rests 6.25 meters below street level.[73] The combination of a floodwall and raised ground level has resulted in the significant reduction of floods that challenge the Campus Martius, but not their elimination.[74] Permanent reminders of the height of floods and of the

Tiber's alluvial impact over the past several centuries can be found on incised stone markers throughout the area.[75]

WATER FROM THE EAST

On June 9, 19 B.C.E., clear, cold water rose from the soil beneath an estate formerly owned by one of Rome's great generals and politicians, Lucius Licinius Lucullus. Located near the eighth milestone east of the city limits, the spring was thought by some ancient writers to have been revealed by a young maiden to soldiers who were searching for water. In her honor, it was called the "Virgo," the Virgin.[76] With construction overseen by Agrippa for the final two years of work, the Aqua Virgo sent its waters on a lengthy and circuitous journey to the heart of the Campus Martius.[77] By coincidence or otherwise, June 9 was the feast day of Vesta, the goddess of the Vestal Virgins, and just as the flame on the hearth of the *Vestales* was to be eternal, the Virgin's water bubbling from the spring and flowing toward Rome on that early summer day has, in fact, never ceased. The water first entered a catch basin from the various underground springs with just under one cubic meter of water pouring forth every second into the Virgo's channel (*specus*).[78] From there, it flowed through an underground conduit that had been built along a nearby road, now the Via Collatina, and traveled west down a slight slope toward the city.

Near the later-built Porta Maggiore, the water was channeled north and then west again under the Pincian Hill, crossing under another of Lucullus's properties, his famous gardens, the Horti Luculliani.[79] Curving south, the flow of water continued through the *specus* down the hill near the modern Spanish Steps. There the conduit emerged and was carried over 139 stone arches for approximately one kilometer through the city.[80] It traveled first south about 536 meters to its modern terminus, the site of the famous Trevi Fountain built seventeen centuries later. A relief panel on the fountain commemorates Agrippa's construction project (Figure 30). From the area of the Trevi the water wended west across the Via Flaminia, and at last arrived in the central Campus Martius.[81] Just east of the Pantheon and north of the Saepta Julia, the water poured into a distribution chamber (*castellum*), before leaving in different directions through lead pipes (*fistulae*) to meet the needs of the rapidly developing Field of Mars.[82] Entering Rome at only 20 meters above sea level, the Aqua Virgo was one of the lowest aqueducts, but then its waters were heading to one of the lowest parts of the city.[83]

On this June morning in the early imperial era, most of the Aqua Virgo's supply traveled a short distance from the *castellum* before splashing into the empty pools that had been built into a large bathhouse just south of the Pantheon. Begun under the direction of Marcus Agrippa just six years earlier as a dry sweat bath, the Thermae Agrippae could now offer visitors to the

30. Agrippa supervising the Aqua Virgo construction, Trevi Fountain, Rome (eighteenth century). (Photo: Paul Jacobs)

Campus Martius a full bathing experience.[84] From the bathhouse area the water ran directly west to the Stagnum Agrippae that, in turn, drained into the Euripus Thermarum Agrippae.[85] The Virgo also poured as much as nineteen cubic meters that first day, one-fifth of the total flow that reached the city, into another *euripus*, the newly constructed Euripus Virginis, a channel that, according to the first-century C.E. Roman water commissioner Sextus Julius Frontinus, derived its name from the source of the water pouring through it.[86] Unlike the Euripus Thermarum Agrippae, the Euripus Virginis was apparently employed as a recreational swimming facility.[87] The term *euripus* was derived from the name for a narrow strait between the island of Euboea and mainland Greece, and as noted by Dyson, "This type of fanciful geographical identification was there especially associated with villa architecture and further emphasized the shift in the Campus Martius from *virtus* to *otium*."[88]

Within the Euripus Virginis, the Virgo's water flowed west and then south around the Theater of Pompey before reaching the Tiber in the area of a bridge thought to be the Pons Agrippae.[89] Whether on that June day or some time later, the Virgo's spring water was carried over the Pons Agrippae, to serve the villas on the Tiber's west bank, the Transtiberim.[90] Whatever the extent of the Virgo's ultimate reach on that first day, approximately 74,000 cubic meters of groundwater entered Rome through the aqueduct and, with few interruptions, have been doing so for more than two millennia.[91]

The Aqua Virgo was designed to provide for the intensive water needs of this section of the city, ultimately filling 90 percent of the Field of Mars's supply.[92] According to Frontinus, it was one of three major aqueduct projects initiated by Marcus Agrippa that, in combination, more than doubled the available fresh water for a burgeoning population.[93] But while the other two supplied a large part of their bounty to private homes and public basins and troughs, the Virgo's waters, according to Frontinus, went primarily for public works (*opera publica*), an undefined category that likely included Agrippa's baths, the Stagnum, and the various entertainment venues, as well as their gardens, such as the *quadriporticus* connected to the Theater of Pompey.[94] The Aqua Virgo's supply to public works is impressive, with 60 percent of the water volume consumed by all of the *opera publica* in the city being furnished by this aqueduct, almost four times the volume of the next highest provider, the Aqua Claudia / Aqua Anio Novus.[95] By contrast, Frontinus reported that only 4 percent of the *lacus*, public basins that provided, among other purposes, domestic drinking water for those without plumbing, was to be found in the Campus Martius.[96]

As Pliny the Elder makes clear, the aqueducts and the great volumes of water they carried to the city were a source of marvel to ancient Romans. "If we take into careful account the abundant supplies of water in public buildings, baths, pools, conduits, houses, gardens, suburban estates, if we reckon from how far the water comes, the raised arches, the tunneled mountains, the leveled valleys, we shall admit there has never been anything more marvelous in the whole world."[97] According to Suetonius, even Augustus highlighted the far-reaching benefit of Agrippa's Aqua Virgo, for he records that when people complained about the high price and scarcity of wine, the emperor retorted, "My own son-in-law Agrippa has taken good care, by building several aqueducts, that men shall not go thirsty."[98] As late as the sixth century C.E., the writer Cassiodorus praised the Virgo, long revered for its purity: "Purest and most delightful of all streams glides along the Aqua Virgo, so named because no defilement ever stains it. For while all the others, after heavy rain show some contaminating mixture of earth, this alone by its ever pure stream would cheat us into believing that the sky was always blue above us. Ah! how express these things in words worthy of them?"[99]

Apart from the significant contribution of the Virgo's waters to the development of the Campus Martius, the monumental structure through which it traveled had a significant visual impact on the space. Following the northern

31. Section of the Aqua Virgo with Claudian inscription, Via del Nazareno, Rome. (Photo: Paul Jacobs)

line of the Saepta Julia, the aqueduct separated the development in the central Campus Martius from the relatively open northern portion of the plain. The point at which the arches of the Aqua Virgo crossed the Via Flaminia provided a visual boundary to those traveling to Rome from the north, and this arcaded signpost begged for imperial decoration (Plan 3, No. 4). In 51 or 52 C.E., Claudius rebuilt one of the arches of the Aqua Virgo as it crossed the Via Flaminia, redesigning it as a single triumphal arch celebrating his successes in Britain eight years earlier.[100] A dedication to the emperor, believed to be from the arch, is now visible in the Capitoline Museum courtyard.[101] This was not the only section of the Aqua Virgo adorned by Claudius. An extant section of the Aqua Virgo northeast of the location of the arch that once crossed the Via Flaminia also displays an honorary inscription to Claudius. The fading but still legible words praise the emperor for restoring the Aqua Virgo after his predecessor Caligula had removed some of its stones for a building project (Figure 31).[102]

Before the construction of the Aqua Virgo, water-related spectacles were held in the Campus Martius near the Tiber's edge. The aqueduct's construction made them possible in numerous venues. Three decades before the Virgo was built, Julius Caesar ordered the creation of a shell-shaped lake near the Tiber, likely connected to the river by a channel, in honor of his triumph of 46 B.C.E., using it to reenact naval battles between the Egyptian and Tyrian fleets.[103] Suetonius tells us that for this event "a large force of fighting men" manned ships that had as many as four levels of oarsmen. Because these vessels did not sit low in the water, the basin may only have been about one and a half meters deep.[104] The basin was left in place for approximately three years.[105] Obviously, the Virgo made such aquatic events possible farther from the Tiber's edge. Augustus flooded the Circus Flaminius in 2 B.C.E. to display thirty-six crocodiles.[106] Caligula filled the Saepta Julia with water in order to display a single ship, and because of its location by the *castellum* of the Virgo, the Saepta undoubtedly was fed by that source.[107] Nero held a *naumachia* in his wooden amphitheater, complete with fish and other sea life, and reenacted the Battle of Salamis.[108] If his structure was located northwest of the Pantheon, the Aqua Virgo likely supplied the water on which the ships floated.[109]

With the addition of the Aqua Virgo's spring water, Agrippa also turned the low-lying Goat Marsh into a well-manicured parkland (Horti Agrippae). Large landholdings of Pompey in the Campus Martius that passed into the hands of Mark Antony and then into those of Agrippa during the turmoil of the Civil War became the site of his building projects.[110] Bordered by the Theater of Pompey to the south, the Pantheon and Baths of Agrippa on the east, the later-built Stadium of Domitian on the west, and Baths of Nero on the north, Agrippa's property was turned into a park with the Euripus Virginis and the Stagnum as its most prominent water features.[111] The gardens contained the famous Fallen Lion by the sculptor Lysippus, brought to Rome from Greece by Agrippa, and the Stagnum was used on at least one occasion to float a pleasure barge.[112] Originally part of Pompey's villa by his theater, the park was, according to Katherine von Stackelberg, transformed by Agrippa "into a showcase for his aquatic achievements" with the water features serving as "a monument to Augustus's admiral, the man who brought water to Rome."[113] Bequeathed in Agrippa's will to the public for its enjoyment, the park provided a relaxing, verdant venue for pedestrians where wild swamp grasses had once grown.[114] Nero later introduced exotic birds and wild animals, turning the public area into something of a zoological park.[115] Following the Roman penchant for forcing the natural environment to submit to the needs of urban expansion, Agrippa channeled the Virgo's spring to suit his development plans and, in doing so, assisted in the transformation of the swampland into a well-ordered entertainment district.

The greatest role of the aqueduct, however, was to serve as the water source for Rome's first grand public baths, the Thermae Agrippae. Covering more than 8,000 square meters, the baths, in conjunction with the Stagnum, the Euripus Virginis, and Agrippa's gardens to the west, created a complex for swimming, boating, exercise, and strolling. Until the completion of the Thermae Agrippae, Romans would have bathed at one of approximately 170 privately owned bathhouses known as *balneae* tucked away in small spaces throughout the city.[116] How many *balneae* were in the Campus Martius at the time Agrippa built his baths is unknown, although Cicero refers to one that may have been in the vicinity of the later-built Theater of Balbus.[117] Although many private bathhouses were dry sweat baths without hot water plunges, those that had pools may have received their water supplies from the runoff of public troughs.[118] Swimming generally took place in the Tiber, although a swimming pool was constructed on the southern side of the city as early as the fourth century B.C.E.[119] Agrippa permanently changed the bathing experience for most Romans by creating an indoor-outdoor leisure facility that combined large areas for bathing, gymnastics and games, swimming, social commerce, dining, business negotiations, shopping, and displays of art.[120] Where once Romans came to muster or witness military parade formations in a swampy and austere environment or practice their swimming skills in the muddy Tiber, now with an abundant supply of fresh spring water, they bathed and swam in clean pools and promenaded in lush but tamed green spaces surrounded by marble baths, theaters, and manubial temples. Augustus's comrade embellished the baths with decorative stucco, mosaics, encaustic painting, and 300 statues, including the famous *Apoxyomenos* by Lysippus. When it was removed a few years later by Tiberius to decorate his bedroom on the Palatine, a riot nearly broke out, resulting in its return to the Thermae Agrippae.[121]

While the baths originally charged a fee to its users, on Agrippa's death in 12 B.C.E., the facility and the adjoining park were given over to the Roman people for their free use.[122] Constructed as part of his building program for the central Campus Martius, the Baths of Agrippa was the first bathing complex in Rome to be maintained by the state.[123] By bringing water to the center of the Field of Mars, Agrippa helped anchor it as space to be shaped by imperial prerogative but available to a public that was daily reminded of the emperor's largesse.

Given the presence of his large landholdings in the Campus Martius and Agrippa's overall vision for its development, his decision to build a monumental bathhouse in this vicinity is logical. Nevertheless, unlike other nearby building projects with which Agrippa was associated such as the Saepta Julia and the Pantheon, the baths required complicated infrastructure improvements, equipment, and a constant and large supply of water and regular maintenance. Water was already available in other parts of the city where the baths could have been supplied more easily without the need to negotiate with landowners for the right to lay a channel through many kilometers of private property.[124] Why, then, add a large bathhouse, exercise space, and swimming facilities to his grouping of structures in the central Campus Martius? A possible answer is found in the fact that the Virgo was important to bringing drinking water to the other side of the Tiber. Baths between the source and the Transtiberim could make good and noticeable use of this bountiful supply, allowing Agrippa to simultaneously accomplish several significant goals.[125]

A different reason that reflects the sacred past of the space helps further to explain the choice of the Field of Mars for the first imperial bath. At the same time that Agrippa was reorganizing the space of the Campus Martius, he was advising Augustus to reorder society with new institutions, including a sports and paramilitary training program for adolescents of the upper classes designed to create a new generation of military and civic leaders.[126] Cassius Dio records Agrippa's recommendations:

> With regard, then to the senators and the knights, this is the advice I have to give you, – yes, and this also, that while they are still children they should attend the schools, and when they come out of childhood into youth they should turn their minds to horses and arms, and have paid public teachers in each of these departments. In this way from their very boyhood they will have had both instruction and practice in all that they will themselves be required to do on reaching manhood, and will thus prove more serviceable to you for every undertaking.[127]

There was probably no more meaningful space to build an exercise facility on a grand scale than in the area where Romulus and Cincinnatus had gathered their troops and Augustus himself had practiced his equestrian exercises as a youth.[128]

The Baths of Agrippa also would have provided an added attraction to the formal entertainment venues in the area. The Theater of Pompey and its portico-enclosed grounds for ambulations and assemblies were nearly adjacent to the bathhouse. Dedicated shortly after the Virgo began to deliver water to the baths, the theaters built by Cornelius Balbus and by Augustus in honor of his nephew Marcellus were only a few minutes' walk south. Patrons of Agrippa's baths would not have limited their visits to those days when shows were being performed, however. Attendance at bathhouses was part of a daily ritual of congregation that involved cleansing, exercise, relaxation, and conversation.[129] Roman citizens worked from daybreak to noon, had a light lunch and rest, and then went to the baths in the early afternoon for a couple hours when the pools were heated to their ideal temperatures.[130] A trip to the theater might follow the bathhouse experience.[131] While Agrippa's baths were on the outskirts of the city, and there were numerous small bathhouses elsewhere, for about eight decades, until Nero's imperial baths were constructed close by in the Campus Martius, they were the largest and likely the most prestigious place for Romans to gather for the bathing experience.[132] And for most of their history, Agrippa's baths were free of charge. Even after other, larger baths opened, they remained popular. Martial complained wearily that while he preferred the new Baths of Titus located near the Colosseum, his patron Fabianus insisted that the poet accompany him to the then century-old Baths of Agrippa for a late afternoon wash.[133]

32. G. B. Piranesi, detail of the Baths of Agrippa from *The Campus Martius of Ancient Rome* (1762). (Private collection)

Those partaking of Agrippa's baths for an afternoon of relaxation may have entered through an opening in the west side of the structure near the Stagnum.[134] Entering a courtyard with a pool in the center, bathers would have turned left and proceeded into a two-story building used as a changing room (*apodyterium*). Street clothes were placed in cabinets, on shelves, or left in the safekeeping of personal slaves, and a light garment, possibly of linen, would be donned for exercise. From there exercises could be taken in the courtyard or in front of the changing room. These moderate activities might include handball, running, walking, and boxing, performed with only enough vigor to create a slight sweat.[135] With the ringing of a bell to signal the availability of the hot baths, bathers would stop their exercises and head first to the warm bath (*tepidarium*) located in a room to the left of the changing room.[136] Relaxation in the warm bath would be followed by the hot bath (*caldarium*) and perhaps a trip to the sweat bath (*sudatorium*). Finally, the bather cooled down by plunging in the cold bath (*frigidarium*). A rotunda more than twenty-four meters in diameter anchored the main east–west axis of the bathhouse and is visible on a fragment of the Severan Marble Plan.[137] The large circular hall likely functioned as a central circulation space for visitors to greet friends and with its six exits provided a means to communicate to the various appended rooms. It possibly served also as the location of the *frigidarium*.[138] The ruins of this once-grand hall as envisioned by the artist Piranesi in 1762 capture the essence of what remains visible today (Figure 32).[139]

Bathhouses were raucous places, not locations for quiet contemplation. Seneca compared the unpredictability of life to the atmosphere of a bathhouse: "Sometimes things will be thrown at you, and sometimes they will strike you by accident."[140] Living near a bathhouse, Seneca complained of the noise emanating from within, providing an extraordinary picture of the bathing experience in Rome:

> So picture to yourself the assortment of sounds, which are strong enough to make me hate my very powers of hearing! When your strenuous gentleman, for example, is exercising himself by flourishing leaden weights; when he is working hard, or else pretends to be working hard, I can hear him grunt; and whenever he releases his imprisoned breath, I can hear him panting in wheezy and high-pitched tones. Or perhaps I notice some lazy fellow, content with a cheap rubdown, and hear the crack of the pummeling hand on his shoulder, varying in sound according as the hand is laid on flat or hollow. Then, perhaps, a professional comes along, shouting out the score: that is the finishing touch. Add to this the arresting of an occasional roysterer or pickpocket, the racket of the man who always likes to hear his own voice in the bathroom, or the enthusiast who plunges into the swimming-tank with unconscionable noise and splashing. Besides all those whose voices, if nothing else, are good, imagine the hair-plucker with his penetrating, shrill voice, – for purposes of advertisement, – continually giving it vent and never holding his tongue except when he is plucking the armpits and making his victim yell instead. Then the cakeseller with his varied cries, the sausageman, the confectioner, and all the vendors of food hawking their wares, each with his own distinctive intonation.[141]

Crowded with patrons seeking an afternoon of relaxation, socializing, and exercise, Agrippa's baths provided a source of employment for many. As Seneca notes, sellers of food and drink would have strolled the halls, and bathers could buy oils and other bathing necessities, rent towels, and hire services such as massages.[142] Shops provided additional goods for bathhouse guests. The baths themselves needed a large work force, both freedmen and slaves, to supply and store wood for the furnaces, maintain the machinery and *fistulae*, launder hundreds if not thousands of towels each day, clean the rooms, and generally maintain the structure.[143] Workers would have arrived early and stayed late seven days a week, keeping the central Campus Martius a constant center of bustling activity. Agrippa's bathhouse would have also attracted prostitutes, who often plied their trade in and near the baths.[144] As noted in Chapter 4, the third-century C.E. emperor Elagabalus was purported to have rounded up prostitutes from the bathhouses as well as other public places.[145] Describing a floating orgy on the Stagnum near the Agrippan baths during Nero's reign, the writer Tacitus noted that "on the quays of the lake stood brothels, filled with women of high rank; and, opposite, naked harlots met the view."[146]

While Agrippa's baths were clearly successful, Romans continued to use the smaller, privately run bathing establishments such as the Balneum Claudii Etrusci supplied by the Aqua Virgo and known for the richness of its marbles.[147] Notwithstanding the popularity of the Thermae Agrippae and the presence of many smaller bathing facilities, the emperor Nero built Rome's second major bathhouse in the Campus Martius about 400 meters northwest of Agrippa's baths. Why Nero selected a site so close to the Agrippan complex on which to establish his own *thermae* is unknown, although three factors could have played a role. At the time, this area of the Campus Martius remained mostly open and undeveloped, the baths were near a ready supply of water from the Aqua Virgo, and they opened north on a road that ran west from the Via Flaminia in the direction of the Tiber, possibly connecting to the bridge known later as the Pons Neronianus.[148] Whereas the Baths of Agrippa had small areas for exercise within the *thermae* walls, Nero's had a large Greek-style gymnasium integrated with the bathhouse.[149] Later, Domitian would build a facility just next door for viewing Greek-style games, the Stadium of Domitian. The configuration of Nero's structure is uncertain and may have comprised an "irregular grouping of buildings" that took advantage of Agrippa's gardens and the Stagnum in much the same way as did Agrippa's baths.[150]

The opening of the baths by Emperor Nero was a grand affair, underscoring the significance of these new imperial bathhouses in Rome's social life. To celebrate its completion, the emperor staged games called the Neronia with three contests: gymnastics, horse racing, and music. The gymnastic contest was held not in the bathhouse itself but in the Saepta Julia, as discussed in Chapter 4.[151] As part of the celebration, Nero awarded all members of the Senate and equestrian class with bath oils.[152] Not all Romans appreciated Nero's generosity, however. A philosopher named Demetrius entered the bath's gymnasium on opening day and commenced a tirade "against people who bathed, declaring that they enfeebled and polluted themselves; and he showed that such institutions were a useless expense."[153] Luckily for Demetrius, the emperor was singing in a tavern next door to the bathhouse and did not hear the outburst, or Demetrius's death would have been immediate. The story did, however, make its way to Nero's friend Tigellinus, now head of the imperial guard, who had Demetrius banished, claiming he "had ruined and overthrown the bath by the words he used."[154] Others who were not fans of Nero nevertheless enjoyed his baths. Remarking on the contrast between Nero and his eponymous *thermae*, Martial wrote: "What was worse than Nero? What is better than Nero's warm baths?"[155]

After the construction of Nero's complex, no other major bathhouse was built in the Campus Martius for more than a century and a half. Emperors Titus, Trajan, and Caracalla sited their imperial baths elsewhere in the city. Additionally, private bathhouses continued to play a significant role in the

Roman bathing experience. The fourth-century C.E. regionary catalogs note that the number of *balneae* had grown almost sixfold from the time of Agrippa, with sixty-three scattered throughout the Campus Martius alone. Part of that growth may have come from the emperor Alexander Severus, who made sure in the early third century C.E. that every Roman neighborhood had at least one private bathhouse.[156] In 227 C.E., however, Alexander Severus decided to make use of Nero's 163-year-old structure to impress his own major mark in the Field of Mars: he renovated and renamed the baths after himself and created a parklike *nemus* or garden in the vicinity, an action that may have been inspired by the similar projects of Agrippa in that sector of the plain. Although the Aqua Virgo likely fed the earlier bathhouse, its water resources must have been inadequate by the third century C.E. to meet the demands of an expanded structure, because we are told in the *Historia Augusta* that Alexander Severus built a new aqueduct to supply it – the Aqua Alexandrina.[157] The aqueduct brought the water from a source almost 18 kilometers east of the city to the vicinity of the eastern gate later known as the Porta Maggiore and then another 3.2 kilometers through the city to the baths.[158] Whereas Nero likely built his original facility in empty fields, Alexander had to purchase and raze surrounding buildings in order to add a park to the baths. The once-open Field of Mars now required reclamation to create green space. Whereas Agrippa had given his baths to the public for free use, Alexander Severus imposed taxes to maintain his. He did, however, illuminate his baths so that bathers could enjoy the facilities at night, helping to ensure that the Campus Martius was an area not only for nocturnal work but also for evening entertainment.[159]

When the expansion and renovation was completed, the baths of Alexander Severus covered more than 22,000 square meters, almost three times the size of Agrippa's baths.[160] To ensure enough wood was readily available to heat the enlarged facility, the emperor designated entire forests solely for its use.[161] On the basis of plans of extant ruins drawn by the eighteenth-century architect Palladio, it is thought that the patrons entered from the north into a courtyard with a large swimming pool. Colonnaded courtyards for exercise flanked the pool. The building was symmetrical with the east-west axis anchored by the *frigidarium* and the *tepidarium*. The *caldarium* may have protruded from the center axis on the south side.[162]

The Campus Martius's two major bathhouses continued to serve Rome's public bathing needs for centuries. Agrippa's baths were repaired after suffering damage in the fire of 80 C.E. and restored again as late as 345 C.E. After Alexander Severus expanded Nero's bathhouse, those baths likely continued in operation until the sixth century C.E., when invading Goths cut the water supply and the Roman general Belisarius blocked with masonry the aqueducts, including the Aqua Virgo, to prevent their use as a means by which to enter the city.[163] With aqueducts destroyed or blocked, baths were forced to close. Drinking water was obtained by digging wells.[164] The aqueducts were functioning again within about sixty years, but it is unclear whether they then supplied the former imperial bathhouses.[165] Only the Virgo's connection to Rome has continued into the modern era, supplying fresh water daily to the beautiful Trevi Fountain just to the east of the ancient eastern boundary of the Campus Martius. Agrippa's baths later became a center for lime burning, with marble from surrounding ruins thrown in the ovens and cooked down to a chalky powder that was then remixed for later construction.[166] Much of the ruins of the Neronian/Severan baths were incorporated into other structures, in particular the fifteenth-century Palazzo Madama, now the location of the Italian Senate. Substantial remains of the structure were visible in the seventeenth century, and a few glimpses of its outer walls remain, as well as large columns discovered below street level (Figure 33).[167]

By the third century C.E., the Campus Martius was drained of its low marshes and filled with structures, and stagnant pools were replaced with the Aqua Virgo's cold, fresh water. These alterations to the environment did not end the risk of malaria, however. Ironically, this is possibly due to the fact that *Anopheles* mosquitoes that carry human malaria prefer clear, well-oxygenated water.[168] That keen observer of nature, Pliny the Elder, noticed that "culices," a term that can mean mosquitoes, liked to buzz around irrigated gardens, a problem that would have applied to the Campus Martius's parks and quadriporticoes with their well-watered trees and exotic plants.[169] The large Stagnum as well as the slow flowing Euripus Virginus also must have attracted mosquitoes.[170] Even workers in an area such as the Roman Forum, despite it being well drained and built up by the late first century B.C.E., were at risk of fever, according to the Roman writer Horace.[171] Whether the mosquito problem impacted traffic to the Campus Martius in the later summer when the risk of malarial infection peaked is unknown, but it is doubtful that any one, low area of the city was worse than another. Wealthy nobles owning extramural country estates could flee the hot and mosquito-infested city altogether, but such an option did not exist for most inhabitants of the capital. Later visitors to Rome warned of the risk of mosquito bites in the warm weather months. The English writer Horace Walpole noted in 1740, "There is a horrid thing called the malaria, that comes to Rome every summer, and kills one, and I did not care for being killed so far from Christian burial."[172]

WATER FROM AFAR

Water had not only a significant physical presence in the Campus Martius but a metaphorical one as well. The war god's field was filled with reminders of military success on the waters of the Mediterranean basin. The most obvious, perhaps, was the presence of warships and their berths. Along the Tiber's edge

33. Columns from the Neronian/Severan baths (Via di Sant'Eustachio, Rome). (Photo: Paul Jacobs)

in the western Campus Martius stood the military ship sheds or *navalia*. First mentioned in 179 B.C.E., they were expanded over the years and were significant structures with peaked roofs sheltering each ship.[173] Romans would line the riverbank to watch Roman war vessels make their way to the offloading ramps

34. Detail of the decorative frieze of marine thiasos from the Paris/Munich reliefs (formerly known as the Altar of Ahenobarbus) (first century B.C.E.), Glyptothek, Staatlich Antikensamm-lung, Munich, Germany. (Photo: Foto Marburg / Art Resource, New York)

carrying extraordinary booty from foreign lands. Enemy vessels captured at sea and brought to the city for display afforded another spectacle for Rome's inhabitants.[174]

Numerous temples in the Campus Martius, vowed to the gods during skirmishes on the seas, memorialized past naval triumphs. Some of the honored gods had mythological connections to water or war. Following the defeat of the Carthaginian fleet off of Sicily in 260 B.C.E., the Temple of Janus was dedicated in the Forum Holitorium at the southern end of the Field of Mars near the Pons Fabricius, the bridge crossing to the Tiber Island.[175] At the time the temple was built, Rome did not have a "sea" god, and Janus's association with water crossings and bridges could have suggested to a victor in naval warfare that he was an appropriate deity to honor with a shrine.[176]

As discussed in Chapter 3, a temple of the nymph Juturna was vowed in 242 B.C.E. in connection with the defeat of the Carthaginian navy in a battle that ended the First Punic War. The temple was located in the central Campus Martius as was another, the Temple of Vulcan, which commemorated the Roman fleet's landing and taking of the Aeolian island of Lipari.[177] A vow made in the successful naval battle against Antiochus the Great resulted in the construction of the temple of the "Lares of the Sea" with its lengthy inscription describing the enemy's defeat, including the capture of forty-two ships and all of their crew.[178] A temple of Neptune, a protector of waters, may have stood along the edge of the Circus Flaminius.[179]

Not surprisingly, nautical motifs were visible throughout the Campus Martius. At the field's southern end, the Tiber Island was surmounted by a wall fashioned to look like a ship's stern.[180] The Temple of Neptune was decorated, according to Pliny the Elder, with Nereids riding the backs of dolphins, Tritons, and numerous sea creatures.[181] A frieze from a large base or altar thought to have been in the vicinity of the temple in the Circus Flaminius displayed a marine *thiasos* (celebratory procession) and, possibly, featured Amphitrite and Neptune (Figure 34).[182] Wedged between the Pantheon and the Baths of Agrippa, a large rectangular building, known as the Basilica of Neptune

35. Detail of the decorative frieze from the Basilica of Neptune, Via della Palombella, Rome. (Photo: Paul Jacobs)

and the Stoa of Poseidon, was decorated with sea creatures and dolphins (Figure 35).[183] The basilica possibly had an entrance on the east side, opening onto another structure with symbolic connections to the sea. Decorated with paintings relating the adventures of Jason and the Argonauts, the Porticus Argonautarum offered visitors to the marble space a mythological history of the sea routes now traveled by Roman cargo ships.[184]

To the east of the Saepta Julia were the temples of the Egyptian gods Isis and Serapis. Here the waters of the Nile, transported from Egypt in jars, were used in cultic practices.[185] In close vicinity to the temples stood statues of the water gods, Nile and Tiberis (Figures 36 and 37). Later perhaps, three others, including the god Oceanus, were added.[186] Interpreted as the personification of these rivers in full flood, the statues of the Tiber and the Nile possibly date to the early second century C.E. and display well-understood attributes of the two rivers.[187] The Nile god reclines with a sphinx and a cornucopia at its elbow and crocodiles under its legs. Sixteen children, perhaps representations of Roman provinces or conquered nations, climb about his trunk and limbs.[188] Pygmies and wildlife are carved in the sides and back of the base. Like Nile, Tiber rests by a horn of plenty. Here, however, the sphinx is appropriately replaced by the she-wolf nursing Romulus and Remus. A base relief possibly displays Aeneas as part of the foundation legend of Rome as well as workers unloading cargo from riverboats.[189] As Swetnam-Burland has noted, each of these statues viewed by both perambulators in the park and participants in the Egyptian cults "blend[ed] complementary threads of visual, historical, and mythic traditions

36. Nile River (early second century C.E.?). Braccio Nuovo, Museo Chiaramonti, Vatican Museums, Vatican State. (Photo: Album / Art Resource, New York)

into a single artwork that embodies positive associations between the river and those who depend on it for life and livelihood."[190] Their placement in the Campus Martius where river floods were more than a theoretical issue would not have been lost on the imperial viewer.

As the marble cornucopia at the Nile god's elbow represented the foreign bounty now flowing to Rome, so, too, the daily commercial traffic floating along the Campus Martius's meandering western border provided a constant reminder of Rome's supremacy over the Mediterranean and the riches under its control. It also placed the Field of Mars literally within the stream of commerce. The legendary grain of Tarquinius Superbus that washed downstream from the Campus Martius to form the Tiber Island was substantially multiplied centuries later: more than one-half million tons of grain was brought up the Tiber to

37. Tiber River (early second century C.E.?). Louvre, Paris. (Photo: RMN-Grand Palais / Art Resource, New York)

Rome annually from farmlands throughout the empire.[191] Although, as Pliny noted, the Tiber was "accessible to ships of the largest size from the Italian sea," goods would be off-loaded at the port of Ostia and then barged upriver to Rome on smaller vessels.[192] Stored in warehouses, or *horrea*, on the edge of the Campus Martius by the Forum Holitorium, the grain was carried to the Transtiberim to be fed into the mills that used the Tiber's flow to operate the millstones that ground the wheat. The flour was then taken across the river and moved along the roads of the Campus Martius to be distributed to Romans from the Porticus Minucia Frumentaria.[193] Over eighty thousand cubic meters of wine entered the city annually, much of which was transferred to the docks along the Campus Martius, and beginning with the reign of Aurelian (r. 270–5 C.E.), was transported across the Field of Mars and up the Quirinal Hill for distribution from the portico that ran along the Temple of Sol.[194] Tons of foreign marble were barged to the area around the Pons Aelius to be cut and moved to construction sites within the city.[195] Wine from Greece, exotic marbles from Anatolia, granite from Egypt, and even wild animals from Africa removed from the holds of river vessels docking at the Tiber's banks along the Field of Mars served to emphasize that the Mediterranean was just one more road that led to Rome and that the Campus Martius was an important way station for the empire's riches.

CONCLUSION

No other area of Rome faced greater risks from the impact of water nor offered greater opportunity to employ it for the benefit of its citizens than the Campus Martius. The low, marshy, and open plain that lay prone to the Tiber's floodwaters was at first defenseless to the seasonal inundations, but it made little difference when the Field of Mars served primarily as a seasonal mustering ground and voting precinct. Winter floods and summer mosquitoes could be avoided. As the Romans sought to make greater use of the space, however, they had to shape the landscape in an attempt to mitigate damages and dangers. Drainage channels, buildings of brick and concrete, and use of fill dirt were deployed to resist the Tiber, albeit with modest success. Despite such efforts, the Campus Martius continued to flood and yet the Romans continued to build; the space was simply too important to leave undeveloped. Even the threat posed by malaria-bearing mosquitoes in late summer did not dissuade the Romans from turning the space into a year-round venue for entertainment and commerce. Grain, marble, and wine moved down the gangplanks on the Tiber's edge and trundled in carts through the streets of the Campus Martius. Much of the marble moved only a few hundred meters to be used to construct temples, porticoes, and theaters whose erection in the Field of Mars continued, unrelenting.

If the first grandiose bathhouse was to be built anywhere in Rome during the Augustan Era, it made sense to locate it where the other Agrippan projects were underway, on land controlled by Augustus's admiral. Yet this meant creating an enormous and costly infrastructure to bring in a secure source of fresh water and then devising a system to channel it to the Tiber. In fact, using those channels to meet the water needs of development across the Tiber made the whole scheme practical. These goals were accomplished with the completion of the Aqua Virgo in 19 B.C.E. and the construction of the Stagnum, the Euripus Virginis, the Euripus Thermarum Agrippae, and other conduits. Agrippa's dedication to engineering improvements made the Virgo's water available for bathing, aquatic displays, swimming, and other water-related activities in the Field of Mars and beyond. Fed by the Virgo, Rome's first imperial baths, followed by a second bath complex and another aqueduct, helped ensure that the Campus Martius, once an occasional venue for public gatherings, was a daily destination for work, residency, and relaxation. Where stagnant water once saturated marshy soil, by the imperial era fresh spring water filled bathing pools and coursed through channels of concrete carved into manicured parks, wending around columned temples and theaters.

CHAPTER SEVEN

"A ZEAL FOR BUILDINGS": RESHAPING OF THE SPACE BY THE EMPERORS

In late summer, 43 B.C.E., Octavian, then using the self-appointed title of Caesar, rode with his army to the Field of Mars to confront his Senate enemies within the city walls.[1] Much had occurred since his first trip to Rome after his adoptive father's assassination. At that time (late May 44 B.C.E.) he had met in the Campus Martius with Mark Antony in gardens that previously belonged to Pompey the Great in order to claim, unsuccessfully, his inheritance.[2] Now the young Caesar returned in force. Facing legions camped in the mostly open plain, the Senate wisely yielded to Octavian's demands. Donatives were awarded to his men, and Caesar's heir was made consul, allowing him to enter the city as Rome's sanctioned co-leader. While Octavian was performing sacrifices with respect to his election to consul, twelve vultures were seen, according to Appian and Suetonius, the same number that oversaw the laying of the city's foundation by Romulus.[3]

Fifty-seven years later, Octavian, now the emperor Augustus, died. His funeral bier was carried on the shoulders of senators through the Campus Martius to be cremated. The space through which the mourners walked was very different from the field that had housed the young Octavian's troops in 43 B.C.E. A series of buildings now rose parallel to the Via Flaminia: the Diribitorium, Saepta Julia, Thermae Agrippae, Stoa of Poseidon, and Pantheon. The arcades of the Aqua Virgo crossed the main road north. Along the western side of the Via Flaminia stood an altar to Augustan Peace, the Ara Pacis, and nearby an imported Egyptian obelisk dedicated to the emperor's triumph over

Antony and Cleopatra cast a shadow along a bronze meridian set in travertine. Numerous temples in the area of the Circus Flaminius were rebuilt and rededicated, and two additional permanent theaters were added. The emperor's final resting place, a giant tumulus in a verdant park, waited for his ashes at the far reaches of the Field of Mars. In a span of more than five decades, the Campus Martius was radically altered from a swampy military camp and an infrequently attended memorial to individual valor of republican generals to a thriving and crowded wonderland of communicating architecture for daily sports and recreation and celebrations of the achievements and divinization of the imperial family and the power of the expanding Roman Empire. Later emperors would continue to populate the Field of Mars with extraordinary structures, forever transforming the open, flat plain.

AUGUSTUS

With a clear-eyed focus on his immortality, Octavian constructed his own tomb on the northern edge of the Campus Martius as one of his first building projects (Plan 3, No. 1).[4] According to Suetonius, the structure was underway, if not completed, in 28 B.C.E., a year before the young man in his mid-thirties took the title Augustus. By the time the tomb was complete, Octavian had returned from his eastern campaigns and celebrated a grand triple triumph (the same number as Romulus) for his victories over Antony and Cleopatra.[5] Placed where the Tiber and the Via Flaminia nearly converge, the structure was viewed easily by both river and land travelers. At a height of forty-four meters and a diameter of approximately eighty-nine meters, the building dominated the northern reaches of the plain in the same way that Pompey's theater overshadowed structures in the central Campus Martius.[6]

Clearly the siting of the enormous tomb along a heavily trafficked roadway that Augustus would shortly restore was both deliberate and meaningful.[7] As the Via Flaminia was often used for military campaign marches to the northern and western regions of the empire, the gigantic mausoleum relayed themes of victory over one's enemies as well as triumph over death through apotheosis. Its accessibility to a major road helped to ensure that visitors to the mausoleum contemplated these messages.[8] It was further offset by its immediate surroundings. In accordance with tradition, the mausoleum was placed within a verdant space in which walkways meandered through groves of trees.[9] So located, the monument would, in essence, be a signpost to both the Field of Mars and the city. Not only the size and location but also the selection of the architectural design for the tomb likely provided symbolic significance. Possibly influenced by Ptolemaic models, the Mausoleum of Augustus was, according to one author, as much a war trophy as a final resting place.[10]

38. South side of the Mausoleum of Augustus. (Photo: Paul Jacobs)

Although reconstructions of the now partially preserved circular structure are many and often controversial, Strabo's roughly contemporaneous account illustrates how Augustus's mausoleum rose above the flat plain as another hill of Rome: "The most noteworthy [tomb in the Campus Martius] is what is called the Mausoleum, a great mound near the river on a lofty foundation of white marble, thickly covered with ever-green trees to the very summit."[11] The outermost wall of the round tomb was some twelve meters high and was originally faced on both sides with travertine; what remains today is merely an exposed core of tufa reticulate and mortar construction (Figure 38). Interior concentric walls connected by semicircular buttresses and covered in earth rose above the outer wall, giving the appearance of an earthen mound.[12] The thick walls were penetrated by a narrow passageway running from the entrance to a circular, vaulted corridor. The central burial chamber was designed as a circular hall with a pillar in the center. Niches in the walls of the burial chamber and in the central pillar provided space for deposit of imperial remains. A structure for cremation (*ustrinum*) was constructed nearby.[13]

At or about the same time that Augustus was focused on his immortal future in the northern Campus Martius, he looked to the past in the southern Campus Martius and refurbished a space that had once reflected the glory of

39. Detail, frieze, Temple of Apollo Sosianus (ca. 29 B.C.E.). (Photo: with permission of Roma, Musei Capitolini, Centrale Montemartini)

republican military success to one that declared his new power and status. Controlling what Strabo termed the "zeal for buildings" of his "sons and friends and wife and sister," Augustus undertook to leave his mark on the area around the Circus Flaminius.[14] One such "friend" was the general Gaius Sosius, a former partisan of Antony who was arrested after the Battle of Actium but ultimately pardoned by Octavian. Having previously initiated a restoration of the four-centuries-old Temple of Apollo Medicus to honor his own battlefield success, Sosius wisely altered the sculptural program after his reconciliation to depict Octavian's eastern successes and triple triumph in 29 B.C.E. (Figure 39).[15] The Temple of Bellona next to the Apollo temple was also rebuilt, possibly under the direction of Appius Claudius Pulcher, an ally of Octavian and a relative of his wife, Livia, and in 33 B.C.E., Octavian's nephew Marcus Claudius Marcellus undertook to rebuild the Porticus Metelli (Plan 3, Inset B). Possibly financed by Octavian, the portico project was dedicated by Marcellus's mother Octavia, Augustus's sister, after Marcellus's death in 23 B.C.E. and named the Porticus Octaviae.[16] Octavia also refurbished the temples of Juno Regina and Jupiter Stator and added libraries, and on the northwestern end of the Circus Flaminius, Octavian's stepfather, L. Marcus Philippus, enclosed the Temple of Hercules Musarum in a portico named the Porticus Philippi (Plan 3, Inset B).[17] At approximately the same time, Octavian restored the portico just to the west of the Porticus Philippi that had been constructed more than a century earlier by his ancestor Gnaeus Octavius.[18] Joining the reconstructed temples and porticoes in the area of the Circus Flaminius were the newly built theaters, one dedicated to the emperor's nephew Marcellus and the other built by a supporter of Augustus, Cornelius Balbus. This clustering of edifices built or reconstructed under the new emperor's effective control created a node of Augustan political display in the southern Campus Martius. Augustus's successors would expand on this theme with an arch to his great-nephew Germanicus, complete with eleven statues of the latter's immediate family, later erected between the Portico of Octavia and the Theater of Marcellus.[19]

While the southern campus was the site of mostly refurbishment and rebuilding projects accomplished by Augustus and his allies, the central Field of Mars gained new and extraordinary monuments. These efforts were undertaken by Augustus's most trusted and capable construction overseer, Marcus Agrippa. Agrippa contended with a low-lying, marshy area that was often flooded, a challenge that might have made this location less than appealing had it not been also charged with symbolic capital as the site of the apotheosis of Romulus. Appointed aedile in 33 B.C.E., Agrippa undertook major waterworks in the Campus Martius, including improved drainage systems and water supply channels and construction of the Aqua Virgo.[20] He was the first manager of the waters (*curator aquarum*), a lifetime appointment created by Augustus to address earlier disregard for maintenance of Rome's neglected infrastructure.[21] Just north of Pompey's theater complex, he erected in the once swampy area two structures to receive the Virgo's waters, the Thermae Agrippae and the Stagnum Agrippae.[22] By combining practical, utilitarian constructions with enhanced areas for leisure and entertainment, Agrippa's program no doubt augmented the popularity of the plain for Roman citizens of all ranks.

Agrippa's baths and Stagnum followed a north-south orientation, in line with the Saepta Julia completed by Agrippa the previous year and the Diribitorium dedicated in 7 B.C.E., five year's after Agrippa's death.[23] To the north of his baths, Agrippa also built two additional structures, both of which were damaged or destroyed and substantially reconstructed later in the imperial period: the Pantheon and the building variously identified as the Basilica of Neptune and Stoa of Poseidon.[24] The basilica/stoa was constructed between the Baths of Agrippa and Agrippa's Pantheon.[25] A large hall on the Via della Palombella, rebuilt by Hadrian, has been identified as originally belonging to this Agrippan building. Like most basilicas, the structure appears to have served primarily a commercial function, further enhancing the practical functions of Agrippa's constructions in the Campus Martius.[26] The general details regarding Agrippa's Pantheon, a structure also mentioned in some detail by Cassius Dio, are no less controversial.[27] The function of the building, as well as its original shape and orientation, has caused much debate. Although he likely confused aspects of the surviving Hadrianic structure with the earlier Agrippan building, Cassius Dio reported the reasons for its initial construction:

> Also, he [Agrippa] completed the building called the Pantheon. It has this name, perhaps because it received among the images which decorated it the statues of many gods, including Mars and Venus; but my own opinion of the name is that, because of its vaulted roof, it resembles the heavens. Agrippa, for his part, wished to place a statue of Augustus there also and to bestow upon him the honor of having the structure named after him; but when the emperor would not accept either honor, he placed in the temple itself a statue of the former Caesar [Julius Caesar] and in the ante-room [porch] statues of Augustus and himself.[28]

On the basis of Dio's commentary, Agrippa's structure seems to have been planned as a quasi-dynastic structure, linking Augustus not only to his divine father but also to the divine Romulus, whose legendary apotheosis took place near the Caprae Palus.[29] The shape of Agrippa's lost Pantheon continues to be controversial: some scholars argue for a T-shaped design with a transverse cult space (*cella*) facing south, while others propose a north-facing structure with a foundation footprint closely resembling the later Hadrianic building, albeit most often without the concrete domed ceiling, an innovative form later celebrated in Hadrian's domed rotunda of the same name.[30] In addition to statues of the imperial family and various divinities mentioned in Dio's accounts, Pliny referred to the caryatid sculptures (subjects unknown) by Diogenes of Athens, as well as bronze Corinthian capitals.[31] Clearly the structure was adorned with symbols and statues connected with burgeoning Augustan iconography; less clear and more controversial are the design and function of this enigmatic building.

Augustus focused on the northern Campus Martius for the sites of his final two major monuments in the Field of Mars – the horologium and the Ara Pacis Augustae (Altar of Augustan Peace). Following the emperor's return to Rome in 13 B.C.E. after three years of successful campaigns and negotiations in the western provinces (Spain and Gaul), the Roman Senate voted to erect an altar of Augustan Peace. The altar and its enclosure wall were built along the western edge of the Via Flaminia south of the mausoleum (Plan 3, No. 3). While for most monuments in Rome there is a dearth of textual evidence, for the Ara Pacis there survives ample textual evidence, the most prominent of which is a reference in the *Res Gestae*.[32]

The Ara Pacis Augustae complex consisted of two main parts: a U-shaped altar proper in the center where sacrifices took place and the walls surrounding the altar, known as the *saeptum*, that physically demarcated the sacred precinct area.[33] Two wide doors allowed entrance from the east (Via Flaminia) and from the west (Campus Martius). The interior surfaces of the marble *saeptum* walls were carved with imitation wooden slats with pilasters at the corners; suspended garlands of leaves, pinecones, and fruit; the skulls of sacrificed bulls (*bucrania*); and sacrificial bowls (*patera*). This decorative scheme might have been an idealized stone version of an archaic Roman wooden templum with dual levels of symbolism: new fertility of the land under Augustus and a return to traditional Roman religious practices and structures. On the exterior, a floral frieze of vines and flowers arranged in a careful, controlled composition with Apollo's swans covered the entire lower zone on all four sides, referencing the new god of the Augustan golden age.[34] Four rectangular panels on either side of the doorways in the upper zone carried mythological and allegorical scenes related to the foundation myths of the city: the infants Romulus and Remus suckled by the she-wolf (northwest); Aeneas or Numa sacrificing a

40. Detail, frieze, Ara Pacis. Museum of the Ara Pacis, Rome. (Photo: Album / Art Resource, New York)

sow (southwest); the goddess Roma seated on a pile of weapons (northeast); and "Tellus" holding two infants while surrounded by various plants, fruits, and domestic animals (southeast).[35] The iconography of these sculpted panels was clear – agricultural prosperity and human fertility would thrive through legitimate warfare and victory under Augustus.[36]

The final areas of carved decoration were the two processional friezes on the exterior north and south sides of the long *saeptum* walls. These famous sculptures show heavily draped Romans participating in a *supplicatio* ceremony, a thanksgiving ritual for the safe return of Augustus (Figure 40).[37] Both processions move toward the west and the plain of the Campus Martius. Figures identified in the friezes include Augustus, Agrippa, members of the imperial family, the *pontifices* (college of priests), the Rex Sacrorum, the *quindecemviri sacris faciundis* (college of fifteen men in charge of the Sibylline Books) and the *septemviri epulonum* (the seven men in charge of public feasts), lictors carrying the *fasces*, and other attendants.[38] Finally, the altar proper bore relief sculptures depicting the Vestals, a sacrificial procession, and perhaps images of nations and peoples. Thus, the sculptures that once covered the altar were related to actual events of the dedication ceremonies of the altar performed on January 30, 9 B.C.E., the birthday of Augustus's wife Livia. These rites and rituals were to be repeated annually by magistrates and Vestals for the continuation of peace and prosperity.[39]

41. Horologium gnomon, Piazza di Montecitorio, Rome. (Photo: Paul Jacobs)

Shortly before or after the dedication of the Ara Pacis, Augustus caused to be erected approximately 90 meters southwest of the altar an obelisk of red granite.[40] Augustus ordered the sixth-century B.C.E. obelisk shipped from Heliopolis in Egypt to Rome to be incorporated into his plans for the northern Campus Martius (Plan 3, No. 2).[41] Measuring just over 21.8 meters high, it is found today, reerected, in the Piazza di Montecitorio about 200 meters south of its original location standing before the Italian Chamber of Deputies (Figure 41).[42] An inscription carved on two sides of the base is still visible and notes that Augustus as Pontifex Maximus was dedicating the obelisk to Sol, the sun god, after Egypt was brought under the power of the Roman people.[43] According to Pliny the Elder, the needle of Egyptian granite in the northern Campus Martius was surmounted by a gilt ball that allowed a sharp shadow to be cast on a system of bronze markers on the ground.[44]

42. Horologium bronze marker, Via del Campo Marzio No. 48, Rome. (Photo: Paul Jacobs)

Known today as the Horologium Solarium Augusti, the monument has generated significant controversy with respect to its function as well as to its physical and symbolic relationship to the Ara Pacis. Through much of the twentieth century, scholars envisioned the bronze markers as arcuated lines radiating from a central line north of the gnomon generally in the shape of a double ax approximately 150 meters wide.[45] Under this configuration, the cast shadow would mark the passage of time, creating, in essence, a sundial.[46] Excavations in the area beginning in the late 1970s revealed, however, but one crosshatched bronze line incised in travertine 6.25 meters below street level. The line faced north–south and was within reach of the shadow cast from the original location of the obelisk. Inscriptions in Greek note "Etesian winds stop" and the "beginning of summer" as well as references to the zodiac (Figure 42).[47]

The failure to find bronze lines other than the excavated north–south line has resulted in the conclusion by some scholars that the monument functioned solely as a solar meridian to measure noon on each day of the year.[48] As a solar meridian was used, in part, to verify the accuracy of the civil calendar with the solar year, the horologium would have held symbolic significance at this time because Augustus was awarded three years earlier the title

Pontifex Maximus, a religious position that included responsibility for Rome's calendar.[49] In addition to the horologium's connection to Augustus's official duties, arguments have been advanced for a functional relationship between the meridian and the monument to Augustan peace. It has been proposed that on the fall equinox, the date of Augustus's official birthday (September 23), the shadow cast by the gnomon's ball follows a line perpendicular to the meridian and points to the entrance of the Ara Pacis. This claim has drawn considerable scholarly criticism, as well.[50] While the theory of the gnomon's shadow on the fall equinox has drawn fire, it appears that the three major Augustan monuments in the northern Campus Martius were configured in a manner that would have provided a clear visual interrelationship.[51] Because the Ara Pacis and the horologium were constructed so closely in time and space, there can be little doubt that their relationship with the mausoleum to the north was an intentional manifestation of Augustan power. Late in the principate the red granite shaft from Heliopolis harkened back to the defeat of Egypt and the beginning of an era of peace, resonating with the nearby mausoleum that was built when the defeat was fresh and peace still not guaranteed after a long civil war. The horologium, in combination with the nearby Ara Pacis, expressed and augmented Augustan concepts: the cyclical nature of time, the return of the golden age, and the significance of contemporary astrology for the maintenance of the order and the wealth and fertility brought by Augustus's providential rule. With the large circular mound of the mausoleum within sight to the north, the entire northern Campus Martius, previously devoid of any significant structures, became laden with a complex series of intertwined messages of imperial power, divine consent, and immortality through apotheosis.

With the completion of the horologium and Ara Pacis, more than thirty-two structures in the Campus Martius had been newly constructed or refurbished under the emperor's watchful eye. Augustus treated the northern flatland as a *tabula rasa* on which to imprint monumental symbols of imperial power.[52] At the same time he reorganized the space physically, the emperor altered the campus administratively. In 7 B.C.E., the Field of Mars was officially "incorporated" into the bureaucratic control of the capital as one of the fourteen districts (*Urbs XIV Regionum*) under a plan that was innovative and without republican precedent. Seven of these newly created regions, including the Campus Martius, lay outside the traditional boundaries of the *pomerium*, although the restrictions imposed on those entering the city had been modified with respect to the emperor. For instance, in 23 B.C.E. Augustus was authorized to utilize tribunal powers, normally reserved for the city limits, within a mile of the pomerial line, an area that would include the Campus Martius. Additionally, from 19 B.C.E. Augustus, and then later emperors, had consular *imperium*, a status that allowed them to command troops and to appear in military uniform within the city.[53] Not only the physical but now also the religious lines between the city proper and the Campus Martius were becoming blurred.

Following Augustus's death in 14 C.E., two matching pillars were erected outside the entrance to his mausoleum.[54] They were adorned with bronze tablets inscribed with the *Res Gestae*, a document composed by the *princeps* himself that detailed his political, military, architectural, and civic achievements. He noted with pride certain of his projects in the Campus Martius – the Ara Pacis, the Porticus Octaviae, the Theater of Marcellus, and reconstruction of the Theater of Pompey and the Via Flaminia.[55] At the top of the tomb's exterior, a statue of the emperor, likely a colossal gilded portrait, was held aloft by the central pillar – the same pillar that housed the cremated remains of members of Augustus's family and perhaps the emperor's funerary urn.[56] The elevated position of this portrait statue, rising above the tomb and the plain of the northern Campus Martius, no doubt celebrated and reinforced the apotheosis of the *princeps*. Just as Romulus had once risen to the heavens from the Field of Mars to join the Roman pantheon of gods, so too did Augustus.[57]

DOMITIAN

Other than the imperial bath complex commissioned by Nero discussed previously (Thermae Neronianae), little major building or restoration activity altered the general topography of the Campus Martius during the era of the Julio-Claudians (r. 14–68 C.E.). Claudius, however, extended the *pomerium* into the central plain, an act that brought an area dedicated to the military within the city limits for the first time.[58] Likewise, Vespasian (r. 69–79 C.E.) and Titus (r. 79–81 C.E.), the first two rulers of the Flavian Dynasty, concentrated their construction efforts elsewhere. The destructive conflagration of 80, however, ravaged large portions of the Field of Mars and likely encouraged the prolific architectural patron, Domitian (r. 81–96 C.E.), to undertake costly repairs as well as the financing of new construction.[59] Structures listed as destroyed or damaged include but were certainly not limited to the temples of Isis (Iseum Campense) and Serapis (Serapeum), the Saepta and Diribitorium, the Basilica of Neptune and the Baths of Agrippa, Agrippa's Pantheon, the theaters of Balbus and Pompey, and the Porticus Octaviae. As becomes clear, Domitian's interests in the Campus Martius did not continue the major trends begun by Augustus. Rather than emphasizing universal triumph and imperial apotheosis, Domitian built and repaired structures that were far more personal in nature. Nevertheless, Domitian's constructions permanently reconfigured and further enhanced the activities and rituals that took place on the plain.

The Serapeum and Iseum Campense (occasionally referred to as the Temple of Isis Campensis) were originally built as early as the late republic. They stood

43. Detail, tomb of the Haterii, depicting "Arcus ad Isis" (so-called Arco di Camigliano?) (late first century C.E.). Museo Gregoriano Profano, Vatican Museums. (Photo: Scala / Art Resource, New York)

within the same precinct and represented the official cult center for Isis and Serapis in Rome.[60] It is not surprising that Domitian took particular interest in rebuilding their shrines; ample evidence demonstrates his fascination with Ptolemaic Egyptian religion and with Isis in particular.[61] What we know of the design of this temple complex comes from the remaining fragments of the Severan Marble Plan as well as from a late first century C.E. relief from the tomb of the Haterii, a family of builders, that possibly shows a small, triple arcade from the precinct area, the "Arco di Camigliano" (Figure 43).[62] Located between the Saepta and the Via Flaminia, much of the details of the plan of the Iseum are gone and therefore difficult to reconstruct. The Serapeum, better preserved on the Marble Plan, appears to have been a large rectangular courtyard connected on its western side by means of a grand portal to the Saepta Julia. A portico with four apsidal exedras projected from a portico shaped like an inverted D south of the courtyard (Plan 4, Nos. 6 and 7).[63]

While we have only a few tantalizing hints as to the architecture of this Egyptian complex, a surprisingly large quantity of artwork that decorated the precinct has survived. Statues of water gods (Nile, Tiber, and Oceanus; see Figures 36 and 37) as well as a basalt sculpture of a baboon survive, as do several obelisks (Obelisci Isei Campensis), including those currently located at the Piazza Santa Maria sopra Minerva (Figure 44), the Viale delle Terme Diocletiane, and the famous obelisk decorating the ornate fountain in the Piazza della Rotunda (Plate I). Another Egyptian obelisk that may have once stood inside the Iseum precinct, the Pamphili Obelisk, is carved with unusual hieroglyphs and images that celebrate Domitian as both the emperor of Rome and the pharaoh of Egypt.[64] A large marble foot from an acrolith and known as the Pie' di Marmo rests on a pedestal outside in the area where the complex once stood (Figure 45).

Just to the east of the temples of Isis and Serapis is a second set of structures associated with Domitian's rebuilding program in the Campus Martius following the fire of 80 C.E. Again, the character of these constructions represents a departure from Augustus's program and is closely tied to the personal and dynastic interests of the last Flavian emperor. A possible replacement for the remaining space in the much diminished Villa Publica and similar in general design to the Forum Pacis, the Divorum consisted of a large, open *quadriporticus* within which stood two temples, one dedicated to Divus Vespasianus and one to Divus Titus, and possibly the (repaired?) altar to Mars (Plan 4, No. 9).[65] To the north of the Divorum and east of the Temple of Isis and Serapis was another precinct that once contained a round temple (*tholos*) of Minerva Chalcidica (Plan 4, No. 8). It serves as yet another example of Domitian's devotion to the warlike goddess Minerva, for whom he built temples and shrines throughout the city and with whose image he decorated multiple issues of his coinage as well as state reliefs.[66]

In addition to this concentration of religious structures east of the Saepta, Domitian constructed new entertainment facilities west of the Baths of Agrippa and Nero, in keeping with the uses established in the central Campus Martius over the previous century. Used for contests and spectacles, these structures were known as the Stadium of Domitian and the Odeum of Domitian (Plan 4, Nos. 19 and 20). The second structure, the Odeum of Domitian, has disappeared; although scholars have a general sense of its location south of the stadium, its overall shape (rectangular vs. semicircular) remains controversial. Both of these projects can be connected with Domitian's philhellenism and his reintroduction of Greek-style contests known as the Capitoline Games in honor of Jupiter. Like Minerva, Jupiter was a favorite deity of Domitian, and these constructions in the central area of the plain are testament to his attempts to promote Greek agonistic festivals as well as his personal interest in Greek literature, culture, and sport. With the completion of Domitian's stadium and

44. Obelisk from Iseum incorporated in Bernini's *Elephant and Obelisk*, Piazza Santa Maria sopra Minerva, Rome. (Photo: Paul Jacobs)

45. Marble foot from an acrolith (so-called Pie' di Marmo), Via di Pie' di Marmo, Rome. (Photo: Paul Jacobs)

odeum, we see a pattern of building distribution emerging in the imperial period: religious precincts added to the eastern side of the central zone, new leisure and entertainment facilities constructed to the west. The last vestige of an open space in that part of the field that had witnessed for centuries so many popular gatherings outside of the *pomerium*, namely the Villa Publica, was now enclosed within a regularized portico structure. Meanwhile, the northern campus (physically separated from the central field by an east-west road) still remained a vast and open "Augustan park," with grand buildings and ornately decorated monuments that celebrated the more abstract concepts of perpetual triumph and imperial apotheosis.

HADRIAN AND THE ANTONINES

Following the assassination of Domitian in 96 C.E., the emperors Nerva and Trajan undertook projects that consisted of either completing or restoring earlier Domitianic construction (Forum Transitorium, Forum of Julius Caesar) or initiating new projects (Forum of Trajan, Baths of Trajan). However, during the years 98–117, little significant attention was paid to constructions or restorations in the Campus Martius. Renewed activity on the plain took place in earnest, however, during the early years of the reign of Hadrian. The *Historia Augusta* provides a brief description of Hadrian's building projects in the capital: "At Rome he restored the Pantheon [Pantheum], the Voting-enclosure [Saepta], the Basilica of Neptune, very many temples, the Forum of Augustus, the Baths of Agrippa, and dedicated all of them in the names of their original builders."[67]

Hadrian spent ample resources in the central Campus to restore earlier structures and, like much of his program, his interests focused on projects associated with Augustus and the Julian *gens*. His work on the Augustan Saepta appears to have involved a reconstruction of the west portico of the building, including an access route between the northwest corner of the Saepta portico and the facade of the Pantheon.[68] Also associated with Hadrian's constructions in this area is the large hall located south of the Pantheon and most often associated with the Agrippan Basilica of Neptune.[69] Hadrian's restoration of the Baths of Agrippa should also be seen as part of this overall program of renewal and refurbishment of structures associated with Augustus and Agrippa in the central zone of the Campus Martius.

One of the best-preserved ancient structures in Rome is also one of the most enigmatic – Hadrian's Pantheon (Plan 4, No. 14).[70] Like Agrippa's earlier structure on whose site it rests, Hadrian's Pantheon is the object of intense scholarly discourse as to its function and meaning. Unlike the Augustan era structure, the Hadrianic building at least has an observable architecture, but after centuries of alterations, questions about dating and form still remain (Plate I).[71] The structure comprises three primary elements: the porch, an intermediate block, and a drum or rotunda. Originally, the Pantheon was set atop a podium with five marble steps leading to the *pronaos*, but the rise in the level of the ground around the building has buried this area to the level of the porch paving. The *pronaos* bears a total of sixteen columns with monolithic shafts of Egyptian granite, with eight gray granite columns across the facade (*octostyle*). Four rows of two red granite columns each are arranged to divide the porch area into three distinct aisles. All of the columns display *entasis* (subtle diminution of diameter as they rise) and all bear Corinthian capitals and bases of white marble. The columns are 40 Roman feet (11.8 meters) high, which is large but not uncommon in ancient Roman construction.[72] The wider central aisle leads to the main doorway, while the side aisles terminate in large niches that possibly held statues of Augustus and Agrippa, perhaps preserved from the earlier structure.[73] All of the porch columns carry entablatures, which over the two inner rows of columns support piers and arches. This system, together with the exterior columns and their entablatures, once bore a bronze roof structure removed in the seventeenth century. Today, the tiled roof is supported by wooden framing that is visible from below, although in Hadrian's day it was likely covered by an imitation barrel vault.[74] The restored porch pavement consists of dark granite and white marble forming patterns of oblongs, squares, and circles. The pediment of the porch (which is now blank) reveals attachment holes, some ancient, indicating that decorative elements were applied to the space. It has been conjectured that a bronze eagle within a wreath graced the center.[75] Bronze letters, although not original, do remain in place on the architrave proclaiming: M AGRIPPA L F COS TERTIVM FECIT

(Marcus Agrippa, the son of Lucius, three times consul, built this). While Agrippa was given credit in the inscription for the construction, Augustus's friend and builder of the original Pantheon was long dead when this structure was erected.[76] One ancient source states that it was the emperor's modesty that caused him to proclaim Agrippa as the builder.[77]

Tying the rectangular porch to the cylindrical central structure is a transitional block that is the same width as the porch but the same height as the rotunda. Like the domed rotunda behind, the rectangular connector was constructed almost entirely out of brick and mortar. The transitional block has two side chambers that extend all the way up to the top of the structure with staircases leading to several vaulted chambers. One of the oddities of the relationship of the porch to the intermediate block is that the latter is as high as the top of the drum behind it, while the *pronaos* is not, resulting in "two stacked, interfering pediments of the pronaos and transitional block" (Figure 46).[78] The differential would have been solved if the builders had used columns for the porch that were fifty Roman feet in height instead of forty, and it has been proposed that the resulting configuration was the product of an architectural compromise when the larger shafts could not be obtained to meet the construction schedule.[79]

Behind the intermediate block is the domed rotunda that is nearly twice as high and two-thirds as wide as the pedimental porch. The interior volume is contained within an almost perfect sphere measuring 147 Roman feet (43.5 meters) from the floor to the ceiling, as the hemispherical dome is as tall as the drum on which it rests.[80] The dome itself, made of solid concrete fashioned from pumice, a relatively light volcanic stone aggregate, was poured over a huge wooden form shaped like the resulting hemisphere and supported by wooden scaffolds.[81] Each coffer likely contained a gilded rosette in the center and a molding around its edge.[82] At the top of the dome, an opening (*oculus*) 30 Roman feet (8.9 meters) in diameter and edged in gilded bronze allowed in natural light as well as the elements.[83] It continues to do so today (Figure 47).

There are two stories beneath the vast expanse of the dome. The first story consists of eight large recessed bays between eight hidden piers. Six of the bays are screened by two columns each. Between the niches and in front of each pier is a *tabernacle* or *aedicule* on a raised podium. The space is faced in various colored marbles from throughout the empire. As William MacDonald has noted, "The result is a scenic, theatre-like wall, richly worked with light and shade, cornerless and continuous."[84] The second story, substantially modified in the eighteenth century, contained a pattern of alternating blind windows and pilasters over a band of marble.[85] The floor was decorated with thin slabs of colored stones (granites, marbles, and porphyry) arranged in a large geometric pattern much like a checkerboard.[86]

46. Detail, Pantheon porch and transitional block. (Photo: Paul Jacobs)

Efforts have been made over the centuries to find intentional symbolism in the interior's geometry. Writing decades after Hadrian's death, Cassius Dio thought the dome "resembles the heavens," but more recently it has been argued that the design of the Pantheon interior was an expression of Hadrianic intellectual and sensual interest in arithmetic ideals and geometry, with the arrangement of the coffers in 28 vertical lines, creating a deliberate visual manifestation of the second perfect number (28 equals the sum of its

47. Pantheon interior. (Photo: Paul Jacobs)

divisors, excluding itself: 1+2+4+7+14=28).[87] The obvious play of sunlight through the oculus has not gone unnoticed. At local noon on April 21, the sun's rays entering the oculus strike the north-facing door. This occurrence on Rome's birthday in a building sited in the area of Romulus's apotheosis and on the same day that the sunrise is in line with the east entrance to the Ara Pacis raises huge possibilities for intentional imperial symbolism.[88]

The Pantheon we see today was completed early in Hadrian's reign, likely sometime in the period 125–28 c.e.[89] It has been generally accepted that the project began in 118/19 c.e.[90] Approximately the same height as Augustus's mausoleum, the Pantheon's dome could be appreciated at a distance, but the drum was mostly hidden by surrounding structures.[91] A forecourt framed by a colonnade extended some 100 to 150 meters north, and visitors would reach the *pronaos* through either lateral stairs or the flanking colonnade.[92] The fact that the exterior design was well hidden must have made the interior that much more surprising and extraordinary to those allowed entrance. While its name in Greek, Pantheon (*Pantheum* in Latin), technically referred to a temple dedicated to all the gods, there is disagreement whether this label was a nickname or an official designation.[93] Cassius Dio recorded that sometime after 125 c.e., Hadrian used the space as an imperial audience hall, reading proclamations from a tribunal upon his return to the capital following one of his tours of the empire.[94]

In addition to his construction of the Pantheon, Hadrian commissioned a precinct in the central Campus Martius for the worship of his deified mother-in-law, Matidia (Plan 4, No. 13). The complex, which may have also included basilicas dedicated to Matidia and Marciana, appears to have been a large peripteral temple surrounded by deep porticoes, the columns of which may have been constructed from different-colored imported granite.[95] Taken together, the Pantheon and the nearby Diva Matidia complex offer additional support for the hypothesis that Hadrian deliberately refurbished Augustan structures and constructed new dynastic buildings to celebrate his family and their connections with the glorious past of Augustan Rome. No district of the capital was more suited for such a building program than the central Campus Martius.[96]

Following Hadrian's death in 138 c.e., work commenced on a temple in the central Campus Martius just east of the Temple of Matidia. It was dedicated to the Divine Hadrian (Divus Hadrianus) in 145 c.e. by his successor Antoninus Pius (r. 138–61) (Plan 4, No. 4).[97] Eleven of the original thirteen fluted, Proconnesian marble columns of the northern flank of the peristyle can be seen on the northern side of the Palazzo della Borsa (former Roman Stock Exchange) in Piazza di Pietra (Figure 48).[98] Originally, the temple had a frontal staircase on the east, all raised on a podium made of peperino tufa and faced with marble. The *cella* was roofed by a coffered barrel vault (similar to the coffered vestibule of the intermediate block of the Pantheon), a section of which is still preserved inside the former Borsa. The interior was accentuated by engaged columns.[99] In the area around the temple, twenty-four marble panels and pedestals have been discovered that have been associated with the temple

48. Temple of Divine Hadrian, Piazza di Pietra, Rome. (Photo: Paul Jacobs)

or an enclosing portico.[100] They display reliefs of allegorical figures believed to represent the Roman provinces alternating with reliefs of weapons and trophies (Figure 49). The entablature of the interior *cella* colonnade had a frieze of spiraling acanthus candelabras possibly presenting a deliberate association with common Augustan decorative iconography.[101]

Following the death of Antoninus Pius, an unfluted, red granite column was raised to his memory and that of his wife Faustina in the northern Campus Martius southwest of Augustus's horologium complex.[102] Approximately 14.75 meters high, the shaft sat on a white marble base, now in the Vatican (Figure 50).[103] In keeping with the imperial theme of apotheosis with which the Campus Martius had become associated, the base displayed a relief of Antoninus Pius and his wife lifted to heaven on the wings of a figure thought

49. Marble panels from the area of the Temple of Divine Hadrian, Musei Capitolini. (Photo: Scala / Art Resource, New York)

50. Column of Antoninus Pius, base relief (ca. 161 B.C.E.). Apotheosis of Antoninus Pius and his wife Faustina. Vatican Museum. (Photo: Album / Art Resource, New York)

to be Aion, a god of eternity. An eagle above each of the god's wings symbolized the spirits of the divine couple ascending to the heavens. To the lower right is the goddess Roma, seated and surrounded by weapons; to the left is a reclining seminude personification of the Campus Martius holding an obelisk with an orb, likely the obelisk that served as the gnomon for the Horologium Augusti.[104] Flanking reliefs on the base show funeral rites (*decursio*) performed prior to lighting the pyre. Given the types and locations of funerary monuments in this zone of the central Campus Martius, one scholar has labeled this area of the plain as an Antonine "apotheosis landscape."[105]

While the base of the Antoninus Pius column and nearby commemorative funerary altars reminded Romans that its greatest leaders left for heaven from the Field of Mars, another nearby Antonine monument reflected the space's military themes. In honor of the defeat of the Sarmatians and the Marcomanni in 172–75 C.E. by the emperor Marcus Aurelius (r. 161–80), the Senate commissioned a large column to be erected just west of the Via Flaminia in the northern Campus Martius (Figure 51).[106] Comprising twenty-six drums of Luna marble with an internal spiral staircase of 200 steps, the monument on its base rises 100 Roman feet (29.77 meters).[107] Clearly based on the design of the earlier column of Trajan in the Forum of Trajan, scenes of the two campaigns of Marcus Aurelius are deeply carved into the marble and are separated by a

51. Column of Marcus Aurelius, Piazza Colonna, Rome. (Photo: Paul Jacobs)

52. Detail, Column of Marcus Aurelius, "Miracle of the Rain," Piazza Colonna, Rome. (Photo: Paul Jacobs)

personification of Victoria. The depictions of violence are graphic, including the beheading of barbarian men and the brutal capture of provincial women and children. Most famous is the "Miracle of the Rain" scene, which depicts a bearded god with outstretched arms dispensing a torrential storm to aid the entrenched Roman legions (Figure 52). The position of the column and its decorated pedestal base on the Via Flaminia was deliberate and purposeful. The most important scenes in the helical reliefs (Victory, Rain Miracle, Crossing the Danube) as well as the pedestal entrance doorway to the internal spiral staircase were easily seen from the roadway.[108]

162 CAMPUS MARTIUS

THE SEVERANS AND LATE ANTIQUITY

As was the case with the first two Flavian emperors, as well as Nerva and Trajan, the Severans did not commit many resources to constructions in the already crowded central and southern zones of the Campus Martius. Their interests in commissioning new structures were focused on other regions of the capital, and Severan restorations of structures on the plain are limited, such as poorly understood minor repairs of the Hadrianic Pantheon.[109] This early third-century restoration of the Pantheon was a minuscule manifestation of the much broader program of Septimius Severus to connect his dynasty with areas of and structures in Rome associated with the Divine Augustus.[110] The last emperor of the Severan dynasty, Alexander Severus (r. 222–35), rebuilt and enlarged the earlier Baths of Nero in 227 C.E. as discussed in Chapter 6.

The next major architectural changes to the Campus would not be realized until the reign of Aurelian (r. 270–5 C.E.). Construction of an 11-kilometer-long, 6.5-meter-high brick wall, fortified with defensive turrets at regular intervals, was begun sometime before Aurelian's wars against Zenobia in 271–2 C.E. Work on the massive structure continued for another ten years; it was finally dedicated by Aurelian's successor, Probus (r. 276–82 C.E.), while extensive restorations and additions continued in the fourth and early fifth centuries.[111] The erection of Aurelian's Wall marks the first time that the fortified physical boundary of the city incorporated the Campus Martius, as previously the so-called Servian Wall had not included the plain within its much smaller perimeter. Following Aurelian's defensive construction, the Campus was integrated once and for all within the official, imperial-sanctioned boundary of the capital city.

SPACES BETWEEN THE MONUMENTS

Over three centuries, the emperors left their deep imprint on the Field of Mars, filling most of the plain with baths, temples, porticoes, and theaters. There remained, however, room in the interstices among the grand structures in which to squeeze residential and commercial establishments. This helped assure that the Campus Martius would function as a living space as well as a destination for entertainment and relaxation. As early as the first century B.C.E., public land in the plain was sold to raise money for the treasury, and Caesar planned to enlarge the Campus Martius and create living space for an increasingly crowded city.[112] His scheme was not realized, of course, and apart from several notable villas, housing in the Field of Mars was kept in check by the large areas devoted to massive public buildings and parks. Nevertheless, as the great monuments were erected in the imperial era, residents also moved in. By the fourth century C.E., the northern plain reportedly contained almost

2,800 *insulae*, approximately 6 percent of all such units in the city at the time, and 140 or almost 8 percent of the city's private homes.[113] Although these numbers appear impressive, given the size of the Campus Martius, the density of *insulae* there has been calculated to be the lowest of the fourteen regions and the density of *domus* near the lowest, reflecting the large area occupied by public buildings.[114] Glimpses of some of these buildings can still be found under the modern city. Beneath a cinema just east of the Corso and close by the Trevi Fountain are the remains of a three- or four-story apartment building constructed following the great fire of 64 C.E. In the fourth century, the structure was converted to a luxurious home.[115] Northwest of the Circus Flaminius, a *horrea* dating to the late first century C.E. was converted in the late second to early third century C.E. to an *insula*. Portions of the structure are still visible under a palazzo on the Via di S. Paolo alla Regola.[116] Just north of the Stadium of Domitian and beneath the Renaissance Palazzo Altemps, now a museum, can be found walls from a reception room of a grand first-century C.E. *domus*.[117]

In the northern Campus Martius near the horologium and Ara Pacis, beautiful homes began to occupy the still-open spaces in the late second century C.E., only to be replaced by large *insulae* in the third century. Parallel to the Via Lata and just north of the Ara Pacis, a large *insula* was constructed. At least two stories in height, it contained commercial establishments or businesses for small industry on the ground floor. The remains beneath the Church of San Lorenzo in Lucina disclose a row of nine rooms running north and south with a staircase. Brick stamps date the construction to the time of Caracalla (r. 198–217 C.E.), and the building was in use until the early church basilica was constructed in the fourth century C.E.[118] Evidence of another large second-century C.E. structure, possibly an *insula*, has been found just north of the Church of San Lorenzo in Lucina.[119] The deliberately triangulated space created by Augustus two centuries earlier to express the glories of his reign was now giving way to pedestrian structures that reflected a Campus Martius for the masses.

CONCLUSION

With the concentration of state power in the hands of the emperors, the Campus Martius converted from a mostly open and occasionally visited marshland to an integral part of the city, imbued with symbols of its past and altered to accommodate the exigencies of the expanding urban space. Development under Augustus was no longer small scale and piecemeal, as the wealth and political will of the principate could be brought to bear, transforming large spaces within decades rather than centuries. Where republican military might had been accommodated seasonally in a flat, open topography of swamp and grasses, imperial strength became reflected daily in a landscape of organized, marbled edifices stretching skyward. What had been the area for war, tribal elections, and celebrations of individual accomplishments during the republic became the people's marble park, a crowded but salubrious space where inhabitants could stroll, play, negotiate, and live in the shade of imperial cult temples and permanent stone memorials. Grandiose imperial spaces enveloped the small nodes of republican development. Drainage channels and aqueducts allowed imperial style bathhouses and artificial lakes to replace ponds. Whereas some emperors such as Nero and Domitian focused their resources on building public entertainment and leisure facilities, others followed Augustus's lead and commissioned magnificent temples and funerary monuments designed to declare and perpetuate the ideologies of imperial apotheosis and dynastic continuity. In the field that saw the ascension of Romulus, where Rome's first king dissipated in a mist, later emperors created monuments to ensure the permanent record of their own apotheoses. The imperial structures were designed to attract visitors and, in turn, created the conditions for residential and commercial development in the spaces between the monuments. The zeal for building had overtaken the grassy spaces of Strabo where one could exercise without hindrance, and after three centuries the Field of Mars endured, but fully urbanized, converted and transformed in use and import, subsumed by its "mere accessory."

CONCLUSION: "THE REST OF THE CITY A MERE ACCESSORY"

From the time of its mythical founding in the mid-eighth century B.C.E. and for the next 500 years, Rome expanded its living and working spaces across its hills and valleys and, with a seasonal rhythm, ventured beyond its protected position to confront and defeat other tribes throughout the Italian Peninsula. A large swath of real estate just to the north of Rome's walls remained, however, in its natural state, unconquered and untamed. While other low-lying portions of Rome were drained and built upon, the area between the Tiber and the Pincian and Quirinal Hills stayed a swampy, mosquito-infested clearing to which citizens came periodically to muster for military exercises, to be counted in the census and to vote, and, at the far southern end, to shop at a vegetable market. The natural and austere conditions of the marshland for that half millennium suited perfectly the needs of a growing military power that required a large unencumbered space in which to gather and train its troops. Religious and very practical social policies forbade armed soldiers to cross the sacred line or *pomerium* and to enter the *urbis*, except in the event of a military triumph. When awarded a parade for valor in battle, a consul would gather his troops in the northern field to march into the city with captives and booty. The populace could be counted in the plain while protected by the army, and the surrounding hills provided excellent observation points for all to be carefully watched. It mattered little that the marshland flooded in the winter or was infested in the summer, as the designated activities generally could be timed to avoid those issues.

Used for centuries as a location to prepare for battle and triumphal parades, the campus developed early associations with Rome's god of war, Mars. Horses raced across the plain in his honor in the spring and in the fall, while on the Ides of March, the deity's eponymous month, revelers raced to the area to celebrate the New Year. An altar to Mars was constructed there, and by the mid- to late first century B.C.E., writers were referring to that portion of the field west of the Via Flaminia as the Campus Martius. When the myths of Rome's founding by a son of Mars, Romulus, were developed in the early third century B.C.E., it was the northern flatland that was selected as the site of the ruler's apotheosis. The anniversary of this event was celebrated with running and shouting, mock battles, and dining in the campus. In another myth, the republic was said to have been founded upon the seizure of the last king's grain growing there. The stalks were tossed into the plain's watery western boundary, and when captured by the rocks at the southern end, the accumulated grasses helped create the Tiber Island.

As the myths linking the Campus Martius to Rome's foundation were emerging, the military imperative to maintain the real estate in its natural environment was diminishing. In the 100-year period from the mid-third to the mid-second centuries B.C.E., the era of the three Punic Wars, Rome began to send its troops far from the Italian mainland and for more than seasonal duty. With reduced use by the military, the field beckoned for development. At first only permanent structures deemed consistent with its mythical and martial past, namely victory monuments, were erected. Consuls in the heat of battle prayed to gods. Returning victoriously to Rome, they honored the solicited deity with a temple. Approximately half of all temples vowed during the century of Punic Wars were located in the Field of Mars. If the open plain north of the city was deemed sacred to Mars, such "sacredness" certainly did not hinder its development; if anything, it encouraged it.

Placed in three large nodes where they could be admired during the gatherings of the census or at the collection point for triumphal parades, these temples, ostentatiously endowed with statuary and other symbols of foreign conquest, brought honor to their patrons and to the city. Two of those areas, the Circus Flaminius and the Forum Holitorium, became better defined by the temples erected along the edges of each. During the same period, the Via Flaminia cut through the heart of the plain, establishing thereafter the campus's eastern line and facilitating both military and commercial travel from the city walls to the northern horizon. Porticoes employed as ceremonial walkways or embellishments to sacred precincts made their debut in Rome during this period, finding their first expression in the northern plain. As the space was beyond the *pomerium*, the Field of Mars was still an important location for soldiers to form up for triumphal parades, for foreign ambassadors to await the right to enter the city and for citizens to vote and to be counted in the census. There was still ample room for these activities, and the placement of temples and porticoes was clearly made with those continuing functions in mind.

It does appear evident from the ancient sources that a certain level of architectural experimentation was undertaken in the republican structures erected in the Field of Mars. Captivated by the building design and decoration seen in their forays to the East, Rome's generals used the marshy soil of the Campus Martius as test plots to develop these architectural forms that then took root throughout the city. At first, Greek elements were grafted to the older Etruscan styles. Later, other eastern architectural elements found their initial expression in the northern plain with the first structure in the city made entirely of marble and the first victory monument in Rome to be fashioned in the form of a colonnade. A confluence of factors likely explains the choice of the Campus Martius for the exploitation of new architectural forms, but certainly the location of the space beyond the pomerial line may have afforded license to challenge the traditional forms in a way that was not possible within the city proper.

Topography played an indirect role in temple construction in the Campus Martius in the sense that the open flat plain was well suited for the periodic large public gatherings, and the builders of such structures would want to place them in close proximity to those sites. It did not appear to place great constraints, however, on the orientation and relationship of the temples as the wide plain allowed the three primary nodes to develop without clear reference to each other. The Circus Flaminius ran from the southeast to the northwest, roughly following the line of the Tiber at that point, and the temples around it were oriented toward the center of the space. The temples in the Largo Argentina faced due east in the direction of the morning sun and the nearby Villa Publica. The temples in the Forum Holitorium opened to the northeast, far to the south of the Largo Argentina. If they communicated at all, it was in the shared themes of military glory and as possible way stations on the triumphal parade route. The buildings themselves did little to alter the topography and did not likely disrupt the prior rhythm of popular use of the space. Rome's residents flocked to the Campus Martius for holidays and special events; the temples were embellishments and would not have changed the established activities that occurred in the field.

In the mid-first century B.C.E., topography played a more central role in the site determination of more grandiose buildings, and these, in turn, altered both the landscape and the uses of the Field of Mars. Until that time, theatrical performances were held in the campus near temples as part of religious festivals as well as in large temporary theaters. With respect to the latter venues, space within the city walls was at a premium in the middle to late republican period, and a wooden stage could be erected on a temporary basis in the Field of Mars without much effort and removed just as easily when its presence was deemed offensive to the public good. When objection to permanent theatrical structures waned in the late republic, the flat space of the Campus Martius was perfect for creating a new form of freestanding entertainment site. It was here that Pompey the Great erected Rome's first permanent stone theater. Engineered to withstand massive loads above marshy soil and employing materials impervious to rising floodwaters, the theater met and withstood the challenges of building in the Campus Martius. Constructed beyond the city walls, the theater did not require the demolition of existing structures, an issue that could provoke political backlash. It was also raised at a time and place that lessened the risk for criticism, although Pompey's effort still had its detractors.

The theater's construction in the plain was transformative. At about the same height as the Capitoline and more than half its area, Pompey's enormous stone structure was a "veritable mountain," and with its appended *quadriportico* it dominated the Field of Mars like no previous building and like very few since.[1] Its size, significance, and uses, as well as the authority of its builder, created its own gravity that soon drew other large structures in its direction and oriented them on an orthogonal grid. For the first time, the Field of Mars had an attraction that gave Rome's populace a reason to venture north of the *pomerium*. Now, the city's inhabitants came frequently and in large numbers for entertainment and relaxation in beautiful gardens. The Campus Martius was no longer simply a site at which to practice for war or honor victors or past victories. It was a magnet for quotidian pleasures.

Built as the republic was in its death throes and before the empire arose, the theater's construction in the plain was also transitional. Located close to one of the established republican temple nodes, the theater also carried on its shoulders a series of religious spaces, but its size and function presaged the many large utilitarian and secular spaces to be developed there by the emperors. Its chronological and physical positions in the development of the northern marshland as well as its architecture allowed Pompey's theater to serve as a bridge between the republican past and the imperial future of the Field of Mars.

There was, however, one other general with the prestige and financial means to equal if not best Pompey in construction in the Campus Martius, and he had the plans to do so. Julius Caesar built a basin for the similacra of sea battles, cleared land for a theater, and proposed a new voting precinct, the Saepta. He even conceived the idea of shifting the Tiber west to add more land to the northern field. None of these projects save the naumachia, however, was ever brought to fruition by Caesar. Instead (ironically), he died in an annex to Pompey's own portico structure, and his dreams for the plain were not to be realized for at least another decade, when his heir Octavian, fresh from his victory over Mark Antony, turned his attention to the northern field.

Octavian, the future Augustus, tackled the Campus Martius from three different directions and, in a sense, in three different ways. On the northern narrow throat where all must pass along the important Via Flaminia, he built his mausoleum. It was as high as Pompey's theater and with its surrounding parks challenged it for dominance of the plain. As a burial site, its *extrapomerial* location was appropriate, and its massive structure countered the "gravity" of the Theater of Pompey. At the far southern end of the plain, the Augustan theater dedicated to Marcellus counterbalanced the mausoleum, and like Pompey's theater, it helped anchor traditional republican temple nodes, resting between and dominating the Circus Flaminius and Forum Holitorium. As the mausoleum provided a very visible demarcation to the northern edge of the Campus Martius, the Theater of Marcellus was similarly sited at the southern end. Indeed, Augustus became the gatekeeper with respect to triumphal parades moving south. No longer could such spectacles move through the Circus Flaminius to the city gates without first going through his family's theater. The emperor's improvements in that area did not stop with the theater, however. Temples were rebuilt and expanded with libraries and new porticoes added. Statues to the deified Augustus were erected there, as well as later an arch to the deceased Germanicus. The symbols of Augustan power were everywhere, and the individualized monuments to a republican past were transformed into a unified glorification of an imperial present.

It was in the central Campus Martius that Augustus left, perhaps, his most profound mark. Near where both the founder of Rome, Romulus, and Julius Caesar had died, he oversaw the draining of a swampland and the construction of marvels of engineering, the traces of which can be seen today in the streets leading north from the Largo Argentina. Entrusted to carry out the work, Augustus's comrade Marcus Agrippa built the Pantheon with statues honoring his emperor, the Saepta Julia with its extraordinary parallel porticoes, and the Diribitorium with the largest roof under a single beam, as well as Rome's first imperial-style public bathhouse. Basins, pools, and fountains were added. To provide the massive amount of fresh water needed for the space and for other development across the river, an aqueduct was constructed. To counter the Tiber's floodwater, the buildings were of brick and concrete and drainage pipes were added. Large spaces, confined within porticoes, were embellished with trees and adorned with statuary and were connected to each other by still other porticoes. Where citizens previously had come to walk quietly through open fields, now they strolled or jostled within a network of marbled colonnades. While still consolidating the reins of power, Octavian had encouraged those allied with him to build within the Campus Martius, and two other entertainment venues were constructed there, an amphitheater and another theater. With voting of lessening significance in the imperial age, the Saepta Julia was turned into another site for shows. In a few short decades the Campus Martius had gone from a spacious war memorial and periodic gathering place to a crowded entertainment district. Now sufficiently developed, the plain was included in Augustus's revamped *regiones* as Region IX, Circus Flaminius, subdivided into neighborhoods with elected magistrates. Still beyond the *pomerium*, it was beginning, nevertheless, to have the look and feel of an urban district.

The one part of the Field of Mars that maintained its openness, although now more manicured, was the area between the Aqua Virgo and the mausoleum. Augustus returned to this space late in life and erected symbols of Rome's past and imperial present. Between the area where Romulus ascended to heaven and where Augustus was to be buried, he erected an Egyptian obelisk that cast the sun's shadow on a bronze meridian inlaid in a travertine block pavement. Dedicated to the sun god Sol and proclaiming his defeat of Egypt decades earlier, as well as his recently achieved title as Pontifex Maximus, the horologium was built contemporaneously with an altar celebrating an era of Augustan peace. The Ara Pacis was covered with sculpted images of Rome's legendary founders, Romulus, Remus, and Aeneas or Numa as well as Augustus, Agrippa, and members of the emperor's family. Whether or not the gnomon's shadow pointed to the altar on the emperor's birthday, the horologium, altar, and mausoleum were clearly meant to imbue the northernmost portion of the plain with rich symbols linking the field's mythical past with the imperial present. In its totality, the Augustan Campus Martius must have been to citizens and visitors alike a marbled wonderland that allowed Strabo without hesitation to denigrate the rest of the city as "a mere accessory."

With the model established by Rome's first emperor, Augustus's successors did not hesitate to expend large sums on refurbishing older structures there and adding to an increasingly crowded landscape. Some of the work was necessitated by devastating fires that ruined structures in a manner that periodic flooding could not. A few buildings such as the Pantheon were built on a grander scale after their destruction, others such as the Diribitorium were just left open to the sky when its roof collapsed, and still others such as the Amphitheater of Statilius Taurus were never rebuilt. The shrunken remaining space of the Villa Publica that had served as a republican gathering space for so many centuries was enclosed after the fire of 80 C.E. into the Divorum, a temple complex that possibly contained the altar to Mars that had sat alone in the field centuries earlier.

While there was sufficient clear space in the center of the plain in the midfirst century C.E. for the Neronian baths to be constructed but a few hundred meters from those of Agrippa, by the time that they were expanded a century and a half later by Alexander Severus, nearby buildings were demolished to make room. The Aqua Virgo that had met most of the freshwater needs of the Campus Martius was now insufficient. A second aqueduct had to be erected to supply Alexander's baths. Room was found for additional temples, and entertainment venues were also wedged into the space with Domitian adding a stadium for Greek games and the Odeum for musical performances and other spectacles.

Reinforcing the themes of imperial divinity and apotheosis that had been established by Augustus, Hadrian and his Antonine successors added a temple to Hadrian's mother-in-law, the Divine Matidia, and a temple to the Divine Hadrian built by Antoninus Pius. Two memorial columns were erected. One displayed scenes along the shaft of Marcus Aurelius's battlefield victories. On the base of another, Antoninus Pius and his wife were shown rising heavenward while a personification of the Campus Martius held up the horologium gnomon. Monuments memorializing their *ustrina* are believed to have been in the same vicinity.

As the Campus Martius became more tightly integrated with the city proper to the south, the significance of the pomerial boundary became blurred. Claudius redrew the sacred lines that pushed the ceremonial limits into the central Campus Martius, and in the late third century C.E., the Aurelian Wall brought the entire Campus Martius within the physical embrace of the city. Apart from the monumental structures that nestled tightly together, remaining room existed in the spaces between colonnades, baths, and temples to be filled by more utilitarian edifices. Apartment buildings contributed to the density and verticality of the Field of Mars. Whatever distinctions relegated the city to "accessory" status at the time of Augustus, by the late third century C.E., the once-open field and the city proper were one and the same, with as many as a million people coursing through the tight arteries connecting the various portions of the urban space. A millennium had passed since the city's mythical founder rose in a cloud from the swampy field, and centuries had elapsed since troops mustered there for battles against northern tribes. Memorials to that storied past still remained and were likely admired by those not otherwise racing to a show, the baths, or their next meal. Over time, however, they too would fall, leaving only a palimpsest for the modern city to trace.

EPILOGUE

Before another millennium had passed, the Campus Martius of the early common era was barely recognizable, but the standing structures and the detritus of a once great empire left a profound impression on those who wandered through the space. Writing in the twelfth or thirteenth century, a learned visitor to Rome from England, Magister Gregorius, marveled at those edifices in the Field of Mars whose antiquity was clear but whose names were not as certain.[2] Gregorius admired statues collected from fallen temples in the area of the Pantheon and arranged in front of the rotunda, later to be recorded in drawings by other visitors to the city, some of whom even took the time to measure the impressive width of the building.[3] Yet by this date, few of Rome's monumental imperial edifices remained intact. Looking down at the city from the heights of one of Rome's hills, Gregorius recorded that the grand structures of the ancient world had been replaced by a "forest of [medieval] towers."[4] Another visitor needed no sylvan metaphor to describe the urban disintegration. Now overgrown, parts of the city were "thick woods [with] wild beasts, hares, foxes, deer and even so it is said porcupines breed in the caves."[5] The level topography of the once marshy field that had been so dramatically altered by great marble-faced buildings was transformed further as newer structures were erected on the ruins of the old. In 1581, the great French essayist Michel Montaigne traveled to Rome and noted in his journal that "upon the very wrecks of the ancient buildings, as they fall to ruin, the builders set out casually the foundations of new houses, as if these fragments were great masses of rock, firm and trustworthy. It is evident that many of the old streets lie more than thirty feet below the level of those now in existence."[6]

The destruction of the imperial Field of Mars, however, occurred slowly. To any one generation, change was almost imperceptible and certainly did not take place in a linear manner. For instance, in the fourth century C.E., while stones from the Theater of Marcellus were being taken to repair the Pons Cestius and a glassmaking shop was set up in the portico adjacent to Balbus's theater, an enormous portico, the Porticus Maximae, was built from the Circus Flaminius to the Pons Aelius. Concurrently, a large temple and portico to Bonus Eventus was erected near Agrippa's baths, and the Theater of Pompey, still a site for popular entertainment, was repaired.[7] The emperor had moved from Rome to Constantinople, but the show, as it were, went on. When the emperor Constantius II traveled to the former imperial capital in the mid-fourth century C.E., he visited the Theater of Pompey and the Stadium of Domitian and marveled at the Pantheon appearing "like a self-contained district under its high and lovely dome."[8] The year before his arrival, however, the pagan temples that had been financed by republican generals in thanks for battles won were closed. Buildings dedicated to the Christian prince of peace now began to occupy the space. Some temples became the supporting material for early Roman churches. S. Nicola in Carcere, built in the sixth century, sits over the Temple of Juno Sospita in the Forum Holitorium with the ruins of Spes and Janus hard up against it. Rather than being razed, the Pantheon became S. Maria ad Martyres in the early seventh century. In 663 its bronze roof tiles were removed, later to be replaced with lead, an act that Gregorius decried as the result of "excessive avarice and the 'excessive greed for gold.'"[9]

Once protected by its walls and its military might, Rome was clearly susceptible to attack after its capital moved. It was burned and sacked twice in the fifth century, first for three days by the Visigoths in 410, and then for fourteen by the Vandals in 455. In 472, the city suffered a five-month siege. What structures invaders did not completely destroy were weakened or leveled by the forces of nature. Three powerful earthquakes racked the city between 408 and 508, and two major floods washed over the low-lying spaces in 398 and 411.[10] The fallen marble facing and columns were often just tossed into kilns (calcaria) and burned into lime powder for reuse in mortar for newer buildings. Set up near the Baths of Agrippa, the kilns gave the district its nickname, calcarium, and were used into the Renaissance.[11] In some respects the ancient Campus Martius did not simply fall down, it melted away.

By the ninth century new roads had been cut through the ancient porticoes, obscuring the orthogonal lines set during the late republic and early imperial era in the central Campus Martius.[12] The massive stone theaters were converted from entertainment venues to strongholds and residences. Balbus's theater became known as the Castrum Aureum or "Golden Castle" and the Theater of Marcellus, which was in ruins by the eighth century, became a fortress in the twelfth century and was then transformed into a palazzo in the sixteenth. The great Theater of Pompey was restored and held performances as late as the sixth century, but it, too, was in ruins by the eighth century and then succumbed to the development needs of one of the wealthy Roman families. In the thirteenth century, the Orsini turned the cavea into a fortress.[13]

The population of Rome shrank in the early medieval period to just a few thousand residents, perhaps as low as 5,000. While it has been generally assumed that this handful of people was concentrated primarily in the Campus Martius, recent scholarship suggests that the plain was essentially deserted until the tenth century when clerics and nobles moved in, seizing large unoccupied areas for monasteries and palaces.[14] A millennium after Augustus, a new generation of powerful men recognized the potential of the Campus Martius for development and erected imposing structures on the plain north of the Capitoline. Although the construction in the Field of Mars during the age of the emperors was dictated in large part by the space's mythical past, the medieval and Renaissance building projects were in spite of it. Over time, the rubble-filled plain developed mounds, or monti, now referenced in several street names and buildings, as the ground level rose above the foundations and walls of ancient structures. The Theater of Marcellus became the "Monte Savello," and on a rise in the street behind the location of the Circus Flaminius is the Monte dei Cenci.[15]

Many visitors to Rome over the centuries have despaired over the loss of the antique. Gregorius lamented, "For although all of Rome lies in ruin, nothing intact can be compared to this. . . . I believe this ruin teaches us clearly that all temporal things will soon pass away, especially as Rome, the epitome of earthly glory, languishes and declines so much every day."[16] Some reached for metaphors to describe, perhaps wistfully, the ruins around them. In 1535, the humanist Alexander Steuco wrote, "Often . . . wandering through the ruins of the ancient city, I was not able to contain either my tears or sighs, partly commiserating over the miserable destruction of so great a city, partly deploring the instability of human things. . . . Everything is cadaverous, in ruins, just like the bones of a once beautiful body."[17] Four hundred years later Charles Dickens described the "battered pillars of old Pagan temples, dug up from the ground, and forced, like giant captives, to support the roof of Christian churches."[18] Slowly, over time, the ancient calcium "bones" were absorbed into the surrounding structures. By Dickens's day, the surviving scattered column drums, capitals, and other marble pieces, not otherwise scooped up to fill private collections or grace *palazzi*, could be seen protruding from stuccoed walls. As the English novelist observed, "It is strange to see, how every fragment, whenever it is possible, has been blended into some modern structure, and made to serve some modern purpose – a wall, a dwelling place, a granary, a stable – some use for which it never was designed, and associated with which it cannot otherwise than lamely assort."[19]

Having been on the outskirts of Rome proper for so many centuries, the former Campus Martius today is the *centro storico*, the historic center. It is now mostly a baroque space punctuated throughout with Renaissance, medieval, and ancient structures. Preoccupation in the early twentieth century with the ancient past at the expense, perhaps, of its medieval successor resulted in the recovery of many ancient monuments that had been covered in part with the Tiber's deposits. Excavations around the Theater of Marcellus and in the Largo Argentina were conducted under the watchful eye of a latter-day emperor, Benito Mussolini, who also cleared the space around the mausoleum of Augustus to showcase his own imperial style of architecture. After 2,000 years, the Campus Martius still had the power to attract grandiose schemes. But while some have decried the disappearance of the ancient city and occasionally, like Mussolini, have tried to bring it back to the surface, the fact of the matter is that it never totally disappeared. Despite a few "monti," the field still opens as a wide plain below the surrounding hills, and its buildings preserve a profile not much different from that found at the height of the empire. Many of the ancient arterial routes can still be traced and the outlines of major monuments such as Pompey's theater and Domitian's stadium remain visible. But the real proof can be found in wandering the crowded streets of the *centro storico* during an early evening *passagiata* when the modern Romans, walking arm-in-arm, carry on the same conversations that animated their ancestors two millennia ago. The hawkers of street goods and food vendors continue to fill the travel paths. Selius can still be seen racing around looking for his next meal. Martial continues to complain about being dragged off to a passé establishment instead of a trendier one. The ancient Romans never left; they are all there. To those standing in the shadow of the Pantheon observing the birds circling above, lit by the setting sun, it is obvious today as it was to Strabo, the rest of the city is a "mere accessory."

APPENDIX A

CHRONOLOGY OF DEVELOPMENT IN THE CAMPUS MARTIUS TO THE EARLY FOURTH CENTURY C.E.

B.C.E.

753 – Traditional date for founding of Rome

435 – Villa Publica in use

431 – Temple of Apollo Medicus dedicated

390 – Rome sacked by the Gauls

298–290 – Third Samnite War

296 – Temple of Bellona vowed

290/225 – Alternative dates for vowing of Temple of Feronia

264 – Commencement of First Punic War

260 – Temple of Janus vowed

258–249 – Temple of Spes vowed

242 – Temple of Juturna vowed

241 – End of First Punic War

241 – Temple of Juno Curitis constructed after this date

221 – Circus Flaminius constructed

220 – Via Flaminia constructed

218 – Temple of Hercules Magnus Custos constructed before this date

218 – Commencement of Second Punic War

214 – Temple of Vulcan constructed before this date

206 – Temple of Neptune known in the Circus Flaminius

201 – End of Second Punic War

200 – 196 Second Macedonian War

194 – Temple of Juno Sospita dedicated; before this date structures in Villa Publica in use

193 – Construction of Porticus Aemilia from the Porta Fontinalis to the Ara Martis

181 – Temple of Pietas dedicated

179 – Temples of Lares Permarini, Diana, and Juno Regina (Juno the Queen) dedicated; Temple to Hercules Musarum (Hercules of the Muses) underway or completed

173 – Temple of Fortuna Equestris dedicated

172–168 – Third Macedonian War

168 – Construction of Porticus Octavia (Portico of Octavius)

149–148 – Fourth Macedonian War

149–146 – Third Punic War

146 – Porticus Metelli constructed after this date by the temples of Jupiter Stator and Juno Regina

133 – Approximate construction date for Temple of Mars in Circus Flaminius

110 – Approximate construction date of the Porticus Minucia Vetus

101 – Temple of Fortuna Huiusce Diei vowed

100/70 – Alternative dates for construction of Temple of Castor and Pollux

90 – Temple of Juno Sospita restored

90–88 – Social Wars

60 – Beginning of First Triumvirate of J. Caesar, M. Crassus, and Gn. Pompey

58 – Temporary Theater of Scaurus constructed

55 – Theater of Pompey dedicated

53 – End of First Triumvirate

53 – Temporary Theatra Curionis constructed

46 – Naumachia Caesaris constructed

44 – Death of Julius Caesar

43 – Naumachia Caesaris filled in

43 – Second Triumvirate of Octavian, M. Lepidus, and M. Antony

42 – Temple of Neptune possibly rebuilt after this date

33 – End of Second Triumvirate

33 – Porticus Octavia rebuilt

32 – Octavian restores Theater of Pompey; Temple of Apollo Sosianus rebuilt after this date

31 – Defeat of Antony and Cleopatra at Battle of Actium

31 – Temple of Spes burned and restored

29 – Temple of Hercules Musarum restored and surrounded by Porticus Philippi; Amphitheater of Statilius Taurus dedicated

28 – Mausoleum of Augustus under construction

27 – Octavian given title of Augustus and Princeps

27/25 – Agrippa's Pantheon constructed

26 – Saepta Julia dedicated

25 – Baths of Agrippa begun; Stoa of Poseidon/Basilica of Neptune built

23 – Dedication of Porticus Octaviae and refurbishment of temples of Juno Regina and Jupiter Stator

19 – Aqua Virgo completed; Baths of Agrippa, Stagnum Agrippae, Euripus Virginis, and Euripus Thermarum Agrippae receive Virgo waters

13 – Theater of Balbus and Crypta Balbi dedicated

13/11 – Theater of Marcellus dedicated

10/9 – Horologium Augusti gnomon erected

9 – Ara Pacis dedicated

7 – Diribitorium completed

C.E.

14 – Death of Augustus

14–37 – Reign of Tiberius

19 – Approximate date of construction of commemorative arch to Germanicus in Circus Flaminius

21 – Theater of Pompey burned and repaired

37–41 – Reign of Caligula

37 – Temples to Isis and Serapis known to exist after this date

41–54 – Reign of Claudius

51–52 – Arch of Claudius across Via Flaminia constructed

54–68 – Reign of Nero

57 – Temporary Theater of Nero built

60 – Baths of Nero dedicated

64 – Burning of Amphitheater of Statilius Taurus

69–79 – Reign of Vespasian

79–81 – Reign of Titus

80 – Pantheon, Porticus Octaviae, Theater of Pompey *scaenae frons*, Baths of Agrippa, Basilica of Neptune, Saepta Julia, Diribitorium, Temple of Isis, Crypta Balbi, temples in Largo Argentina, and other Campus Martius structures burned

81–96 – Reign of Domitian

81 – After this date Divorum built, Porticus Octaviae and temples of Jupiter Stator and Juno Regina restored, Temple of Isis restored, Temple of Minerva Chalcidica built, Horologium Augusti rebuilt, Odeum constructed, Porticus Minucia Vetus restored, Stadium of Domitian built, Theater of Balbus and Crypta Balbi restored, Theater of Pompey restored, and Baths of Agrippa restored

96–98 – Reign of Nerva

98–117 – Reign of Trajan

117–38 – Reign of Hadrian

117 – After this date, Temple of Divine Matidia built, Basilica of Neptune restored, Pantheon rebuilt, Saepta Julia restored, Baths of Agrippa restored

138–61 – Reign of Antoninus Pius

145 – Temple to Divine Hadrian dedicated

161–80 – Reign of Marcus Aurelius

161 – After this date Column of Antoninus Pius erected

175 – After this date Column of Marcus Aurelius erected

180–93 – Reign of Commodus

193–211 – Reign of Septimius Severus

202 – Pantheon restored

203 – Porticus Octaviae and temples of Jupiter Stator and Juno Regina restored

209–11 – Restoration work on the Theater of Pompey

211–17 – Reign of Caracalla

218–22 – Reign of Elagabalus

222–35 – Reign of Alexander Severus

222 – After this date Aqua Alexandrina constructed; Stadium of Domitian restored

227 – Baths of Nero enlarged and renamed Baths of Alexander

238 – Reign of Gordian I and II

238–44 – Reign of Gordian III

244–249 – Reign of Philip the Arab

247 – Theater of Pompey and Hecatostylon burned

249–51 – Reign of Decius

251–53 – Reign of Gallus

253–60 – Reign of Valerian

253–68 – Reign of Gallienus

268–70 – Reign of Claudius Gothicus

270–75 – Reign of Aurelian

272 – Aurelian Wall begun before this date

276–82 – Reign of Probus

276 – After this date Aurelian Wall completed

283 – Fire destroys Theater of Pompey and Porticus of Pompey

284–305 – Reign of Diocletian

284 – After this date Theater of Pompey and Porticus of Pompey restored

306–12 – Reign of Maxentius

312–37 – Reign of Constantine

312 – After this date Aqua Virgo repaired

APPENDIX B

GLOSSARY OF ARCHITECTURAL TERMS

aedes. A dwelling for deities; though most often used synonymously with "temple," *aedes* can also refer to a sanctuary or shrine.

aedicule (pl. *aediculae*). An architectural frame of two (engaged) columns and a pediment.

amphiprostyle. Having columns in front of the chamber on both the front and the rear.

amphitheater. An architectural form originally called *spectacula* and developed for the viewing of entertainment from all sides; consists of an arena encircled by seats set upon vaulting, built on mounds, or carved from the earth. Especially associated with wild animal hunts (*venatio*), mock sea battles (*naumachia*), and gladiatorial fights (*munera*).

apodyterium. The changing room in a bath complex.

aqueduct. A channel engineered to bring water from natural springs to settlements using gravity. While aqueducts are most famous for the built arches running through the countryside to support their channels, most aqueduct channels run underground.

ara. Altar.

arcade. A series of connected arches within or along the exterior facade of a building, or independent of other structures, often covered as a ***colonnade***, where people may stroll and vendors may set up shop; the series of arches supporting an aqueduct may also be called an arcade.

balnea (pl. balneae). Privately owned bathhouses (as opposed to imperially funded *thermae*); the term applied whether the bathhouse offered a dry sweat bath or a wet, hot water plunge.

balteus. The wall running along the concourse (*praecinctio*) that divides the upper and lower seating in the *cavea* of a theater.

barrel vault. Roof of a semicircular shape, created by placing arches directly adjacent and parallel to each other.

basilica. A rectangular structure with colonnades along its interior, creating space for commerce, banking, and legal hearings, often with an apse at one end. This form was adopted by Christian architects when erecting churches.

bay. The space between two vertical supports such as (but not limited to) columns, *pilasters*, or *piers*.

bibliotheca. Library.

caldarium. The chamber of a bathhouse housing the hot bath.

campus. A flat area of (open) ground, generally translated as a field, roughly equivalent to Greek *pedion*.

castellum (aquae). Distribution chamber for water brought in by *aqueduct*; from the *castellum*; the water would leave through pipes (*fistulae*), destined for specific locations and purposes.

cavea (pl. caveae). The sloped seating area of a theater; in the Greek tradition, built on a hillside; in the Roman tradition, built on man-made vaults.

cella. The sacred chamber of a temple (Greek *naos*).

cippus (pl. cippi). Stone boundary marker, often engraved with the defining terms of the boundary.

circus. A racetrack for horse and chariot races, originally applied to a defined circuit with temporary, if any, architecture for seating, eventually codified as a Roman architectural genre incorporating specific elements such as starting gates (*carceres*), a central dividing wall (*spina* or *euripus*), and sloped seating on a hillside or vaults.

cloaca. Sewer.

coffer. A sunken panel, as on the ceiling of the Pantheon.

colonnade. A row of columns set at a uniform distance from each other and supporting a roof (cf. *stoa*, *portico*).

Corinthian column. A column with a flared capital decorated with leaves; of a style generally accepted as having developed after the Doric and Ionic orders. The order may have been first used in Rome in the Portico of Octavius. It was later used on the columns of the top level of the Colosseum and (thought to be also on) the top level of the Theater of Marcellus.

crypta. A covered corridor lit from windows placed high in the wall near the vault (Crypta Balbi).

curia. Assembly house.

Doric column. A column with no base and a pillow-like capital; the style of column (order) of the Parthenon in Athens, found on the ground level of the Colosseum and the Theater of Marcellus.

encaustic painting. A decorative art whereby heated, pigmented wax is applied to a surface to create designs and pictures.

entablature. The portion of a building between the capitals and the pediment, generally broken into three ascending layers: the architrave, the frieze, and the cornice.

entasis. A calculated tapering of a column from bottom to top.

euripus. An artificial channel of water created along the ground, named for a narrow strait between the island of Euboea and mainland Greece.

exedra. A semicircular recess.

extrapomerial. Outside the sacred boundary of the ***pomerium***.

fistula (pl. fistulae). Pipes.

Forma Urbis Romae. *See Severan Marble Plan.*

forum (pl. fora). Open area generally surrounded with public buildings, shops, and temples and originally used as a public square and marketplace and later for lawcourts, meetings of the Senate and public administration. The three major fora in republican Rome were the Roman Forum, southeast of the Capitoline and north of the Palatine Hills; the Forum Holitorium, on the southern end of the Campus Martius; and the Forum Boarium, between the base of the Capitoline and base of the Aventine.

frigidarium. The chamber of a bathhouse housing the cold bath.

giallo antico. A marble (usually yellowish) from North Africa.

gymnasium. A space dedicated to physical training and exercise, originally a Greek construct, and eventually associated with bath complexes. Nero introduced the first gymnasium in Rome in connection with the Thermae Neronianae.

hexastyle. Having six columns.

horologium. A device for marking the passage of the sun based on the shadow cast by a gnomon along a line that runs north-south, and often used as a solar meridian to note noon at different times of the year.

horrea. Warehouses for the storage of goods, especially grain.

hortus (pl. horti). Garden.

insula (pl. insulae). A term for a group of apartments or possibly a single, large apartment building where families lived in separate living quarters.

Ionic column. A column on a base topped by a capital with volutes (curls), slimmer than a Doric column and more abstract than a Corinthian column; the Ionic order was considered to fall between the Doric and the Corinthian and can be found on the second levels of the Colosseum and the Theater of Marcellus.

lacus. Public basin providing drinking water.

manubial temple. A temple financed through the acquisition of war booty (*manubiae*).

mausoleum. An above-ground tomb. This term derives from the tomb of Mausolus at Halicarnassus, counted by Herodotus as one of the Seven Wonders of the World. The tomb of Augustus built on the Campus Martius is a mausoleum.

naos. The sacred chamber of a temple; Roman *cella*.

naumachia. Greek for sea battle, used for describing both mock sea battles and the structures built to house them (ex. Julius Caesar's *Naumachia Caesaris* built in 46 B.C.E.).

navalia. Shipyards.

niche. A recess built into a wall, either small, as if to hold a statue or small shrine, or large, as an exedra.

obelisk. A large, monolithic column of stone (usually granite) with a pyramidal tapered point, often covered in Egyptian hieroglyphs. Augustus brought the first obelisks to Rome from Egypt as trophies, erecting the Obelisk of Psammetichus II as the gnomon for his horologium and placing the Obelisk of Seti I / Ramses II on the center barrier (*euripus/spina*) of the Circus Maximus.

octostyle. Having eight columns.

oculus. A round opening in the ceiling of a structure, as in the Pantheon.

odeum. A small, roofed theater for musical performance and recitations.

opera publica. Translated as "public works," this is a category of buildings in Rome as described by Frontinus that were supplied by the aqueducts.

opus latericium. Ancient Roman brickwork, often facing concrete.

orchestra. The circular floor of a theater where the chorus would dance and sing; developed into the semicircular space in front of the stage in the Roman theater.

orthogonal. Arranged at right angles; Roman city planning began to plot streets at right angles to each other, resulting in an orthogonal, or gridlike, plan.

ovilia (ovile). Meaning "sheep pens," this term applied to the enclosed voting precinct in the Campus Martius later replaced by the Saepta Julia (though still sometimes called *ovilia/ovile*).

pediment. The triangular space created by a pitched roof above the facade of a building and atop the *entablature*; also a similarly shaped decorative element above *aediculae*.

peripteral. Having columns along the exterior walls of the *cella*.

peristyle. A courtyard surrounded by four porticoes (*quadriporticus*), often found in Roman domestic architecture to provide a central garden sheltered from the exterior.

pier. Architectural support having a square or rectangular base, often used for supporting arches.

pilaster. An ornamental detail along a wall mimicking an engaged column but not actually bearing weight.

plinth. The support for a column, pedestal, or statue.

podium (pl. podia). The base of a temple, elevating the floor of the chamber from ground level.

pomerium. The mythical plow line that defined the limits of the city proper. Certain activities, such as burial and arming of troops, were required to take place outside of the *pomerium*.

porticus (portico). A roofed walkway, generally with a solid wall supporting the roof along one side and a series of columns (*colonnade*) on the other side (cf. *stoa*, *colonnade*, *quadriporticus*), less commonly with rows of columns along both sides.

pronaos. The porch of a temple, literally the area "before the *naos*."

propylon (propylaeum). A monumental gate.

proscaenium. A stone stage raised above the *orchestra* where actors would perform.

prostyle. Having columns in front of the *cella*.

quadriporticus. Four porticoes connected at the corners, open to a courtyard in the center, often containing a *temple* or other structure.

rotunda. A circular building, often roofed with a dome (ex. Pantheon).

scaenae frons. The set building of a theater.

scholae. Lecture halls.

Servian Wall. Fourth-century B.C.E. wall likely built after the 390 B.C.E. sack of Rome by the Gauls. Livy erroneously attributes this wall to the sixth-century B.C.E. king Servius Tullius and the association has remained.

Severan Marble Plan (Forma Urbis Romae). A highly detailed map of Rome and the buildings within the city believed to have been created between 203 and 211 C.E. during the reign of Septimius Severus. It was incised on 150 marble slabs that were attached with iron clamps to a wall in the Forum Pacis.

spectacula. The original name for *amphitheaters*.

specus. The channel that carries the water within an aqueduct.

stabula. Stables for horses; there were four stables in Rome, collectively referred to as the *Stabula IIII Factionum*.

stadium. A venue built for viewing foot races, shaped like an elongated horseshoe with sloped seating above the arena. Domitian built Rome's first stadium. Originally a Greek architectural type placing the seats on banked earth, Domitian's stadium put the seating atop vaults of stone.

stoa. A covered walkway with a roof supported by columns on one side and a wall along the other (cf. *porticus*, *colonnade*).

sudatorium. The chamber of a bathhouse housing the sweat bath.

tabernacle. An architectural frame of two (engaged) columns and a *pediment* (see *aedicule*).

temple. A sacred building erected to serve as the house of a deity and containing its image and treasure.

tepidarium. The chamber of a bathhouse housing the warm bath.

tetrastyle. Having four columns.

theater. A building for viewing dramatic performances, consisting of an *orchestra*, a stage (*proscaenium*), a set building (*scaenae frons*), and tiered seating (*cavea*). Originally a Greek architectural type built into hillsides to support the sloped seating, Roman engineering eventually employed vaults under the seating to create a freestanding structure (*ex.* Theater of Pompey).

thermae. Large bathhouses somewhat like modern recreation centers.

tholos. A circular building with a conical or vaulted roof (*cf. rotunda*).

travertine. A limestone used extensively in Roman construction (*ex.* **Colosseum**).

tumulus. A mound of earth or stones built over a grave.

Tuscan column. An unfluted column with a circular base and simple, unadorned capital; less embellished than the Doric order, the Tuscan order is a Roman aesthetic.

ustrinum (bustrum). Funerary pyre.

vela. Originally Latin for "sail," this word also came to be used for the large canvas awnings that provided shade at entertainment venues.

vicus (pl. vici). Neighborhoods whose areas were defined by imperial order in 7 B.C.E.

NOTES

INTRODUCTION: "THIS PLACE WAS HOLIEST OF ALL"

1. There has been great debate as to the precise dates of the writing of *Geographica* as well as where it was written. Some argue that the work was started in the last decade B.C.E., and others that it was composed entirely two decades later between 16 and 18 C.E. See discussion in Dueck 2000, 146–50, who argues that it was composed even later between the years 18 and 24 C.E.
2. Strabo 5.3.2.
3. Ibid.
4. Strabo 5.3.8.
5. Ibid.
6. Varro *Ling.* 5.143; Richardson 1992, 293–6. See Beard, North, and Price, vol. 1, 177–81.
7. See, e.g., Livy 30.21.12, 33.24.5, 42.36.2. See also Richardson 1992, 58; Dyson, 23.
8. Livy 2.5.2. Livy, and William Masfen Roberts, *The History of Rome* (New York: Dutton, 1912).
9. Livy 1.60.3.
10. Livy 2.5.2. The reference to the sixth century B.C.E. space as the Campus Martius was likely anachronistic. See Chapter 2.
11. As Katherine Welch notes in her introduction to Dillon and Welch, 1, "War suffused Roman life to a degree unparalleled in other ancient societies."

ONE: "THE SIZE OF THE PLAIN IS REMARKABLE": DEFINING THE LIMITS OF THE CAMPUS MARTIUS IN TIME AND SPACE

1. For an excellent discussion of the Capitoline's geology, see Heiken, Funiciello, and De Rita, 27–34.
2. Christopher Smith, "Early and Archaic Rome," in Coulston and Dodge, 18. The earliest known settlements date to approximately

1700 B.C.E. See also A. Grandazzi, "The Emergence of the City," in Erdkamp, 11.
3. Richardson 1992, 287–8.
4. C. Smith, "Early and Archaic Rome," 18.
5. Boatwright, Gargola, and Talbert, 34. The date of 753 B.C.E. is generally assigned by Marcus Terentius Varro, who wrote six centuries later.
6. Palatine: C. Smith, "Early and Archaic Rome," 23; Grandazzi, "Emergence," 14; Forum: Boatwright et al., 34–5.
7. Plut. *Vit. Rom.* 27.5, believed that Romulus built a temple to Vulcan (Aedes Volcanus) in the southern Campus Martius, but there is no archaeological verification for this assertion. See Chapter 3.
8. C. Smith, "Early and Archaic Rome," 27; Grandazzi, "Emergence," 20.
9. C. Smith, "Early and Archaic Rome," 25; Richardson 1992, 91.
10. See Stamper, 31–2. The temple was begun as early as the late seventh century B.C.E. Grandazzi, "Emergence," 18.
11. Richardson 1992, 222.
12. C. Smith, "Early and Archaic Rome," 26. The Comitia Calata met at the Curia Calabra, likely a precinct or enclosed area within the Area Capitolina. Ibid.
13. See Chapter 2 with respect to the Ara Martis.
14. Cornell, 191; Livy 4.22.7.
15. The structures were added some time before 194 B.C.E. Livy 34.44.5. See Richardson 1992, 430.
16. The Temple of Apollo was built by a certain C. Julius. Livy 4.29.7; Richardson 1992, 12.
17. Richardson 1992, 57; Platner and Ashby, 82.
18. Varro *Ling.* 5.146. Richardson 1992, 164, 206. See Tac. *Ann.* 2.49.
19. See discussion in Chapter 3.
20. Richardson 1976, 60–6; Haselberger, Romano, and Dumser, 205.
21. See Richardson 1992, 383–5.

22. See Cic. *Att.* 13.33a.

23. Aldrete, 182–3.

24. Richardson 1992, 67.

25. Suet. *Aug.* 81 (Octavian's equestrian exercises); App. *B.Civ.* 3.94 (claim of inheritance).

26. Thornton, 50.

27. Richardson 1992, 70.

28. See discussion in Haselberger 2007, 136, 138.

29. The area is calculated from the approximate boundaries of the Villa Publica suggested by Richardson 1992, 430.

30. As Diane Favro has noted, "The field of the war god Mars became a lush parkland." Favro 1996, 179.

31. Aldrete, 165.

32. Richardson 1992, 394.

33. Cassius Dio 66.24.1; Suet. *Titus* 8.

34. Cassius Dio 66.24.1.

35. Suet. *Claud.* 18.1; Cassius Dio 55.8.4, 66.24.2. Thereafter, the Diribitorium was left open to the sky.

36. Richardson 1992, 211. See discussion in Chapter 7.

37. Cassius Dio 66.24.1.

38. Richardson 1992, 191.

39. Richardson 1992, 256.

40. According to Lanciani 1897, 446, the twelve largest colonnades enclosed approximately 100,000 square meters of space.

41. See M. Andreussi, "Pomerium," in *Lexicon topographicum urbis romae* (hereafter *LTUR*), vol. 4, 96–105; Richardson 1992, 296.

42. Livy 40.52.4, notes the dedication of a "temple to the Lares of the Sea in the Campus" (*Larium permarinum in Campo*). See also Cic. *Cat.* 2.1; Hor. *Carm.* 1.8.4, 3.1.11.

43. Suetonius, *Aug.* 100.3–4, placed Augustus's Mausoleum *inter Flaminiam viam ripamque Tiberis* (between the Via Flaminia and the bank of the Tiber), while the funeral procession traveled *in campum*. Livy, 21.30.11, employed the phrase *campum interiacentem Tiberi ac moenibus Romanis* (in the field that lay between the Tiber and the walls of Rome) to describe the area of Rome promised by Hannibal to his troops, but in several other passages he merely referred to the *campus Martius*. See, e.g., Livy 1.44.1; 3.10.1; 3.27.4; 3.43.6; 6.20.10; 22.33.2; and 31.7.1. In another passage, Livy, 2.5.2, described the land of the Tarquinii that was "consecrated to Mars" as "lying between the City and the Tiber" (*inter urbem ac Tiberim fuit*).

See also Ov. *Fasti* 3.519–20. See Richardson 1980, 1.

44. One channel was the Petronia Amnis, whose waters traveled from the Quirinal on the east to the Tiber by the Isola Tibertina. The other, now known as the Aqua Sallustiana, began between the Quirinal and the Pincian Hills and emptied into the river near the modern Ponte Umberto I. See Richardson 1992, 66.

45. See Richardson 1992, 4 (oak grove); Ov. *Fast.* 2.491, Richardson 1992, 70 (Caprae Palus); Livy 2.5.2, Plut. *Publ.* 8.1 (grain of Tarquinius Superbus).

46. T. P. Wiseman, "Campus Martius," *LTUR*, vol. 1, 220; Coarelli 2007, 261.

47. T. P. Wiseman, "Campus Martius," *LTUR*, vol. 1, 220–1.

48. Livy, 40.52.2–4, notes that Marcus Aemilius Lepidus dedicated temples to Diana and Juno Regina *in circo Flaminio* and also dedicated one to the Lares Permarini *in Campo*.

49. Richardson 1992, 65. Coarelli 2007, 261–70, includes the Circus Flaminius as part of the southern Campus Martius but also notes that, even after Augustus tied all of the land west of the Via Flaminia into Region IX, the Circus Flaminius space "was always considered a separate entity." Ibid. 261.

50. While Livy, 40.52.1, placed the Temple to Juno Regina in the Circus Flaminius as did Obsequens (Obseq. 16), the Fasti Antiates Maiores placed it *in campo*. A temple of Vulcan is described as *aedem in campo Volcani* by Livy, 24.10.10, and *in circo Flaminio* in Fasti Vallenses. See Wiseman 1974, 5, 8 and nn. 27, 31.

51. See Strabo 5.3.8. T. P. Wiseman (*LTUR*, vol. 1, 221), however, believes that Strabo was mistaken, stating that the Greek author's inclusion of the Theater of Marcellus in the Campus Martius "cannot be pressed as a technical description."

52. T. P. Wiseman, "Campus Martius," *LTUR*, vol. 1, 221. This delineation would have excluded about 100,000 square meters of land along the river, possibly placing outside of its limits the naval sheds (*navalia*) along the banks. The *navalia*, however, are described as *in campo Martio* (Livy 45.42.12; Enn., *ann.* fr.504 Sk), and Richardson 1992, 266, places them in the lower Campus Martius southeast of the Tarentum. See also Platner and Ashby, 358; Coarelli

1977, 823; Coarelli 2007, 260. T. P. Wiseman (*LTUR*, vol. 1, 220) is able to include the *navalia* within the Campus Martius by placing them "well upstream" of the Tarentum.

53. Coarelli 2007, 261, has proposed that the Campus Martius included the first emperor's tomb as well as the parkland that surrounded it, while T. P. Wiseman, "Campus Martius," *LTUR*, vol. 1, 220, asserts that the line fell just south of the tomb. Richardson 1992, 65, has argued that the border of the field faded in the horizon about 1.6 kilometers past the modern Piazza del Popolo.

54. It may have been the northern limit of Region IX, however, and to the extent that the two were coterminous at that point, it would have formed a boundary for the Campus Martius at the Piazza del Popolo. See discussion in Muzzioli, 184–6.

55. Coarelli 2007, 261, and Richardson 1992, 65. See Coarelli 1997, 5, based on Livy 2.5.2 and Dion. Hal. 5.13.2.

56. T. P. Wiseman, "Campus Martius," *LTUR*, vol. 1, 222.

57. Ov. *Pont.* 1.8.33–8, as quoted in Edwards, 123.

58. T. P. Wiseman, "Campus Martius," *LTUR*, vol. 1, 223, believes it would have left the impression of a city wall.

59. This road is identified as the Via "Recta" or Via "Tecta" by some historians (see, e.g., Albers, 281), while others assign those names to the road that connected the Circus Flaminius to the Pons Neronianus, now the location of the Ponte Sant'Angelo. See Richardson 1992, 419. See also discussion in Patterson, "Via Tecta," *LTUR*, vol. 5, 145–6.

60. T. P. Wiseman, "Campus Martius," *LTUR*, vol. 1, 224.

61. Favro 1996, 137–8.

62. Richardson 1992, 332.

63. Later known as the "Via Lata," this region included the vast parklands that had been owned by Marcus Agrippa.

64. Interestingly, the *Campum Martium* is listed as a place within Region IX along with, e.g., the Pantheon, Basilica of Neptune, and Baths of Agrippa. See Palmer 1990, 32.

65. Richardson 1992, 295.

66. Cic. *Agr.* 2.31.

67. If we use the perimeter of Region IX, the Campus Martius enclosed 1.7 square kilometers or 423 acres. Maria D'Alessio, "Regione

IX. Circus Flaminius," in Carandini and Carafa, eds. vol. 1, 493. See also vol. 2, tav. 207.

TWO: GATHERING TROOPS IN THE WAR GOD'S FIELD

1. Plut. *Vit. Rom.* 27; 29. See also Cic. *Rep.* 1.16.25. Dionysius of Halicarnassus (*Ant. Rom.* 2.56.5) indicated that Romulus disappeared at the time of the celebration of the *Poplifugia*, Flight of the Throng, on July 5, not on the Nones of Quintilis. See discussion in Woodard, 37–41.

2. Livy 1.16. The *Caprae Palus* or Goat Marsh is believed to be the swampy and lowest area of the Campus Martius, which was later drained and is the area in which the Pantheon was built. Richardson 1992, 70. See Plan 1.

3. Livy, 1.16, notes that not all were ready to believe that Romulus was "caught up on high in the blast" but rather had been torn to pieces by the senators present.

4. Plut. *Cam.* 33.2–7; *De Fort. Rom.* 8.

5. Livy 3.26–9.

6. Livy 3.69.8.

7. It was "impious for the assembly of the centuries to be held within the *pomerium*, because the army must be summoned outside of the city, and it is not lawful for it to be summoned within the city." Gell. *NA* 15.27.5.

8. Gell. *NA* 15.27.5. It has also been suggested that guards were used at voting assemblies to prevent voters from casting more than one ballot. L. R. Taylor, 47.

9. Livy 7.23.3.

10. Livy 1.43; Dion. Hal. 4.16–18. See Cornell, 173, 179–81, 191.

11. Livy 1.44.1–3.

12. Livy 1.44.2; Dion. Hal. 4.22.

13. The frieze showing the lustrum ceremony to mark the completion of the census is now in the Louvre; another piece depicting a marine *thiasos* is in the Glyptothek in Munich. See discussion in Chapter 6.

14. First censors: Livy 4.8.2. Villa Publica built: Livy 4.22.7.

15. Centuriate assemblies were initiated by Servius in conjunction with his military reforms. Livy 1.42.

16. Cassius Dio 37.28.3.

17. John Rich, introduction to Rich and Shipley, 1.

18. Livy, 1.44.2, notes that, according to Fabius Pictor, there were 80,000 citizens, although it is reasonably certain that the total population at that time did not exceed 35,000. Cornell, 208.

19. Cornell, 182.

20. Polyb. 6.20.8. Because the number of centuries per legion stayed the same and they generally had half the strength of the original Servian legion, overall strength was accomplished by increasing the number of legions. See Cornell, 182–3 (discussing the theory of Plinio Fraccaro), 193.

21. Polyb. 6.19. See Cornell, 182, 354, citing Livy 9.30.3.

22. During the imperial era, the *cippi* were blocks of stone two meters in height. Beard et al., vol. 1, 177.

23. Livy, 1.44.4, notes that the pomerial line was actually a cleared space on either side of the wall itself, and as the walls moved out, so did the *pomerium*.

24. See Richardson 1992, 262. Livy, 6.32.1, notes that a wall of "hewn stone" was built following the sack. See Katherine Welch, introduction to Dillon and Welch, 3.

25. Cornell, 198; A. Grandazzi, "Emergence," in Erdkamp, 22.

26. Livy, 5.41.4, notes that during the sack of Rome in 390 B.C.E. the Gauls attacked Rome from the north but clearly circumvented the Campus Martius by entering through the open Colline Gate on the east side of the city.

27. See L. R. Taylor, 85; Cassius Dio 37.26–8.

28. Stephen Oakley, "The Roman Conquest of Italy," in Rich and Shipley, 15–16.

29. Ibid., 10.

30. Grandazzi, "Emergence," 9.

31. "An army was levied, marched out to fight for a few months, and then returned to be discharged." Rich, "Fear, Greed and Glory," 44.

32. Ibid., 44–8.

33. Harris, 45.

34. John Patterson, "Military Organization and Social Change in the Later Roman Republic," in Rich and Shipley, 95–6. The high participation rate occurred during the Second Punic War.

35. See Keppie, 55.

36. Harris, 166–67; Woodard, 184. Livy, 1.32, traces the practice back to Rome's third king, Ancus Marcius, in the seventh century B.C.E.

Dionysius of Halicarnassus differs slightly in his description of the procedure with three visits to the enemy territory at ten-day intervals. Dion. Hal. *Ant. Rom.* 2.72.

37. See Livy 8.22 (327 B.C.E.), 9.45 (304 B.C.E.), 10.12 (298 B.C.E.), and 10.45 (293 B.C.E.). In the case of the declaration of war in 298 B.C.E. (the Third Samnite War), the *Fetiales* never made it to enemy-controlled territory as Samnite messengers met them along the route and warned them that a closer approach risked bodily harm. Livy 10.12.

38. A fifth-century C.E. commentator, Servius Auctus, 9.52, explained that in 281 B.C.E. the Romans captured one of Pyrrhus's soldiers and forced him to buy a plot of ground in the area of the Circus Flaminius so that it could be treated as enemy territory for purposes of hurling the spear.

39. See Wiedemann, 481–2. Wiedemann doubts that spears were hurled by the Romans to declare war prior to 32 B.C.E. and that Augustus created the ceremony. With respect to the *columna bellica*, Ovid wrote, "A small open space commands from the temple [of Bellona] a view of the top of the Circus. There stands a little pillar of no little note. From it the custom is to hurl by hand a spear, war's harbinger, when it has been resolved to take arms against a king and peoples." Ov. *Fast.* 6.205.

40. Harris, 167, 267–8.

41. Richardson 1992, 415–16. See discussion in Chapter 1.

42. Richardson 1992, 415.

43. Richardson 1992, 416; Ashby and Fell, 136.

44. Rich, introduction to Rich and Shipley, 2.

45. See David Potter, "The Roman Army and Navy," in Flower, 80–3, and Jurgen von Ungern-Sternberg, "The Crisis of the Republic," in Flower, 95–6.

46. Rich, introduction to Rich and Shipley, 4–5.

47. App. *B.Civ.* 1.89.

48. App. *B.Civ.*, 3.94.

49. Strabo 5.4.11; Cassius Dio 30–5 frag. 109.5–8. See also discussion in Chapter 3.

50. L. R. Taylor, 113. See also Dyson, 110, who puts the figure closer to 55,000.

51. Plut. *Mar.* 34.

52. Lucr. 2.40–4; 2.324–5 ("mighty legions, marching round, fill all the quarters of the plains [*camporum*] below, rousing a mimic warfare . . ."). See also Pratt, 21.

53. Varro *Rust.* 3.2.4, as translated in Makin, 26.

54. Suet. *Aug.* 81.
55. Nash, vol. 2, 117.
56. Richardson 1992, 267.
57. Richardson 1992, 266.
58. Pietilä-Castrén, 44.
59. Pliny *NH* 36.40.
60. Cornell, 308. The myth of Romulus's apotheo-
    sis before the assembled troops during the
    month of July, while not completely consistent
    with the historical rhythm of musters in the
    Field of Mars, nevertheless placed the event in
    a season when the area was driest.
61. Livy 3.10.1.
62. Livy 45.35; Polyb. 36.5.9. See discussion in
    Chapter 5 of the capture of Perseus.
63. Plut. *Mar.* 34.
64. Greg Woolf, "Roman Peace," in Rich and
    Shipley, at 174.
65. Beard 2007, 61–2.
66. Beard et al., vol. 1, 68; Coarelli 1997, 112–13.
67. Bremmer and Horsfall, 28.
68. Beard et al., vol. 1, 33.
69. See, e.g., Livy 22.1.11 ("Mavors"); Verg. *Aen.*
    8.630 ("Mavor"); Ov. *Fast.* 4.828 ("Mavors");
    Carm. arv. ("Marmar" "Marmor"); Fowler
    1911, 131; Adkins and Adkins, 141; Dumézil,
    212.
70. Grant and Hazel, 270.
71. Livy 1.20; Ov. *Fast.* 3.80–1.
72. Fowler 1899, 33, notes that it is not clear that
    January is in fact named for Janus. The earliest
    published calendar of Cn. Flavius in 304 B.C.E.
    has March as the first month of the year. Fowler
    1899, 11.
73. Ov. *Fast.* 3.351; Plut. *Num.* 13; Fowler 1899,
    38–40.
74. Fowler 1899, 330.
75. Ov. *Fast.* 2.860.
76. Fowler 1899, 50; see also Horsfall, 196.
77. Fowler 1899, 53. Anna Perenna tricks Mars
    who came to her for help in wooing Min-
    erva. Instead of finding Minerva, Mars finds
    old Anna in his marriage bed. Ov. *Fast.* 3.675ff.
    See also Dumézil, 213.
78. Fowler 1899, 62; L. R. Taylor, 3–4.
79. Pascal, 275.
80. See discussion in Chapter 4 with respect to the
    location.
81. Timaeus *ap.* Polyb. 12.4b. See discussion in Pas-
    cal, 261ff.
82. Fowler 1899, 242. One author believes that
    it was the male horse's genitalia that were
    removed and carried to the Regia and not

the tail (see Devereux, 298–9). This theory
has been questioned, however. See Pascal,
276 n. 72.
83. Polyb., 12.4b, takes issue with the belief of the
    Greek historian Timaeus (ca. 345–250 B.C.E.)
    that the October Horse commemorated the
    fall of Troy to the Greeks.
84. See discussion in Ogilvie, 73–4; Fowler 1899,
    243–9; Dumézil, 240–1.
85. Pascal, 264–5.
86. See discussions in Fowler 1911, 148; Beard
    et al., vol. 1, 15–16; 47–8; Pascal, 284–5.
87. Fowler 1899, 249.
88. Beard et al., vol. 1, 43. Dumézil, 154, notes that
    the festival "definitely characterizes the earliest
    Mars."
89. This despite having been described by one his-
    torian as a "cult center." Richardson 1992, 245.
90. Festus 204 L; Richardson 1992, 245.
91. Livy 35.10.12. Richardson 1992, 245; T. P.
    Wiseman, "Campus Martius," *LTUR*, vol. 1,
    220; Platner, 73. See discussion in Chapter 5.
92. Livy 40.45.8. The curule chair or *sella curulis*
    was the chair upon which magistrates with
    imperium were entitled to sit. See Livy 1.20.2.
93. Richardson 1992, 111, 245. See discussion in
    Chapter 7.
94. Richardson 1992, 245. Platner and Ashby, 328,
    believe the temple was constructed in 138 B.C.E.
95. Richardson 1992, 245. Pliny *NH* 36.4.
96. Cassius Dio 56.24.3; see Platner and Ashby,
    328. Ziólkowski 1992, 102–3, believes, how-
    ever, that the reference by Cassius Dio is to a
    temple of Mars built by Agrippa in the area of
    the Pantheon.
97. It suffers from the same problematical relation-
    ship to the Campus Martius as the nearby tem-
    ple of Mars built a century and a half later.
    Until the construction of the Circus Flaminius,
    it would be described as *ad Forum Holitorium*
    and not *in circo*. See Ziólkowski 1992, 287, 290.
98. See Dumézil, 391–2.
99. Vitr. *De arch.* 1.7.1. See Chapter 3 with respect
    to other principles set out by Vitruvius for the
    placement of temples.
100. Livy 7.23.3 (Porta Capena); Dion. Hal. *Ant.
     Rom.* 6.13.4 (*equites*). The temple's founding
     provided the eponymous reference to a rise in
     the road leading to it (the Clivus Martis), and
     Suetonius and Cicero described a large area
     around it as *ad Martis*. Cic. *QFr.* 3.7.1; Suet.
     Ter. 5.
101. Dumézil, 209.

102. Richardson 1992, 245. See Ov. *Fast.* 2.859–60; T. P. Wiseman, "Campus Martius," *LTUR*, vol. 1, 222.

103. Suet. *Iul.* 44.1. The Naumachia Caesaris was built in the Codeta Minor, a marshy area within the Campus Martius. Richardson 1992, 265. See also F. Coarelli, "Codeta Minor," *LTUR*, vol. 1, 291; Platner and Ashby, 128. But see Coleman, 50, who believes it was either in Trastevere or the Campus Martius.

104. The naumachia was filled in response to a plague according to Cassius Dio, 45.17.8, and it is not clear that the temple ever got past the concept stage.

105. Wiseman 1995, 107. See Dumézil, 451. Some scholars would push the Romulus legend back 200 years to the sixth century B.C.E. based upon reliance on the antiquity of a bronze statue of a she-wolf, now in the Capitoline Museum. Adriano La Regina, "La lupa dei Campidoglio è medievale la prova è nel test al carbonio," *La Repubblica*, July 9, 2008. See also discussion in Bickerman, 67; Cornell, 61; Mazzoni, 23. Recent scientific analysis indicates that the bronze wolf is datable to the medieval period. See discussion in Mazzoni, 36–9. The suckling twins beneath the she-wolf have long been known to be of Renaissance origin. The so-called "Mirror of Bolsena" dating to approximately 340–330 B.C.E. has engraved on one side what has been described as a she-wolf and two infants, possibly the earliest extant representation of Romulus and Remus. See discussion in Mazzoni, 174–8.

106. Wiseman 1995, 111.

107. Livy 22.1.12; Wiseman 1995, 65 and n. 6.

108. Livy 10.23.12; Carter, 22.

109. Wiseman 1995, 107.

110. Callias wrote that a Trojan woman Rhome married Latinus and that their sons Romulus and Remus founded the city named after her. See Bickerman, 67; Gruen, 15–16; Carter, 22. The Greeks produced a variety of tales for the foundation of Rome with at least twenty-five having been cataloged by ancient writers. See Dion. Hal. *Ant. Rom.* 1.72; Plut. *Rom.* 2; Festus 269 L. See Bickerman, 65.

111. Plut. *Rom.* 4. See Bremmer and Horsfall, 31. Livy, 10.27.9, indicates the wolf to be a beast of Mars. See Wiseman 1995, 65.

112. Livy 10.23.13.

113. Bremmer and Horsfall, 27–8.

114. See Wiseman 1998, 2. Various versions of the rape of Rhea Silvia by Mars would be told centuries later. Dionysius of Halicarnassus told of one "fabulous" legend that the event included the disappearance of the sun and took place in a grove dedicated to Mars. The writers also repeat alternative versions of the birth of the twins in which the war god is not the father. See Plut. *Rom.* 4.4; Dion. Hal. *Ant. Rom.* 1.77.

115. Strabo, 5.3.2, for instance, repeated the tale that Mars was the father of Romulus. Later, Plutarch would do the same. Plut., *Rom.* 2.3.

116. Plut. *Numa* 19. Plutarch notes that Rome's second king, Numa, altered the order of the months to make March the third month instead of the first "because he wished in every case that martial influences should yield precedence to civil and political." Ibid.

117. Wiseman 1995, 141. The cult of Quirinus may date back centuries earlier, before its association with Romulus. See Richardson 1992, 326–7; Dumézil, 249–51.

118. See Bremmer and Horsfall, 45, and Carter, 22. In a fragment, Ennius wrote, "Romulus in caelo cum dis genitalibus aevum degit." See Remains of Old Latin, trans. E. H. Warmington (Cambridge, Mass.: Harvard University Press, 1935), 38.

119. See Wiseman 1995, 128.

120. Livy 1.16.1; Dion. Hal. *Ant. Rom.* 2.56; Plut. *Rom.* 27.6. See Carter, 23. An alternative story of Romulus's death is that he was murdered either in the Campus Martius or the Senate House in the Forum (Dion. Hal. *Ant. Rom.* 2.56) or at the Vulcanal by the Forum. Plut. *Rom.* 27.

121. Coarelli 1997, 57.

122. Livy 1.16.1. See Plut. *Rom.* 27; Ov. *Fast.* 2.475.

123. See Richardson 1992, 70.

124. See Bremmer and Horsfall, 78–9.

125. Plut. *Cam.* 33.2–6. Coarelli 1997, 34, describes this holiday as laden with sexual connotations and one of role reversals. He suggests that the wild fig may have been located in the Campus Martius. Ibid. 57. The holiday may be closely linked to the tale of a *poplifugium*, or flight of the people, commemorating the bravery of a servant girl who, taken prisoner by the Latins along with other maids of the city, climbed a wild fig tree at night and signaled to the Roman soldiers to

attack while the enemy slept. See discussion in Woodward, 39–41.

126. Plut. *Cam.* 33.2–6. See also discussion in Chapter 3 with respect to the possible connections between the *Nonae Capratinae* and Largo Argentina temples.

127. Bremmer and Horsfall, 84.

128. A shrine referenced in the fourth-century C.E. regionary catalogs and known as the Aedicula Capraria as well as a street that ran south of the Aqua Virgo called the Vicus Caprarius may echo the festival's name and/or the goat marsh. A chamber found about a quarter of a mile east of the Pantheon in 1924 may be the Aedicula Capraria. Richardson 1992, 3, 421–2.

129. Plut. *Rom.* 28–9. Plutarch notes that some believe the name Quirinus means Romulus while others claim that it refers to a spearhead called by the ancients "*Quiris.*"

130. The inscription (*CIL* 10.809) states, "Romulus, son of Mars, founded the city of Rome and ruled 38 years. He [as] first leader consecrated rich spoils to Jupiter Feretrius, having destroyed the general of the enemy, Acron [aka Acro], king of the Caeninenses. And having been received in the number of the gods, he is called Quirinus." Translation by Joanna Schmitz.

131. Ov. *Fast.* 2.505–8. See also Cic. *Rep.* 2.10.24.

132. Plut. *Rom.* 8.7.

133. Carter, 24; Scott, 99–100. Cicero, however, notes that Proculus Julius was an untutored peasant, not a patrician as Plutarch reports. See Cic. *Rep.* 2.10.

134. Wiseman 1995, 50.

135. Wiseman 1995, 54.

136. Gruen, 28. See also Bremmer and Horsfall, 18, who write that "No reliable indications, literary, religious, inscriptional, or artistic, therefore exist for the Romans' own interest in Aeneas before, indeed, 300 B.C.[E.]."

137. Gruen, 32.

138. Gruen, 39.

139. Livy 1.3.6.

140. See Strabo 5.3; Ov. *Fast.* 1.527, 4.251; Plut. *Rom.* 3.2; Verg. *Aen.* 271ff.

141. Bremmer and Horsfall, 24.

142. Ibid.

143. Verg. *Aen.* 1.286–96, emphasis added.

144. Dumézil, 257–8. The phrase "brother Remus" may refer to Agrippa. See note 167 in this chapter.

145. Livy 2.5.2.

146. Plut. *Publ.* 8.1.

147. Livy 2.5.2; Plut. *Publ.* 8.1.

148. Plut. *Publ.* 8.1.

149. Plut. *Publ.* 8.2.

150. Livy 2.5.3–4; Suet. *Claud.* 25; Plut. *Publ.* 8.3.

151. Bremmer and Horsfall, 85.

152. Livy 1.44.1. When referring to the location of Romulus's ascension, he merely calls it *in campo ad Caprae paludem.* Livy 1.16.1.

153. See, e.g., Cic. *Agr.* 2.85.1 (*campus martius*) and *Pro Rabirio Perduellionis Reo* 11.3 (*in campo martio*) and *Mur.* 33 (*in campum martium*); Varro *Ling.* 5.28.5 (*itaque Tiberis amnis quod ambit martium campum et urbem*), *Rust.* 3.2.5.2 (*in campo martio extremo*); Livy 2.5.2 (*martius deinde campus fuit*), 3.69.6 (*omnes iuniores postero die prima luce in campo martio adessent*); and Strabo 5.3.8 (Μάρτιος ἔχει κάμπος).

154. Cicero appears to be, perhaps, the earliest writer employing the phrase beginning around 63 B.C.E. in *De lege agraria* (2.85) and *Pro Rabirio Perduellionis Reo* (4 and 10). Earlier writings mention only the "campus." See Cic. *Att.* 1.1 from July 65 B.C.E. In later writings, the use of Mars as a descriptor is clearly used to distinguish the space from another in order to avoid confusion. In a letter of July 45 B.C.E., Cicero, *Att.* 13.33a, describes a conversation in which "Capito happened to be talking of the enlargement of the city, saying that the Tiber is being diverted at the Mulvian Bridge to run alongside of the Vatican hills, that the Campus Martius is being built over and the other Campus, the Vaticanus, is becoming a new Campus Martius" (... *illum autem campus Vaticanum fieri quasi Martium campum*). See also Cic. *Att.* 12.8.

155. Straightening the Tiber: see Cic. *Att.* 13.33a; filling in the Naumachia: see Suet. *Iul.* 44.1.

156. Plut. *Vit. Rom.* 26.2; Cassius Dio 44.6, 43.45. See also Scott, 83.

157. Scott, 84.

158. Cic. *Att.* 12.45.3, 12.47.3, 13.28.3. See Scott, 83.

159. Richardson 1992, 326; Palmer 1976, 54–5. The Domitianic relief shows Romulus, Remus, Mars, Jupiter, and vultures, among other figures.

160. See Cassius Dio 46.46.2–3. Wiseman 1995, 144, notes that Octavian was "arrogat[ing] to himself both Remus' augury for the citizen body, and Romulus', for the army."

161. See Favro 1996, 96. The temple was vowed in 42 B.C.E. at the Battle of Philippi and its name

derives from Octavian's desire to avenge the death of his adoptive father two years earlier. Suet. *Aug.* 29.2.

162. Richardson 1992, 161 (eight columns); Ov. *Fast.* 5.559.

163. Richardson 1992, 162.

164. See Livy 4.20.3; Favro 1996, 92.

165. Favro 1996, 104; *Res Gestae* 19.

166. Dating to the late first century B.C.E., the tomb of the family of T. Statilius Taurus was located near the present Porta Maggiore.

167. Verg. *Aen.* 1.291–6; Prop. 4.1.9–10. See discussion in Wiseman 1995, 145–6.

168. Wilson Jones, 180.

169. Cassius Dio 53.27. See Wilson Jones, 179–80.

170. See Adam Ziółkowski, "What did Agrippa's Pantheon look Like? New Answers to an Old Question," in Graßhoff, Heinzelmann, and Wäfler, at 36. Ziółkowski suggests that, while there may have been other statues in the Pantheon, the only cult deities were Mars and Venus.

171. Rehak 2001, 197.

172. See catalog of scholarship accepting the identification of the primary figure on the right panel as Aeneas in Rehak 2001, 190 and n. 6.

173. Rehak 2001, 190ff.

174. Rehak 2001, 196.

175. Rehak 2001, 199.

176. Suet. *Aug.* 7; Favro 1996, 104.

177. Suet. *Aug.* 7.

178. Ov. *Fast.* 2.132. See Favro 1996, 124.

179. Cassius Dio 56.34.

180. Cassius Dio 56.36.

181. Cassius Dio 56.42.

182. Cassius Dio 56.46.

183. *Res Gestae* 12.

184. Suet. *Claud.* 21.6.

THREE: "VERY COSTLY TEMPLES": THE CAMPUS MARTIUS AND REPUBLICAN TEMPLE CONSTRUCTION

1. Lepidus and Gaius Flaminius were selected on the twelfth day before the Kalends of March, 188 B.C.E. Livy 38.42.2–3.

2. Livy 38.42.8.

3. Livy 38.43.1.

4. Livy 38.42.11.

5. Livy 38.42.13.

6. Livy 39.1.3.

7. Livy 39.1.5.

8. Livy 39.1.2.

9. Livy 39.1.8.

10. Livy 39.2.8.

11. Along the way, he had his men build the eponymous Via Aemilia, a road that stretched 160 miles from Placentia (modern Piacenza) to Ariminum (modern Rimini) and connected to the Via Flaminia built three decades earlier by his co-consul's father. Livy 39.2.10.

12. Livy 39.2.11.

13. See Pietilä-Castrén, 106–7.

14. See Pietilä-Castrén, 106.

15. M. Furius Camillus vowed the temple following Veii's destruction in 396 B.C.E., and it was dedicated four years later. Livy 5.21.2–3. See also Pietilä-Castrén, 106.

16. Livy 39.4.2.

17. Livy 39.4–5.

18. Livy 39.22.2. See Welch, 23.

19. Richardson 1992, 216.

20. While we do not have certain information for Lepidus's temple of Diana, possible locations include the southern side of the Circus Flaminius, opposite the Juno Regina temple, or perhaps further east and closer to where the Theater of Marcellus was later built. See Pietilä-Castrén, 104. With respect to the Severan Marble Plan, also known as the Forma Urbis Romae, see the Stanford Digital Forma Urbis Romae Project at http://formaurbis.stanford.edu (accessed January 28, 2011). See also Wallace-Hadrill, 301–12.

21. Pietilä-Castrén, 106; Richardson 1992, 233.

22. Pliny *NH* 35.36; Ov. *Fast.* 6.797–812; Richardson 1992, 187.

23. Pietilä-Castrén, 102. Why Fulvius chose to honor Hercules, particularly after choosing to vow games to Jupiter, is unknown, although the consul apparently learned of Hercules' role as a Musagetes (leader or guide of the Muses) while in Greece and made the choice to build a temple to that version of the hero. Richardson 1992, 186–7. The Muses were patrons of Pythagoreans, and Fulvius had included in his Aetolian travels the poet Ennius, who was an adherent to Pythagorean principles. Pietilä-Castrén, 98–100.

24. The only battlefield vow of Fulvius that is mentioned by Livy, 39.5.7, is the promise to hold games, although it has been argued that Fulvius likely vowed a temple at the same time.

See Pietilä-Castrén, 97, 101; Orlin 2002A, 65; Richardson 1992, 187.

25. Orlin 2002A, 139.

26. See discussion in Orlin 2002A, 76–80 (Sibylline books); Hekster and Rich, 152, 155 (aedeles).

27. While approximately eighty temples were built during this period, the means employed to found the temple has been determined only with respect to forty-eight of them. Orlin 2002A 18. At least twenty-six temples, or 54 percent of the known foundings, were the result of military vows. Orlin 2002A, 19–20.

28. Ziólkowski 1992, 311.

29. There is disagreement whether the *vota nuncupata* was binding upon the state. Compare Ziólkowski 1992, 195–8, and Orlin 2002A, 46–7.

30. Ziólkowski 1992, 203–8, takes the position that *locatio* refers to the selection of the temple, while Orlin 2002A, 139–40 nn. 94, 141, believes that *locatio* applies only to the letting of the construction contract and not to actual site selection.

31. Beard et al., vol. 1, 34.

32. Livy 10.19.17. Famous for the saying "every man is the architect of his own fortune," Appius built, in addition to the Bellona temple, Rome's first great road, the Via Appia, and Rome's first aqueduct, the Aqua Appia, both constructed in 312 B.C.E. Richardson 1992, 15, 414.

33. Cic. *Nat.D.* 1.82.

34. Livy 32.30.10.

35. This was the case when Postumus vowed a temple to Castor after breaking enemy lines at Lake Regillus in 496 B.C.E. Livy 2.20.11–12. See Orlin 2002A, 30.

36. One of the most notable examples of a general who eschewed formality to his mortal detriment is that of Gaius Flaminius Nepos who, after constructing the Via Flaminia, failed to make the proper vows to Mars before assuming his post in Ariminum (ancient Rimini) and later died with 15,000 of his men at the hands of Hannibal's forces at the Battle of Lake Trasimene. Livy 22.7.1–5; 22.9.7–11; Polyb. 3.84.

37. See discussion in Ziólkowski 1992, 266–7.

38. This so-called rule has numerous exceptions, and at least one scholar discounts its viability entirely because of the lack of mention by any ancient author of its application. See discussion in Orlin 2002B, 2, 5. See also Ziólkowski 1992, 266–8, and Dumézil, 446–7 (exception to rule for gods accepted early into Roman culture).

39. See Orlin 2002B, 5, 14. See Orlin 2002A, 63–4, with respect to the consideration of Juno Sospita as "foreign."

40. Vitr. *De arch.* 1.7.1.

41. Ibid. The precept suggested by Vitruvius did not always result in a rule as evidence of Vulcan's first shrine: the Vulcanal has been located in excavations in the northwest corner of the Roman Forum (Beard et al., vol. 1, 12, and vol. 2, 21–2), although at the time of its construction, that location may have been outside the *pomerium*. See H. J. Rose, 46.

42. Vitr. *De arch.* 1.7.30; Ziólkowski 1992, 55.

43. See J. Davies, 1999.

44. Orlin 2002A, 61.

45. The temple approved by the Senate in 179 B.C.E. was that of Fortuna Equestris vowed by Q. Fulvius Flaccus a year earlier. Livy 40.44.8. The games denied were those to be held by P. Cornelius Scipio Nasica in 191 B.C.E. Livy 36.36.2.

46. Orlin believes that very few vows would have been rejected and that no Roman general is believed to have introduced a deity that the Senate found wanting. Orlin 2002A, 61.

47. See Ziólkowski 1992, 241; Shatzman, 177, 180, 184, 204; Hekster and Rich, 152. Orlin 2002A, 130–4, disputes the notion that *manubiae* was generally the source for temple construction noting that of eighty vowed temples, we only have reports of five built with *manubiae* whereas there are six reported to have been built out of tributes collected by aediles.

48. See generally Shatzman, 177, 180, 184, 204.

49. See Ziólkowski 1992, 241.

50. Ziólkowski 1992, 309. Ziólkowski counts forty manubial temples out of fifty built.

51. Ziólkowski 1992, 253. Temples of Janus, Feronia, and Hercules Magnus Custos were built under such circumstances. Vowing the capture of a city such as Lipara that resulted in the building of the Temple of Vulcan was another circumstance. See ibid.

52. Ziólkowski 1992. 244. According to Ziólkowski, more than half of the Roman temples vowed by generals come from the eighty-year period from the beginning of the

Third Samnite War in 298 B.C.E. to the start of the war with Hannibal.

53. Ziólkowski 1992, 308, argues that the only limitation on a general's site selection was the availability of public land. Orlin 2002A, 148, argues that the use of *duumviri* in temple contracting suggests a high degree of senatorial involvement. See also Beard et al., vol. 1, 88, who note that while booty was generally used to finance temples, "the religious authorities could control or limit the commander's wishes if they were seen as in conflict with the rules of the sacred law."

54. Ziólkowski 1992, 193, 308.

55. Orlin 2002A, 178–9, notes that eleven of seventeen were dedicated by the vower or his son. When Lepidus's dedication of the Temple of the Lares Permarini that had been vowed by his relative L. Aemilius Regillus is included, that raises the total to twelve of seventeen.

56. Livy 40.52.1.

57. While some scholars believe that the Temple of Apollo Medicus was founded after consultation with the Sibylline Books, this theory has been questioned. See discussion in Orlin 2002A, 97–8.

58. These included three in the Circus Maximus. See Ziólkowski 1992, 187.

59. Those that have been claimed to be within the Campus Martius are the following with vow dates in parentheses: Janus (260), Spes (258, 254), Neptunus (257–229), Volcanus (252), Juturna (242/1), Juno Curitis (241), Feronia (225), Hercules Magnus Custos (223), Juno Sospita (197), Pietas (191), Lares Permarini (190), Diana (187), Juno Regina (187), Hercules Musarum (187), Fortuna Equestris (182), and Jupiter Stator (147). Those that have been claimed to be outside of the Campus Martius are the following: Tempestates (259), Fides (254), Ops Opifera (250), Fortuna Publica in Colle Quirinale (241), Flora ad Circus Maximus (241), Honos (233), Fons (231), Honos et Virtus (222), Fortuna Primigenia (204), Vediovis (200), Victoria Virgo (195), Venus Erycina (184), Juno Moneta (173), Felicitas (151), Hercules (147), and Hercules Victor (146). See Pietilä-Castrén, 145–52; Ziólkowski 1992, 187–8. With respect to the question as to whether the temple of Hercules Musarum was actually vowed in battle, see note 24.

60. Varro *Ling.* 5.146. See Richardson 1992, 164.

61. Pietilä-Castrén, 34, 154. See also Coarelli 2007, 314; F. Coarelli, "Ianus, Aedes," *LTUR*, vol. 3, 90–1; Stamper, 59–60; Haselberger et al., 234.

62. It is believed that he vowed a temple to Janus during the battle, and Tacitus tells us that he built the temple in the Forum Holitorium. Pietilä-Castrén, 34; Tac. *Ann.* 2.49. Duilius received the first known Roman triumph for a naval victory.

63. Spes was vowed by the consul A. Atilius Caiatinus while he was fighting in Sicily at various times between 258 and 249 B.C.E. Caiatinus served as consul in 258 and 254 as well as praetor in 257 and dictator in 249. He earned a triumph for his exploits in Sicily in 258–257, but the sources do not make clear when he vowed the two temples he built to honor Spes and Fides. See Ziólkowski 1992, 29, 152; Pietilä-Castrén, 39.

64. Livy 21.62.4.

65. The general Cornelius Cethegus vowed the temple in 197 B.C.E. while fighting the Insubrians, and he was honored with a triumph that same year. Livy 32.30.10; 33.23.4.

66. Although it is generally believed that the temples in the Forum Holitorium (going north to south) were Janus, Juno Sospita, and Spes, one author, Richardson 1992, 206, 217, takes the position that the Temple of Janus was in the Forum Boarium and that the three temples in the Forum Holitorium are Juno Sospita, Spes, and Pietas.

67. The temple in honor of Juturna is believed to have been built by the consul C. Lutatius Catulus whose naval victory over the Carthaginians in 242 B.C.E. ended the First Punic War. See Ziólkowski 1992, 94; Pietilä-Castrén, 46. Although it was described by Livy (24.10.9) simply as *in campo*, its remains have been variously identified as Temples A or C in the Largo Argentina and in an unidentified spot further north where the Aqua Virgo terminated by the later-built Saepta. One author (Ziólkowski 1992, 94–7) favors Temple C while others (Pietilä-Castrén, 47 and F. Coarelli, "Iuturna, Templum," *LTUR*, vol. 3, 162–3) prefer Temple A. Richardson 1992, 228, and Platner and Ashby, 308, believe it was located just to the west of the Via Flaminia near the later-built Temple to the Divine Hadrian.

68. See Ziólkowski 1992, 64; Richardson 1992, 214; Platner and Ashby, 288.

69. Two different battles have been associated with the vowing of Feronia: the defeat of the Sabines in 290 B.C.E. by the consul Manius Curius Dentatus and the defeat of the Gauls in 225 B.C.E. by L. Aemilius Papus. Stamper, 44, contends that Feronia is Temple C built by Curius Dentatus while Ziólkowski 1986, 638–9, believes that Feronia is the slightly younger Temple A built by Aemilius Papus.

70. Livy 40.52.4.

71. Livy 40.52.5–6. The inscription read as follows: "For finishing a great war, for subduing kings, this battle, fought for the purpose of winning peace (gave victory) to Lucius Aemilius, the son of Marcus Aemilius, as he left the field. Under his auspices and command, with his good fortune and generalship, in the area bounded by Ephesus, Samos and Chios, under the eyes of Antiochus himself, of all his army, his cavalry and his elephants, the fleet of King Antiochus, hitherto undefeated, was routed, shattered and put to flight, and there on that day forty-two ships were taken with all their crews. As a result of the finishing of this battle, King Antiochus was defeated and his naval empire (overthrown). By reason of this victory, he vowed a temple to the Lares of the Sea [Lares Permarini]."

72. Richardson 1992, 233, and G. Rickman ("Porticus Minucia," in De Fine Licht, 107) believe the Lares Permarini is the small temple, the ruins of which are on the Via delle Botteghe Oscura across from the Theater of Balbus complex, while Coarelli 2007, 279, 281, Pietilä-Castrén, 94, and Ziólkowski 1986, 623, favor Temple D. Coarelli believes the site across from the Theater of Balbus to be the Temple of the Nymphs in part because one stood in the Villa Publica. See also discussion in Haselberger et al., 160; Nicolet 1976, 37–8.

73. Livy 3.54.15. The *prata flaminia* was supposedly named after an ancient ancestor of the builder of the circus. Varro *Ling.* V.154; Wiseman 1974, 5. With respect to the construction date, see A. Viscogliosi, "Circus Flaminius," *LTUR*, vol. 1, 269–72; Richardson 1992, 83. Coarelli 2007, 267, prefers a construction date of one year earlier in 220 B.C.E.

74. See Varro *Ling.* 5.154; Richardson 1992, 83. See discussion in Chapter 5.

75. Ziólkowski 1992, 52. Ovid (*Fasti* 6.209–12) suggests that Sulla, in the first century B.C.E., was responsible for construction of the

temple, but this is generally thought to be a restoration of a preexisting *aedes*. See discussion in Richardson 1992, 186. Livy 21.62.9 records a *supplicatio* at the Temple of Hercules in 218 B.C.E.

76. Ziólkowski 1992, 53–5, proposes that the *aedes* was first ordered by the Sibylline Books at the beginning of the Great Gallic War but was not immediately built as the crisis soon passed. Later, it was re-vowed by Flaminius while he was fighting a tribe in Lombardy in 223 B.C.E.

77. Vitr. *De arch.* 1.7.30; Ziólkowski 1992, 55.

78. Cassius Dio 57.60 fr. 17. Livy, 28.11.4, mentions only an altar and not a temple. With respect to possible locations, see Coarelli 1997, 420; Tucci, 15–42; Richardson 1992, 267.

79. Favro 1996, 90; Shipley 1933, 44; Richardson 1992, 267. The coin was issued between 42 and 38 B.C.E. by the Roman general and later consul Gnaeus Domitius Ahenobarbus. It shows a temple and a legend indicating that it is dedicated to the sea god.

80. Although it is generally accepted that the Temple of Juno Regina shown on the Severan Marble Plan next to Jupiter Stator is the one dedicated by Lepidus in 179 B.C.E. (see discussion in Richardson 1992, 217; A. Viscogliosi, "Iuno Regina, Aedes in Campo, ad Circum Flaminium," *LTUR*, vol. 3, 126–8; Stamper, 54; Boyd, 154), it has been argued that it was actually constructed by Metellus at the time he built the portico enclosing the temples to Jupiter Stator and Juno Regina in 146 B.C.E. Morgan, 480ff. Under this hypothesis, the temple of Juno Regina that is known to have been constructed by Lepidus was located in a still-undetermined space on or by the Circus Flaminius.

81. Pliny *NH* 7.121; Cassius Dio 43.49.2–3.

82. Livy 40.34.4–6. Glabrio captured a huge cache of valuable objects and for his efforts was awarded a triumph in 190 B.C.E. His extravagant triumphal parade apparently stirred controversy, since when he ran for censor a year later, he was accused of pilfering some of the treasure seized from Antiochus and had to drop out of the election or risk a large fine. Livy 37.57.12; 37.58.1. See Shatzman, 191–2.

83. Livy 40.34.5. Pliny attributes the dedication to Pietas to a legend of a lactating mother who nourished her own mother with breast milk

when the latter languished starving in prison. Pliny *NH* 7.121. Near the Temple of Pietas was a Columna Lactaria where babies could be brought to receive milk. Richardson 1992, 94.

84. Richardson 1992, 245.

85. While Richardson 1992, 76, believes a date of 100 B.C.E. is appropriate, others have suggested 70 B.C.E. (Haselberger et al. 2002, 84) and mid-second century B.C.E. (Patterson, 197).

86. Pliny *NH* 34.54; 34.60. See Richardson 1992, 156.

87. Lomas and Cornell, 31. While only 10 percent of the approximately 400 consuls that served from the end of the sixth century B.C.E. to the beginning of the first century B.C.E. ever vowed a temple, those who did were mostly committing temples to the gods during the mid-third century to the mid- to late second century. Orlin 2002A, 31, 198–202.

88. J. Muccigrosso, "Religion and Politics: Did the Romans Scruple about the Placement of Their Temples?," in Harvey and Schulz, 191. The free population of Rome may have grown as much as fourfold from 225 to 28 B.C.E. See Willem Jongman, "Slavery and the Growth of Rome: The Transformation of Italy in the Second and First Centuries BCE," in Edwards and Woolf, 103 and n. 23.

89. Those temples dedicated in the Campus Martius during this period were Juno Sospita (194 B.C.E.), Pietas (181 B.C.E.), Lares Permarini (179 B.C.E.), Diana (179 B.C.E.), Juno Regina (179 B.C.E.), Hercules Musarum (c. 179 B.C.E.), and Fortuna Equestris (173 B.C.E.). See Pietilä-Castrén, 69, 88, 93, 101, 105, and 115–16. The Temple of Fortuna Equestris was vowed by Q. Fulvius Flaccus while fighting in Spain and is believed to have been located in the vicinity of the later-built Theater of Pompey. Richardson 1992, 155.

90. Richardson 1992, 216.

91. See Hardie, 561, who relates the Temple of Hercules Musarum to Juno Regina through the concept of *concordia*.

92. While Eumenius states that the Temple of Hercules Musarum was built *ex pecunia censoria* (Eumen. *Pro Instaur. Scholis* 7–8), Cicero (*Arch.* 11.27) claims it was constructed *ex manubiae*. See Richardson 1992, 187; Orlin 2002A, 132–3. If the latter source of funds is correct, it is less likely to have been started so late, particularly since, unlike Aemilius

Lepidus who had completed and dedicated two temples by 179 B.C.E., Marcus Fulvius brought back a large cache of booty from Ambracia and, hence, was not dependent on fines for funding. See also A. Viscogliosi, "Hercules Musarum, Aedes," *LTUR*, vol. 3, 17–19.

93. Plut. *Vit. Rom.* 16.5.

94. Pietilä-Castrén, 25–6.

95. Val. Max. 2.8.1.

96. An exception would be during the mid-fourth century when a number of successes resulted in eight triumphs awarded between 361 and 354 B.C.E. See Cornell, 324.

97. Cornell, 308; Harris, 26.

98. John Rich, "Fear, Greed and Glory: The Causes of Roman War-Making in the Middle Republic," in Rich and Shipley, 50.

99. Livy 39.5.11–14. See Rosivach, 274.

100. Plut. *Aem.* 32.2.

101. See Plut. *Pomp.* 45.5.

102. App. *Mith.* 17.116. Along with illustrations of the dead Mithridates were depictions of his daughters who chose to die with him, conveying, as one scholar has put it, the message of "how the mighty have fallen." See Kathleen M. Coleman, "'Informers' on Parade," in Bergmann and Kondoleon, 240.

103. After two efforts to fit the yoked pachyderms through the city gates, the effort had to be abandoned, and they were switched out for horses. See the excellent description of Pompey's third triumph in Beard 2007, 7–41.

104. See discussion in Beard 2007, 163–7, in which she notes that of 320 triumphs claimed between the time of Romulus and Vespasian's triumph in 71 C.E., only a few could have included displays of extraordinary war booty.

105. Makin, 26. See discussion in Beard 2007, 93–6.

106. See discussion in Makin, 26–8. The building where Titus and Vespasian spent the night may be the same one shown on a coin of mid first century B.C.E. Ibid. As Beard 2007, 95–6, notes, the Greek does not make certain whether the generals stayed in or near the Temple of Isis, while the nearby Villa Publica was an alternative but is not mentioned. The grounds of the Villa Publica certainly provided a large area for their attending troops to camp.

107. Josephus *BJ* 7.96. Translation in Beard 2007, 93–4.

108. See, e.g., Pietilä-Castrén, 25; Richardson 1992, 83; Coarelli 2007, 267. Ancient writers, however, note that while the Circus Flaminius was used for activities related to the triumph, they do not clearly state that it was the actual parade gathering point. Livy, 39.5.17, for instance, notes that on the day of his parade, Fulvius used the Circus Flaminius to hand out military decorations and cash to his soldiers. Plutarch describes the decoration of the Circus Flaminius with enemy arms and war machines in connection with a triumph by the general Lucullus. Plut. *Lucul.* 37.2.

109. Much debate has occurred as to precisely where in the city walls the triumph entered and whether the opening in the walls was the *porta triumphalis* to which reference is made in a few passages of ancient literature. For an excellent discussion of this problem, see Beard 2007, 96–105. The Porta Carmentalis was one of the sites pointed out to Aeneas on his tour of Rome in Vergil's *Aeneid*. Verg. *Aen* 8.337–68.

110. Coulston and Dodge, 104 n. 71; Pietilä-Castrén, 25.

111. See, e.g., Livy 31.47.7 (200 B.C.E.); 28.38.1–2 (206 B.C.E.); 28.9.5 (207 B.C.E.); 26.21.1 (211 B.C.E.). The Senate debates over the award of a triumph were often hard fought. In the case of Marcus Marcellus in 211 B.C.E., the triumph was denied, but he was granted the lesser award of an *ovatio*, requiring him to enter the city on horse or on foot but not in a chariot. Livy 26.21.1–5. Publius Cornelius Scipio Africanus went to the Temple of Bellona and sought a triumph in 206 B.C.E., but it was not granted as he was not a magistrate at the time he commanded his troops. Livy 28.38.1–4. See also Beard 2007, 201.

112. Livy 39.4.1. See also Livy 37.58.3 (189 B.C.E.); 41.17.4 (176 B.C.E.).

113. Other spaces on the triumphal route were, however, still available, and yet the Circus Flaminius was apparently viewed as an attractive place for temple construction along the route. A temple of Felicitas was dedicated circa 142 B.C.E. in the Velabrum, and a temple of Hercules was dedicated in the Forum Boarium at approximately the same time, both on the triumphal route. See Pietilä-Castrén, 154.

114. Pietilä-Castrén, 41, 154–5; Richardson 1992, 151.

115. See Orlin 2002A, 132.

116. The Ligurian shield was noted as being present on the Temple of Juno Regina when it was struck by lightning in 134 B.C.E. Obseq. 27. See also Richardson 1992, 217.

117. While Vespasian and Titus spent the night in the central Campus Martius before their triumph, there is no evidence that earlier *triumphatores* did the same, and the record is silent as to the parade route forming there.

118. As Patterson, 196, notes, "It is hard to avoid the conclusion that these temples were so positioned as to impress the voters thronging the Campus at election time." Varro *Rust.* 3.5.12, set in the Villa Publica, makes reference to the Temple of Fortuna Huiusce Diei nearby in the Largo Argentina.

119. Patterson, 196.

120. J. Muccigrosso, "Religion and Politics: Did the Romans Scruple about the Placement of Their Temples?," in Harvey and Schulz, 190.

121. The Temple of the Nymphs housed records of the census, and since the census was taken in the Villa Publica, it is believed that the temple must have been close to the villa. The temple located on the Via delle Botteghe Oscure would, at one time, have been within the grounds of the Villa Publica. The temple burned down in the mid-first century B.C.E. Manacorda 2000, 16.

122. See note 67 in this chapter with respect to the different arguments for the location of this temple. If, as has been suggested, the Temple of the Lares Permarini is Temple D and that of Juturna resided next door in Temple C, then the placement of the former may be seen also as an attempt by L. Aemilius Regillus to associate his extraordinary naval victory over Antiochus with the naval battle that ended the First Punic War. Ziółkowski 1986, 633.

123. Plut. *Vit. Rom.* 29.2. See Woodard, 196–7; D. Manacorda, "Iuno Curitis," *LTUR*, vol. 3, 121; Coarelli 1997, 33. See discussion in Chapter 2.

124. Plut. *Quaest Rom.* 47. The Temple of Vulcan was vowed by the consul C. Aurelius Cotta, who was awarded a triumph for his taking of Lipara (now Lipari), one of the Aeolian Islands north of Sicily. Ziółkowski 1992, 181. Livy (24.10.9) places the temple simply in the Campus Martius, while the Fasti Vallenses places it specifically in the area of the Circus Flaminius. Richardson 1992, 432. It possibly stood in the center of the area later

developed as the Crypta Balbi, which would place it near the edge of the Circus Flaminius and close by the Largo Argentina and Villa Publica. See Woodard, 61; Coarelli 2007, 283. Although its construction date is uncertain, it certainly antedated 214 B.C.E. when Livy notes that it was struck by lightening. Livy 24.10.9.

125. Ballentine, 92.
126. Stamper, 34.
127. Stamper, 44.
128. Stamper, 54–5.
129. Stamper, 49.
130. See Chapter 6 with respect to the benefits of the high temple platform to avoid the periodic flooding that occurred in the Campus Martius.
131. Stamper, 60–2.
132. Stamper, 61.
133. Stamper, 59–63. The Temple of Janus on the north was rebuilt during the early first century B.C.E., and its Ionic columns from that period are still visible. Stamper, 59–60; F. Coarelli, "Ianus, Aedes," *LTUR*, vol. 3, 91.
134. Pliny *NH* 36.24. There were also statues of Juno by Greek sculptors Dionysius, Polycles, and Praxiteles. Dionysius and Polycles collaborated on the statue of Jupiter in that god's temple next door. Pliny *NH* 36.4.
135. Vitr. *De arch.* 3.2.5.
136. Vell. Pat. 1.11.5; Stamper, 53–4; Dyson, 54.
137. Nepos ap. Priscian 8.17.
138. Richardson 1992, 76; Vitr. *De arch.* 4.8.4. While the founder of the Temple of Castor and Pollux is unknown, we have good information regarding its appearance as it was etched in a fragment of marble found in 1983 known as the Via Anicia Plan. See Patterson, 197.
139. As one scholar notes, temples of Hercules were often round. See Pietilä-Castrén, 102; Richardson 1992, 187.
140. Richardson 1992, 156; Stamper, 75–7; Stambaugh, 39.
141. "Some made fun of the Romans' traditions and customs . . . others of the appearance of the city itself, not yet beautiful in either public or private domains." Livy 40.5.7. See Stambaugh, 28.
142. Stamper, 45–6, 80.
143. Stamper, 80–1.
144. Stamper, 119.
145. Stamper, 120–1.
146. Richardson 1992, 317.

147. Stamper, 124. For a discussion of the porticoes, see Chapter 5.

FOUR: "CHARIOT RACES," "THREE THEATRES," "AN AMPHITHEATRE," AND MORE: ENTERTAINMENT IN THE CAMPUS MARTIUS

1. Calp. *Ecl.* 7.23–72.
2. The dating of Calpurnius's *Eclogues* and the location of the amphitheater are not agreed upon by all. Champlin, 107, argues that the poem describes the Colosseum of the third century C.E. Townend, 169, offers a solid rebuttal, dating the visit of Calpurnius to 57 C.E. and the location as the Amphitheater of Nero.
3. Calp. *Ecl.* 7.23–5; Pliny *NH* 16.200.
4. See Richardson 1992, 10; Futrell 2006, 59, with respect to the amphitheater's possible location northwest of the Pantheon, which would have put Calpurnius's observation point about one kilometer northwest of the Capitoline.
5. Pliny *NH* 19.24.
6. Calp. *Ecl.* 7.23–4.
7. Ibid.
8. As noted in Chapter 2, the *Fasti Triumphales* record triumphs going back to the monarchy. See Beard 2007, 61–2.
9. See Scullard, 82; 89. Livy claimed that horse races in Rome were conducted as early as the eighth century B.C.E. when, at the festival of Consualia during the reign of Romulus, the Romans used equestrian events to distract the Sabine men so that the Romans could carry off their women. Livy 1.9. See Scullard, 177–8; Boatwright et al., 383.
10. Scullard, 82; Rawson 1981, 1 n. 4.
11. Scullard, 193; Pascal, 275. Its possible location will be discussed later in this chapter.
12. Horse racing events were often combined with soldiers engaging in military maneuvers to entertain the crowds between races. Livy 44.9.
13. See Humphrey, 61. The valley was known during the late empire as the Vallis Murcia. See also Futrell 2006, 68. While Livy, 1.35.8, attributes the construction to Tarquinius Priscus (617–578 B.C.E.), Dionysius of Halicarnassus (*Ant. Rom.* 4.44.1) believed the circus was completed by Tarquinius's grandson, Tarquinius Superbus (534–510 B.C.E.). See discussion in Humphrey, 64–7. Other

circus facilities constructed in Rome during the imperial period include the Circus Gaii et Neronis where the Vatican now stands and the Circus Varianus inside the Aurelian Walls near the Church of S. Croce in Geruslemme. See Richardson 1992, 83–4, 87.

14. With respect to dimensions of the arena in its final form, see Richardson 1992, 86. With respect to capacity, see Dion. Hal. *Ant. Rom.* 3.68 (150,000) and Pliny *NH* 36.102 (250,000). See discussion in Richardson 1992, 86–7. Although races were originally seven laps, Suetonius (*Dom.* 4.3) tells us that the Emperor Domitian reduced the length to five laps in order to fit in as many as 100 races. The Circus Maximus continued to be the site of circus games until 549 C.E., 1,100 years after its traditional founding. See discussions in Humphrey, 126–31; Richardson 1992, 84–7; Balsdon, 252.

15. Richardson 1992, 86.

16. Futrell 2006, 2. The *ludi Romani* were held annually from September 5 to 19 and were to honor Jupiter. Boatwright 1990, 187.

17. Although dating to as early as the sixth century B.C.E. (Humphrey, 66–7), they received annual state sponsorship in 366 B.C.E. See Futrell 2006, 2.

18. Dupont, 207.

19. Rawson 1981, 16.

20. A late Roman writer Tertullian (Tert. *De spect.* 9.5) stated that during the period of the Roman Kings there were two competing teams – Red and White. See discussion in Balsdon, 314; Poynton, 78. Modern scholars are less certain with arguments for the establishment of racing teams spanning the period from the mid-fifth century B.C.E. to the end of the Second Punic War. Compare Rawson 1981, 16, and Humphrey, 137–138. See also Kathleen M. Coleman, "Entertaining Rome," in Coulston and Dodge, 215. Four teams were clearly in place by the end of the republic. Rawson 1981, 6.

21. Balsdon, 316.

22. Humphrey, 137. Each of the four colors could field as many as three chariots per race.

23. Balsdon, 248, also 268.

24. See Boatwright et al., 385; Futrell 2006, 198. Unless horse teams were raced more than once a day, more than 1,100 horses would be needed to meet the demand. Between races, audiences were entertained with displays of trick riders. Poynton, 77.

25. During the *ludi Taurii* horses were mounted by jockeys and not hitched to chariots. Humphrey, 543–4; Wiseman 1974, 4; Wiseman 1976, 44. Varro *Ling.* 5.154 is our source for the location in the Circus Flaminius. Dedicated to the gods of the underworld, the quinquennial games would have been appropriate near the location of the altar to Dis and Proserpina northwest of the Circus Flaminius.

26. Val. Max. 1.7.4. See Humphrey, 543. Coleman, "Entertaining," 217, suggests the races may have started in the Circus Flaminius and then moved later to the Circus Maximus. See also Scullard, 196.

27. Strabo 5.3.8.

28. See Richardson 1992, 83; Coleman, "Entertaining," 217; Wiseman 1974, 4–5. The term *circus* may have referred to the original circular shape of the space confined by certain structures such as the temples of Bellona and Apollo Medicus on the south. Once significant development began in the area in the late third and early second centuries B.C.E., the structures within the area could then be described as *in circo Flaminio*. See Wiseman 1974, 5; Humphrey, 541–2.

29. See Humphrey, 543–4, who indicates that once confined it was only about half its original length. Carandini and Carafa, eds., vol. 2, *tavole fuori testo* 18–19, suggests a slightly greater length in the fourth century C.E., approximately 335 meters.

30. This is based on Humphrey's measurement of the circus's length (see note 29) and a velocity of about 34 kilometers per hour. With respect to the velocity, see Boatwright et al., 385, who calculate that *quadrigae* in the Circus Maximus covered the 8.4-kilometers distance of a race in about fifteen minutes, which translates to approximately 34 kilometers per hour.

31. At a width of approximately 40 meters at the turning post, the Circus Maximus provided approximately 3.3 meters of width for each chariot. That suggests that four *quadrigae* could be accommodated in about 13.2 meters of width. The shaded area of the Circus Flaminius, as shown in the *Atlante di Roma Antica* (Carandini and Carafa, eds., vol. 2, *tavole fuori testo* 18–19), indicates a width of approximately 60 meters, more than twice the total width necessary at the turning post to accommodate one chariot from each of the four teams.

32. With respect to the October Horse location, the fourth-century C.E. calendar of Philocalus notes, *equus ad nixas fit*. CIL I², p. 274. There has been great debate as to whether this is the same location as the reference in the regionary catalogs for Region IX to *ciconias nixas*. See Richardson 1992, 81–2, who believes the *ciconiae* was where wine was offloaded just south of the Ponte Cavour in the northern Campus Martius and that *nixas* refers to a different location in Region IX. Palmer 1990, 34, 62, places an altar to the *Nixae* in the vicinity of the Tarentum where he believes the October Horse was sacrificed, specifically on the Via degli Aquasparta near the Ponte Umberto I north of the Via Coronari. Pascal, 285–6 connects the two words to the same location and would have the October Horse run about 300 meters south of the Mausoleum of Augustus in the approximate area of the Piazza Borghese.

33. See Coarelli 1977, 839; Rawson 1981, 1 n. 4. *But* see Palmer 1990, 33. With respect to possible sources of the name, see Richardson 1992, 401.

34. It has been argued that the *trigarium* was simply an open area set aside as a practice track with occasional formal races held. See Coarelli 1977, 839.

35. This location would have been between the Circus Flaminius and the altar to Dis and Proserpina. See Coarelli 2007, 263. See also Carandini and Carafa, eds., vol. 2, *tavole fuori testo* 13 and *tav.* 275. Palmer 1990, 30, challenges this location, in part, because of its susceptibility to flooding, but we do know that on occasion the Equirria races were flooded out and were then held on the Caelian Hill, so the presence of the race course in low-lying portions of the plain cannot be ruled out. See Ov. *Fast.* 3.519–23, Festus 117 L; Scullard, 82; Palmer 1990, 16. The regionary catalogs list a "Trigarium," although its location is not determinable from this source. Palmer 1990, 31–3.

36. A stone font from the Church of S. Lorenzo in Damaso, now part of the Palazzo della Cancelleria, bears the fourth-century church's earlier name, S. Laurentii in Prasino, a reference to the stables of the Green faction. See also discussion by F. Coarelli, "Trigarium," *LTUR*, vol. 5, 89–90. See Richardson 1992, 366; Dyson, 237–8.

37. Suet. *Calig.* 55.2–3; Cassius Dio 59.14.6–7.
38. Suet. *Calig.* 55.2–3. Resting under purple blankets and bejeweled with a collar of precious stones, Incitatus was also provided by Caligula with a furnished house and slaves to be used "for the more elegant entertainment of the guests invited in his name; and it is also said that [the Emperor] planned to make him consul." Ibid.
39. Suet. *Aug.* 81; Plut. *Mar.* 34.
40. Strabo 5.3.8.
41. Livy 7.2 gives the precise date as 361 B.C.E. Beacham, 10, gives September 363; Gruen, 185, gives the year 364.
42. Livy 7.2. See discussion in Beacham, 11–13.
43. Beacham, 12–13.
44. The earliest performances were called *satura*, a term later used for satire. Beacham, 11–12. The playwright Livius Andronicus is credited with the introduction of scripted drama in 240 B.C.E. Beacham, 13; Gruen, 185. Among other works, Andronicus introduced the *Odyssey* translated into Latin. Beacham, 19.
45. The *fabulae praetextae* included stories about the birth of the twins Romulus and Remus and their victory over their great uncle Amulius and the abduction of the Sabine women. The plays about the birth of Romulus and Remus and defeat of Amulius were by the author Naevius. The abduction of the Sabine women under Romulus was by Ennius. Wiseman 1998, 2–3; Beacham, 24. With respect to festivals, apart from the *ludi Romani*, there were the *ludi Florales* (begun in 240 B.C.E., annually in 173 B.C.E.), the *ludi Plebeii* (begun in 216 B.C.E.), the *ludi Apollinares* (begun in 214 or 212 B.C.E.), and the *ludi Megalenses* (begun in 204 B.C.E.). See Gruen, 185–6; Beacham, 20.
46. Boatwright 1990, 187; Scullard, 196; Sear 2006, 54.
47. With respect to the number in mid-second century B.C.E., see Gruen, 187, who estimates that oftentimes another five or six days were added annually for the reshowing of performances. Balsdon, 248, notes that theatrical performances were held on fifty-six of the seventy-seven days set aside at the time of Augustus for public games.
48. Beacham, 154.
49. Coleman, "Entertaining," 220; Beacham, 20; Hanson, 17–18.

50. Manuwald, 57; Coleman, "Entertaining," 220. While there has been debate as to whether early theatrical performances were viewed sitting or standing, certainly by the third century B.C.E., when Plautus was writing, spectators watched from seats. See Sear 2006, 54.

51. See Livy 40.51.3 See also Sear 2006, 54–5; Saunders, 91; C. Campbell 2003, 68. It has been suggested that the theater was "semipermanent" in the sense that the *cavea* was left in place while the scene building was torn down and rebuilt periodically for performances. The seating may have been reused five years later in connection with a stage built in 174 B.C.E. Livy 41.27.5. Sear 2006, 55. Gruen, 206, however, questions whether the project ever "got off the ground."

52. See Livy, 42.10.5, who notes that the dedication also included one day of circus games. Richardson 1992, 155, places the temple to Fortuna Equestris close to the Theater of Pompey and believes that it was destroyed in a fire of 21 B.C.E. that also engulfed the *scaenae frons* of Pompey's theater.

53. Polyb. 30.22.12. The stage was erected for the triumph of Lucius Anicius Gallus who served as praetor in 168 B.C.E. See Beacham, 64. Satires were performed at the triumph of Scipio Africanus in 201 B.C.E. Beacham, 12. See also Balsdon, 261.

54. App. *Pun.* 9.66, describing the triumph of Scipio Africanus in 201 B.C.E., as translated in Mary Beard, "The Triumph of the Absurd: Roman Street Theatre," in Edwards and Woolf, 33–4.

55. Suet. *Iul.* 39.

56. Balsdon, 274–7; Boatwright 1990, 188. The story of the old hag Anna Perenna and the trick played upon Mars discussed in Chapter 2 was performed as a mime. Entitled *Anna Perenna*, the play was written by the first-century B.C.E. playwright Laberius. See Wiseman 1998, 72.

57. Sear 2006, 48–53.

58. Sear 2006, 130–1.

59. Beacham, 57–8. See also Sear 2006, 25–7, regarding the calculation of capacity and the relative size of theaters.

60. Beacham, 8, 58–60.

61. See C. Campbell 2003, 69–70, for summary of arguments. See also Claire Holleran, "The Development of Public Entertainment Venues in Rome and Italy," in Lomas and Cornell, 58; Gruen, 205–10.

62. See discussion in C. Campbell 2003, 70, with respect to the theory regarding honoring gods in their own precincts as well as her own proposal regarding the problems with Roman concrete, 76.

63. Livy *Per.* 48. See discussion in Gruen, 206–7. The theater was being constructed southwest of the Palatine, and if completed, it would have placed Rome's first permanent theater outside of the Campus Martius. See C. Campbell 2003, 73.

64. Val. Max.2.4.2; Hanson, 24.

65. App. *B.Civ.* 1.28.

66. Gruen, 209–10. For an excellent discussion of the demolition of this theater in the context of the various reasons provided for avoiding permanent theaters until the construction of Pompey's grand edifice, see Wallace-Hadrill, 160–9.

67. Livy 34.44, 34.54; Val. Max. 2.4.3; Balsdon, 260.

68. Beacham, 66 and note 41. Ironically, the consul at the time was the father of Aemilius Scaurus who, sixty-seven years later, would build the extraordinarily elaborate temporary theater discussed next. See Beacham, 67–8.

69. For an analysis of the Lex Iulia Theatralis, see Rawson 1987.

70. See discussion in Beacham, 66.

71. Beacham, 66–7. Some time before 100 B.C.E. the aedile L. Licinius Crassus erected columns of Hymettus marble within a temporary theater. Richardson 1992, 380.

72. Pliny, *NH*, 36.35, claimed it held 80,000 people, a likely fourfold exaggeration. See Richardson 1992, 385.

73. Richardson 1992, 380, 385.

74. Erected by the tribune for 50 B.C.E., C. Scribonius Curio, these were the Theatra Curionis used for funeral games in 53 B.C.E. After a few days, however, the pivoting device wore down and the stages would no longer turn. See Richardson 1992, 381.

75. Pliny *NH* 36.15.117–20, as quoted in Futrell 2006, 57–8.

76. Holleran, "Public Entertainment Venues," 52–3.

77. Plut. *Vit. Pomp.* 42.4.

78. One ancient writer, Velleius Paterculus (Vell. Pat. 2.48.2), notes that Pompey used his own money, but others suggest the funds came from one of Pompey's freedmen. See Cassius Dio 39.38.6; Plut. *Vit. Pomp.* 40.4–5.

79. See Richardson 1992, 384; Sear 2006, 57; P. Gros, "Theatrum Pompei," *LTUR*, vol. 5, 35.

80. Sear 2006, 57, calculates approximately 150 meters; Monterroso Checa, 197, concludes it had a diameter of 165 meters.

81. Monterroso Checa, 313 (height). The theater complex, including the *quadriportico*, covered 53,790 square meters (ibid., 393) more than one-half the Capitoline's area of approximately 100,000 square meters (Heiken et al., 27–34).

82. Sear 2006, 57.

83. Pliny *NH*, 36.115, claims it held 40,000 spectators, a number that many modern scholars reject. The fourth-century C.E. regionary catalogs provide the capacity as 17,580 *loca*, but there is no uniformity of opinion as to how to turn that number into actual seats. Two authors treat *loca* as a measurement of length and assign approximately 18 inches for a seat, resulting in the number between 11,000 (Richardson 1992, 385) and 11,600 (Sear 2006, 57 and n. 65). Two others, Coarelli 2007, 283, and P. Gros, "Theatrum Pompei," *LTUR*, vol. 5, 36, use the number provided in the regionary catalogs as the number of seats. Most recently, Monterroso, 296, calculates a total capacity of 21,008 consisting of 18,635 seats in the *ima* and *media cavea*, 1888 in the *summa cavea*, and 485 senatorial seats.

84. Richardson 1992, 385.

85. Richardson 1992, 385. Sear notes that the Marble Plan shows the *cavea* divided into sixteen segments, and while he believes these to be indications of the passageways, there was insufficient room on the plan to detail all of them. Sear 2006, 60.

86. Richardson 1992, 385; P. Gros, "Theatrum Pompei," *LTUR*, vol. 5, 37; Cod. Vat. Lat. 3439 f.22r and 23r.

87. The satyr (figure 16), one of a pair said to have been found in the vicinity of Pompey's theater, may date to the second century C.E. and was possibly part of the decoration of the rebuilt theater. See discussion in Haskell and Penny, 301–2. The statue of a seated muse (figure 17) was found by the Via Arenula east of the theater.

88. Amm. Marc. 16.10.14.

89. The other temples were to Honor (Honos), Virtue (Virtus), Luck (Felicitas), and, perhaps, Victory (Victoria). See Richardson 1992, 384; Gagliardo and Packer, 95. See Suet. *Claud.* 21.1. It is uncertain that the temples other

than that of Venus Victrix were part of the original construction. The roof of the temple of Venus is estimated to have been forty-five meters above ground level, or the approximate height of the Capitoline Hill. Coleman, "Entertaining," 221.

90. Tert. *De spect.* 10.

91. See Tac. *Ann.* 14.20; Richardson 1992, 384. Although the first in Rome, Pompey's theater was not unique for having temples atop the *cavea*. See discussion in Sear 2006, 58.

92. Dyson, 103.

93. Plut. *Vit. Pomp.* 68.

94. Beacham, 162. See Cassius Dio 44.6.2.

95. See Cic. *Div.* 2.23; Plut. *Vit. Caes.* 66.1–2; *Brut.* 14.1–2.

96. Richardson 1992, 384. With respect to walling up the *curia*, see Suet. *Iul.* 88, *Aug.* 31.5.

97. As to the conversion to a latrine, see Cassius Dio 47.19.1; Richardson 1992, 104.

98. Dyson, 102.

99. See Florus 2.13.4.2.91 (Julius Caesar); Suet. *Claud.* 21.1 (Claudius).

100. Tac. *Ann.* 13.54.3–4.

101. Pliny *NH* 33.54; Cassius Dio 63.6.

102. Sear 2006, 59.

103. Plut. *Vit. Pomp.* 40.4–5.

104. Vitruvius noted that theaters could be built either against hills or on flat ground if solid foundations are provided. Vitr. *De arch.* 5.3.3.

105. It has been argued that the earlier attempts at permanent theaters failed in Rome in part because the quality of concrete architecture was insufficient in second-century B.C.E. Rome to create the kind of concrete vaulting that supported a structure such as Pompey's. See C. Campbell 2003, 74–8.

106. Personification of nations: Edwards in "Incorporating the Alien: The Art of Conquest," in Edwards and Woolf, 65; Venus: Beard 2013, 195.

107. Suet. *Iul.* 44.

108. Cic. *Att.* 4.16. Favro 1996, 67. Richardson 1992, 340, notes that it is uncertain that Caesar even commenced construction of the project.

109. Cassius Dio, 43.49.2; Suet. *Iul.* 44 See Richardson 1992, 382.

110. Marcellus had served as aedile, the office in charge of maintaining public buildings and festivities. When Marcellus organized a successful festival in 23 B.C.E., Augustus honored him by covering the entire Roman Forum in awnings.

That same year Marcellus died. Cassius Dio 53.30–31.

111. Coarelli 2007, 267.

112. Sear 2006, 62.

113. There is no firm agreement on the construction period for Sosianus's project. Richardson 1992, 13, dates the structure to 30–28 B.C.E. Strong, 80–1, suggests that some of the decorative elements date to ca. 20 B.C.E., an indication that the temple was not completed by the time that Augustus commenced work on the theater.

114. One theory is that it housed the republican *perirrhanterion*, a sacred font that stood in front of the earlier Temple of Apollo. See E. La Rocca, "Perirrhanterion," *LTUR*, vol. 4, 80. According to Plutarch, it is here that Lucius Catilina (108–62 B.C.E.) or Catiline washed the blood off his hands after showing the dictator Sulla the head of his political rival, Marius, during a meeting in the Senate. Plut. *Vit. Sull.* 32.

115. Sear 2006, 62.

116. Richardson 1992, 382; Sear 2006, 62.

117. See Hanson, 22–3. See also Richardson 1992, 383.

118. Coarelli 2007, 268. If Coarelli is correct, the proximity of the temples of Apollo and Bellona could have been less of a factor in the theater's site selection.

119. See Favro 1996, 157, with respect to the triumphal route through the theater. See Hill, 83–4, with respect to the statue of Augustus. The statue was erected by Tiberius, and it is believed to be depicted on a coin issued by Augustus's immediate successor showing Augustus seated by an altar with a branch and a scepter in his hands. Ibid.

120. See Favro 1996, 108; Patterson, 198.

121. While the Theater of Pompey had a *cavea* diameter between 150 and 165 meters (see note 80), the diameter of the Theater of Marcellus was about 129 meters. Sear 2006, 21. The regionary catalogs list the capacity of the Theater of Marcellus at 20,500 *loca* compared to the Theater of Pompey with 17,580. Depending on the calculation used for *loca* (see note 83), this results in a difference in capacity of between 2,000 (Richardson 1992, 382, 385) and 3,500 (Sear 2006, 62).

122. Favro 1996, 164.

123. Richardson 1992, 383; Sear 2006, 63. The stacking of the three orders is seen most clearly today in the remains of the Colosseum, built

more than a century after the Theater of Marcellus. One scholar believes the architects of the Colosseum must have studied the theater closely for its exterior design elements. See Richardson 1992, 383.

124. Sear 2006, 64.

125. Sear 2006, 65.

126. Cic. *Scaur.* 45; Sear 2006, 65. Richardson 1992, 382, notes that while the columns were likely in the central entrance to the stage, they may have been part of one of the appended structures.

127. Richardson 1992, 383. Coarelli has suggested that one or both of the small squares represent temples, with one being a rebuilt Temple of Pietas, but there is no evidence for this proposition. See Coarelli 2007, 267–8.

128. Favro 1996, 145. According to Cassius Dio 54.26.1, the dedication occurred in 13 B.C.E.; Pliny, *NH*, 8.65, indicates that it was in 11 B.C.E.

129. According to myth, a Sabine seeking a cure for his sick children offered the original sacrifice. Later this initial sacrifice was celebrated with sacrifices over three consecutive nights. Augustus changed the ceremony to honor Terra Mater (Mother Earth), the Fates, and Ilythiae, the goddess of childbirth, as well as Jupiter, Juno, Apollo, and Diana. See Beard et al., vol. 1, 203–5. Adkins and Adkins, 134. Septimius Severus would later reinstitute the *ludi saeculares* with a commemorative record set up in the Tarentum, near the altar of Dis and Proserpina, with Mars featured in honor of the emperor's military victories. Dyson, 206.

130. Beard et al., vol. 1, 203–4. See Hazel Dodge, "Amusing the Masses: Buildings for Entertainment and Leisure in the Roman World," in Potter and Mattingly, 206–7, for discussion of Greek games in Rome.

131. Cassius Dio 54.25.2; Richardson 1992, 381–2.

132. According to the regionary catalogs, the theater had 11,510 *loca*. Richardson 1992, 381, calculates this as 7,700 seats and Sear 2006, 66, calculates the total as 8,460. With respect to the relative diameters, see Coarelli 2007, 281.

133. Pliny *NH* 36.60.

134. The word *crypta* indicates a covered passage. Vendettelli, 54; Manacorda, 12.

135. Vendettelli, 54; Coarelli 2007, 283, suggests that it may be the third-century B.C.E.

Temple of Vulcan. See discussion in Chapter 3, note 124.

136. Cassius Dio 54.25; Pliny *NH* 36.60.

137. With respect to the Trojan Games, see C. B. Rose 2005, 42–3. See also Verg. *Aen.* 5.545–603. The future emperor Gaius (Caligula) participated in these games. In addition to the Troy Games, there were wild beasts displayed. Cassius Dio 54.261.

138. Pliny *NH* 8.65; Suet. *Iul.* 88, *Aug.* 31.5; Cassius Dio 53.30.6.

139. Balsdon, 248; Coleman, "Entertaining," 226.

140. Balsdon, 267–8. With respect to Rome's imperial population, see Robinson, 8–9.

141. The calculations are based on the theater areas given by Sear 2006, 21, for the theaters of Pompey and Marcellus and a similar calculation for the Theater of Balbus (ibid. 66) and the areas of the porticoes connected to Pompey's theater and the Crypta Balbi.

142. Richardson 1992, 276; Coarelli 2007, 295–6. Still later, Strabo would have briefly seen a fifth theater in the Campus Martius, the Theatrum Traiani, a theater constructed by Trajan but destroyed by Hadrian. Richardson 1992, 385.

143. Coleman, "Entertaining," 243. Coarelli 2007, 296, notes a column that has survived. See also Richardson 1992, 276.

144. Robinson, 163; Suet. *Dom.* 4; Coleman, "Entertaining," 241.

145. Richardson 1992, 276.

146. Richardson 1992, 40–1. With respect to discovery of the site of the Athenaeum, see http://www.huffingtonpost.com/2009/10/21/ancient-auditorium-called_n_328657.html (accessed February 2, 2013); Coates-Stephens, 290–1.

147. Suet. *Vesp.* 19. One tragic actor received 400,000 *sesterces*, which in modern bullion would be convertible to approximately $875,000. The repairs may have been necessitated by damage from a fire that spread from the Capitoline in 69 C.E. during the brief reign of Vitellius. See P. Ciancio Rossetto, "Theatrum Marcelli," *LTUR*, vol. 5, 32.

148. The taxes were obtained from, among other sources, "prostitutes, both male and female." SHA *Alex. Sev.* 24, 44. See Richardson 1992, 382; Dudley, 142.

149. See table 1 "Documented Restorations of Pompey Theatre," in Gagliardo and Packer, 96.

150. Sear 2006, 66.

151. Richardson 1992, 276; Suet. *Dom.* 5; Cassius Dio 69.4.1; Polemius Silvius, Mommsen, *MGH*, (1892), 545; Amm. Marc. 16.10.14.

152. Livy *Epit.* 16; Val. Max. 2.4.7. See Futrell 1997, 20–1. The source for gladiatorial combat has been argued to be either the Samnites in the south or the Etruscans in the north. See Welch, 11–18; Holleran, "Public Entertainment Venues," 49.

153. Coleman, "Entertaining," 227.

154. Cassius Dio 47.40.6; Robinson, 145–6.

155. Welch, 19; Robinson, 145–6.

156. Cassius Dio 37.8; Suet. *Caes.* 10.1.

157. Cassius Dio 43.22.2–3. See Kathleen M. Coleman, "Euergetism in Its Place – Where Was the Amphitheatre in Augustan Rome?," in Lomas and Cornell, 63–4.

158. Cassius Dio 54.2; Balsdon, 251.

159. Robinson, 145.

160. *Res Gestae* 22.

161. Balsdon, 252; Beacham 198.

162. These balconies, called *maeniana superiora*, were possibly named after the censor Maenius, who first came up with the idea later used for tiers of seats in the stone amphitheaters. See Welch, 32.

163. Welch, 76.

164. See note 74 in this chapter.

165. Welch, 73–4.

166. Holleran, "Public Entertainment Venues," 52–3.

167. Welch, 119.

168. Suet. *Aug.* 29.4–5; Welch 110.

169. *Res Gestae* 22.

170. Suet. *Tib.* 7.1; *Calig.* 18.1; Cassius Dio 59.10.5.

171. Suet. *Calig.* 21.

172. Coleman, "Entertaining," 228; Haselberger et al., 44.

173. With respect to the location east of the Via Flaminia, see Richardson 1992, 11. As to its location in the area of Monte dei Cenci, see Haselberger et al., 44–5.

174. Haselberger et al., 44–5. The eighteenth-century architect and artist Piranesi placed the amphitheater in the location of Montecitorio in the central Campus Martius. Connors, 30, 43.

175. Begun around 70–2 C.E. by Vespasian, it was dedicated by him in 79 C.E., shortly before his death, although it was not finished. The work was completed by his successor Titus,

who held a second dedication in 80 C.E. with 100 days of games. Cassius Dio 66.25; Suet. *Tit.* 7.3.

176. For a discussion of the origins of the name, see Canter, 150–64.

177. Livy 39.22.2. Coleman, "Entertaining," 242. These games, conducted over ten days, also included a wild animal hunt. See Rosivach, 276.

178. Robinson, 143; Coleman, "Entertaining," 242; Dodge, "Amusing the Masses," 207.

179. With respect to Pompey, see Cassius Dio 39.38.1–5; Plut. *Vit. Pomp.* 52. As to Augustus, see *Res Gestae* 22.

180. Suet. *Iul.* 39.3, *Aug.* 43; Cassius Dio 53.1.5.

181. Suet. *Ner.* 12.3.

182. Coleman, "Entertaining," 241. The term "stadium" derived from the Greek *stade*, a unit of measure roughly 198 meters in length. See Vaughan Hart, "Stadium," in Grafton, Most, and Settis, 907.

183. Coleman, "Entertaining," 241–2.

184. Damsky 1990, 91.

185. Damsky 1990, 89–90.

186. Damsky 1990, 95–9.

187. Cassius Dio 79.25.

188. Amm. Marc. 16.10.14. During the medieval period, it was known variously as the Circus Flaminius, Theatrum Alexandri, and Circus Alexandri. Nash, vol. 2, 387. The last title stuck until the nineteenth century, when its connection to Domitian was recognized.

189. L. R. Taylor, 47, 113. See also Lucan 2.197, Juvenal 6.528–9.

190. Livy 26.22.11. See L. R. Taylor, 47. Concerning its relationship to the Villa Publica, see Richardson 1992, 278.

191. Cassius Dio 55.8. The Forum would have otherwise been the site had it not been badly damaged in a fire.

192. Cassius Dio 55.10.

193. Suet. *Calig.* 18.1.

194. Suet. *Claud.* 21.4.

195. Suet. *Ner.* 12.

196. Cassius Dio 66.24.2; Richardson 1992, 340.

197. Richardson 1992, 110, 340.

198. Cassius Dio 55.8.4; Pliny *NH* 16.201, 36.102.

199. Cassius Dio 55.8.4; 66.24.2.

200. Stat. *Silv.* 1.6.9–50; Cassius Dio 66.25.

201. Cassiod. *Var.* 1.27.4–5.

202. Amm. Marc. 28.4.28–33. The Tauri lived in southern Crimea.

203. Suet. *Aug.* 44, *Dom.* 4.

204. Cassius Dio 76.16.

205. SHA *Elag.* 26.3, translated in Aicher, 89.8.

206. A church to the saint now fronts onto the piazza where the stadium once stood. References to St. Agnes in Agone are found throughout the piazza, from the eponymous church on the west side to the modern name of the piazza, "Navona," which appears to be a corruption of *agone*, the Greek word for contest or competition. For much of the period following the decline of ancient Rome, the area was known as the "Circus Agonius," as shown on early maps. Palladio, 33 and n. 154.

FIVE: "COLONNADES ABOUT IT IN VERY GREAT NUMBERS": THE PORTICOES OF THE CAMPUS MARTIUS

1. Livy 43.17.2–10; 43.18.1.

2. Livy 43.18.1–11.

3. Livy 43.19.5.

4. Livy 44.17.7–10.

5. Livy 44.17.9–10. This was not Octavius's first encounter with the Hellenistic world, however. He had been one of the envoys to Greece the previous year, and he spoke Greek. Livy 43.17.2; 45.29.3.

6. Livy 44.35.9; 44.35.15; 44.46.3; 45.5.1.

7. Livy 45.6.9–12. See Lehmann, 79, 88, 90ff. and plan III.

8. See McCredie 1965, 102, 104.

9. See McCredie 1968, 202, fig. 1, 203.

10. Livy 45.6.10.

11. Livy 45.33.5.

12. Livy 45.35.2–4.

13. Livy 45.42.2.

14. Aemilius Paullus's triumph almost did not occur as his enemies tried to derail it. In a lengthy and impassioned argument in favor of the honor, Marcus Servilius asked, "Will King Perseus of Macedonia, together with his sons, the throng of other prisoners, and the spoils of Macedonia, be left behind in the Circus Flaminius?" Livy 45.39.13–14. Ultimately, the triumph occurred as planned.

15. Richardson 1992, 317.

16. See Senseney, 426; Richardson 1992, 267.

17. Pliny *NH* 34.7; Vell. Pat. 2.1.2; Richardson 1976, 60, speculates that it was likely the first colonnade with Corinthian capitals in Rome and possibly the first Corinthian building in the city.

18. As Kontokosta, 10, points out, there is no literary evidence that the porticus was the result of fulfillment of a battlefield vow.

19. Pliny *NH* 34.7. See Senseney, 428.

20. Senseney, 432. The stoa sat on the eastern and northern sides of the fourth-century B.C.E. Temple of Athena Nikephoros (330s–320s B.C.E.).

21. Senseney, 428.

22. App. *Ill.* 28; *Res Gestae* 19.

23. *Res Gestae* 4.19; Richardson 1992, 317.

24. Senseney, 421.

25. Livy 35.10.12; Richardson 1992, 303, 311.

26. Richardson 1992, 303.

27. Richardson 1976, 57.

28. Richardson 1992, 311.

29. With respect to the cost and financing, see Livy 35.10.12; see also Richardson 1976, 57. For a brief review of the debates concerning the designation Aemiliana, see Richardson 1992, 3. During the fire of Nero, many porticoes were destroyed in this area of Rome. Tac. *Ann.* 15.40.

30. Livy 35.10.12; MacDonald 1982, 5–6.

31. Livy 40.51.6; Richardson 1992, 317; Senseney, 429.

32. See Coulton, 4. Dating to the seventh century B.C.E., the earliest Greek stoas were as much as sixty meters long, with some having two colonnades. From the second half of the fifth century through the second century B.C.E., the freestanding colonnade was a significant element of Greek architecture, particularly in Athens. Later, the colonnade became integrated with other structures to create, for instance, *peristyles*. Coulton, 7, 18.

33. The Stoa at Perachora built circa 300 B.C.E. was L-shaped (Coulton, 56) and certainly would have been known to the Romans at the time of their defeat of the Achaean League in 146 B.C.E. At Pergamon, there were numerous stoas, including those on three sides of the sanctuary of Athena, with one colonnade and two storeys. Coulton, 67.

34. Coulton, 9.

35. Richardson 1976, 58. Richardson suggests the Stoa of Eumenes II along the southern slope of the Acropolis as a possible model, but Eumenes' rule from 197 to 156 B.C.E. makes the dating tight, and one author (Corso, 391) dates the construction of the *stoa* to a period between 180 and 160 B.C.E., at least a decade after the Porticus Aemilia *a Porta Fontinali ad Martis aram* was constructed.

36. Coulton, 168.

37. Strabo 5.3.8. As Wallace-Hadrill, 175, has noted, porticoes "transformed the urban face of Rome, making the Campus Martius by Strabo's day one of the most magnificent sites in the world."

38. See, e.g., Livy 35.10.12 (*porticum unam extra portam trigeminam*); Pliny *NH* 34.13 (*porticum duplicem*); *Res Gestae* 19 (*porticum ad circum Flaminium*).

39. Richardson 1992, 315. See also Morgan, 499–504. As for the number of sides of the *porticus*, Vitruvius (3.2.5) described the Temple of Jupiter Stator as being in the *porticus* (*in porticu*), suggesting the *porticus* wrapped around the temple on at least three sides, an orientation supported by Velleius Paterculus, 1.11.2–5, who notes that the portico surrounded (*circumdatae*) the temples. See Favro 1996, 170 and 316 n. 61; Richardson 1992, 317; Platner and Ashby, 424.

40. Pollitt 1978, 156–7. See Vell. Pat. 1.11.3–4. See also Serena Ensoli, "Lisippo a Roma," in Moreno, 299–303.

41. Pliny *NH* 34.31; Plut. *Vit. C. Gracch.* 4.3.

42. Pliny, *NH* 34.28, also mentions an archaic equestrian statue of Cloelia, a gallant maiden who escaped from the Tuscan king Lars Porsena, who had invaded Rome and taken her captive. Coarelli 2007, 272, however, describes the Cornelia statue as "the first public statue of a woman in Rome." See also J. D. Evans 2009, 135.

43. Vell. Pat. 2.8.3; Velleius associated the *porticus* with the victories of Minucius over the Scordisci.

44. See Carandini and Carafa, eds., vol. 2, tav. 216–17, identifying this portico with a question mark just to the east of the Largo Argentina temples. Patterson 1992, 214, indicates that the portico surrounded the Largo Argentina temples, but Richardson 1992, 316, believes it was a *quadriporticus* east of the Largo Argentina temples, aligning with the portico identified as "Minucia" on the Marble Plan. See also F. Coarelli, "Porticus Minucia Vetus," *LTUR*, vol. 4, 137–8.

45. The *porticus* has been measured to enclose a space 180 by 135 meters. Sear 2006, 61.

46. Pompey traveled throughout the East, including Cilicia, Bithynia, Syria, Cyprus, Ephesos, and possibly Athens and Rhodes before returning to Rome in 62 B.C.E. See J. D. Evans 2009, 124.

47. Vitr. *De arch.* 5.9.1. See discussion in Corso, 389–96.

48. Vitr. *De arch.* 5.9.1, trans. Rowland. While theoretically possible, it is difficult to envision 11,000 or more theatergoers leaving the protection of the theater's arcades and running around the building to find the entrances to the portico and then squeezing under its narrow roofline for cover.

49. As for its suitability for sexual encounters, see Catull. 55.6–14; Kuttner 1999, 350–1.

50. Pliny *NH* 35.37; 35.40.

51. Tatianus *Ad Gr.* 33–4. With respect to the statues as courtesans rather than women poets, see J. D. Evans 2009, 129–35.

52. See Pliny *NH* 35.132 (Alexander, Kalypso, both by Nikias); *NH* 35.126 (Sacrifice of Oxen, by Pausias); and *NH* 35.114 (Kadmos and Europa, by Antiphilus).

53. See Prop. 2.32.11–12; Val. Max. 2.4.6; Mart. *Ep.* 2.14. J. D. Evans 2009, 126. See also Kuttner 1995, 171–2.

54. Vitr. *De arch.* 5.9.5, trans. Rowland.

55. See Carandini and Carafa, eds., vol. 2, tav. 220, although Lanciani 1990, no. 21, indicates that it extended no further than the edge of the east side of Pompey's portico.

56. See Richardson 1992, 185; F. Coarelli, "Hecatostylum," *LTUR*, vol. 3, 9.

57. See Richardson 1992, 185. Martial, *Ep.* 3.19.1–2, indicates that the portico had ties to an area with plane trees in which bronze cast animals were displayed. This could be either Pompey's portico or a park adjacent to the Stagnum Agrippae by the Baths of Agrippa. Richardson 1992, 185.

58. Known from an inscription, the portico may have been built by the Lentulii family at approximately the time of construction of Pompey's complex (P. Cornelius Lentulus Spinther was consul in 57 B.C.E. and P. Cornelius Lentulus Crus was consul in 49 B.C.E.) or when two brothers from the same family were co-consuls in 18 B.C.E. at a time when Augustus encouraged such undertakings. See Suet *Aug.* 29. For discussion of the possible connection of the Porticus Lentulorum and the Hecatostylon and the arguments concerning dating, see S. Orlandi, "Porticus Lentulorum," *LTUR*, vol. 4, 125.

59. See Servius *Ad Aen.* 8.721. See also Suet. *Nero* 46. With respect to the argument connecting the Porticus ad Nationes to the Porticus Lentulorum and the Hecatostylon, see F. Coarelli, "Porticus ad Nationes," *LTUR*, vol. 4, 138–9.

60. Pliny *NH* 36.39. The indication of an entrance to the Porticus ad Nationes would seem to rule out the single-wing Hecatostylon next to Pompey's theater portico as its location, although, as Favro points out, a portico lined with statues of conquered nations served as "an overt counterpoint to the similar exhibition of Pompey in his theater." See Favro 1996, 174, 317 n. 73.

61. Manacorda, 12. Manacorda suggests that the Crypta Balbi served as a model for the building of Eumachia in the Forum of Pompeii. For a proposed elevation drawing of the Crypta Balbi of 13 B.C.E., see Carandini and Carafa, eds., vol. 2, tav. 228.

62. At the time of the rebuilding under Hadrian, the enclosed *crypta* may have been converted into an open portico, but the enclosed second story that was added allowed the term to continue to apply. Manacorda, 12.

63. Ov. *Ars am.* 1.69–70. See also, Richardson 1992, 317; A. Viscogliosi, "Porticus Octaviae," *LTUR*, vol. 4, 141.

64. Significant portions of the plan of the Porticus Octaviae survive in the fragments of the Marble Plan (fragments 31u, 31cc, 31bb, 31vaa). Richardson 1992, 317–18.

65. Richardson 1992, 317.

66. Richardson 1992, 317–18; *LTUR*, vol. 1, 386, fig. 51.

67. Pliny *NH* 34.31 (*Octaviae opera*); Plut. *Marc.* 30.6 (*bibliotheca Porticus Octaviae*); Cassius Dio 55.8.1 (*Curia*); Pliny *NH* 35.114 (*schola*). See Favro 1996, 171 (table 4) with respect to the area of the *porticus*.

68. Pliny *NH* 35.114. Antiphilus was a painter from Naucratis, Egypt, and active in the time of Alexander the Great. A contemporary of Apelles, he was known for his talents with light and shadow (Pliny *NH* 35.138), genre scenes, and caricatures (Pliny *NH* 35.114).

69. Pliny *NH* 35.139 (paintings of Androbius, country of origin and dates unknown).

70. Pliny *NH* 36.15 (Pheidias's Venus); 36.22 (Praxiteles' Cupid, also mentioned by Cicero in his Verrine Orations, IV.2.4 and IV 60.135); 36.24 (Cephisodotus the Younger's Aesclepius and Diana); 36.35 (Dionysius's Juno). Cephisodotus and Timarchides were Greek sculptors working during the final decades of the fourth century B.C.E. They are recorded as the sons of Praxiteles.
71. Richardson 1976, 63–4.
72. Richardson 1992, 187, 318.
73. Scenes of the Trojan War by Theorus and a Helen of Troy by Zeuxis were also placed within the *porticus*. Pliny *NH* 35.66, 114, 144.
74. *FUR* fgg. 31bb, 31cc, 31dd, 31eeff, 31hh. See Richardson 1977, 359.
75. Favro 1996, 173. The level of uniformity would have changed over time depending upon the extent to which the Porticus Octaviae was completely colonnaded on the side facing the Circus Flaminius.
76. Favro 1996, 169–70; Richardson 1992, 165. See also discussion in Chapter 3.
77. Vitr. *De arch.* 5.9.2.
78. Cic. *Att.* 4.16.14. It, too, featured famous works of art. See Pliny *NH* 36.29.
79. The Saepta Julia was a rectangle of 310 by 120 meters, so the length of the perimeter (all four sides) was approximately 860 meters (a little more than a half-mile). Richardson 1992, 340.
80. Cassius Dio 53.23.2. Richardson 1992, 341.
81. Richardson 1992, 340.
82. Richardson 1992, 312. On the eastern side of Hadrian's Pantheon, along the Via della Minerva, the remains of a structure built in *opus latericium* with a series of rectangular niches has been identified as a section of the west wall of the Porticus Argonautarum.
83. Mart. *Ep.* 2.14.16; 3.20.11; 9.59.2; 11.1.12.
84. Richardson 1992, 341.
85. Richardson 1992, 315.
86. See Senseney, 422.
87. See Favro 1996, 69, 171 (table 4).
88. The calculations are based on the dimensions provided by Favro 1996, 171 (table 4), as well as consideration of the area of the Porticus Pompeii and Porticus Minucia Vetus (PMV).
89. With respect to the dating (reign of Claudius v. Domitian) and location of the Porticus Minucia Frumentaria (PMF) east of the Largo Argentina, see D. Manacorda, "Porticus Minucia Frumentaria," *LTUR*, vol. 4, 132–7. The siting of the PMF adjacent to the Largo Argentina and the PMV is not universal. Richardson 1992, 315, would place the PMF along the west side of the Via Flaminia where remains of a vaulted structure with "a forest of rusticated piers" have been discovered. This identification would mean that the "portico" was not a colonnade but more in the nature of the early Porticus Aemilia *extra Portam Trigeminam*, as described by MacDonald 1982, 5–6. Richardson 1992, 316, would place the PMV in the space just east of the Largo Argentina.
90. D. Manacorda, "Porticus Minucia Frumentaria," *LTUR*, vol. 4, 134.
91. Vitr. *De arch.* 5.9.9, trans. Rowland.
92. See F. Coarelli, "Divorum, Porticus, Templum," *LTUR*, vol. 2, 19–20; Richardson 1992, 111. See Carandini and Carafa, eds., vol. 2, tav. 237, for possible reconstruction.
93. Richardson 1992, 246–7. See Carandini and Carafa, eds., vol. 2, tav. 241, for possible reconstruction.
94. Richardson 1992, 184. See plan for the temple and portico in Carandini and Carafa, eds., vol. 2, tav. 244. Claridge 2010, 224–5, notes, however, that evidence for a portico has been found only on the north side of the temple.
95. Richardson 1992, 184–5.
96. Richardson 1992, 312.
97. See Richardson 1992, 315.
98. Lanciani 1897, 445–6.
99. Ov. *Ars am.* 3.167–8 (wigs); Mart. *Ep.* 9.59 (inlaid furniture, goblets).
100. Mart. *Ep.* 2.14. See Prior, 125–8. Richardson 1992, 267, 313, would place it near the Stagnum Agrippae.
101. Mart. *Ep.* 2.14. Prior, 138.
102. Mart. *Ep.* 2.14: roof supported by 100 columns (*centum pendentia tecta columnis*); Pompey's gift and double wood (*Pompei dona nemusque duplex*).
103. MacDonald 1986, 99.
104. For attributes of an architectural armature, see MacDonald 1986, 17–22.
105. MacDonald 1986, 48.

SIX: BETWEEN THE AQUA VIRGO AND THE TIBER: WATER AND THE FIELD OF MARS

1. Verg. *Aen.* 8.69; Statius *Silvae* 3.5.111; Dion. Per. 351–6, as found in B. Campbell 2012, 310; Mart. *Ep.* 4.64.24.

2. B. Campbell 2012, 21.

3. Livy 2.5.4; Suet. *Claud.* 25; Plut. *Publ.* 8.1–8.3 (sacred grain); Livy 1.4.4 (Romulus and Remus).

4. Verg. *Aen.* 8.31–78.

5. Ov. *Fasti* 2.597–8.

6. Plut. *Vit. Oth.* 4.5.

7. Cassius Dio 53.20.1.

8. Pliny *NH* 3.54–5, translation from Shipley and Salmon.

9. Livy 5.54.4; Juv. 3.60–3.

10. Plut. *Vit. Cat. Mai.* 20.4 (Cato); Veg. *Mil.* 1.10 (soldiers).

11. Celsus *Med.* 3.3.2 (tertian fever); B. Campbell 2012, 335 (sewage).

12. Nicholas Purcell, "Rome and the Management of Water: Environment, Culture and Power," in Shipley and Salmon, 189.

13. R. Taylor 2000, 131.

14. Aldrete, 33.

15. Most of the Campus Martius was at a height of ten meters above sea level. Aldrete, 45–9; Haselberger et al., map insert 1:3000.

16. Aldrete, 45 (fig. 1.7), 47 (fig. 1.8), 49 (fig. 1.10).

17. Fifteen floods are recorded from 415 to 32 B.C.E. The six occurring during Augustus's reign were in 27, 23, 22, and 13 and two in 5 and 12 C.E. Ibid. 15.

18. Aldrete, 80–1.

19. Livy 24.9.6; 38.28.4.

20. Cassius Dio 53.20.1 (27 B.C.E.); 53.33.5 (23 B.C.E.); 55.22.3 (5 C.E.).

21. August. *De civ D.* 3.18.

22. Plut. *Oth.* 4.5 (grain supply); Tac. *Hist.* 1.86 (loss of life).

23. Pliny *Ep.* 8.17, as translated by Aldrete, 29.

24. See Claridge 2010, 201; Carandini and Carafa, eds., vol. 2, tav. 207.

25. Holland, 31.

26. Livy 5.53.9. While the central Campus Martius contained the Caprae Palus, the Roman Forum contained a large swamp that, according to one account provided by Livy, was named the *lacus Curtius* after a Sabine horseman whose horse plunged into the marsh. See Livy 1.12, 1.13.5; Plut. *Rom.* 18.2; Dion. Hal. *Ant. Rom.* 2.42; Ov. *Fast.* 6.395–417.

27. The fora are thought to have been at a level of fifteen meters above sea level, while the valley in which the Circus Maximus lies was at ten. See Aldrete, figs. 1.8–1.10, 47–9.

28. Cassius Dio 56.27.

29. August. *De civ D.* 3.18 (*pene omnia urbis plana subversa sunt*); Livy 38.28.4 (*Tiberis duodeciens campum Martium planaque urbis inundavit*).

30. Cassius Dio 53.20.1; Tac. *Ann.* 1.76.

31. Ov. *Fast.* 2.390; 3.517–22.

32. Cassius Dio 54.25.2; Aldrete, 67.

33. Cassius Dio 56.27.4; Aldrete, 67.

34. See discussion in Aldrete, 66–71. Records from 1700 to the present indicate that more than 77 percent of the Tiber's floods occur from November to February. Indications from the ancient sources that flooding occurred during the winter and early spring months may be the result of calendar shifts. See ibid. 66, 69–71.

35. Columella *Rust.* 1.5.6, as translated by Sallares, 61 n. 41.

36. Writing at the time of Tiberius, Celsus described the disease that we now know as malaria. Because of the periodicity of its fever, which would come one day be gone the next and then reappear on a third or later day, malaria was called "tertian," "semi-tertian," or "quartan" fever. Celsus *Med.* 3.3.2. See Sallares, 14. Romans did not understand, however, that it was the mosquito that bore the virus. Ibid. 47, 49. The second-century C.E. Roman physician Galen noted that malaria was "most frequent at Rome, being very familiar to men in the city." Gal. 17A.121–2K, as translated by Sallares, 222. The frequency and severity of malaria outbreaks in ancient Rome, and more specifically in the swampy, low-lying areas of the city, have not been determined from the available evidence. Dyson, 268–9.

37. Varro *Rust.* 1.12.2, translation from Sallares, 60–1. Fifth-century C.E. bishop Palladius wrote that marshes must be avoided "because of the pestilence or hostile little animals which it generates," as from Sallares, 68.

38. Those studies disclosed that annual outbreaks of malaria occurred in July, with the maximum number of cases in August. No new cases occurred from March to June. See Sallares, 62.

39. Juv. *Sat.* 4.56–59. See Sallares, 217 n. 35.

40. Aldrete, 97. See Tac. *Ann.* 1.79 concerning proposals to divert the Tiber's tributaries to control flooding and the possible ramifications for doing so.

41. Pliny *Ep.* 8.17.

42. Cassius Dio 39.61.1–2. See Aldrete, 122–3. Aldrete, 213–16, also notes that approximately

85 percent of the known upper-class housing in the city was in the hills above the flood plain.

43. Aldrete, 149.

44. Cic. *Rep.* 2.6.11.

45. Veg. *Mil.* 1.10.

46. Richardson 1992, 91.

47. Strabo 5.3.8; Pliny *NH* 36.24.104; Cassius Dio 49.43.

48. Richardson 1992, 91; 289–90; Narducci, 36–7, 40–2.

49. Lloyd, 196 and n. 31; Hopkins, 3. Lanciani 1990, map XV, shows a "cloaca" approaching the Pantheon from the east, then turning north and then west in front of the building, and then south again along the Pantheon's west side.

50. Lloyd, 196 and n. 31.

51. With respect to porticoes in swampy soil, Vitruvius recommended that the sites be excavated as deep as possible and filled with charcoal and sand for drainage. Vitr. *De arch.* 5.9.7.

52. See Lloyd, 196, with respect to receipt of surface water drainage. See Richardson 1992, 367, with respect to water draining from Baths of Agrippa.

53. Richardson 1992, 146–7.

54. Richardson 1992, 147. This channel may be distinguished from another drainage channel known as the Euripus Virginis, which is discussed later in this chapter. See Lloyd, 198–9.

55. Aldrete, 87–9.

56. Aldrete, 175–6, 237. Stone construction also accelerated drying once the floodwaters stopped rising.

57. Pliny *Ep.* 8.17, as translated by Aldrete, 28–9. The flood likely occurred around 107 or 108 C.E. Ibid.

58. Aldrete, 231. Several reasons have been suggested why the Romans did not go to the expense. First, there was high ground nearby that was easily reachable in case of flooding. Second, many of the buildings constructed in the floodplain were of sturdy materials that could withstand floods with minimal damage. Third, grain supplies were warehoused in *horrea* that were designed to protect grain from water damage. Fourth, rapid drainage led to quick recovery from inundations. Ibid. 232–7.

59. Cic. *Att.* 13.33.4; Le Gal 1953A, 114.

60. Tac. *Ann.* 1.79. See Le Gall 1953A, 114; Aldrete, 182–4. Aldrete believes the plan was designed for flood control but makes a strong case that the effort would have failed.

61. Suet. *Aug.* 30. See R. Taylor 2000, 82, 152 n. 64, who suggests that the dredging occurred in 7 B.C.E. If that date is correct, then the next flood known from our ancient sources, in 5 C.E., shows that the effort was unsuccessful. As Cassiodorus wrote, "For eight miserable days there was destruction of men and homes as the Tiber attacked." Cassiod. *Chron.* 604, trans. Aldrete, 25. See also Le Gall 1953A 117.

62. Cassius Dio 57.14.7–8. The flood commission established by Tiberius was called the *curatores riparum et alvei Tiberis*. Later, under Vespasian, it was reduced to one commissioner. See Aldrete, 199.

63. Richardson 1992, 284.

64. Richardson 1992, 385. With respect to the location of the theater in relationship to the Caprae Palus, see Gagliardo and Packer, 93 n. 4.

65. Cassius Dio reported that in 54 B.C.E. brick houses were soaked through and collapsed. Cassius Dio 39.61.1–2.

66. See Aldrete, 181 and n. 18, who cites personal conversation with Albert Ammerman, with respect to the temples in the Forum Holitorium. As to the Apollo Sosianus temple, the elevation of the porch as drawn in Stamper, 121, is approximately five meters above the moderate flood stage of ten meters above sea level.

67. Aldrete, 113–18.

68. Tac. *Hist.* 1.86.

69. See discussion in Chapter 7. Single-family homes (*domus*) tended to avoid the problems posed by the floodplain. See note 42 in this chapter.

70. Aldrete, 178.

71. Richardson 1992, 191; Aldrete, 180.

72. Temple of Divine Hadrian (Claridge 2010, 223); Pantheon (as measured by author). See Figure 28.

73. Haselberger 2011, 55.

74. Cresting at almost seventeen meters above sea level, a flood in 1937 was recorded on four markers in the low lying areas of the city. Aldrete, 246 (table A.1).

75. For instance, markers noting flood levels in the area of the Campus Martius can be found at L'Arco di Banchi (1277), S. Maria Sopra Minerva (1422, 1530, 1557), Palazzo Madama

(1495), S. Eustachio (1495), and Piazza del Popolo (1530), among others. See Katherine Rinne, Aquae Urbis Romae: The Waters of the City of Rome (2006), http://www3 .iath.virginia.edu/waters/main.html (accessed March 31, 2013).

76. Frontin. *Aq.* 1.10. Pliny claimed that the stream, like a virgin, tried to avoid commingling with a stream named for Neptune and received its name for that reason. Pliny *NH* 31.42. Cassiodorus stated that the water received its name because, unlike other sources, it remained pure. Cassiod. *Var.* 7.6.

77. See R. Taylor 2000, 103 (11.5 km length); Hodge, 347 (21 km length).

78. Aicher 1995, 39. The daily flow of the Aqua Virgo entering the city was described by Frontinus (*Aq.* 2.70) as 2,504 *quinariae* measured near the city. Using Taylor's estimate (R. Taylor 2000, 39) of one *quinaria* = 32 cubic meters (m^3)/day, the Virgo's flow was approximately 80,128 m^3/day or 0.93 m^3/sec. See also Hodge, 299–300, who notes that a figure of 40 m^3/day has been accepted for the flow rate of a *quinaria*, a figure that produces a flow of about 1.16 m^3/sec.

79. Frontin. *Aq.* 1.22; Platner and Ashby, 268–9.

80. See Aicher 1995, 71.

81. See description of route in Richardson 1992, 19; Lloyd, 193–4; and Aicher 1995, 71.

82. Lloyd, 195; Aicher 1995, 73.

83. See Hazel Dodge, "'Greater than the Pyramids': The Water Supply of Ancient Rome," in Coulston and Dodge, 171, 176.

84. See Richardson 1992, 386 (*Thermae Agrippae*). As Yegül notes, the baths are often described as the "first public baths" in Rome, but this can be misleading since most baths were open to all and, therefore, to a citizen were considered "public." Yegül, 43, 133. Agrippa's baths, as others, charged admission until his death in 12 B.C.E., when they were left to the Roman people to use without charge. Cassius Dio 54.29.4. See also Fagan, 108.

85. See Richardson 1992, 367 (Stagnum Agrippae). The Stagnum is estimated, to have been 180 by 220 to 300 meters (39,600 to 54,000 square meters) in area. See R. Taylor 2000, 179; Coleman, 50.

86. See Richardson 1992, 146 (*Euripus Virginis*). H. B. Evans 1982, 409, and Aicher 1995, 74, both use Frontin. *Aq.* 2.84: 460 *quinariae* went

to the Euripus (460 *quinariae* = 19.9 percent of the amount distributed within the city: 2,304 *quinariae*). With respect to the source of the name *Euripus Virginis*, see Frontin. *Aq.* 2.84.

87. Richardson 1992, 147. Seneca told of bravely diving into the waters of the Euripus Virginis on a cold January day. Sen. *Ep.* 83.5.

88. Dyson, 143. See also von Stackelberg, 40, noting that "the inclusion of a euripus suggested both glamour and Hellenistic elegance."

89. Richardson 1992, 147; Lloyd, 197. Restored by Antoninus Pius in 147 C.E., the bridge may have been dismantled at the time of Emperor Caracalla for construction of the Pons Aurelius. Lloyd, 201; R. Taylor 2002, 10.

90. Lloyd, 197; R. Taylor 2000, 148.

91. The calculation is based on Frontinus's figure of 2,304 *quinariae* per day reaching the city limits (*Aq.* 2.84) multiplied by 32 cubic meters per *quinaria* as calculated by R. Taylor 2000, 39.

92. H. B. Evans 1982, 409; R. Taylor 2000, 76. Before the construction of the Aqua Virgo, some southern areas of the Campus Martius were provided with limited water from the Aqua Appia and the Aqua Marcia. See H. B. Evans 1982, 408–9.

93. Agrippa also built the Aqua Julia and supervised a major rebuilding of the Aqua Tepula that had been originally constructed in 126–125 B.C.E. and may have been mostly for industrial use. (See H. B. Evans 1982, 404.) Both entered the city from the east. Combined, the two aqueducts supplied Rome with a capacity of about 928 *quinariae* or just 40 percent of the Aqua Virgo's 2,304 *quinariae*. See ibid. 406–9.

94. Frontinus assigns the *euripus* (likely the Euripus Virginis) to the category of *opera publica*, Frontin *Aq.* 2.84, but there is uncertainty as to the other public structures included. Compare H. B. Evans 1997, 9, and Fagan, 69–74. While it is reasonably certain that the Baths of Agrippa fell within the category of *opera publica*, it is not clear if later imperial baths were within that category rather than "in the name of Caesar" (*nomine Caesaris*). See Fagan, 73. Whether or not included in the category of *opera publica*, Rome's second imperial bathhouse, the Baths of Nero, which was in operation in Frontinus's day, was likely fed by the Aqua Virgo. See R. Taylor 2000, 46.

95. The second greatest contributor to public works water supply was the Claudia/Anio Novus at 16 percent. R. Taylor 2000, 46.

96. Only 25 of the 591 *lacus* were in the Campus Martius. H. B. Evans 1997, 11, 108–9. We do know the name of one *lacus* located in the Campus Martius, the Lacus Cunicli, described in an inscription of 375 C.E. See Richardson 1992, 229. For distribution statistics, see Frontin. *Aq.* 2.78–86; H. B. Evans 1997, 34–6. By the fourth century, however, the regionary catalogs would indicate that almost 10 percent of the city's *lacus* were in the Campus Martius. See Wallace-Hadrill, 295 (table 6.1).

97. Pliny *NH* 36.24.123, as translated in Robinson, 99.

98. Suet. *Aug.* 42.1.

99. Cassiod., *Var.*, 7.6.

100. See Richardson 1992, 24. Cassius Dio notes that Claudius was awarded two arches, the second in Gaul. Cassius Dio 60.22.1.

101. Richardson 1992, 24 Arcus Claudii [II]; Nash, vol. 1, 102; Aicher 1995, 73.

102. Nash, vol. 1, fig. 52, The inscription reads, "Tiberius Claudius Caesar Augustus Germanicus, son of Drusus, Pontifex Maximus, in his fifth year of tribunician power, imperator eleven times, father of his country, consul designate for the fourth time, made new and restored from their foundations the arcades of the Aqua Virgo, since they had been knocked down by Gaius Caesar [Caligula]."

103. Suet. *Iul.* 39.4.

104. Suet. *Iul.* 39.4. See Coleman, 53, who suggests that the Naumachia Augusti built in 2 B.C.E. across the Tiber in Trastevere was approximately 1.7 meters deep to accommodate warships for mock battles.

105. Cassius Dio indicates that on direction of the Senate in 43 B.C.E. it was filled in because of a disease outbreak, likely malaria. Cassius Dio 45.17.8.

106. Cassius Dio 55.10.8. See Coleman, 56. Given the proximity of the Petronia Amnis, it is possible that piping from the stream was used to fill the circus rather than the Virgo, but either would have done the job.

107. Cassius Dio 59.10.5.

108. Suet. *Ner.* 12.1; Cassius Dio 61.9.5.

109. See Chapter 4, note 4.

110. Coarelli 2007, 265; Roddaz, 238–9.

111. Richardson 1992, 196.

112. Strabo 13.1.19 (Lysippus statue of lion); Tac. *Ann.* 15.37.2–7 (barge on Stagnum). While Coleman, 51, states that the Stagnum "may have been intended as a swimming-pool," Lloyd, 196, points out that there is "no reference to swimming in it."

113. Von Stackelberg, 82.

114. Cassius Dio 54.29.

115. Tac. *Ann.* 15.37.2.

116. Dyson, 230. See Yegül, 43.

117. Cic. *Rosc. Am.* 18. See Richardson 1992, 49 with respect to the Balneae Pallacinae.

118. See Dodge, "Water Supply," 189. See also Nielsen, vol. 1, 29, 36. Hot water baths had, however, come to Rome by at least 200 B.C.E. *Balnea* without exercise facilities were in Rome by the same approximate period. The hypocaust system that allowed for graduated bath heating did not appear until the beginning of the first century B.C.E.

119. Nielsen, vol. 1, 13. This was the Piscina Publica built in conjunction with the Aqua Appia (312 BC) and was situated outside the Porta Capena. See Livy 23.32.4.

120. Yegül, 136.

121. Pliny *NH* 36.189. With respect to the *Apoxyomenos*, Pliny (*NH* 34.62) recounts how the statue stood outside the *tepidarium* or warm baths, and when Tiberius confiscated the statue, the people at the theater shouted, "Give us back the Apoxyomenos," resulting in its return.

122. Richardson 1992, 386; Yegül, 133–35.

123. Fagan, 109.

124. It was possibly the problem of obtaining rights to lay the aqueduct through property that resulted in the Virgo's lengthy and circuitous route. See R. Taylor 2000, 105–6.

125. Lloyd, 203.

126. See Yegül, 137. See also Nielsen, vol. 1, 58. For a description of the *Juventus* movement, see Mohler, 442–3; Stambaugh, 138.

127. Cassius Dio 52.26.1. See also Verg. *Aen.* 7.162–9: "Youths in their early bloom practice horsemanship, or break in teams amid the dust, or bend the eager bows, or hurl with their arms tough darts."

128. As Yegül, 137, states, "This new and highly patriotic institution was capitalizing on the time-honored military associations of the 'Field for War Sports' as well as addressing the demands of a new and formal program of athletic and military fitness."

129. Stambaugh, 201.
130. See Mart. *Ep.* 4.8; Yegül, 32–3; Nielsen, vol. 1, 135–6.
131. Nielsen, vol. 1, 136.
132. See Fagan, 108–10.
133. Mart. *Ep.* 3.36.
134. The path taken is based on the supposition of Nielsen, vol. 1, 45, and vol. 2, 83, fig. 49. The Marble Plan, drawings by Palladio, and scant ruins allow little more than hypothetical recreations of each room's purpose. See Yegül, 133–7.
135. Yegül, 35–7. Some larger baths had weight rooms, but it is not known if the Baths of Agrippa had such a facility. Ibid.
136. Martial (*Ep.* 14.163) noted that if you did not listen to the bell and played too long, the baths could be closed, and you would have to be satisfied with the Virgo's unheated waters. See Yegül, 38. With respect to the location of the *tepidarium*, see Nielsen, vol. 2, 83.
137. Yegül, 38.
138. The location of the *frigidarium* in Agrippa's baths is a mystery. Yegül, 136, offers several possibilities – the central rotunda, a room southeast of the round hall, or the courtyard pools. Nielsen, vol. 1, 44, believes the rotunda was the *frigidarium*.
139. The remains of the structure can be seen on the Via dell'Arco Ciambella, between Via dei Cestari and Via di Torre Argentina. Aicher, 73.
140. Sen. *Ep.* 107.2. See Fagan, 30–1.
141. Sen. *Ep.* 56.1–2.
142. Yegül, 45.
143. Yegül, 47. Yegül notes that there is evidence that convicts were impressed into service in the baths as well.
144. Yegül, 42; Nielsen, vol. 1, 145.
145. SHA *Elag.* 26.3, translated in Aicher 2004, vol. 1, 233 (89.8).
146. Tac. *Ann.* 15.37.2–7. Allen, 100, suggests that Tacitus was most likely describing an imperial interpretation of a public festival such as Floralia rather than engaging in an immoral display.
147. Martial *Ep.* 6.42. It was supplied by both the Aqua Virgo and Aqua Marcia and was in either Region VII or IX. Richardson 1992, 48.
148. The road, whose ancient name is uncertain, has been located under the Via dei Coronari and Via delle Cappelle. See discussion

in Chapter 1, note 59. The name Pons Neronianus is known from the medieval period, and while it may have connected to the circus where the Vatican is now located, it is not known if it was constructed by Nero. Richardson 1992, 298.
149. Richardson 1992, 394. See also Yegül, 137. The Agrippan baths were able to take advantage of the Stagnum and surrounding gardens.
150. See Yegül, 138–9, for the debate regarding the question whether the symmetry found in the third-century C.E. structure of Alexander Severus also dates to the Neronian period.
151. Suet. *Ner.* 12. We are not told how the emperor fared at the gymnastic games, although at the other contests the fix was in. Nero won the Latin contest unanimously and also the lyre-playing contest, although he magnanimously declined the latter award, laying it at the foot of a statue of Caesar.
152. Ibid.
153. Philostr. *VA* 4.42.
154. Ibid.
155. Mart. *Ep.* 7.34.
156. See Fagan, 357–8 (regionary catalog numbers). See SHA *Alex. Sev.* 39.4; Dyson, 230 (additions by Alexander Severus). The number of *balneae* in the Campus Martius remained relatively low compared to other portions of the city. See Wallace-Hadrill, 295 (table 6.1).
157. SHA *Alex. Sev.* 24.5–6; Richardson 1992, 15, 394; Yegül, 107.
158. The source was near Gabii, eighteen kilometers east of Rome. Richardson 1992, 15; Dodge, "Water Supply," 195.
159. Dyson, 209–10.
160. Richardson 1992, 394. With respect to the various arguments for dating the original construction, see Fagan, 110 and n. 21.
161. SHA *Alex. Sev.* 24.5–6.
162. See description in Yegül, 137–9.
163. Procop. *De Bellis Goth.* 5.19.1–11, 18: Belisarius blocks aqueducts. See Dodge, "Water Supply," 193 n. 226.
164. Procop. *De Bellis Goth* 5.19.28.
165. See Dodge, "Water Supply," 194; Richardson 1992, 38.
166. Richardson 1992, 386.
167. With respect to columns, see Nash, vol. 2, 462–3.
168. Sallares, 68–9.
169. Pliny *NH* 19.58.180.

170. As the Euripus Virginus was used for swimming, its flow was likely reduced. Richardson 1992, 147.

171. Hor. *Ep.* 1.7.8–9.

172. See Sallares, 9. Discussing the fourth-century B.C.E. invasion by the Gauls, Livy (5.48.1–3) noted, "The Gauls suffered also from a pestilence, being encamped between hills on low ground"; see also Sallares, 203, 223–5.

173. See Richardson 1992, 266.

174. Plut. *Cat. Min.* 39.1–3; Livy 45.35.3. In 338 B.C.E., for instance, captured ships of the Antiates were brought upstream to Rome. Livy 8.14.12. See also Holland, 220. The captured treasure of Perseus floating up river on ships to Rome is discussed in Chapter 5.

175. See Chapter 3, note 62.

176. See Holland, 24–6, 65, and 219–21; see also Richardson 1992, 206.

177. See Chapter 3, note 124.

178. Livy 40.52.5–6. See Chapter 3, note 71.

179. See Chapter 3, note 78.

180. Richardson 1992, 210.

181. The works were by the Greek sculptor Skopas. Pliny *NH* 36.26.

182. Nash, vol. 2, 120. The frieze, part in the Glyptothek in Munich and the other in the Louvre in Paris, has been called the Altar of Ahenobarbus, and two consuls by that name have been associated with the Temple of Neptune – Cn. Domitius Ahenobarbus (*cos.* 122 B.C.E.) and Cn. Domitius Ahenobarbus (*cos.* 32 B.C.E.). The latter Ahenobarbus may have rebuilt the temple. See Richardson 1992, 267. P. L. Tucci, "Neptunus, Aedes in Campo, Aedes in Circo," *LTUR*, vol. 5, 279.

183. See Richardson 1992, 54. See discussion in Chapter 6.

184. See Richardson 1992, 312; Dueck and Brodersen, 26–7.

185. Wild, 92, 110.

186. Richardson 1992, 212; Swetnam-Burland, 445. See also Carandini and Carafa, eds., vol. 2 tav. 236, fig. E.

187. See Swetnam-Burland, 441; Le Gall 1944, 131–5.

188. Swetnam-Burland, 445–6.

189. Swetnam-Burland, 453, 455.

190. Swetnam-Burland, 454.

191. See Stephen Tuck, "The Tiber and River Transport," in Erdkamp, 237 (one-half million tons), and Rickman, 10 (one million tons).

192. Pliny *NH* 3.54–5. See Dyson, 243, with respect to barging upriver. It has been estimated that it took a fleet of approximately 2,000 vessels to ship Rome's annual wheat supply to Ostia, with a somewhat smaller fleet of river barges to move the grain on a three-day voyage upriver to Rome. See Temin, 31.

193. R. Taylor 2002, 219 n. 46. See also ibid. 199, for introduction of mills in Commodus's reign or early Severan period. See Dyson, 245, with respect to movement of grain to the Porticus Minucia Frumentaria.

194. Dyson, 248, 345. Richardson 1992, 81, believes the wine was taken ashore in the area of the Lungotevere Marzio in the northern Campus Martius.

195. Dyson, 257. Another area for the offloading and working of marble was around Monte Testaccio and the Aventine. Ibid.

SEVEN: "A ZEAL FOR BUILDINGS":
RESHAPING OF THE SPACE BY
THE EMPERORS

1. App. *B.Civ.* 3.88, 3.94.

2. App. *B.Civ.* 3.14. With respect to the location, see Roddaz, 238–9. With respect to the date, see Syme, 115.

3. App. *B.Civ.* 3.94; Suet. *Aug.* 95.

4. Richardson 1992, 247, asserts that it was Augustus's first project in the Campus Martius, but its start date is unclear (see note 5), and as discussed later with respect to the rebuilding efforts in the area of the Circus Flaminius, other projects in which Augustus clearly had a hand were being undertaken at approximately the same time.

5. Suet. *Aug.* 100.4. The precise start of construction on the Mausoleum is not clear, and as Rehak, 36, notes, its size indicates it took several years to complete. Some scholars argue that it was begun before the Battle of Actium in 31 B.C.E., while others, following a remark in Suetonius, prefer a date of ca. 28 B.C.E. For an interesting, brief discussion of the reasons why Octavian may have begun his tomb so early in life, see Rehak 2006, 32–33. For a discussion of the connection of the Augustan triple triumph and those of Romulus, see Cooley, 123.

6. For the size of the mausoleum, see Richardson 1992, 248.

7. With respect to the repair of the Via Flaminia, see Cassius Dio 53.22.1; *Res Gestae* 4.21; Suet. *Aug.* 30.1. To commemorate Augustus's road project, statues were erected on triumphal arches bearing dedicatory inscriptions that were built on the Milvian Bridge and on another bridge 362 kilometers further north at the other end of the Via Flaminia in the town of Ariminum. Cassius Dio 53.22.1.

8. See P. Davies, 120, who notes that "Romans often sought highly frequented locations for their sepulchers." Because the Campus Martius was generally reserved for the burial of public citizens selected posthumously by the Senate, some scholars have argued that the mausoleum was constructed just north of the Campus Martius and not actually in it. See discussion in P. Davies, 50 and n. 3. Others have argued that the mausoleum and the surrounding parkland were included. See Chapter 1, note 53.

9. Suet. *Aug.* 100.4; P. Davies, 120.

10. See discussion in P. Davies, 51–64, with respect to Ptolemaic influence. Other scholars believe Etruscan tombs provide the inspiration for the mausoleum. See Mark J. Johnson, "The Mausoleum of Augustus: Etruscan and Other Influences on Its Design," in Hall, 227–30. A concise summary of the different opinions on the design of the Mausoleum can be found in P. Davies, 14–15, in addition to the more detailed discussion of potential influences on the design in Rehak 2006, 35–52.

11. Strabo 5.3.8.

12. See discussion in Richardson 1992, 248.

13. Strabo 5.3.8.

14. Ibid.

15. Sosius saved: Cassius Dio, 51.2.4. See Stamper, 119. See Chapter 3 with respect to description of rebuilt temple. Apollo was the favorite deity of Octavian. See Favro 1996, 91, 99–100. The extant relief (Figure 39) shows two barbarians, hands tied, being hoisted on a parade platform with a trophy between them and followed by a trumpeter and bulls led in procession.

16. Bellona: Stamper, 120–1; A. Viscogliosi, "Bellona, Aedes in Circo," in *LTUR*, vol. 1, 191. Porticus Metelli: Stamper, 121 and n. 142. See also Richardson 1992, 317–18. See also discussion in Chapter 5.

17. Platner and Ashby, 428.

18. See discussion in Chapter 5. In the *Res Gestae* 19, Augustus stated, "I built...the portico at the Circus Flaminius which I allowed to be called Octavia after the name of him who had constructed an earlier one on the same site."

19. See Patterson, 198; Richardson 1992, 26. The arch commemorated Germanicus's victory in the Battle of Idistaviso (Valley of the Maidens) in 16 C.E. along the Weser River in present-day Germany. A fragment of the Severan Marble Plan (see Figure 26) shows an arch in front of the *propylaeum* to the Porticus Octaviae, and while it has been suggested that this was the arch dedicated to Germanicus, that theory has its critics. See E. Rodríguez Almeida, "Arcus Germanici in Circo Flaminio," *LTUR*, vol. 1, 94–5; Platner and Ashby, 40. See discussion in Flory, 289 and n. 7.

20. H. B. Evans 1982, 401, 403.

21. H. B. Evans 1982, 410, suggests that, given the complexities of the system, Agrippa may have begun the initial planning and preparations for his water program, including distribution to the Campus Martius, as early as 40 B.C.E., when he was *praetor urbanus* of Rome. See also Aicher 1995, 23; Favro 1996, 134–5; Frontin. *Aq.* 2.100–1.

22. In his will, Agrippa bequeathed the baths to the Roman people and transferred to Augustus ownership of his team of 240 private slaves (*aquarii*), who were responsible for maintenance of the newly repaired or constructed aqueducts, fountains, and other water supplies. Frontin. *Aq.* 2.98–99.

23. Richardson 1992, 340 (Saepta Iulia dedicated 26 B.C.E.); 110 (Diribitorium dedicated 7 B.C.E.).

24. L. Cordischi, "Basilica Neptuni," *LTUR*, vol. 1, 182–3; Richardson 1992, 54. Dio notes that the "stoa" was built by Agrippa in 25 B.C.E. and destroyed in the fire of 79 C.E. Cassius Dio 53.27.1. It was apparently rebuilt and known as the Basilica of Neptune at the time of Hadrian. SHA *Hadr.* 19.10; Cassius Dio 66.24.2.

25. The identification of the remains just south of Hadrian's Pantheon remains somewhat controversial. See Boatwright 1987, 48–9.

26. L. Cordischi, "Basilica Neptuni," *LTUR*, vol. 1, 182–3.

27. Cassius Dio 53.27.2–4. For a recent assemblage of the bibliography on Agrippa's Pantheon, see Wilson Jones, 258–9.

28. Cassius Dio 53.27.2–4.

29. A statue of Romulus might have been included among the images of the gods displayed in the temple. Wilson Jones, 179–80.

30. For a concise summary of the different scholarly camps, see A. Ziólkowski, "Pantheon," *LTUR*, vol. 1, 54–6. See also discussion in Ziólkowski, "What Did Agrippa's Pantheon Look Like? New Answers to an Old Question," in Graßhoff et al., 30–2.

31. Pliny *NH* 36.38 (pediment decoration and caryatids); Pliny *NH* 34.13 (bronze capitals).

32. *Res Gestae* 12. In addition to the description in the *Res Gestae*, there are additional references to the ceremonies of the Ara Pacis preserved on several fragmentary calendars (*fasti*) and in Ovid's *Fasti* (1.709–22; 3.879–82). See also A. Wallace-Hadrill, "Time for Augustus: Ovid, Augustus, and the *Fasti*," in Bramble, Whitby, Hardie, and Whitby, 221–30.

33. The bibliography on the Ara Pacis is understandably massive. For general studies, see La Rocca, Ruesch, and Zanardi 1983; Rossini 2006; S. Settis, "Die Ara Pacis," in Hofter 1988; Zanker 1988.

34. For discussions and interpretations of the Floral/Scroll frieze, see Caneva; Castriota; Cohon; Sauron.

35. For various studies of the mythological and allegorical panels, see most recently Galinsky 1992; de Grummond; Rehak 2001.

36. Kleiner 1978; Billows; Elsner; D. Kleiner, "Semblance and Storytelling in Augustan Rome," in Galinsky 2005, 197–233; C. B. Rose 1990B.

37. Billows, 80–92.

38. The most definitive and detailed discussion of the identification of priestly groups on the Ara Pacis remains Koeppel 1987 and Koeppel 1988.

39. See Barrett, 632, who suggests that the dedication occurred on Livia's fiftieth birthday.

40. The dedication to Augustus on the obelisk was between June 9 and June 10 B.C.E. See Haselberger 2011, 48.

41. Pliny *NH* 36.71; Strabo 17.27.

42. The obelisk was excavated in 1748, but was not reerected in the Piazza di Montecitorio until 1789. It was repaired with fragments from the granite Column of Antoninus Pius. Haselberger 2011, 48.

43. *CIL* vi 702; Haselberger 2011, 48.

44. Pliny *NH* 36.72.

45. Haselberger 2011, 51–3 in particular fig. 5 (Lanciani) and fig. 6 (Buchner).

46. See discussion in Heslin 2007, 4.

47. Haselberger 2011, 54–5. The excavations were conducted by E. Buchner and F. Rakob, the former writing extensively on the theory that the horologium's bronze marker was a wide-spaced grid for measuring the sun and that the shadow of the gnomon cast upon the grid pointed to the altar of the Ara Pacis on the fall equinox. See E. Buchner, "Horologium Augusti," *LTUR*, vol. 3, 35–7.

48. Heslin 2007, 3.

49. Augustus became Pontifex Maximus in 12 B.C.E., giving him official responsibility for the calendar. In 9 B.C.E., following the horologium's construction, the Roman calendar was found to be inaccurate and Augustus required adjustments to be made. The horologium was too new, however, to have been the source of the error's discovery. Heslin 2007, 5–6.

50. See discussion in Haselberger 2011, 64–7, with respect to the different arguments. Schütz 2011, 78–86, questions the viability of Buchner's argument, noting that the proposed equinox line reaches the entrance of the Ara Pacis at an angle instead of directly and that there is no literary evidence that Augustus intended for his birthday to be celebrated in this manner. See also Hannah, 90–1 (supports the theory), and Heslin 2011, 75–7 (disagrees with theory). Recent measurements by Bernard Frischer indicate that Buchner's measurements of the gnomon's location were inaccurate, raising further doubts. See, e.g., http://vimeo.com/85043815 (accessed April 6, 2014).

51. Imaginary lines drawn among the three monuments describe a right triangle. Heslin 2007, 14–15. One author notes that a line from the gnomon through the Ara Pacis meets the sunrise on April 21 (under the Julian Calendar), the date recognized by the Romans as the city's birthday. Schütz 2011, 85–6. Recent computer analysis proposes that when the gnomon is viewed from the Via Flaminia in line with the center of the Ara Pacis, the sun's disk appears to rest on the gnomon on October 9, the festival date for the Temple of Apollo on the Palatine. See http://news.indiana.edu/releases/iu/2013/12/augustus-virtual-reality-project.shtml (accessed December 29, 2013).

52. See Favro 1996, 207. By one measure, the Augustan projects in the Field of Mars constituted more than one-third of all significant construction in Rome during his reign. Thornton, 40–2. Thornton uses a complex determination of "work units" by taking a "typical" building as a base and then comparing other buildings to it.

53. Beard et al., vol. 1, 178–80.

54. A matching pair of two small, red granite obelisks flanked the pillars; they survive and were reincorporated into later monuments in the Piazza S. Maria Maggiore and in front of the Palazzo Quirinale.

55. *Res Gestae* 12, 19, 20.

56. Strabo 5.3.8.

57. It is important to note that Octavian had originally proposed that he be referred to as the second Romulus, the second founder of the city, during the early years of his rise to power (Suet. *Aug.* 7.2; Cassius Dio 53.16.7). See also Rehak 2006, 61: "The Mausoleum of Augustus, with its *Res Gestae* and colossal crowning statue, is not simply a tomb but rather an architectural metaphor for deification."

58. A cippus found in the area of the modern Via dei Banchi Vecchi proclaims that Claudius extended the city's limits after having expanded Rome's empire. Richardson 1992, 294–5.

59. Suet. *Div. Titus.* 8.3; Suet. *Dom.* 12; Cassius Dio 66.24.2. See also Sutherland, 157–60.

60. See Catull. 10.26; Cassius Dio 47.15.4. With respect to the name Isis Campensis, see Apuleius, *Met.* 11.26.

61. For a detailed discussion of Domitian's possible interests in Ptolemaic Egyptian culture and cults, see Darwall-Smith, 150–3. It appears that the cults of Isis and Serapis received significant imperial support during the Flavian age. See also Roullet, 23–35; Richardson 1992, 211–12.

62. Richardson 1992, 211–12 and figs. 46–7. The tomb was located along the Via Labicana.

63. Richardson 1992, 212.

64. Today, the Pamphili obelisk decorates Bernini's celebrated fountain in Piazza Navona. See Darwall-Smith, 145–50; Anderson, 96.

65. Richardson 1992, 111.

66. See, e.g., the Flavian Cancelleria Reliefs, found in an ancient storage building beneath the Palazzo Cancelleria in the Campus Martius and now in the Vatican Museums. Also Magi 1945.

67. SHA *Hadr.* 19.9–10. For a concise discussion of Hadrian's building activities in the Campus Martius, see Boatwright 1987, 33–73.

68. Boatwright 1987, 51.

69. Boatwright 1987, 48–50.

70. MacDonald 1976, 11, has aptly termed the Pantheon as "original, utterly bold, many-layered in associations and meaning, the container of a kind of immanent universality."

71. See MacDonald 1976, 18–19. For greater detail, see Tod Marder, "The Pantheon after Antiquity," in Graßhoff et al., 145–54.

72. Wilson Jones, 208.

73. Cassius Dio, 53.27.2–4, claims that the Pantheon of Agrippa had statues of Augustus and Agrippa on its porch. Since Agrippa's structure was long gone by the time Dio wrote, it is believed that he was describing statues then standing in Hadrian's structure. See discussion in MacDonald 1976, 77.

74. MacDonald 1976, 28.

75. See discussion in L. Haselberger, "The Pantheon: Nagging Questions to No End," in Graßhoff et al., 180.

76. MacDonald 1976, 13. See also Hetland, 95 n. 1.

77. SHA *Hadr.* 19.9–10.

78. Haselberger, "The Pantheon: Nagging Questions to No End," 181.

79. Wilson Jones, 208–11. See Haselberger, "The Pantheon: Nagging Questions to No End," 181–4.

80. "In effect the volumetric proportions of the whole project can be reduced to a hemisphere, a cylinder of the same height and a double cube." Wilson Jones, 185.

81. MacDonald 1976, 38.

82. Ibid.

83. Ibid.

84. MacDonald 1976, 35.

85. A small section of the simpler "false window" Roman design was restored through painted plaster in the 1930s. See MacDonald 1976, 37 and fig. 36.

86. MacDonald 1976, 35.

87. Cassius Dio 53.27.2; See also Amm. Marc. 16.10.14. For arithmetic perfection: A. Ziółkowski, "Pantheon," *LTUR*, vol. 4, 61.

88. Hannah and Magli, 489–502.

89. A. Ziólkowski, "Pantheon," *LTUR*, vol. 4, 56.

90. Hetland, 95–6, however, proposes 114 C.E. as a beginning date on the basis of brick stamps.

91. An annex two stories high and wedged between the drum and the basilica hid the structure from the direction of Agrippa's baths. See M. Wilson Jones, "The Pantheon and the Phasing of Its Construction," in Graßhoff et al., 72–5. The Porticus Argonautarum flanked the rotunda on the east. The likeliest clear view was from the west near the Stagnum.

92. A. Ziólkowski, "Pantheon," *LTUR*, vol. 4, 57. As Boatwright 1987, 46–7, has argued, "there seems to have been an effort to disguise from the front the unconventionality of Hadrian's new building."

93. See A. Ziólkowski, "Pantheon," *LTUR*, vol. 4, 55–6; Haselberger, "The Pantheon: Nagging Questions to No End," 171.

94. Cassius Dio, 69.7.1.

95. See F. de Caprariis, "Matidia, Templum," *LTUR*, vol. 3, 233. With respect to the medallion, see Chapter 5.

96. Cippi from the reign of Hadrian indicate that the central Campus Martius was clearly within the *pomerium* as of 121 C.E. Richardson 1992, 295.

97. Richardson 1992, 184.

98. M. Cipollone, "Hadrianus, Divus, Templum; Hadrianeum," *LTUR*, vol. 3, 7–8.

99. Richardson 1992, 184; Claridge 2010, 224.

100. Claridge 2010, 225, notes that the pedestals and panels are not compatible with the exterior or interior of the temple itself and may have decorated the portico. Evidence for the portico has been found only on the north side. Ibid. 224–5.

101. Richardson 1992, 184.

102. Richardson 1992, 94.

103. Ibid. Just to the southeast of Pius's column stood a commemorative stone altar of Antonine date immortalizing the site of a massive wooden imperial funeral pyre. Beckmann, 45.

104. Beckmann, 45.

105. Zanker 2004, 56, 66–8.

106. Epigraphic evidence suggests that it was finished by 193 C.E., and Beckmann, 36, has argued that the column was not a posthumous construction but rather a monument built to celebrate Marcus Aurelius's triumphal celebrations over the Germans and Sarmatians in 176.

107. Richardson 1992, 95.

108. Beckmann, 48.

109. An inscription below the famous "Agrippa" inscription of Hadrianic date records a restoration in 202 C.E. by Septimius Severus and Caracalla. *CIL* 6.896; A. Ziólkowski, "Pantheon," *LTUR*, vol. 4, 57.

110. For a recent discussion of Severus's deliberate associations through iconography and constructions, see A. Cooley, "Septimius Severus: The Augustan Emperor," in Swain, Harrison, and Elsner, 385–97. Severus and Caracalla repaired the fire-damaged temples of Jupiter Stator and Juno Regina as well as the Porticus Octaviae sometime between 203 and 205. Curran 2000, 24–5.

111. Coarelli 2007, 12; Richardson 1992, 260–2.

112. Platner and Ashby, 93.

113. Richardson 1992, 67, 209. It is uncertain, however, if the totals provided refer to the number of separate apartments, apartment buildings, or something in between. See, e.g., Hermansen, 130–1; Packer, 83.

114. Reynolds, 234–5; 414–15.

115. Claridge 2010, 223. The *insula* was built along an ancient street, the Vicus Caprarius. For a detailed discussion of the structure, see generally Insalaco.

116. Claridge 2010, 253.

117. Nunzio Giustozzi, "Ancient Sculpture: Ground Floor," in Giustozzi, 7.

118. See generally Henrik Bowman, "A Third Century Insula beneath the Basilica of San Lorenzo in Lucina," in Brandt, 81–122. It has also been suggested that the structure was a large *horrea* instead. Ibid. 111.

119. Bowman, "A Third Century Insula," 108–9.

CONCLUSION: "THE REST OF THE CITY A MERE ACCESSORY"

1. Sear 2013, 539 ("veritable mountain"). See Chapter 4, note 79.

2. See Gregorius, 10–15.

3. Gregorius, 29.

4. Gregorius, 18.

5. Partner, 5.

6. Montaigne, 100.

7. Richardson 1992, 382 (Theater of Marcellus); Manacorda, 19 (Crypta Balbi glassworks); Richardson 1992, 60 (Bonus Eventus temple and portico); Richardson 1992, 385 (Theater of Pompey repairs).

8. Amm. Marc. 16.10.

9. With respect to the date of the conversion of the Pantheon to a church, see Richardson 1992, 285. See also Gregorius, 29.

10. See Manacorda, 20.

11. Richardson 1992, 386.

12. Manacorda, 22.

13. Sear 2006, 59.

14. Coates-Stephens 1996, 239, 242.

15. Richardson 1992, 382 (Theater of Marcellus).

16. Gregorius, 18–19.

17. Quoted in R. K. Delph, "Renovatio, Reformatio, and Humanist Ambition in Rome," in Delph, Fontaine, and Martin, 74.

18. Dickens, 186.

19. Dickens, 201.

SELECTED BIBLIOGRAPHY

PRIMARY SOURCES

Unless otherwise indicated in the notes, the following English translations of Greek and Latin sources were employed.

Ammianus Marcellinus. 1986. *The Later Roman Empire (A.D. 354–378)*. Translated by Walter Hamilton. Harmondsworth: Penguin Books.

Appian. 1899. *The Roman History of Appian of Alexandria*. Translated by Horace White. New York: Macmillan.

Augustus. (*Res Gestae*). 1924. *Compendium of Roman History: Res Gestae Divi Augusti*. Translated by Frederick W. Shipley. London: W. Heinemann.

Calpurnius. 1934. *Minor Latin poets*. Translated by J. Wight Duff and A. M. Duff. London: W. Heinemann.

Cassiodorus. (*Variae*). 1886. *The Letters of Cassiodorus*. Translated by Thomas Hodgkin. London: H. Frowde.

Cassius Dio. 1914. *Roman History*. Translated by Earnest Cary and Herbert Baldwin Foster. Cambridge, Mass.: Harvard University Press.

Cicero. (*Att.*). 1965. *Letters to Atticus*. Translated by D. R. Shackleton Bailey. Cambridge: Cambridge University Press.

———. (*Rep.*). 1999. *On the Commonwealth and on the Laws*. Translated by James E. G. Zetzel. Cambridge: Cambridge University Press.

Dionysius of Halicarnassus. 1937. *Roman Antiquities*. Vol. 1. Translated by Earnest Cary. Cambridge, Mass.: Harvard University Press.

Frontinus. 1925. *Strategems: Aqueducts of Rome*. Translated by Charles E. Bennett. Cambridge, Mass.: Harvard University Press.

Gellius. 1927. *Attic Nights*. Translated by John Carew Rolfe. Cambridge, Mass.: Harvard University Press.

Historia Augusta. 1921. *Historia Augusta*. Vol. 1. Translated by David Magie. London: W. Heinemann.

Livy. (Books 1–10 and 21–2). 1919. *History of Rome*. Translated by B. O. Foster. London: W. Heinemann.

———. (Books 40–2). 1938. Translated by Evan T. Sage and Alfred C. Schlesinger. Cambridge, Mass.: Harvard University Press.

———. (Books 43–5). 1989. Translated by Alfred C. Schlesinger. Cambridge, Mass.: Harvard University Press.

Lucretius. 1916. *On the Nature of Things*. Translated by William Ellery Leonard. New York: Dutton.

Martial. 1919. *Epigrams, with an English Translation*. Translated by Walter C. A. Ker. London: W. Heinemann.

Ovid (*Fasti*). 1931. *Ovid's Fasti*. Translated by James George Frazer. Cambridge, Mass.: Harvard University Press.

Philostratus. 1912. *The Life of Apollonius of Tyana*. Translated by F. C. Conybeare. London: W. Heinemann.

Pliny. 1952. *Natural History*. Books 33–5. Translated by H. Rackham. Cambridge, Mass.: Harvard University Press.

———. 1962. *Natural History*. Books 36–7. Translated by D. E. Eichholz. London: W. Heinemann.

Plutarch. 1914. *Lives*. Translated by Bernadotte Perrin. London: W. Heinemann.

Seneca. 1917. *Epistles. 1–65*. Vol. 1. Translated by Richard M. Gummere. London: W. Heinemann.

————. 1925. *Epistles. 93–124.* Vol. 3. Translated by Richard M. Gummere. Cambridge, Mass.: Harvard University Press.

Statius. 1928. *Silvae.* Translated by J. H. Mozley. London: W. Heinemann.

Strabo. 1923. *Geography.* Translated by Horace Leonard Jones. Cambridge, Mass.: Harvard University Press.

Suetonius. 1997. *Suetonius.* Translated by John Carew Rolfe. Cambridge, Mass.: Harvard University Press.

Tacitus (*Annals*). (*Histories*). 1925. *Histories: Books 1–3.* Translated by Clifford Herschel Moore. London: W. Heinemann.

————. 1931. *Histories: Books 4–5 / Annals: Books 1–3.* Translated by Clifford Herschel Moore and John Jackson. London: W. Heinemann.

Vegetius. 1767. *Military Institutions of Vegetius.* Translated by John Clarke. London: W. Griffin.

Velleius Paterculus. 1924. *Compendium of Roman History: Res Gestae divi Augusti.* Translated by Frederick W. Shipley. London: W. Heinemann.

Vergil. 1916. *Aeneid.* Translated by H. Rushton Fairclough. Cambridge, Mass.: Harvard University Press.

Vitruvius. 1826. *The Architecture of Marcus Vitruvius Pollio, in Ten Books.* Translated by Joseph Gwilt. London: Priestly and Weale.

————. 1999. *Vitruvius: Ten Books on Architecture.* Translated by Ingrid D. Rowland. Cambridge: Cambridge University Press.

SECONDARY SOURCES

Adkins, Lesley, and Roy Adkins. 1996. *Dictionary of Roman Religion.* New York: Facts on File.

Aicher, Peter J. 1993. "Terminal Display Fountains ('Mostre') and the Aqueducts of Ancient Rome." *Phoenix* 47(4):339–52.

————. 1995. *Guide to the Aqueducts of Ancient Rome.* Wauconda, Ill.: Bolchazy-Carducci.

————. 2004. *Rome Alive: A Source-Guide to the Ancient City.* 2 vols. Wauconda, Ill.: Bolchazy-Carducci.

Albers, Jon. 2013. *Campus Martius: Die urbane Entwicklung des Marsfeldes von der Republik bis zur mittleren Kaiserzeit.* Wiesbaden: Dr. Ludwig Reichert Verlag.

Albertson, Fred C. 1987. "An Augustan Temple Represented on a Historical Relief Dating to the Time of Claudius." *American Journal of Archaeology* 91(3):441–58.

Aldrete, Gregory S. 2007. *Floods of the Tiber in Ancient Rome.* Baltimore: Johns Hopkins University Press.

Alessandroni, Maria Gabriella, and Gianrenzo Remédia. 2002. "3 Floods: Case Studies – The Most Severe Floods of the Tiber River in Rome." *IAHS Publication* 271:129.

Allen, Walter, Jr., et al. 1962. "Nero's Eccentricities before the Fire (Tac. *Ann.* 15.37)." *Numen* 9(2):99–109.

Anderson, James C. 1983. "A Topographical Tradition in Fourth Century Chronicles: Domitian's Building Program." *Historia: Zeitschrift für Alte Geschichte* 32(1):93–105.

Aragozzini, Giovanna, and Marco Nocca. 1993. *Le piante di Roma: al Cinquecento all' Ottocento.* Rome: Dino Audino.

Ashby, T., and R. A. L. Fell. 1921. "The Via Flaminia." *Journal of Roman Studies* 11:125–90.

Ballentine, Floyd G. 1904. "Some Phases of the Cult of the Nymphs." *Harvard Studies in Classical Philology* 15:77–119.

Balsdon, J. D. 2002. *Life and Leisure in Ancient Rome.* London: Phoenix Press.

Barrett, Anthony A. 1999. "The Year of Livia's Birth." *Classical Quarterly* 49(2):630–2.

Beacham, Richard. 1991. *Roman Theatre and Its Audience.* Cambridge, Mass.: Harvard University Press.

Beard, Mary. 2007. *The Roman Triumph.* Cambridge, Mass.: Belknap Press of Harvard University Press.

————. 2013. *Confronting the Classics: Traditions, Adventures and Innovations.* New York: W. W. Norton.

Beard, Mary, John North, and Simon Price. 1998. *Religions of Rome.* 2 vols. Cambridge: Cambridge University Press.

Beckmann, Martin. 2011. *The Column of Marcus Aurelius: The Genesis and Meaning of a Roman Imperial Monument.* Chapel Hill: University of North Carolina Press.

Bergmann, Bettina Ann, and Christine Kondoleon, eds. 1999. *The Art of Ancient Spectacle.* Washington, D.C.: National Gallery of Art.

Bickerman, Elias J. 1952. "Origines Gentium." *Classical Philology* 47(2):65–81.

Billows, R. 1993. "The Religious Procession of the Ara Pacis Augustae: Augustus's Supplicatio in 13 B.C." *Journal of Roman Archaeology* 6:80–92.

Blake, Marion Elizabeth. 1959. *Roman Construction in Italy from Tiberius through the Flavians.* Washington, D.C.: Carnegie Institution of Washington.

Blake, Marion Elizabeth, and Esther Boise Van Deman. 1947. *Ancient Roman Construction in Italy from the Prehistoric Period to Augustus.* Washington, D.C.: Carnegie Institution of Washington.

Boatwright, Mary Taliaferro. 1985. "The 'Ara Ditis-Ustrinum of Hadrian' in the Western Campus Martius and Other Problematic Roman Ustrina." *American Journal of Archaeology* 89(3):485–97.

———. 1987. *Hadrian and the City of Rome.* Princeton, N.J.: Princeton University Press.

———. 1990. "Theaters in the Roman Empire." *Biblical Archaeologist* 53(4):184–92.

Boatwright, Mary T., Daniel J. Gargola, and Richard J. A. Talbert. 2004. *The Romans from Village to Empire: A History of Rome from Earliest Times to Constantine.* New York: Oxford University Press.

Bober, Phyllis Pray, Ruth Rubinstein, and Susan Woodford. 1986. *Renaissance Artists and Antique Sculpture: A Handbook of Sources.* London: H. Miller.

Boyd, M. J. 1953. "The Porticoes of Metellus and Octavia and Their Two Temples." *Papers of the British School at Rome* 21:152–9.

Bramble, J. C., Michael Whitby, Philip R. Hardie, and Mary Whitby. 1987. *Homo Viator: Classical Essays for John Bramble.* Bristol: Bristol Classical.

Brandt, Olof, ed. 2012. *San Lorenzo in Lucina: The Transformation of a Roman Quarter.* Stockholm: Swedish Institute.

Bremmer, Jan N., and Nicholas Horsfall. 1987. *Roman Myth and Mythography.* London: University of London, Institute of Classical Studies.

Buchner, Edmund. 1976. "Solarium Augusti und Ara Pacis." *Römische Mitteilungen* 83:319–65.

———. 1980. "Horologium Solarium Augusti: Vorbericht über die Ausgrabungen 1979/80." *Römische Mitteilungen* 87:355–73.

Campbell, Brian. 2012. *Rivers and the Power of Ancient Rome.* Chapel Hill: University of North Carolina Press.

Campbell, Constance. 2003. "The Uncompleted Theatres of Rome." *Theatre Journal* 55(1):67–79.

Cancik, Hubert, Helmuth Schneider, Christine F. Salazar, and David E. Orton. 2002. *Brill's New Pauly: Encyclopaedia of the Ancient World.* Leiden: Brill.

Caneva, Giulia. 2010. *Il codice botanico di Augusto. Roma – Ara Pacis: Parlare al popolo attraverso le immagini della natura = The Augustan Botanical Code: Rome, Ara Pacis; Speaking to the People through Images of Nature.* Rome: Gangemi.

Canter, Howard Vernon. 1930. "The Venerable Bede and the Colosseum." *Transactions and Proceedings of the American Philological Association* 61:150–64.

Carandini, Andrea, and Paolo Carafa, eds. 2011. *Atlante di Roma Antica. Immagini della città.* 2 vols. Milan: Electa Elemond.

Carettoni, Gianfilippo, Antonio M. Colini, Lucos Cozza, and Guglielmo Gatti, eds. 1960. *La Pianta Marmorea di Roma Antica, Forma Urbis Romae.* Rome: Comune di Roma.

Carlson, Marvin A. 1988. "The Theatre as Civic Monument." *Theatre Journal* 40(1):12–32.

———. 1989. *Places of Performance: The Semiotics of Theatre Architecture.* Ithaca, N.Y.: Cornell University Press.

Carter, Jesse Benedict. 1909. "The Death of Romulus." *American Journal of Archaeology.* 13(1):19–29.

Castriota, David. 1995. *The Ara Pacis Augustae and the Imagery of Abundance in Later Greek and Early Imperial Roman Art.* Princeton, N.J.: Princeton University Press.

Ceen, Allan, ed. 1984. *Rome 1748: The Pianta Grande di Roma of Giambattista Nolli*. Highmount, N.Y.: J. H. Aronson.

Çelik, Zeynep, Diane Favro, and Richard Ingersoll, eds. 1994. *Streets: Critical Perspectives on Public Space*. Berkeley: University of California Press.

Champlin, Edward. 1978. "The Life and Times of Calpurnius Siculus." *Journal of Roman Studies* 68:95–110.

Ciancio Rossetto, Paola. 1996. "Rinvenimenti e restauri al portico d'Ottavia e in piazza delle Cinque Scole." *Bullettino della Commisione Archeologica Comunale di Roma* 97:267–78.

Claridge, Amanda. 2007. "Hadrian's Lost Temple of Trajan." *Journal of Roman Archaeology* 20:55–94.

———. 2010. *Rome: An Oxford Archaeological Guide*. Oxford: Oxford University Press.

Coarelli, Filippo. 1977. "Il Campo Marzio occidentale. Storia e topografia." *Mélanges de l'Ecole Française de Rome, Antiquité* 89(2):807–46.

———. 1997. *Il Campo Marzio: dalle origini alla fine della Repubblica*. Rome: Quasar.

———. 2007. *Rome and Environs: An Archaeological Guide*. Berkeley: University of California Press.

Coarelli, Filippo, Iiro Kajanto, and Margareta Steinby. 1981. *L'area sacra di Largo Argentina*. 1.1. Rome: Poliglotta Vaticana.

Coates-Stephens, Robert. 1996. "Housing in Early Medieval Rome, 500–1000 AD." *Papers of the British School at Rome* 64:239–59.

———. 2010. "Notes from Rome 2009–10." *Papers of the British School at Rome* 78:289–95.

Cohon, R. 2004. "Forerunners of the Scrollwork on the Ara Pacis Augustae Made by a Western Asiatic Workshop." *Journal of Roman Archaeology* 17:83–106.

Coleman, K. M. 1993. "Launching into History: Aquatic Displays in the Early Empire." *Journal of Roman Studies* 83:48–74.

Colini, Antonio Maria. 1941. *Lo Stadio di Domiziano*. Rome: Governatorato di Roma.

Connors, Joseph. 2011. *Piranesi and the Campus Martius: The Missing Corso*. Milan: Editoriale Jaca Book Spa.

Cooley, Alison E., trans. 2009. *Res Gestae Divi Augusti: Text, Translation and Commentary*. Cambridge: Cambridge University Press.

Cornell, T. J. 1995. *The Beginnings of Rome: Italy and Rome from the Bronze Age to the Punic Wars (c. 1000–264 BC)*. London: Routledge.

Corso, Antonio. 1997. "Vitruvius and Attic Monuments." *Annual of the British School at Athens* 92:373–400.

Coulston, Jon, and Hazel Dodge, eds. 2000. *Ancient Rome: The Archaeology of the Eternal City*. Oxford: Oxford University School of Archaeology.

Coulton, J. J. 1976. *The Architectural Development of the Greek Stoa*. Oxford: Clarendon Press.

Curran, Brian A. 2009. *Obelisk: A History*. Cambridge, Mass.: Burndy Library.

Curran, John. 2000. *Pagan City and Christian Capital: Rome in the Fourth Century*. London: Clarendon Press.

Damsky, Ben L. 1990. "The Stadium Aureus of Septimius Severus." *American Journal of Numismatics, Second series* 2:77–105.

Darwall-Smith, Robin. 1996. *Emperors and Architecture: A Study of Flavian Rome*. Brussels: Latomus.

Davies, Jason. 1999. Review: Eric M. Orlin, *Temples, Religion and Politics in the Roman Republic*. *Bryn Mawr Classical Review*. http://bmcr.brynmawr.edu/1999/1999-01-11.html.

Davies, Penelope. 2004. *Death and the Roman Emperor: Roman Imperial Funerary Monuments from Augustus to Marcus Aurelius*. Austin: University of Texas Press.

De Fine Licht, Kjeld. 1983. *Città e architettura nella Roma imperiale: atti del seminario del 27 Ottobre 1981 nel 25 aniversario dell'Accademia di Danimarca*. Odense: Odense University Press.

De Grummond, Nancy. 1990. "Pax Augusta and the Horae on the Ara Pacis Augustae." *American Journal of Archaeology* 94(4):663–77.

Delph, Ronald K., Michelle M. Fontaine, and John Jeffries Martin, eds. 2006. *Heresy, Culture, and Religion in Early Modern Italy: Contexts and Contestations*. Kirksville, Mo.: Truman State University Press.

De Nuccio, Marilda, and Lucrezia Ungaro. 2002. *I marmi colorati della Roma imperiale*. Venice: Marsilio.

Denard, Hugh. 2002. "Virtuality and Performativity: Recreating Rome's Theatre of Pompey." *Performing Arts Journal* 24(1):25–43.

Dessau, Herman. 1979. *Inscriptiones Latinae Selectae*. Chicago: Ares.

Deutsch, Monroe E. 1924. "Pompey's Three Triumphs." *Classical Philology* 19(3):277–9.

Devereux, George. 1970. "The Equus October Ritual Reconsidered." *Mnemosyne* 23(3):297–301.

Dickens, Charles. 1871. *Pictures from Italy*. New York: Hurd & Houghton.

Dillon, Sheila, and Katherine E. Welch. 2006. *Representations of War in Ancient Rome*. Cambridge: Cambridge University Press.

Dudley, Donald Reynolds. 1967. *Urbs Roma: A Source Book of Classical Texts on the City & its monuments*. London: Phaidon Press.

Dueck, Daniela. 1999. "The Date and Method of Composition of Strabo's 'Geography.'" *Hermes* 127(4):467–78.

———. 2000. *Strabo of Amasia: A Greek Man of Letters in Augustan Rome*. London: Routledge.

Dueck, Daniela, and Kai Brodersen. 2012. *Geography in Classical Antiquity*. Cambridge: Cambridge University Press.

Dumézil, Georges. 1966. *Archaic Roman Religion, with an Appendix on the Religion of the Etruscans*. Chicago: University of Chicago Press.

Dupont, Florence. 1993. *Daily Life in Ancient Rome*. Oxford: Blackwell.

Dyson, Stephen L. 2010. *Rome: A Living Portrait of an Ancient City*. Baltimore: Johns Hopkins University Press.

Edwards, Catherine. 1996. *Writing Rome: Textual Approaches to the City*. Cambridge: Cambridge University Press.

Edwards, Catherine, and Greg Woolf, eds. 2003. *Rome the Cosmopolis*. Cambridge: Cambridge University Press.

Elsner, Jaś. 1991. "Cult and Sacrifice: Sacrifice in the Ara Pacis Augustae." *Journal of Roman Studies* 81:50–61.

Erdkamp, Paul. 2013. *The Cambridge Companion to Ancient Rome*. Cambridge: Cambridge University Press.

Evans, Harry B. 1982. "Agrippa's Water Plan." *American Journal of Archaeology* 86(3):401–11.

———. 1997. *Water Distribution in Ancient Rome: The Evidence of Frontinus*. Ann Arbor: University of Michigan Press.

Evans, Jane DeRose. 2009. "Prostitutes in the Portico of Pompey? A Reconsideration." *Transactions of the American Philological Association* 139(1):123–45.

Everett, Anthony. 2001. *Cicero: The Life and Times of Rome's Greatest Politician*. New York: Random House.

Fagan, Garrett G. 1999. *Bathing in Public in the Roman World*. Ann Arbor: University of Michigan Press.

Favro, Diane. 1992. "'Pater urbis': Augustus as City Father of Rome." *Journal of the Society of Architectural Historians* 51(1):61–84.

———. 1996. *The Urban Image of Augustan Rome*. Cambridge: Cambridge University Press.

Flory, Marleen B. 1996. "Dynastic Ideology, the Domus Augusta and Imperial Women: A Lost Statuary Group in the Circus Flaminius." *Transactions and Proceedings of the American Philological Association* 126:287–306.

Flower, Harriet I. 2004. *The Cambridge Companion to the Roman Republic*. Cambridge: Cambridge University Press.

Fowler, W. Warde. 1899. *The Roman Festivals of the Period of the Republic: An Introduction to the Study of the Religion of the Romans*. London: Macmillan.

———. 1911. *The Religious Experience of the Roman People*. London: Macmillan.

Futrell, Alison. 1997. *Blood in the Arena: The Spectacle of Roman Power*. Austin: University of Texas Press.

———. 2006. *The Roman Games: A Sourcebook*. Malden, Mass.: Blackwell.

Gabriel, Richard A. 2008. *Scipio Africanus: Rome's Greatest General*. Washington, D.C.: Potomac Books.

Gagliardo, Mara C., and James E. Packer. 2006. "A New Look at Pompey's Theater: History, Documentation and Recent Excavation." *American Journal of Archaeology* 110:93–122.

Galinsky, K. 1992. "Venus, Polysemy, and the Ara Pacis Augustae." *American Journal of Archaeology* 96(3):457–75.

———. 2005. *The Cambridge Companion to the Age of Augustus*. Cambridge: Cambridge University Press.

Giustozzi, Nunzio. 2012. *Palazzo Altemps*. Rome: Electa.

Goldsworthy, Adrian Keith. 2006. *Caesar: Life of a Colossus*. New Haven, Conn.: Yale University Press.

Goodman, Martin. 2007. *Rome and Jerusalem*. New York: Alfred A. Knopf.

Grafton, Anthony, Glenn W. Most, and Salvatore Settis, eds. 2010. *The Classical Tradition*. Cambridge, Mass.: Belknap Press of Harvard University Press.

Grant, Michael. 1994. *The Antonines: The Roman Empire in Transition*. London: Routledge.

Grant, Michael, and John Hazel. 1973. *Gods and Mortals in Classical Mythology*. Springfield, Mass.: G. & C. Merriam.

Graßhoff, Gerd, Michael Heinzelmann, and Markus Wäfler, eds. 2009. *The Pantheon in Rome: Contributions to the Conference, Bern, November 9–12, 2006*. Bern: Universität Bern, Wissenschaftstheorie und Wissenschaftsgeschichte.

Gregorius, Magister. 1987. *Narracio de mirabilibus urbis Romae*. Translated by John Osborne in *The Marvels of Rome*. Toronto: Pontifical Institute of Mediaeval Studies.

Gruen, Erich S. 1992. *Culture and National Identity in Republican Rome*. Ithaca, N.Y.: Cornell University Press.

Hall, John Franklin. 1996. *Etruscan Italy: Etruscan Influences on the Civilizations of Italy from Antiquity to the Modern Era*. Provo, Utah: Museum of Art, Brigham Young University.

Hannah, Robert. 2011. "The Horologium of Augustus as a Sundial." *Journal of Roman Archaeology* 24(1):87–95.

Hannah, Robert, and Giulio Magli. 2011. "The Role of the Sun in the Pantheon's Design and Meaning." *Numen* 58(4):486–513.

Hanson, John Arthur. 1959. *Roman Theatre-Temples*. Princeton, N.J.: Princeton University Press.

Hardie, Alex. 2007. "Juno, Hercules, and the Muses at Rome." *American Journal of Philology* 128(4):551–92.

Harris, William V. 1979. *War and Imperialism in Republican Rome: 327–70 B.C.* Oxford: Clarendon Press.

Harvey, Paul B., and Celia E. Schultz, eds. 2006. *Religion in Republican Italy*. Cambridge: Cambridge University Press.

Haselberger, Lothar. 2007. *Urbem Adornare: Die Stadt Rom und ihre Gestaltumwandlung unter Augustus / Rome's Urban Metamorphosis under Augustus*. Journal of Roman Archaeology Supplementary Series 64. Translated by Alexander Thein. Portsmouth, R.I.: Journal of Roman Archaeology.

———. 2011. "A Debate on the Horologium of Augustus: Controversy and Clarifications." *Journal of Roman Archaeology* 24(1):47–73.

Haselberger, Lothar, and John Humphrey, eds. 2006. *Imaging Ancient Rome: Documentation, Visualization, Imagination*. Journal of Roman Archaeology Supplementary Series 61. Portsmouth, R.I.: Journal of Roman Archaeology.

Haselberger, Lothar, David Gilman Romano, and Elisha Ann Dumser, eds. 2002. *Mapping Augustan Rome*. Journal of Roman Archaeology Supplementary Series 50. Portsmouth, RI: Journal of Roman Archaeology.

Haskell, Francis, and Nicholas Penny. 1981. *Taste and the Antique*. New Haven, Conn.: Yale University Press.

Healy, John F. 1999. *Pliny The Elder on Science and Technology*. Oxford: Oxford University Press.

Heiken, Grant, Renato Funiciello, and Donatella De Rita. 2005. *The Seven Hills of Rome: A Geological Tour of the Eternal City*. Princeton, N.J.: Princeton University Press.

Heilbron, J. L. 1999. *The Sun in the Church: Cathedrals as Solar Observatories*. Cambridge, Mass.: Harvard University Press.

Hekster, Olivier, and John Rich. 2006. "Octavian and the Thunderbolt: The Temple of Apollo Palatinus and Roman Traditions of Temple Building." *Classical Quarterly* 56(1):149–68.

Hermansen, G. 1978. "The Population of Imperial Rome: The Regionaries." *Historia: Zeitschrift für Alte Geschichte* 27(1):129–68.

Heslin, Peter. 2007. "Augustus, Domitian and the So-Called Horologium Augusti." *Journal of Roman Studies* 97:1–20.

———. 2011. "The Augustus Code: A Response to L. Haselberger." *Journal of Roman Archaeology* 24(1):74–77.

Hetland, Lise M. 2007. "Dating the Pantheon." *Journal of Roman Archaeology* 20:95–111.

Hill, Philip V. 1989. *The Monuments of Ancient Rome as Coin Types.* London: B. A. Seaby.

Hodge, A. Trevor. 1992. *Roman Aqueducts & Water Supply.* London: Duckworth.

Hofter, Mathias René. 1988. *Kaiser Augustus und die verlorene Republik: Eine Ausstellung im Martin-Gropius-Bau, Berlin, 7. Juni–14. August 1988.* Mainz: Von Zabern.

Holland, Louise Adams. 1961. *Janus and the Bridge.* Rome: American Academy in Rome.

Holliday, Peter J. 1993. *Narrative and Event in Ancient Art.* Cambridge: Cambridge University Press.

Hopkins, John N. N. 2003. "The Cloaca Maxima and the Monumental Manipulation of Water in Archaic Rome." *Waters of Rome* 4:1–15.

Hornblower, Simon, and Antony Spawforth, eds. 2003. *The Oxford Classical Dictionary.* Oxford: Oxford University Press.

Horsfall, Nicholas. 1974. "The Ides of March: Some New Problems." *Greece & Rome* 21(2):191–9.

Humphrey, John H. 1986. *Roman Circuses: Arenas for Chariot Racing.* London: B. T. Batsford.

Insalaco, Antonio. 2005. *La città dell'acqua: archeologia sotterranea a Fontana di Trevi.* Milano: Electa.

Jacks, Philip. 1993. *The Antiquarian and the Myth of Antiquity: The Origins of Rome in Renaissance Thought.* Cambridge: Cambridge University Press.

Joost-Gaugier, Christiane L. 2006. *Measuring Heaven: Pythagoras and His Influence on Thought and Art in Antiquity and the Middle Ages.* Ithaca, N.Y.: Cornell University Press.

Katz, Robert. 2003. *The Battle for Rome.* New York: Simon & Schuster.

Keppie, L. J. F. 1998. *The Making of the Roman Army: From Republic to Empire.* Norman: University of Oklahoma Press.

Kleiner, Diana E. E. 1978. "The Great Friezes of the Ara Pacis Augustae: Greek Sources, Roman Derivatives and Augustan Social Policy." *Mélanges de l'École Française de Rome, Antiquité.* 90:753–85.

———. 2005. *Cleopatra and Rome.* Cambridge, Mass.: Belknap Press of Harvard University Press.

Koeppel, G. 1987. "Die historischen Reliefs der römischen Kaiserzeit V: Ara Pacis Augustae, Teil I." *Bonner Jahrbücher* 187:101–57.

———. 1988. "Die historischen Reliefs der römischen Kaiserzeit V: Ara Pacis Augustae, Teil 2." *Bonner Jahrbücher* 188:97–106.

Kontokosta, Anne Hrychuck. 2013. "Reconsidering the Arches (*fornices*) of the Roman Republic." *Journal of Roman Archaeology* 26:8–35.

Krautheimer, Richard. 1980. *Rome, Profile of a City, 312–1308.* Princeton, N.J.: Princeton University Press.

Kuttner, Ann. 1995. "Republican Rome Looks at Pergamon." *Harvard Studies in Classical Philology* 97:157–78.

———. 1999. "Culture and History at Pompey's Museum." *Transactions of the American Philological Association* 129:343–73.

Lanciani, Rodolfo. 1897. *The Ruins and Excavations of Ancient Rome.* Boston: Houghton, Mifflin.

———. 1899. *The Destruction of Ancient Rome.* London: Macmillan.

———. 1990. *Forma Urbis Romae.* Rome: Quasar.

La Rocca, Eugenio, Vivian Ruesch, and Bruno Zanardi. 1983. *Ara Pacis Augustae: in occasione del restauro della fronte orientale.* Rome: L'Erma di Bretschneider.

Le Gall, Joël. 1944. "Les Bas-Reliefs de la Statue du 'Tibre' au Louvre." *Revue Archéologique* 60(21) (January–June 1944): 115–37.

———. 1953A. *Le Tibre, fleuve de Rome dans l'Antiquité.* Paris: Presses Universitaires de France.

————. 1953B. *Recherches sur le Culte du Tibre.* Paris: Presses Universitaires de France.

Lehmann, Karl. 1955. *Samothrace: A Guide to the Excavations and the Museum.* Locust Valley, N.Y.: Published for the Institute of Fine Arts, New York University by J. J. Augustin.

Ling, Roger. 1998. "Campus Martius." Review of *Il Campo Marzio. Dalle origini alla fine della repubblica,* by F. Coarelli. *Classical Review* 48(2):441–2.

Lloyd, Robert B. 1979. "The Aqua Virgo, Euripus and Pons Agrippae." *American Journal of Archaeology* 83(2):193–204.

Lomas, Kathryn, and Tim Cornell, eds. 2003. *Bread and Circuses: Euergetism and Municipal Patronage in Roman Italy.* London: Routledge.

Lott, J. Bert. 2004. *The Neighborhoods of Augustan Rome.* Cambridge: Cambridge University Press.

MacDonald, William L. 1976. *The Pantheon. Design, Meaning and Progeny.* Cambridge, Mass.: Harvard University Press.

————. 1982. *The Architecture of the Roman Empire: An Introductory Study.* New Haven, Conn.: Yale University Press.

————. 1986. *The Architecture of the Roman Empire: An Urban Appraisal.* New Haven, Conn.: Yale University Press.

MacMillan, Hugh. 1888. *Roman Mosaics or Studies in Rome and Its Neighbourhood.* New York: Macmillan.

Magi, Filippo. 1945. *I rilievi Flavi del Palazzo della Cancelleria.* Edited by Dott. G. Bardi. Rome: Presso la Pontificia accademia romana di archeologi.

Makin, Ena. 1921. "The Triumphal Route, with Particular Reference to the Flavian Triumph." *Journal of Roman Studies* 11:25–36.

Manacorda, Daniele. 2000. *Crypta Balbi: Museo nazionale romano.* Milan: Electa.

Manuwald, Gesine. 2011. *Roman Republican Theatre.* Cambridge: Cambridge University Press.

Mazzoni, Cristina. 2010. *She-Wolf: The Story of A Roman Icon.* Cambridge: Cambridge University Press.

McCredie, James R. 1965. "Samothrace: Preliminary Report on the Campaigns of 1962–1964." *Hesperia* 34(2):100–24.

————. 1968. "Samothrace: Preliminary Report on the Campaigns of 1965–1967." *Hesperia* 37(2):200–34.

Mohler, S. L. 1937. "The Iuvenes and Roman Education." *Transactions and Proceedings of the American Philological Association* 68:442–79.

Montaigne, Michel de. 1983. *Montaigne's Travel Journal.* Translated by Donald Murdoch Frame. San Francisco: North Point Press.

Monterroso Checa, Antonio. 2010. *Theatrum Pompei: forma y arquitectura de la génesis del modelo teatral de Roma.* Madrid: Consejo Superior de Investigaciones Científicas, Escuela Española de Historia y Arqueología en Roma.

Moreno, Paolo, ed. 1995. *Lisippo: l'arte e la Fortuna.* Milan: Fabbri.

Morgan, M. Gwyn. 1971. "The Portico of Metellus: A Reconsideration." *Hermes* 99(4):480–505.

Muzzioli, Maria Pia. 1992. "Fonti per la topografia della IX regione di Roma: alcune osservazioni." *Papers of the British School at Rome* 60:179–211.

Narducci, Pietro. 1889. *Sulla Fognatura della Città di Roma.* Rome: Forzani.

Nash, Ernest. 1968. *Pictorial Dictionary of Ancient Rome.* New York: Praeger.

Nicolet, Claude. 1976. "Le temple des Nymphes et les distributions frumentaires à Rome à l'époque républicaine d'après des découvertes récentes." *Comptes rendus des séances de l'Académie des Inscriptions et Belles-Lettres* 120(1):29–51.

————. 1991. *Space, Geography, and Politics in the Early Roman Empire.* Ann Arbor: University of Michigan Press.

Nichols, Francis Morgan. 1986. *The Marvels of Rome: Mirabilia Urbis Romae.* New York: Italica Press.

Nielsen, Inge. 1990. *Thermae et Balnea: The Architecture and Cultural History of Roman Public Baths.* 2 Vols. Aarhus: Aarhus University Press.

Ogilvie, R. M. 1973. "The Cult of Mars." *Classical Review* 23(1):73–75.

Orlin, Eric M. 2002A. *Temples, Religion, and Politics in the Roman Republic.* Boston: Brill Academic.

————. 2002B. "Foreign Cults in Republican Rome: Rethinking the Pomerial Rule." *Memoirs of the American Academy in Rome* 47: 1–18.

————. 2008. "Octavian and Egyptian Cults: Redrawing the Boundaries of Romanness." *American Journal of Philology* 129(2):231–53.

Packer, James E. 1967. "Housing and Population in Imperial Ostia and Rome." *Journal of Roman Studies* 57(1–2):80–95.

Palladio, Andrea. 2006. *Palladio's Rome: A Translation of Andrea Palladio's Two Guidebooks to Rome.* Edited and translated by Vaughan Hart and Peter Hicks. New Haven, Conn.: Yale University Press.

Palmer, Robert E. A. 1976. "Jupiter Blaze, Gods of the Hills, and the Roman Topography of CIL VI 377." *American Journal of Archaeology* 80(1):43–56.

————. 1990. "Studies of the Northern Campus Martius in Ancient Rome." *Transactions of the American Philosophical Society* 80(2):1–64.

Partner, Peter. 1976. *Renaissance Rome, 1500–1559.* Berkeley: University of California Press.

Pascal, C. Bennett. 1981. "October Horse." *Harvard Studies in Classical Philology* 85:261–91.

Patterson, John R. 1992. "The City of Rome: From Republic to Empire." *Journal of Roman Studies* 82:186–215.

Pelling, C. B. R., trans. 1988. *Plutarch: Life of Antony.* Cambridge: Cambridge University Press.

Pietilä-Castrén, Leena. 1987. *Magnificentia Publica: The Victory Monuments of the Roman Generals in the Era of the Punic Wars.* Helsinki: Societas Scientiarum Fennica.

Piranesi, Giovanni Battista, and Luigi Ficacci. 2000. *Giovanni Battista Piranesi: The Complete Etchings = Gesamtkatalog der Kupferstiche = Catalogue raisonné des eaux-fortes.* Cologne: Taschen.

Platner, Samuel Ball. 1908. "The Ara Martis." *Classical Philology* 3(1):65–73.

Platner, Samuel Ball, and Thomas Ashby. 1926. *A Topographical Dictionary of Rome.* Oxford: Oxford University Press.

Poe, Joe Park. 1984. "The Secular Games, the Aventine, and the Pomerium in the Campus Martius." *Classical Antiquity* 3(1):57–81.

Pollitt, J. J. 1978. "The Impact of Greek Art on Rome." *Transactions of the American Philological Association* 108:155–74.

————. 1986. *Art in the Hellenistic Age.* Cambridge: Cambridge University Press.

Potter, D. S., and D. J. Mattingly, eds. 1999. *Life, Death, and Entertainment in the Roman Empire.* Ann Arbor: University of Michigan Press.

Poynton, J. B. 1938. "The Public Games of the Romans." *Greece & Rome* 7(20):76–85.

Pratt, Kenneth J. 1955. "Roman Antimilitarism." *Classical Journal* 51(1):21–5.

Prior, Richard E. 1996. "Going around Hungry: Topography and Poetics in Martial 2.14." *American Journal of Philology* 117(1):121–41.

Rawson, Elizabeth. 1981. "Chariot Racing in the Roman Republic." *Papers of the British School at Rome* 49:1–16.

————. 1987. "Discrimina Ordinum: The Lex Julia Theatralis." *Papers of the British School at Rome* 55:83–114.

Rehak, Paul. 2001. "Aeneas or Numa? Rethinking the Meaning of the Ara Pacis Augustae." *Art Bulletin* 83(2):190–208.

————. 2006. *Imperium and Cosmos: Augustus and the Northern Campus Martius.* Madison: University of Wisconsin Press.

Reynolds, David West. 1986. "Forma Urbis Romae: The Severan Marble Plan and the Urban Form of Ancient Rome." Ph.D. diss., University of Michigan.

Rich, John, and Graham Shipley. 1993. *War and Society In The Roman World.* London: Routledge.

Richardson, Lawrence, Jr. 1976. "The Evolution of the Porticus Octaviae." *American Journal of Archaeology* 80(1):57–64.

————. 1977. "Hercules Musarum and the Porticus Philippi in Rome." *American Journal of Archaeology* 81(3):355–61.

————. 1980. "Two Topographical Notes." *American Journal of Philology* 101(1):53–56.

————. 1987. "A Note on the Architecture of the Theatrum Pompei in Rome." *American Journal of Archaeology* 91(1):123–6.

———. 1992. *A New Topographical Dictionary of Ancient Rome.* Baltimore: Johns Hopkins University Press.

Rickman, Geoffrey. 1971. *Roman Granaries and Store Buildings.* Cambridge: Cambridge University Press.

Robinson, O. F. 1992. *Ancient Rome: City Planning and Administration.* London: Routledge.

Roddaz, Jean-Michel. 1984. *Marcus Agrippa.* Rome: Écoles françaises de Rome.

Rodríguez Almeida, Emilio. 1981. *Forma Urbis Marmorea. Aggiornamento generale 1980.* Rome: Quasar.

Rose, Charles Brian. 1990A. "The Tabula Siarensis and the Arch of Germanicus in the Circus Flaminius." *American Journal of Archaeology* 94(2):312.

———. 1990B. "'Princes' and Barbarians on the Ara Pacis." *American Journal of Archaeology* 94(3):453–67.

———. 2005. "The Parthians in Augustan Rome." *American Journal of Archaeology* 109(1):21–75.

Rose, H. J. 1933. "The Cult of Volkanus at Rome." *Journal of Roman Studies* 23:46–63.

Rosivach, Vincent J. 2006. "The First Venatio." *New England Classical Journal* 33:271–8.

Rossini, Orietta. 2006. *Ara Pacis.* Milan: Electa.

Roullet, Anne. 1972. *The Egyptian and Egyptianizing Monuments of Imperial Rome.* Leiden: Brill.

Rowe, Greg. 2002. *Princes and Political Cultures: The New Tiberian Senatorial Decrees.* Ann Arbor: University of Michigan Press.

Sallares, Robert. 2002. *Malaria and Rome: A History of Malaria in Ancient Italy.* Oxford: Oxford University Press.

Saunders, Catherine. 1913. "The Site of Dramatic Performances at Rome in the Times of Plautus and Terence." *Transactions and Proceedings of the American Philological Association* 44:87–97.

Sauron, Gilles. 1988. "Le message esthétique des rinceaux de l'Ara Pacis Augustae." *Révue Archéologique* Nouvelle Ser. 1:3–40.

Schütz, Michael. 2011. "The Horologium on the Campus Martius Reconsidered." *Journal of Roman Archaeology* 24:78–86.

Scott, Kenneth. 1925. "The Identification of Augustus with Romulus-Quirinus." *Transactions and Proceedings of the American Philological Association* 56:82–105.

Scullard, H. H. 1981. *Festivals and Ceremonies of the Roman Republic.* Ithaca, N.Y.: Cornell University Press.

Sear, Frank. 1990. "Vitruvius and Roman Theater Design." *American Journal of Archaeology* 94(2):249–58.

———. 1993. "The Scaenae Frons of the Theatre of Pompey." *American Journal of Archaeology* 97(4):687–701.

———. 2006. *Roman Theatres: An Architectural Study.* Oxford: Oxford University Press.

———. 2013. "A New Monograph on the Theatre of Pompey." *Journal of Roman Archaeology* 26:539–42.

Senseney, John R. 2011. "Adrift toward Empire: The Lost Porticus Octavia in Rome and the Origins of the Imperial Fora." *Journal of the Society of Architectural Historians* 70(4):421–41.

Serlio, Sebastiano. 1996. *Sebastiano Serlio on Architecture.* Translated by Vaughan Hart and Peter Hicks. New Haven, Conn.: Yale University Press.

Shatzman, Israel. 1972. "The Roman General's Authority over Booty." *Historia: Zeitschrift für Alte Geschichte* 21(2):177–205.

Shipley, Frederick W. 1931. "Chronology of the Building Operations in Rome from the Death of Caesar to the Death of Augustus." *Memoirs of the American Academy in Rome* 9:7–60.

———. 1933. *Agrippa's Building Activities in Rome.* St. Louis: Washington University.

Shipley, Graham, and John Salmon, eds. 1996. *Human Landscapes in Classical Antiquity: Environment and Culture.* London: Routledge.

Smallwood, E. Mary. 1981. *The Jews Under Roman Rule: From Pompey to Diocletian; A Study in Political Relations.* Leiden: Brill.

Smith, William. 1870. *Dictionary of Greek and Roman Biography and Mythology.* Boston: Little and Brown.

Stambaugh, John E. 1988. *The Ancient Roman City.* Baltimore: Johns Hopkins University Press.

Stamper, John W. 2005. *The Architecture of Roman Temples: The Republic to the Middle Empire*. Cambridge: Cambridge University Press.

Steinby, Eva Margareta. 1993–2000. *Lexicon topographicum urbis Romae*. Rome: Edizioni Quasar.

Stilp, Florian. 2001. *Mariage et Suovetaurilia: étude sur le soi-disant "Autel de Domitius Ahenobarbus."* Rome: G. Bretschneider.

Storey, Glenn R. 2003. "The 'Skyscrapers' of the Ancient Roman World." *Latomus* 62(1):3–26.

Strong, D. E. 1963. "Some Observations on Early Roman Corinthian." *Journal of Roman Studies* 53:73–84.

Sutherland, C. H. V. 1935. "The State of the Imperial Treasury at the Death of Domitian." *Journal of Roman Studies* 25:150–62.

Swain, Simon, Stephen Harrison, and Jaś Elsner, eds. 2007. *Severan Culture*. Cambridge: Cambridge University Press.

Swetnam-Burland, Molly. 2009. "Egypt Embodied: The Vatican Nile." *American Journal of Archaeology* 113(3):439–57.

Syme, Ronald. 2002. *Roman Revolution*. Oxford: Oxford University Press.

Taylor, Lily Ross. 1990. *Roman Voting Assemblies from the Hannibalic War to the Dictatorship of Caesar*. Ann Arbor: University of Michigan Press.

Taylor, Rabun. 2000. *Public Needs and Private Pleasures: Water Distribution, the Tiber River and the Urban Development of Ancient Rome*. Rome: L'Erma di Bretschneider.

———. 2002. "Tiber River Bridges and the Development of the Ancient City of Rome." *Waters of Rome* 2:1–20.

Temin, Peter. 2013. *The Roman Market Economy*. Princeton, N.J.: Princeton University Press.

Thomas, Edmund. 2007. *Monumentality and the Roman Empire: Architecture in the Antonine Age*. Oxford: Oxford University Press.

Thommen, Lukas. 2012. *An Environmental History of Ancient Greece and Rome*. Cambridge: Cambridge University Press.

Thornton, M. K. 1986. "Julio-Claudian Building Programs: Eat, Drink, and Be Merry." *Historia: Zeitschrift für Alte Geschichte* 35(1):28–44.

Tierney, J. J. 1963. "The Map of Agrippa." *Proceedings of the Royal Irish Academy* 63:151–66.

Townend, G. B. 1980. "Calpurnius Siculus and Munus Neronis." *Journal of Roman Studies* 70:166–74.

Tucci, Pier Luigi. 1997. "Dov'erano il tempio di Nettuno e la nave di Enea?" *Bullettino della Commissione Archeologica Comunale di Roma* 98:15–42.

Turcan, Robert. 1996. *The Cults of the Roman Empire*. Oxford: Blackwell.

Vendittelli, Laura. 2005. "From the Excavated Site to the Museum Display: Historical Interpretation and Conservation." Paper presented at Urban Pasts and Urban Futures: Bringing Urban Archaeology to Life Enhancing Urban Archaeological Remains, International and Interdisciplinary Symposium – APPEAR, Brussels, October 4–5, *Appendices* 54–8. http://www.international.icomos.org/appear-annexes.pdf.

Vogel, Lise. 1973. *The Column of Antoninus Pius*. Cambridge, Mass.: Harvard University Press.

von Stackelberg, Katherine T. 2009. *The Roman Garden: Space, Sense, and Society*. London: Routledge.

Wallace-Hadrill, Andrew. 2008. *Rome's Cultural Revolution*. Cambridge: Cambridge University Press.

Warrior, Valerie M. 2002. *Roman Religion: A Sourcebook*. Newburyport, Mass.: Focus Pub. / R. Pullins.

Welch, Katherine E. 2007. *The Roman Amphitheatre from Its Origins to the Colosseum*. Cambridge: Cambridge University Press.

Wiedemann, Thomas. 1986. "The Fetiales: A Reconsideration." *Classical Quarterly* 36(2):478–90.

Wild, Robert A. 1981. *Water in the Cultic Worship of Isis and Sarapis*. Leiden: Brill.

Wilson Jones, Mark. 2000. *Principles of Roman Architecture*. New Haven, Conn.: Yale University Press.

Wiseman, T. P. 1974. "The Circus Flaminius." *Papers of the British School at Rome* 42:3–26.

———. 1976. "Two Questions on the Circus Flaminius." *Papers of the British School at Rome* 44:44–47.

———. 1980. "Professor Richardson and the Other Campus." *American Journal of Philology* 101(4):483–5.

———. 1995. *Remus: A Roman Myth*. Cambridge: Cambridge University Press.

———. 1998. *Roman Drama and Roman History*. Exeter: University of Exeter.

Woodard, Roger D. 2013. *Myth, Ritual and the Warrior in Roman and Indo-European Antiquity*. Cambridge: Cambridge University Press.

Yegül, Fikret. 1992. *Baths and Bathing in Classical Antiquity*. Cambridge, Mass.: MIT Press.

Zanker, Paul. 1988. *The Power of Images in the Age of Augustus*. Ann Arbor: University of Michigan Press.

———. 2004. *Die Apotheose der römischen Kaiser: Ritual und städtische Bühne*. Munich: Carl Friedrich von Siemens Stiftung.

Ziólkowski, Adam. 1986. "Les Temples A et C du Largo Argentina: quelques considérations." *Mélanges de l'Ecole Française de Rome, Antiquité* 98(2):623–41.

———. 1992. *The Temples of Mid-Republican Rome and their Historical and Topographical Context*. Rome: Bretschneider.

———. 1994. "Was Agrippa's Pantheon the Temple of Mars *in campo?*" *Papers of the British School at Rome* 62:261–77.

INDEX